PARTICIPATION AND POLITICAL EQUALITY

To our colleagues in the Cross-National Program
on Political and Social Change

PARTICIPATION AND POLITICAL EQUALITY

A SEVEN-NATION COMPARISON

SIDNEY VERBA
Professor of Government, Harvard University

NORMAN H. NIE
Professor of Political Science, University of Chicago

JAE-ON KIM
Associate Professor of Sociology, University of Iowa

CAMBRIDGE UNIVERSITY PRESS

CAMBRIDGE

LONDON · NEW YORK · MELBOURNE

Published by the Syndics of the Cambridge University Press
The Pitt Building, Trumpington Street, Cambridge CB2 1RP
Bentley House, 200 Euston Road, London NW1 2DB
32 East 57th Street, New York, NY 10022, USA
296 Beaconsfield Parade, Middle Park, Melbourne 3206, Australia

© Cambridge University Press 1978

First published 1978

Printed in the United States of America
Typeset by Photo Graphics, Inc., Baltimore, Maryland
Printed and bound by Vail-Ballou Press, Inc., Binghamton, New York

Library of Congress Cataloging in Publication Data
Verba, Sidney.

Participation and political equality.

Bibliography: p.

Includes index.

1. Political participation.   I.   Nie, Norman H.,
joint author.   II.   Kim, Jae-On, joint author.
III.   Title.
JF2011.V46   301.5'92   77-88679
ISBN 0 521 21905 1

CONTENTS

TABLES AND FIGURES

Tables

Figures

PREFACE

This book is based on the analysis of data from the Cross-National Program in Political and Social Change. The Cross-National Program was a collaborative program of survey studies in seven nations. The studies dealt with a wide range of questions but focused primarily on citizen involvement in political life. Other works – some dealing with one or a few of the nations studied, others more generally comparative – have appeared. (See the List of Publications of the Cross-National Program in Participation.) This work attempts to deal comprehensively with one aspect of our study across all seven nations: the ways citizens participate and the processes that lead them to do so.

The study began over a decade ago as a follow-up to Almond and Verba's *The Civic Culture*. The original goal was to replicate that study in some other nations. Over the years the present study has evolved in a somewhat different direction for several reasons. For one thing, we decided to build on rather than replicate the earlier study. In this way, we could take advantage of lessons learned from the earlier work. This choice involves some loss, since replications are valuable ways of achieving continuity in research. But the loss is balanced by our ability to move beyond the previous work. Another source of change in the focus of the study is its organizational structure. From the beginning, it was decided that the study ought to be a cooperative one in which research groups from each of the participating nations would join in research planning and design. The cooperation would go beyond the design of the specific instruments to the choice of a general theoretical orientation. The collaborating groups did join in this process, and the study design developed in new directions in response to their interest.

The resulting study, nevertheless, deals with many of the themes of the earlier work: the citizen as participant, the social sources of that participation, and the values associated with the role of citizen. There are, however, several new emphases. We are more concerned with participatory behaviors – in the wide range of ways in which individuals can participate in politics – than in participatory attitudes. We believe that participatory behaviors have a more immediate impact on politics and that they are somewhat easier to measure in a valid and reliable way across nations. Furthermore, we seek to explain patterns of political participation in terms of the contemporaneous social and psychological characteristics of individuals, not in terms of earlier socialization. Lastly, unlike the approach used in *The Civic Culture*, our concern here is with the problems of social and political equality within nations.

The study began as an attempt to use survey techniques in a number of nations different from the five studied in *The Civic Culture*, particularly some Asian and African nations. The original participating nations were: India, Japan, Mexico, Nigeria, and the United States. Two nations had been in the earlier study, three were new. Over time the set changed somewhat. The Mexican group withdrew during the planning phase. (The withdrawal was largely in response to the Project Camelot affair. Project Camelot was a large-scale planned study of insurgency and social stability sponsored by the Pentagon. The revelation of this base of Camelot's support in Chile had repercussions across many Latin American nations and on many research enterprises having no connection with it.) In the later stages of the research three additional nations joined in: Austria, Yugoslavia, and the Netherlands. The result is a quite heterogeneous set of nations – something that (as we shall try to explain in Chapter 2) is an important asset to our work.

We remain within the tradition of *The Civic Culture* in that we use survey studies to deal with macropolitical problems. We are not primarily interested in explaining the behavior of the individual citizen but in understanding the political system and the way in which individual behavior shapes that system. But despite that macroconcern, our explanatory sights have been set somewhat lower than those of the earlier work. We do not try to explain why some democracies are stable and effective whereas others are less so. To answer such a question as that raised in *The Civic Culture* required quite a leap from the data on citizen attitudes and behavior to conclusions about the political system. We want to explain why the participant population in a society takes the shape it does – why some groups are overrepresented and others underrepresented – and what the consequences are of the particular composition of the participant population. Our substantive concern is with the equality of political access and influence *within* each of the political systems we study, not with the overall survival *of* the political system. As we shall see, the equality of political access and influence within a political system is a political phenomenon quite closely tied to the data we have, and our manipulation of those data allows us to explain differences among the nations.

Data

The data reported in this volume come from large-scale sample surveys conducted in each of the participating nations. The surveys took place at various times between 1966 and 1971, with the sample size ranging from 1,775 in Austria to 2,600 in the United States. The samples were designed to produce a representative cross section of the citizenry in each nation. Exceptions to national coverage exist in three of the nations. In India the sample is limited to four states: Andhra Pradesh, Gujarat, Uttar Pradesh, and West Bengal. In Yugoslavia, it is limited to four republics: Croatia, Macedonia, Serbia, and Slovenia. In each case considerations of cost as well as cultural and linguistic diversity determined the limitation. In Nigeria, our original plan had been for a study in each of the four major regions into which Nigeria was then (1966) divided: the East, Midwest, West, and North. During our field work, violence broke out in a number of northern cities. This had little effect on our sample elsewhere, but made it impossible to complete the northern field work. We have, therefore, limited our analysis to the data from the three nonnorthern regions.

The samples in each nation were designed with multiple purposes in mind, given the varied interests of the researchers. Though the goal was national representativeness (or representativeness within the areas studied), we oversampled in certain target communities and interviewed local political leaders in these communities. This volume is based largely on the cross-section data. A more complete description of the samples is found in Appendix C.

History

The first initiatives for the research project took place during a trip by Gabriel A. Almond to a variety of countries in 1963 during which he had conversations with scholars about the possibility of collaborative research following up that done for *The Civic Culture*. In the spring of 1964 invitations were sent out to scholars from India, Japan, Nigeria, and Mexico for a meeting to last six weeks at the Center for Advanced Studies in the Behavioral Sciences at Stanford. The meeting there was a rather open forum for the discussion of a variety of research approaches and topics. Gradually the group converged on the subject of the interrelationship between social and economic change and political participation.

The group worked out an overall sketch of a research design, but no precise delineation of what was to be done. One important product of the meeting was a rather long and cumbersome interview form. Each group promised to test it on a few dozen respondents in each country as a means of determining whether the information we were interested in was, in fact, obtainable. The interview was not a very useful research instrument, and very little of it survived into the final field work. On the other hand, it was organizationally useful. It meant that all of the research groups spent a large part of the next academic year worrying about the same set of problems and refining their ideas on the subject.

In the summer of 1965, the same research groups met again at the University of Ibadan. The meeting lasted a little over a month and was the most crucial meeting for the development of the project. During this meeting, we agreed on a dual-level survey design (interviewing a cross-section sample as well as local leaders) and upon the overall focus of the interviews. On the basis of this meeting a fairly precise set of interview schedules was worked out. We planned pretest activities for the coming year that would involve the simulation of the entire research task in several communities in each of the countries. During the academic year 1965, pilot studies were conducted in each of the individual countries. The interviews were coded, punched, and sent to Stanford University for preliminary analysis.

In the summer of 1966 there was a briefer meeting of the research groups at Uppsala, Sweden. This meeting led to the drafting of our final questionnaires, which were then sent to each of the participating nations. The field work began in the summer of 1966 and lasted until the spring of 1967.[1] Much of the calendar year of 1967 was spent on coding the data and preparing the data for analysis. In the fall of 1967 the senior researchers from each of the countries came to Palo Alto. Some of them were fellows of the Center for Advanced Studies in the Behavioral Sciences for 1968, and others were at the Institute of Political Studies at Stanford. This gave us an extended period together planning and carrying out the preliminary analysis. Our original goal had been to accomplish a great deal of the data analysis jointly during the period when the various researchers were all together, but we were somewhat overambitious in our timing. The coding and cleaning of the data took longer than anticipated. This, coupled with the transition from the IBM 7090 to the IBM 360 delayed the availability of the data, so that only preliminary analysis could be done at that time.

However, much planning of the analysis was possible and some analysis was carried out. In addition, several members of the research teams from the other countries spent an additional six months at the University of Chicago when the American locale of the project moved there at the beginning of 1969.

In the summer of 1969, we held a meeting in Bled, Yugoslavia, to plan possible extensions of the study to several other countries. The initiative for this extension had come, in each case, from the scholars of the respective countries (or, in the case of Austria, from two American scholars who specialized in Austrian politics). The meeting in Yugoslavia focused on two main problems: (1) how to design a study that would

---

[1] The field work in any single nation took less time.

take advantage of what had been learned in the first wave of our research but that would remain comparable to the early research, and (2) how to adjust a study of political participation for application in a socialist society where the institutional structures were somewhat different.

On the basis of this meeting, a parallel study was conducted in Austria in the winter of 1969. In addition, the year 1969–70 was used for some preliminary studies in Yugoslavia and the Netherlands. During that time, one member of the Yugoslavian group spent six months in Chicago working on the research design. During the academic year 1970–1, field work was carried on in Yugoslavia and the Netherlands.

Data analysis has taken place at a variety of sites. The group that prepared the present volume has analyzed these data at computer centers at Stanford, the University of Chicago, the University of Alberta, the University of Leiden, the Max Planck Institute at Garsching, in West Germany, and the University of Iowa. (If surfers travel the world to find that perfect wave, and mountain climbers do the same to climb the unclimbable, cross-national survey researchers, burdened with the immense data files, travel anywhere to find the cheaper computer.) At these places, data were also analyzed at the request of other national groups – members of which often joined us at one or another place.

Funding

The first part of the study was funded by the Ford Foundation and the Carnegie Corporation of New York. The former supported the field research outside of the United States; the latter supported the research within the United States. In addition, there were funds supplied in each of the countries through the local research centers. Though the major funding for the first wave of studies came from the United States, the use of the funds in each of the countries was under the control of the local research team. The data analysis in the United States has been supported by the National Science Foundation. The Japanese group and the Indian group have both received funds within their own nations for data analysis. The director of the Nigerian study – formerly chairman of the Sociology Department at the University of Ibadan – now occupies the Chair of Sociology at Uppsala, where the data analysis is being supported by Swedish funds.

The studies in Yugoslavia and the Netherlands are supported by funds raised in those two countries. The Austrian study was jointly supported by funds from the Institute of International Studies of the University of California at Berkeley and the Institute for Empirical Social Research in Vienna. Thus, over time, the program has moved toward a more dispersed structure of funding.

Organization

The program was, from the beginning, organized around the principle of maximum possible egalitarian cooperation. Our hope was to have fully cooperative participation in the research design, research administration, and research analysis phases. The major intellectual problems of the study and the major design of the research instruments were determined at the series of conferences among the senior researchers from each of the countries. Within each of the countries, the local team was fully responsible for the conduct of the research.[2]

Comparative survey research is a slow and complex business. Cooperative research designed and conducted by an international group is slower and more complex by a factor probably equal to the number of collaborating groups (in our case seven). Such a research approach is often defended in terms of the sociology and politics of international social science: Intrusive research by foreigners into another country (particularly by researchers from the United States) is a form of intellectual imperialism; a more equitable approach is one in which multinational groups collaborate. The argument has much validity, and "safari research" where the foreign scholar enters to gather some data with the help of local assistants and carries it off home is and should be largely a thing of the past.

But the main justification for a cooperative style of research is intellectual. One major problem in comparative research is how can one do systematic comparisons across nations (which involves simplification and abstraction from the specific setting of any particular nation) and at the same time do justice to the significant special features of each of the nations being considered (which involves sensitivity to complex contextual factors within each nation). Too much research falls at one extreme or the other: either abstracting a few variables from each country, which may lead to superficial results, or returning to the tradition of the configurative case study, which leads to noncomparable results.

An organizational structure for research that forces scholars who have worked intensively on their own countries to consider their country within a comparative framework is one way of attempting to achieve the two somewhat incompatible goals of comparative research. The specialized knowledge that they bring of their own societies (knowledge that is necessary for meaningful understanding), coupled with the need to compare that society with others, leads to a fairly reasonable compromise between the two polar extremes of research.

Our group discussions constantly moved up and down the ladder of

[2] The only exception was the Austrian study that was conducted under the supervision of two American researchers who had worked in Austria. (See the Acknowledgments for a list of collaborators.)

specificity: We would discuss some general dimension of interest to us and how we might tap it; one participant would comment, "But that makes no sense in my country"; we would discuss the situation in that country and then attempt to climb up again to our general dimension armed with some understanding that would allow it to make more sense in that country. We tried to avoid forcing the individual nations into categories that had no relevance to their specific situations, but at the same time we tried to avoid the "in our country it is different" kind of parochialism.

Our ability to accomplish this was enhanced by our dedication to a rather flexible research strategy. No attempt was made to have identical research instruments in each nation; we were interested in functional not formal equivalence (see Chapter 2). Our goal was to deal with the same set of theoretical issues and to measure the same set of theoretically relevant dimensions but, if need be, to measure them somewhat differently in each case. Furthermore, the research instruments were not limited to the core of common concerns. In the various nations, additional sections of the questionnaires were devoted to more specific topics of interest to the local research team.

Was the enterprise worth it? In particular, has the collaboration paid off? The answer must be yes and no. In some respects our dream of a fully cooperative research venture across national boundaries worked out as we had hoped. The design of the study bears the imprint of the multiple collaborators. The design was not as neat as one created by a smaller group would have been, and, at times, the variety of concerns we carried almost drowned us. But most likely it is a better design than any that could have been created by one or the other of the national groups. The comparativist may find that we adjusted too much to national differences; the specialist on one or the other nations will certainly find that we have paid insufficient attention to national peculiarities. But one must set the balance between universalism and particularism somewhere, and we are not unhappy about our choice.

Our cooperative dream, however, has been less completely fulfilled at the analysis stage. The project involved a quite explicit agreement on data access. The main principle was that the data from all of the countries would be fully available to the senior participants in each of the countries, who would be free to do as they wished with them – with the requirement that they keep collaborators elsewhere informed. Thus each of the senior researchers in each of the countries has had, in principle, full rights to conduct any kind of analysis he wishes of the data. In fact, however, things do not work out in quite so egalitarian a manner.

It is easier to express the general principle of equality of access to the data and equal opportunities for analysis than to put these into actual practice. The members of the national groups differ in terms of the amount of time they have available to them for such activities and in terms of the computer and other facilities available to them. It is a rather empty gesture to provide raw data to collaborators who do not have access to the computer facilities needed for the analysis of those data.

Our research project made provisions for these problems. Members of the research teams spent extended periods in the United States working on the data; the U.S. group provided assistance in organizing data analyses in the various nations; and we carried out numerous data analysis requests for the various national groups. The result has been, we believe, an impressive cross-national research product. Large-scale works on each of the nations have been produced or are in progress by the national teams, and a number of collaborative works have been produced by scholars from the different countries. (A full list is provided in the list of publications of the Cross-National Program in Participation; see page 384.) Further national and comparative studies are in progress in several of the nations.

But the project never achieved the full cross-national cooperative result for which we had hoped. In part this was due to problems beyond our control. National groups differ in the kinds of resources available to them – computer facilities, time, technical assistance. Attempts to balance things by international transfers help. But, as most cross-national researchers know, everything always takes more time and costs more money. The result is that the imbalance is never fully corrected.

Perhaps we have achieved all that one could realistically have hoped to achieve. The works produced by our project are large in volume and, we hope, high in quality as well. And as a glance at the List of Publications will make clear, the product is cross-national. Yet we would be less than honest if we did not share our lingering concern that, though international cooperation may be easier in the social sciences than in politics, it is not all that easy.

Though our data come from seven nations, this is not a book about these nations so much as it is a book about some general social processes for which each nation is the setting. This is not to say that we ignore context. As we shall try to demonstrate, certain general social processes lead to different results within different contexts. The seven nations provide us with the appropriate variation in context. We do not, however, attempt to deal with the nations per se. The result is that no nation receives adequate coverage in this volume, even from the point of view of our main concerns with participation and stratification. The choice to focus on the general problem was deliberate. Fuller considerations of the individual nations on the basis of these data can be found in some of the publications listed toward the end of the book.

Acknowledgments

All scholars who have conducted cross-national social science research will agree that it takes more time, costs more money, and involves more people. There is little we can do about the time but regret its passage. We can, however, acknowledge the institutions that provided the money and, more important, the people whose ideas and help enabled us to use it effectively.

We begin with our collaborators in the Cross-National Program in Political and Social Change. Our research program has been collaborative from its beginning. The original ideas, the research design, and the analysis have been shaped in cooperation with scholars who are specialists on and, in most cases, nationals of the collaborating nations. They will not all agree with what we have done with the data. But we thank them for sharing with us their effort in collecting the data as well as their ideas at every stage.

The scholars involved included: Rajni Kothari and Bashiruddin Ahmed of the Centre for the Study of Developing Societies, Delhi; Hajime Ikeuchi, and Jun-Ichi Kyogoku of the University of Tokyo; Joji Watanuki of Sophia University, Tokyo; Ichiro Miyake of Doshisha University, Kyoto; Ulf Himmelstrand and Albert Imohiosen, formerly both of the University of Ibadan; G. Bingham Powell of the University of Rochester; Hans Daalder, Galen Irwin, and Henk Molleman of the University of Leiden; Anna Barbic, and Katja Boh of the Institute of Sociology, University of Ljubljana; Dmiter Mircev of the University of Skopje; Pavle Novosel of the University of Zagreb; and Luba Stoic of Belgrade.

Gabriel A. Almond played a key role in initiating the cross-national participation project, and Robert Somers was an important collaborator in the design and organization of the study. Jan Triska was instrumental in the arrangements that led to the Yugoslavian portion of the study. Kenneth Prewitt and G. Bingham Powell assisted us at numerous points in formulating our ideas. They were frequent and constructive critics of our research.

There are five individuals without whose dedicated efforts and intellectual contributions, this book could never have been written. John Petrocik, Kristi Andersen, Goldie Shabad, and James Rabjohn served for extended periods of time as our senior research assistants. They carried the heavy mechanical burden of the data analysis and made important substantive contributions. Ioanna Crawford, our coordinator for the past three years, managed our many data files. Without her, we would have drowned in a sea of data.

David Lawrence and Susan B. Hansen also made significant contributions to both the substance and mechanics of the data analysis. In addition, we benefited from the help of James Curry, Eugene Durman, Ester Fuchs, Calvin Jones, Ann Lugtejheid, Bill McAllister, Jaap von Pool Gaste, Lawrence Rose, Jaap Rozema, Barry Rundquist, Robert Shapiro, James Smith, and Carol Uhlaner.

Arlee Ellis at Stanford University and Shirley Saldanha at the National Opinion Research Center performed heroic service in keeping three disorganized authors and dozens of others functioning. Rachel Macurdy at Harvard took the major responsibility for preparing this manuscript, and along with Linda Budd and Barbara Pawlowski typed and retyped the chapters and tolerated our tinkering with charts and graphs. Helen Parker, Eileen Petrohelos, Karin VanSant, Lynn Schell, Cynthia Miller Lawrence, Lyn Nell Perret, and Narumi Ohora also helped with these tasks.

William C. Mitchell, C. Hadlai Hull, and Jean Jenkins designed numerous special purpose computer programs required for our analysis. The technical staff of SPSS gave us assistance on numerous occasions.

Our work has been aided by a number of institutions. The first meeting of the research program was held at the Center for Advanced Study in the Behavioral Sciences at Stanford, which was also the site for extended stays in the United States for some of our non-American collaborators. The Institute of Political Studies at Stanford University was the first home of the project. The University of Alberta provided computer time and facilities for some of the early data analysis. The University of Leiden made a similar contribution during the eighteen months in which the project was located in the Netherlands. Dale H. Bent and Christian Bay at the University of Alberta and Hans Daalder and Chris P. Haveman at the University of Leiden made these contributions possible.

The National Opinion Research Center at the University of Chicago played a special role in the development and support of this project. The Center for International Affairs at Harvard facilitated its final stages. The University of Iowa provided computer time and research assistance. No research project of this magnitude or complexity could be carried out without the understanding and active support of our respective departments and research institutions. We are grateful to all who have assisted us.

The Ford Foundation supported the early organization of the study and the data collection in Nigeria, Japan, and India. The Carnegie Corporation of New York funded the collection of the data in the United States. It also supported extended stays in the United States for the principal investigators from Nigeria, Japan, and India. The National Science Foundation (under grants GS3155 and GS38647) generously supported the data analysis. NSF has also provided funding (under grant S0C76-18690) for archiving of the data, so that both data and documentation can be made available to the scientific community.

The field work for the second wave of participating countries, the Netherlands, Austria, and Yugoslavia, was supported largely by local sources. The Dutch National Science Foundation generously supported both the field work and analysis in the Netherlands. The Austrian study was supported by the Institut für Sozialforschung in Vienna. We are grateful to Karl Blecher and Ernst Gehmacher. The Institute of International Studies at Berkeley also supported the Austrian field work. The Yugoslavian study was supported by the Federal Fund for Scientific Research in Belgrade. Nie took advantage of a Fulbright grant and Verba took advantage of a Ford Foundation faculty fellowship in the later years of the project.

Our research project has known no boundaries among nations. It also has known no boundary between professional and personal life. We have brought the project into our homes and brought our homes along to follow the project. Our spouses and children have endured numerous relocations and cultural adjustments. We owe our greatest debt to them: to Cynthia, Carole, and Suki, to Margy and Ericka, who were all there from the beginning; and to Tina, Lara, Annie, Miera, and Jonathan, who joined us along the way. They kept us going.

Sidney Verba
Norman H. Nie
Jae-On Kim

1

Introduction

Most democratic political systems are, in principle, equalitarian. They are based on universal suffrage whereby each person has equal influence. In practice, it does not work that way. There is a wide variation in the political influence exercised by citizens. One reason for this is that most – probably all – modern democracies are neither in principle nor in practice equalitarian when it comes to social and economic matters. Wide differences exist among individuals in income, educational attainment, and occupational status. Such differences mean that citizens are differentially endowed with resources that can be used for political activity and influence. As citizens convert such resources into political influence, political inequality appears.

The political advantage of those citizens more advantaged in socioeconomic terms is found in all nations, certainly in all those for which we have data. But there is a great variation across nations in the extent to which those who have greater socioeconomic resources outparticipate those having fewer resources. In this book we shall compare a very heterogeneous set of nations to determine how people attempt to influence political decisions and what process brings them into political activity. Our purpose is to describe and explain the variations across nations in the extent to which socioeconomic stratification is linked to political participation.

By political participation we refer to those legal acts by private citizens that are more or less directly aimed at influencing the selection of governmental personnel and/or the actions that they take. There are other definitions of participation, some broader, some narrower (see Verba and Nie, 1972, pp. 2–3), but this definition is appropriate for our purposes. We are interested in participation that involves attempts (successful or otherwise) to influence the government. Purely ceremonial participation is outside our sphere of concern though it is very important in many societies. And we limit ourselves to the use of "regular" legal political channels. We do not deal with protests, extralegal violence, or rebellions. We do not deny that these are important ways in which a citizenry can influence the government. But to deal with these would be to write a different book. The history of democracy is in large part the

1

history of the development of regular and legal channels through which citizens can express their preferences and apply pressure on the government to comply with those preferences. The extent to which such channels are available, the extent to which they are used, and (the special concern of our book) the extent to which they are *differentially available* and *differentially used* across social groups are crucial in understanding the effectiveness of democracy. Nor is such a subject unrelated to the subject of more intense "out-of-channels" protests; for the use of such alternative means of political influence often results from the perceived inadequacy or the unequal availability of more regular channels.

Stratification and political participation

Students of society have long debated the relationship among various stratification hierarchies. For Marx, economic position as indicated by one's relation to the means of production represented the dominant dimension of stratification that determined, in the long run, all other stratification patterns. Weber, on the other hand, stressed the distinction among economic, political, and social stratification hierarchies. Positions on such hierarchies can vary independently of each other. One individual or group may be more politically influential than another but less well off in economic terms. Or an individual or group may have wealth but less social prestige.

In general, political and socioeconomic stratification hierarchies are likely to be closely aligned. This is because one's position on one hierarchy affects positions on other hierarchies. Wealth is not the same as political power, but it can (usually) purchase political power as it can (usually with enough time) purchase social respect. Conversely, political power can be converted into wealth. Where political and nonpolitical stratification hierarchies are closely congruent, they mutually support each other. Those citizens who are wealthier, better educated, or who come from more prestigious ethnic or racial or linguistic groups will hold a disproportionate share of political influence. The political stratification system in turn reinforces the socioeconomic one: The economically and socially better-off dominate politics. Government policy, in turn, maintains and reinforces the position of those who are better off.

Where, however, the two hierarchies do not reinforce each other – where they are at least partially independent – the possibility exists that the political can modify the socioeconomic. This can happen where the political stratification system is more egalitarian than the socioeconomic one. Under such conditions, those low on the socioeconomic hierarchies will have – relatively speaking – better political positions. They can use such positions to influence governmental policies to change the socioeconomic stratification patterns. Such was the result that many expected from political democratization. The universalization of the franchise and the expansion of the right of workers, peasants, and other disadvantaged groups to form political movements would create political equality and in turn provide the opportunity for those less well off in society to press for redistributive policies. In this process the less-well-off would use their major political resource, numbers. Their success would be furthered by a disjunction between political and socioeconomic ideologies. The spread of political rights down the socioeconomic hierarchy has usually rested on an equalitarian ideology as to the proper distribution of political rights. Such an equalitarian ideology in the political sphere has often coexisted with a hierarchical one in the socioeconomic sphere. In capitalist societies such as the United States, equalitarianism as a political ideal has gone hand in hand with the legitimacy of hierarchy in economic terms. In traditionally stratified societies such as India, political equality as an ideal has coexisted with a relatively rigid social hierarchy. Equality as a political ideal would legitimate demands for equality in social and economic terms.

In fact, things have not worked out quite that way. It is difficult to measure the impact of democratization on redistribution, but the best available evidence suggests that the impact is by no means large and certainly not uniform. There have been a number of cross-national aggregate data studies of the relationship between the extent of democratization and welfare expenditures. The studies tend to converge on the finding that the level of economic development is more important than the level of democracy in determining the extent of welfare spending. (See, for instance, Cutright, 1965; Aaron, 1967; Pryor, 1968; Wilensky, 1975; Jackman, 1975; and Adelman and Morris, 1973.) Jackman, for example, concludes that the extent of democracy in a society – as measured by the percent voting, the competitiveness of the party system, the absence of electoral irregularity, and freedom of the press – is bivariately related to redistributive policies and economic equality. But when one adds the level of economic development to the analysis, the relationship between the political democracy variables and the measures of economic equality disappears (Jackman, 1975, chap. 4). Similarly, Wilensky divides societies on the basis of two characteristics: (1) "the degree to which the mass of citizens participate in decision making, a continuum from populist to oligarchical" and (2) the "degree to which the state allows or encourages the voluntary action of numerous alternative groups," a continuum that runs from liberal democracies with free speech and party competition to totalitarian systems (Wilensky, 1975, p. 21). These two dimensions are quite similar to the two dimensions that Robert Dahl uses to measure the extent of polyarchy, liberalization (the extent of legitimate political contestation), and inclusiveness (the proportion of the population taking part in political life) (Dahl,

1971, chap. 1). Wilensky finds that welfare spending is largely a function of per capita GNP and the age distribution of a population. The nature of the political system contributes almost nothing to the explanation of the extent of welfare spending (Wilensky, 1971, pp. 22–25). Lastly, one might cite similar results in the work of Adelman and Morris. Measures relating to political participation do relate to income equality, but they rank quite low as explanatory factors for the equality of income distribution across societies (Adelman and Morris, 1973, p. 184).

There is, however, some work in which a relationship between political characteristics and socioeconomic outcomes appears. Douglas Hibbs shows a fairly close connection between the nature of the party or parties that govern a country and macroeconomic policy (Hibbs, 1975, 1976). As he puts it,

> Countries regularly governed by labor-oriented, working-class-based Social Democratic parties have typically experienced average unemployment levels below the West European, North American median and average rates of inflation above the West European, North American median. In contrast, nations dominated by business-oriented, middle-class-based center and right-wing political parties have more often than not experienced above median unemployment rates and below median inflation rates [Hibbs, 1976, p. 78]

In addition, he finds that these differences across nations are replicated longitudinally within nations. Using data from the United States and Britain, he shows that lower unemployment and higher inflation rates occur under Democratic and Labour regimes than under Republican and Conservative regimes respectively. Furthermore, he argues, the macroeconomic choice between unemployment and inflation has redistributive consequences. Policies that minimize unemployment but pay less attention to curbing inflation tend to have redistributive results downward, whereas anti-inflationary policies that allow higher unemployment rates have redistributive effects upward.

Thus if the degree of democratization has little consequence for redistributive policies, the nature of the party system and the kind of party in power do. The studies we have been summarizing are based on highly aggregated cross-national data. Our study based on disaggregated micropolitical data on individuals forms a link between the two sets of studies – those that show little relationship between politics and redistributive policies and those that show a relationship. We shall seek an explanation of the weak link between the extent of democracy and redistributive policies by considering the way in which socioeconomic inequality affects the workings of political democracy and, in particular, the way in which opportunities to take part in democratic political life are used more effectively by more advantaged groups in society. This in turn dampens down the potential redistributive impact of democratization. We shall also consider the question of why there should be a stronger link between the kind of party in power and redistributive policies. We shall explore this link by considering the way in which the pattern of social cleavage in a society and the institutional manifestations of that cleavage in party competition undercut the propensity for dominant socioeconomic groups to make more effective use of the instruments of democracy.

Democracies have evolved in two ways: by expanding the number of political rights and the number of people who have the rights. Citizens come to possess the full panoply of political rights that are needed for political influence: the right to vote, to form and work for political parties and organizations, to petition the government, and to stand for governmental office, as well as the concomitant rights of free speech, press, and assembly that make the former rights meaningful. In addition, these rights are universalized so that all citizens possess them equally. The history of the franchise, for instance, is the history of the removal of barriers based on economic condition or sex or skill and often the lowering of the age threshold (Rokkan, 1962 and 1970; Bendix, 1964, chap. 3). The result is a system with wide political rights equally available to all citizens.

Such political rights, however, represent opportunities available to individuals. Citizens may or may not choose to take advantage of such opportunities; they may or may not have the resources to take advantage of such opportunities. Political rights give disadvantaged groups the opportunity to use their numbers as a political resource. Numbers, however, represent an important resource only when the members of the numerous segments of society take advantage of the rights provided to an extent equal to the advantage taken by other groups. Numbers are important when the numerous are there to be counted and when they are counted with equal weight. Where citizens differ in the extent to which they take advantage of political opportunities — some are active and some are not, or some of the activists are more active than others — numbers may play less of a role.

If activity depends on resources and motivation, then the advantage of numbers may be counterbalanced by the unequal use of participatory opportunities on the part of those who are better off. As we shall show, those high on social and economic stratification hierarchies possess greater resources and motivation to be politically active. They, therefore, take greater advantage of political participatory opportunities than those lower on the socioeconomic stratification hierarchy. The messages communicated to political leaders through the participatory system will reflect the preferences of the advantaged groups. The result is that those who are already well off tend to benefit more from governmental policies because they have greater influence on such policies.

We begin with the assumption that in all societies motivations and resources are unequally distributed among individuals. If such individual differences are the only relevant social and psychological forces affecting political participation and if participatory rights are universalized, one shall find a situation such as is illustrated in Figure 1–1: Political activity will be a function of individual motivations and resources. The result will be a participant population coming disproportionately from those high on the socioeconomic scale. The extent of the skewing in the participant population would depend on how unequally motivations and resources were distributed.

The equalization of opportunities for political activity coexists with inequalities in the *use* of such opportunities. To achieve equality in the use of participatory opportunities may involve greater governmental intervention, intervention that sets a ceiling and/or a floor on political activity. A ceiling on activity limits the amount of activity for each individual. Such a ceiling is most usually found in connection with the vote. Each citizen is allowed one and only one vote, thereby removing any differences among citizens in their amount of influence over the electoral outcome. Such a ceiling goes a long way toward equalizing political participation, but it does not eliminate the possibility that citizens will differ in their use of the franchise. Turnout is usually related to socioeconomic status. Thus it may be necessary to place a floor under political activity as well, to make it compulsory.

Figure 1–2 illustrates what would happen if participation were indeed equalized by law. If all individuals were required to participate (as in compulsory voting systems) and if there were a limit on the amount of

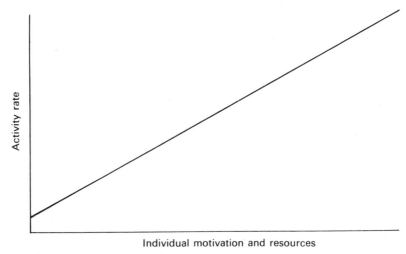

Individual motivation and resources

Figure 1-1. Individual effects only.

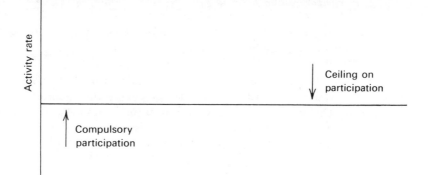

Figure 1-2. Participation equalized by law (one man, one vote, and compulsory voting).

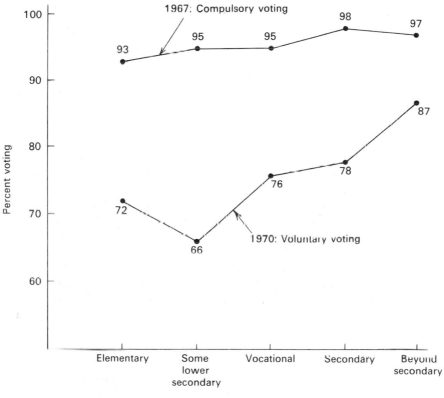

Figure 1-3. Voting turnout by education under compulsory voting and under voluntary system: the Netherlands, 1967 and 1970. Data from Irwin (1974), p. 299.

their participation (one person, one vote), there would be no relationship between individual motivation and resources and the amount of political activity. The floor under political activity would raise the activity level of those low on the resource and motivation scale to a level above that which they would ordinarily attain, and the ceiling on political activity would lower the activity rate of those high in motivation and resources. If one has a system in which the right to vote is universal, all citizens are limited to a single vote, and all citizens are required to vote, there will indeed be legally mandated equality of political activity across all social groups.

Figure 1–3 illustrates such a situation with some real data. Galen Irwin compared the relationship between education and voting turnout in the Netherlands in two elections: the 1967 parliamentary election under the system of compulsory voting that was in effect at that time, and the 1970 election under the system of voluntary voting in effect since 1967. Note that the two elections compared on Figure 1–3 are similar in two respects: Under each, voting rights were universal and individuals only had one vote. Where they differ is in that there was a floor (i.e., compulsory voting) in 1967; in 1970 the floor had been removed.

Voting turnout, as one might expect, was higher under the compulsory system. But our interest is in the relationship between socioeconomic resources and turnout. If we use education as a measure of socioeconomic resources, we see that under voluntary voting the education/turnout relationship is moderately strong; under compulsory voting, turnout is almost equal across educational levels. Compulsory voting pushes up the political activity of those lower on the educational scale. If we take the 1970 figures to indicate what turnout would have been without compulsory voting for various educational levels in 1967, we can see that compulsory voting increases turnout by 20 to 30 percent for those low in education but only by 10 percent for those high in education.[1]

A comparison of Figures 1–1 and 1–2 makes clear why the removal of constraints on participation can have the effect of making participation more unequal. If there are significant differences in resources and motivation, new participatory opportunities can mean more inequality in participation as those with the resources and motivation use the

---

[1] The figure does not illustrate the impact of a ceiling on participation, since each electoral system was a one-man, one-vote system. But one can imagine the curve if there were a floor but no ceiling – for example, a requirement that each citizen contribute some minimum amount to political campaigns but no limit on how much additional money they could contribute. All would be above a minimal threshold, but there would be status-related differences in above-the-minimum contributions.

opportunities available to them.[2] The example of legal constraints on political activity illustrates the two ways such constraints can lead to equality in activity: Those who would otherwise be inactive (those low in resources and motivation) can be boosted in their activity or those who would otherwise be active (those high on that scale) can be reduced somewhat in their activity. In either case, citizens differ in their rate of activity from what one would predict on the basis of their individual resources and motivation.

Legal constraints, however, are not effective equalizing forces. The attempt to equalize the amount of activity that citizens can engage in by placing a ceiling fails for two reasons. For one thing, as we have noted, not all citizens take advantage of rights. Secondly, such limitations work best in connection with the vote, but voting is only one of many ways in which citizens exercise political influence. Other modes of activity may be more effective and, furthermore, are much more flexible in terms of the amount of activity in which an individual can engage. The size of campaign contributions, the amount of time spent in political campaigning, the number of letters written or contacts made with political leaders, the amount of effort given to political groups – all these activities can vary widely in magnitude.

One can attempt to hold the amount of such citizen activity within limits: ceilings can be placed on campaign contributions, or such contributions can be prohibited, or they can be made less important by governmental support for campaigns. Similarly, access to office can be limited by rules against reelection. Witness recent legislative efforts to limit campaign contributions in the United States (see Adamany and Agree, 1975) or attempts to limit campaign activities as in the elaborate Japanese campaign law (Curtis, 1971). Such ceilings, however, are difficult to enforce and are often observed more in the breach (Curtis, 1971). Furthermore,(such restrictions can quickly run up against guarantees of free speech and freedom to organize politically.) The U.S. Supreme Court recently upheld limitations on contributions to candi-

---

[2] Studies of participation in industry have shown this to be the case. An increase in participation within the firm is often accompanied by an increase in the power differential across members of the firm. Mauk Mulder links this to the possession of expertise, one of the political resources in our scheme. "When there are relatively large differences in the expert power of members of a system, an increase in participation will increase the power differences between members. . . . The introduction of greater participation provides the more powerful with an opportunity to exercise their influence over the less powerful, and thereby make their greater power a reality" (Mulder, 1971, p. 34). See also Marrow, Barrows, and Seashore (1968), and, on the Yugoslavian workers' councils, see Kolaja (1965) as well as Chapter 11 in this book.

dates, at the same time when it allowed individuals to spend unlimited funds in direct support of a candidate. The possible inconsistency between the two rulings illustrates both the difficulty in drawing clear boundaries around political activity and the fact that too strict limitations seriously undercut other democratic rights.

⌐ Let us take another example: A policy that limited the amount of political knowledge a citizen could acquire or that restricted the right of an individual to be as convincing and articulate as possible in expressing his or her preferences to a political leader would hardly be consistent with democratic rights. Yet knowledge and articulateness are important determinants of effective political activity. Furthermore, they are by no ∟ means equally distributed across socioeconomic groups in the citizenry.

The effective application of a floor on political activity is even more difficult, especially for activity beyond the vote. Meaningful political participation inevitably is voluntary; at least it is difficult to imagine compulsory letter writing or compulsory local organizational involvement consistent with our notion of democratic participation. (In fact, our definition excludes involuntary acts from the rubric of participation.) And, if activity is voluntary, some will be active and others will not. In short, legal arrangements cannot guarantee equality of political activity; inequality of political activity (and in turn political influence) is likely to exist in all democratic societies.

There are, however, other forces that affect political activity and that can in turn affect the extent to which participation is equally distributed across individuals and groups. Such forces emerge from the structure of political competition and conflict in society. To understand the kinds of forces we have in mind, one must understand a distinction we make between *individual-based* inequalities in participation and *group-based* inequalities. This distinction can be applied to the process by which people come to be political activists and to the results of that process. Let us consider the individual–group distinction from the perspective of results first.

One may find differences in political activity among individual citizens but differences that are randomly distributed across the major social groupings in a society. Some individuals are more active than others, but average activity rates across significant social categories may be the same: members of one religion as active as members of others; farmers as active as workers or managers; men as active as women; rich as active as poor; and so on. Political inequality takes on a different meaning, however, when there are systematic differences in political activity across significant a social groups. What makes a social category "significant" is something we shall deal with at some length later. But for the moment suffice it to refer to any social category whose members would differ from members of other social categories in terms of preferences for governmental policy. If adherents of different religions differ in policy preferences, religion is a significant social category; if not, not. If there are differences in policy preferences between rich and poor, that becomes a significant category.

The group–individual distinction also applies to the processes by which people are mobilized to political activity. An individual-based process of political mobilization depends on individual motivation and resources; a group-based process depends on group-based motivation and resources. Let us consider individual motivation and resources first and then group-based motivation and resources.

The most important characteristic of individual motivations is that they do not involve preferences for policies beneficial to some group of which one is a member. They are "issue-neutral" motivations. Such issue-neutral motivations include a belief in one's political efficacy, general interest or involvement in public affairs, and a sense of obligation to be a political activist. Each of these "civic attitudes" increases the likelihood of political activity.[3] In addition, individuals may be motivated to become politically active because of specific personal problems or grievances with which they want the government to deal. This motivation as well involves no group affiliation. The resources associated with this individual-based process of political mobilization are held by the individual as individual. These include resources such as money or other material resources, time, prestige, and political skill.

The motivations and resources associated with the individual-based process of political mobilization are more likely to be possessed by individuals of upper status. Education provides such issue-neutral motivation as efficacy, interest, and a sense of obligation to be active.[4] Education, wealth, and high-status occupation – the usual components of upper status – provide the resources that individuals can convert into political activity. If an individual-based mobilization process is operating, upper-status citizens will form a disproportionate amount of the activist population.

The motivations and resources associated with the group-based mobilization process are somewhat different. Motivation comes from a preference for policies relevant to a social category of which one is a member. This implies consciousness of one's membership in such a social category and of the way government impinges on or could benefit

---

[3] This is not to imply that the result of such issue-neutral motivation is not some benefit for a group, nor that those with such issue-neutral motivations may not at the same time have preferences for policies to aid some group of which they are members. As we shall point out, issue-neutral motivations are far from issue neutral in their consequences.

[4] One exception is personal grievance, which is as likely to be found at all socioeconomic levels. (See Verba, 1978.)

the group. Group-based political mobilization can be based on economic position, race, ethnicity, language, region, religion, or other factors. What counts is that the motivation to be politically active derives from membership in a particular social group. The resource that is relevant to the group-based mobilization process is organization. The more or-ganized a social category is – into an association or a political party – the more capable is it of taking effective part in political life.

The distinction between individual- and group-based motivation may be better understood if we make a small diversion and address our attention to some findings in the small group experimental literature (where similar sets of forces have been noted). Give a group a task to perform for which the relevant criteria for task performance are un-certain, and those group members with higher status outside of the group (higher education, higher-status occupations) will be more active in trying to perform the task. In the absence of more specific cues as to what is relevant for the task at hand, the more general status and skills associated with education and higher occupational position leads those who have those attributes to volunteer their participation, and leads the others in the group who do not have those attributes to acquiesce to the leading role of the higher-status participants. What is crucial is the absence of cues as to what is relevant to the task at hand (Berger, Zelditch, and Anderson, 1966).

Let us give the situation a bit more political content, but keep it within the realm of the group experiment. Imagine an experimental group set up to discuss and recommend solutions to a simulated set of urban problems. Put a group of white Americans together to discuss the prob-lem, and in all likelihood the more educated and higher-status members of the group will take the lead in the group discussion – even if they have no specific competence in relation to the problem nor any partic-ular policy preferences. They will have general skill in discussion and perhaps feel an obligation to keep the discussion going. But mix the group racially, and it is likely that the black members of the group – even if they are the less well educated members – will not defer to whites of higher socioeconomic level. The additional cue of race will cause the blacks to participate beyond that which one would expect from white group members of similar status. The blacks will have – and be *aware* of having – policy preferences relevant to their identification as blacks.

We have not conducted such an experiment. But we think we are correct in our prediction of the difference between racially unmixed groups that are socioeconomically heterogeneous and racially mixed groups similarly heterogeneous in socioeconomic terms. Our analysis of changes in group participation rates over the past two decades in the United States is consistent with our argument. We found a striking change in the black/white gap in political activity. In the early 1950s, black Americans were much less politically active than whites. By the mid-1960s, they had closed that gap and were roughly as active as whites. For contrast, we traced the gap in participation between whites with less than a high school education and college-educated whites. During the same period, the gap remains constant (Verba and Nie, 1972, chaps. 10 and 14). Our explanation is simply that during the 1950s and 1960s American blacks developed a sense of race consciousness that acted as a group-based motivation. This motivation led them to increase their political activity rather than leave political initiatives to the more affluent and better educated. (See also Aberbach and Walker, 1973.) There is evidence that blacks increased their group-based resources at the same time. During the period in question, the number of black political and community organizations rose precipitously (Miller, 1977).

Group motivation and group resources can vary independently of each other. The members of a social category may have a high level of group-based motivation but be unorganized. Or a well-organized category may have no strongly felt sense of political motivation. The two are likely to go together, however. Groups with a consciousness of common purpose are more likely to form organizations; organizations are likely to try to generate and maintain a sense of common purpose among their members. Where the two go together, one would expect the greatest amount of group-based political mobilization. The well-organized group whose members are motivated to take part in political life because of interests they want to further is likely to be a group with a particularly high level of political activity. In some cases, group motivations may result in organizations that survive after the motivations have declined somewhat. Lipset and Rokkan suggest that this has been the case with many political parties. When formed, they reflect the political cleavages that are relevant, but they may survive and "freeze" those cleavages even after they have become less salient. In such a case, the organization can still mobilize individuals to political activity even if the individuals no longer share the particular concerns that led to the formation of the group in the first place (Lipset and Rokkan, 1967).

Certain social characteristics can function both within the individual-based process of political mobilization and the group-based process; examples are characteristics of social status such as education or wealth or occupational level. On the individual level, as we have pointed out, such social-status characteristics provide issue-neutral motivation and individual resources for political activity. On a group level, such socioeconomic characteristics can be the basis for group interest and/or organization. Thus individuals at a particular income level (the wealthy, the poor, or the "squeezed" middle class) or people with common edu-

cational attainment (the college-educated, those who have been educationally deprived, or people with particular technical skills) might enter
politics in order to further the interests of those particular groups. The
socioeconomic characteristics work differently in the two processes. Insofar as they affect the political activity of people through an individual-
based process, they work only in one direction: They increase disproportionately the activity of those in the upper reaches of the socioeconomic scale. When socioeconomic characteristics operate through a
group-based process, they can affect the political activity of people at
any level of the socioeconomic scale, depending on which groups – the
wealthy or the poor, the well-educated or the less-well-educated – develop consciousness of common interests and/or organization.

How are group- and individual-based processes related to group- and
individual-based results? A group-based process leads to a group-based
result. If particular groups with particular policy preferences are mobilized as groups, the result inevitably is that the participant population
consists disproportionately of individuals from such groups. In contrast,
an individual-based process of mobilization to participation does not
necessarily lead to an individual-based result in terms of the participant
population. Even if people are mobilized to politics on the basis of issue-
neutral motivations and individual resources, there will still be systematic
differences across important social categories in political activity. The
reason is that individual resources and issue-neutral motivation are not
distributed at random across social groups. Those with higher socioeconomic status are more likely to be well endowed with the requisite
individual resources and motivation. The result of the individual-based
process, therefore, is the disproportionate participation of upper-status
groups in politics. Insofar as upper-status citizens have distinctive policy
preferences, these will receive greater representation. The result is similar to what would occur if upper-status citizens were mobilized on a
group basis rather than an individual one.

There is, our discussion suggests, an interesting asymmetry between
the processes by which upper-status and lower-status citizens become
politically active. It does not require any explicit group-based process of
mobilization for upper-status citizens to take a disproportionate role in
political life. Political mobilization can take place on an individual level.
The process is implicit and not easily recognized. (Upper-status people
can also, of course, be mobilized on a group basis.) Lower-status groups,
in contrast, need a group-based process of political mobilization if they
are to catch up to the upper-status groups in terms of political activity.
They need a self-conscious ideology as motivation and need organization
as a resource. The processes that bring them to political activity are
more explicit and easily recognized. They are more likely to involve

explicit conflict with other groups. Our argument is consistent with Michels's contention that organization – and we might add ideology – is the weapon of the weak.

In a previous book (Verba and Nie, 1972) the process of political mobilization in the United States was analyzed from this perspective. It was concluded that processes in the United States tended to be individual ones, resulting in a disproportion of upper-status individuals in the participant population. Group-based processes – with the exception of those associated with black Americans – tended to increase the participation disparity between haves and have-nots, largely because upper-status individuals in America also have more group-based resources and motivation.

In the present book we expand the analysis into a comparative context so as to observe variations in the group-based processes of political mobilization. As we illustrated, the legal constraints – a ceiling or floor – on political activity can modify the positive relationship between socioeconomic level and political activity. Group-based political mobilization can do so as well. How the shape of that relationship changes depends on which groups in society are motivated to be active and have the relevant resources. If a group whose members would otherwise be low in individual motivation and resources has high group motivation and is highly organized (and if other groups higher on the individual motivation and resource scale are not equally motivated and organized as groups), the situation might resemble that in Figure 1-4. The group forces would boost up the activity rates of those with least motivation

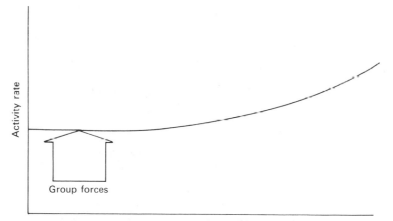

Figure 1-4. Group motivation and resources equalizing activity.

and resources on the individual level, and participation would be more equal. We shall show how this happens in societies where those low on the stratification scale are well organized.

On the other hand, group motivation and resources might be found among those citizens who already have substantial individual motivation and resources. In that case, the situation would look like that in Figure 1–5. Inequality in participation would be greater because of the reinforcing effects of individual and group forces. An example is the im-

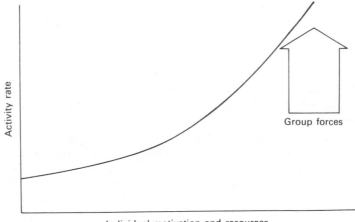

Figure 1-5. Group motivation and resources making activity less equal by reinforcing individual differences.

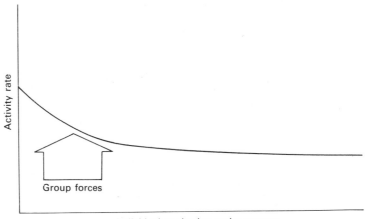

Figure 1-6. Group motivation and resources counterbalancing and overwhelming individual forces.

portance of a free-enterprise ideology and affiliation with the Republican Party that we found to be an important source of campaign mobilization for upper-status groups in the United States (Verba and Nie, p. 227).

Another example is provided by Figure 1–6. Group motivation and resources might so counterbalance the individual forces that they would create a new inequality. Citizens who would as individuals not be likely to be politically active might, through their group membership, become so politically active that they would outparticipate those whose individual motivations and resources would ordinarily make them the leading participants.

The conclusion is that group forces have the potential of reducing the kind of inequality illustrated in Figure 1–1, where those best endowed as individuals with motivations and resources are the most active. Figure 1–4 illustrates such an equalizing force. But group forces can replace inequality based on individual forces with another inequality as illustrated in Figure 1–6. Or group forces may reinforce the individual forces as in Figure 1–5.

One additional way participatory equalization can be achieved ought to be mentioned. Where one or another social category is well organized, the activity of its members will be boosted up above the rate that the individual characteristics of the members would predict. If much of the political activity in a society is based on group forces, those citizens who are not members of organized social categories are unlikely to be politically active even if they have individual motivations and resources. Lacking the requisite organizational base, they may withdraw from political life. This type of equalization is illustrated in Figure 1–7. This situation is, as we shall see, not uncommon where elections are dominated by a mass-based party. Upper-status people may withdraw from that political arena.

Overview of this book

The argument

Our main goal is to explain differences across nations in the degree to which the participant population is representative of the population as a whole. As we shall see, there are substantial differences across nations in this respect, differences in the social characteristics in which the participant population deviates and differences in the extent of that deviation. We shall look most closely at the degree to which the participant population is representative in socioeconomic terms, but shall consider other social characteristics as well.

The book attempts to solve a puzzle posed at the end of a previous book, *Participation in America* (Verba and Nie, 1972). In that book we

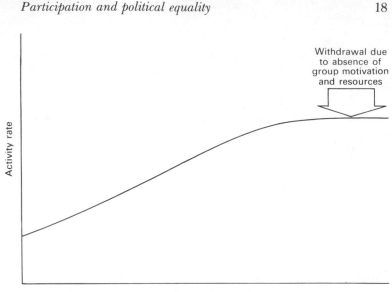

Figure 1-7. Absence of group motivation and resources causing upper-status citizens to withdraw from politics.

showed the close connection between socioeconomic status and political activity in the United States. We ended it with data on the correlation between socioeconomic status and a scale of political activity. The data were from the countries studied in the *Civic Culture* study and from our more recent cross-national studies. They showed that the socioeconomic status/political participation correlation was larger in the United States than in any developed democracy for which we had data and was matched only by the data from India and Yugoslavia. The figures for Austria, Japan, and the Netherlands were much lower. (These data are in Table 4–1.) Why should there be this variation in the relation between status and activity? And why should three nations as different as the United States, India, and Yugoslavia appear so similar in this respect? We posed that problem at the end of *Participation in America*. In this book we attempt to solve the problem.

Our explanation of the differences and similarities in the correlation between political activity and socioeconomic status lies in the juxtaposition of individual- and group-based mobilization processes. Our argument begins with the assumption that everything else being equal, those individuals who possess greater motivation and resources for political activity will be more active. If individual forces are the only ones operating, one will find much similarity across nations, with those who have such resources and motivation (the wealthier and better-educated members of the society) outparticipating those less-well-endowed in these respects.

However, all else is not equal. In particular, group-based forces differ from nation to nation. These differences are reflected in the pattern of cleavage in societies and in the way in which such cleavages are institutionalized in parties and organizations. Societies differ in the extent to which parties and voluntary organizations are tied to any particular population groups and, if they have such ties, in the particular groups to which they are tied. Group-based forces embodied in institutions such as parties and organizations can modify the participation pattern that one would have if only individual forces were operating. They do this by mobilizing some individuals to political activity over and above the level one would expect on the basis of their individual resources and motivation or by inhibiting the activity of others to a level below that which one would expect on the basis of their individual resources. The way in which institutional constraints on participation modify individual propensities to be politically active takes us a long way in explaining differences across nations in the representativeness of the participant population.

In short, we shall begin by demonstrating that individual motivation and resources give a participatory advantage to some in the society. We shall then show how this advantage can be modified by the way in which institutions such as parties and organizations mobilize individuals to political activity. The result of such institutional effects in terms of the composition of the activist population depends upon which groups are affected by institutional forces. And this, as we shall show, depends on the pattern of group affiliation with institutions. The description is probably too schematic. We shall now spell it out more fully.

The nations

The seven nations to which we shall apply our model of the forces that shape the participant population are quite a heterogeneous set: Austria, India, Japan, the Netherlands, Nigeria, the United States, and Yugoslavia. In Chapter 2 we shall discuss the criteria for this selection more fully. But for our introductory purposes it suffices to mention the ways in which they are similar and different that are relevant to the model we are testing. The nations are similar in providing whatever opportunities to participate that they do provide on a universal basis. This gives us the opportunity to observe what kind of person takes advantage of these opportunities. On the other hand, the nations differ in the kinds of group-based forces that exist. This allows us to test our model of the effects of varying configurations of such forces.

The societies we study vary in the extent to which they provide the full panoply of political rights. Four of the nations, Austria, Japan, the Netherlands, and the United States, provide the full array of such rights – the right to vote in meaningful elections, the right to form and join political associations, the right to petition the government, coupled with the auxiliary rights of free speech, a free press, and free assembly. In India, the central government has from time to time suspended certain rights in states it considers troubled; and in 1975 it suspended most democratic rights. At the time of our field work in 1966–67, however, India could certainly be listed with the preceding four nations. Unlike the case in India, our field work in Nigeria took place in the summer of 1966, shortly after the suspension of political rights by a military regime. Our questions, however, were about political activities prior to this suspension. (The particular timing of the Nigerian study poses serious problems for the analysis of those data to which we shall soon allude.)

The situation in Yugoslavia is somewhat more complicated, since it is a "democracy of a different sort." The franchise is universalized, and there are often contests for particular elective positions. But organized opposition via competing parties is barred. Speech and publication critical of the government is allowed, though only up to a point. (There appeared to be more political openness when our study was conducted, in 1971, than more recently.) On the other hand, the Yugoslavian system provides alternative institutions – local councils, workers' councils, and the like – that foster high rates of citizen participation. We shall, in our analysis, take account of these variations among the nations.

But what is crucial for our analysis is that all of these nations provide whatever rights they do provide on a universal basis – to all adult citizens with no sex, income, occupational, racial, ethnic, religious, or other limitations. If there are differences in the extent to which these rights are used, the source of the difference lies outside of the legal requirements.[5]

The framework of universal political rights allows us to observe variations in who takes advantage of these rights. We can observe how individual-based processes (which we believe to be uniform from society to society) and group-based forces (which we shall demonstrate are varied across these societies) shape the participant population. We begin our analysis with a pan-cultural generalization: All else being equal, those individuals with more resources and motivation will be more active. This generalization, as we shall try to demonstrate, holds across the heterogeneous set of nations with which we deal. Though this sociol-

[5] One qualification – that does not affect our overall argument – is the limitation of the availability of certain self-management institutions in Yugoslavia to those in certain sectors of the economy. See Chapter 11.

ogical generalization holds uniformly across nations, the result is different from nation to nation due to the "interference" of the particular patterns of cleavage and the way cleavage has been institutionalized. These patterns differ from nation to nation due to the particularities of political development in each. Thus similar sociological processes lead to different results because they are channeled through different institutions.

Participation and development: a note

The relationship among participation, socioeconomic stratification, and equality is analyzed in this book using data from relatively more and less developed societies. The problems of participation differ between the two types of society. In developing nations the problem is often posed as one of development or mobilization; in more developed nations the problem is more directly one of equity.[6] In the less developed nations, the problem of participation involves the mobilization of apolitical parochials to active citizens. This political mobilization is the result of a number of forces. Changes in the social structure increase the numbers who are literate and educated. The development of the economy increases the numbers who are employed in more modern settings; the factory, according to Inkeles (1969), can substitute for formal education as a school for citizenship. These changes provide the motivation and resources for political development on the part of individuals; they become aware of the wider world of politics, learn norms of citizen participation, and develop the cognitive skills needed for political activity. In addition to these changes in the social situation of individuals and in their psychological predispositions toward political involvement, political institutions affect the political involvement of citizens. Universal suffrage and mass election campaigns open participatory opportunities. The existence of such elections – where they represent meaningful contests – leads political parties to try to mobilize citizen activity. The result is both psychological mobilization (people become more aware of and involved in political life) and behavioral mobilization (they take a more active political role).

In more developed societies the problem of participation is more one of equality than of mobilization. Where education has been widespread and literacy universal, where political parties are well established and electoral politics well institutionalized, the problem is less one of mobilizing an apolitical mass to political life. Rather, it is one of the unequal access to and unequal use of political opportunities.

---

[6] Apter (1971) makes this a central distinction in his work on choice and allocation.

Our analysis is relevant to each of these sets of issues: the mobilization of apoliticals in developing societies and the equality of political activity in developed societies. However, we have blended both of these concerns together in our analysis, for we believe that they are related to each other. In developing nations the problem is only in part the mobilization of citizens to new forms of political life. We consider a wide range of activities – participation in national elections and campaigns as well as activity within the local community. The mobilization model is more appropriate for the former than the latter. For activities within the local community – activities in which the individual relates to his or her government on more narrow, parochial matters – the mobilization model is less relevant. Such activity appears to be widespread among groups not mobilized to politics in the broader sense, nor is its incidence clearly related to those forces – education, awareness of politics in the broader sense – that explain the mobilization of citizens to take part in national elections. (See Verba, 1978.) For these activities, however, the question of equality can be raised even if the mobilization model is of little use.

More important, the mobilization model as applied to those broader political activities for which it is explanatory, also has implications for equality. As we have indicated, economic development may increase the degree of inequity in societies as social groups take differential advantage of developmental opportunities. The same holds true for political mobilization. Citizens are reached unequally by mobilization forces, nor do all take equal advantage of mobilizational opportunities. Indeed, it is at this point that the concerns for mobilization in developing societies and equality in developed societies converge, because just those changes that produce political mobilization (the spread of education, the movement of individuals into occupations in the industrial sector and up the occupational hierarchy within that sector) become the bases for social stratification in the developed society. By looking at mobilization processes in terms of their stratification implications, we can fruitfully compare the processes by which citizens come to be active in less developed and more developed societies.

2
Comparing participatory systems

The strategy of inquiry

No single method is appropriate for all research questions. Our particular research concern is one for which large-scale survey research appeared particularly, though not exclusively, appropriate. As we have pointed out in the previous chapter, and as we shall explicate more fully in this one, we are concerned with the processes that lead to participation in a society. The analysis begins with a consideration of the process by which individual citizens come to be political activists. However, the goal of this analysis is the explanation of macropolitical phenomena. Our dependent variable is the shape of the participant population; more specifically, we are interested in characteristics of the participant population such as the participation disparity (the difference in activity rates) among different groups or the degree to which particular social groups are over- or underrepresented. Thus we need information about individuals that can be systematically aggregated to provide us data on the sub-groups within each of the nations. Sample surveys serve the purpose quite well.

The surveys we have conducted are cross-national. This is also relevant to our research concern. A single-nation study provides a sample of individuals, certainly large enough to allow generalization. But the generalization will be about individuals. We want to generalize about "participatory systems," and need more than one such system to compare. Our concerns are macropolitical, and we need macrounits to compare.

Much of our analysis deals with the individual as individual – the usual case in survey research. We are concerned with the individual characteristics of our respondents that are associated with political activity – their social backgrounds, their resources for political activity, their attitudes toward such activity. We move from these individual-level analyses to the macrolevel in several ways. For one thing, the sum of individual decisions about participation is a social outcome – that is, the individual decisions result in a participant population with a particular composition in demographic terms. The relation between individual demographic or attitudinal characteristics and political activity on the individual level will determine in part the extent to which and the way in which the composition of the participant population differs from the composition of the population as a whole.

The macrocharacteristics of the several political systems appear in our analyses as intervening variables as well. Our model of the forces that lead an individual to be politically active juxtaposes individual characteristics (the social characteristics, resources, and motivations of the individual) with institutional constraints (the effects of those institutions that recruit individuals to political life). These institutional constraints vary from nation to nation. In interaction with the individual characteristics they shape the participant population. This blending of individual forces and institutional constraints allows us to deal with one of the dilemmas of comparative political analysis: How can uniform sociological laws of political behavior (the location and testing of which is one of the goals of comparative politics as a generalizing science) be compatible with the great variety of outcomes that one finds across political systems (as close analysis of the politics in any society tells us is the case)? How, in short, is the diversity of political results compatible with general patterns of political behavior? Our model attempts to couple general laws about political behavior with the particularities of individual political systems to show how similar processes can produce different outcomes. The similar processes are those we locate on the individual level; the particularities are the institutions that exist within the various nations – especially the institutions that recruit citizens to political activity. These institutions (which differ from nation to nation) modify the impact of individual forces that we assume to be uniform from nation to nation. This is why our research puzzle requires us to have data on individuals as well as variation in the institutional systems within which the individuals operate.

As we indicated in the Preface and in Chapter 1, our choice of the seven nations discussed in this book was conditioned by a number of pragmatic considerations. But the choice of a set of nations as heterogeneous as those we have is directly related to our research strategy. We needed, first of all, a set of nations in which we could observe the phenomenon in which we were interested – the individual's political participation, his or her position on various socioeconomic hierarchies, and the organizations that could mobilize citizens to political activity. The specific form that political activity takes and the issues around which it revolves differ substantially from nation to nation. The nature and extent of socioeconomic hierarchies differ from nation to nation. And the political organizations differ. But from the point of view of our theoretical concern with political participation and the processes that lead to it, there are identifiably similar phenomena in each nation. Even in a nation like Yugoslavia, where the participatory and organizational systems are substantially different from those elsewhere, we can identify political activities and organizations comparable to those elsewhere.

Aside from the requirement that we be able to identify and measure these similar phenomena across the nations, we wanted a heterogeneous set of nations. The fact that the nations studied vary in size, culture, level of socioeconomic development, religion, and history is all to the good as far as our research design is concerned. The "maximum-difference" research design for which we have opted is powerful but risky. It is a powerful design if one is seeking, as we are, uniformities across nations. The uniformities we are seeking are in the processes by which citizens are brought to political activity. The heterogeneity of the nations works against such uniform results. If one finds uniformity across as varied a set of nations as ours, one has some warrant for believing that the uniformity has general applicability. Indeed, the maximum-difference tactic makes a virtue out of some of the necessary features of cross-cultural research. In cross-cultural research one must use different languages for interviewing, interviewer-respondent relations differ from nation to nation, citizens across nations differ systematically in the way in which they approach interviews (how trusting they are, how much they try to give the interviewer the answers they think he wants), and so on. These features lead us to a lack of equivalence in instruments and incomparability in measurements. Such is the bane of the existence of the cross-cultural survey researcher. But if out of all these confounding forces one finds similar patterns of relations among variables (and if it can be demonstrated that these are not an artifact of the application of a similar research design across the varied nations), one has a powerful result indeed. (See Przeworski and Teune, 1970.)

The approach is a risky one because it works only if one uncovers uniformities across nations. If one finds no such uniformity, the results become unintelligible. (See Zelditch, 1971.) The features that make uniformity of result powerful, make difference across the nations uninterpretable. The nations differ in many ways, and the research designs inevitably differ from nation to nation. Thus any difference one finds in the relations among variables from nation to nation can be the result of any one of the many substantive differences among the nations or as easily a mere artifact of one of the many differences in research procedures. As we shall try to demonstrate, our ability to interpret certain important differences across the nations depends on a prior demonstration of substantial uniformity.

The cross-national heterogeneity we have just been discussing is essentially an unspecified heterogeneity. By this we mean that the nations differ in many ways that we do not attempt to catalog: Each has a complex and unique history, culture, and social structure. These unspecified differences provide noisy backgrounds against which uniformities of relations among variables stand out and become more credible.

There is, however, another way in which the nations are heterogeneous. They vary in institutional structure in ways that are specifiable and measurable. These ways include the degree to which institutions control access to participatory channels and the distinctiveness of the support bases of the institutions. (See Chapter 6 for a discussion of these characteristics.) The seven nations provide us a wide range in terms of these institutional characteristics. These characteristics are entered into our analysis as initial conditions that help explain the outcome in which we are interested – that is, the shape of the participant population.

The approach allows us to take account of the way in which some complex configurative institutional patterns in each of the nations affect the likelihood that individuals will take part in political life; but it also allows us to treat these configurative patterns in a disciplined way. The history or the structure of the party system in each nation is not invoked as a general and nonspecified explanation of participatory differences among nations; nor are characteristics of the party system brought in in an ad hoc way as a means of explaining particular patterns found in one nation rather than another. We look, instead, for the impact on participation of the specified and measured characteristics of the institutional systems in each nation.

The approach, as we have said, blends cross-cultural generalization about human behavior with historical particularities about specific societies. The generalization has to do with the individual forces that lead to political participation; these we expect to operate uniformly from nation to nation. The historical particularities are the institutional patterns in each nation, in each case the result of a long and complex historical evolution, but manifested in the current setting in the specific characteristics we enter into our analysis. The interaction between the uniform processes and the varying institutional constraints deriving from the different sets of historically produced institutions leads to divergences among the nations in the participatory outcome. (This description is abstract; more concrete illustrations will be presented in subsequent chapters.)

For the kind of analysis we propose, the nature of our dependent variable is crucial. As we have indicated, we are not interested in explaining the decision on the part of the individual whether or not to take part in politics. Our interests are in a macropolitical outcome. But it is a macropolitical outcome fairly closely tied to the survey data, which consists of responses of individual microunits. One of the main problems in the use of survey research to deal with macropolitical phenomena is the danger of committing what Scheuch (1968) has labeled the individualistic fallacy. On the basis of aggregations of individual attitudes or behaviors, one explains some macropolitical outcome. But often there is quite a gap between the data analyzed and the outcome: One has data on attitudes toward democratic procedures and relates them to the stability of a democratic system; or one has data on attitudes on economic growth and relates those to the rate of economic growth. The macro-dependent variable floats a long distance above the actual data manipulated: the data are on individual attitudes or behavior; that which is explained is some institutional pattern. Our ultimate dependent variable is the "shape" of the participant population – that is, what kinds of people participate and how representative of the population as a whole is the participant population. This is a dependent variable based on our data. As our independent variables and intervening variables change, the dependent variable changes in a measurable way.

Surveys versus other techniques

Large-scale cross-national surveys do not represent the only research technique that could be applied to our problem. Consider two alternative ways in which we might have approached the research problem. One approach would be to gather aggregate data from a wide range of democratic nations. Data are available on the socioeconomic characteristics of nations: urbanization, industrialization, media, literacy, ethnic homogeneity, and so on. Data are also available on political activities, though these are usually limited to voting turnout. In addition, other aspects of the participatory systems of the nations can be coded from the literature: the competitiveness of parties, the extent of freedoms, the role of the military, and so on. Such data allow cross-national analyses of the correlates of political participation.

Such analyses have a number of advantages over the survey studies we report. They cover a wider range of nations, a fact that is of great importance if one wants to generalize about patterns of politics on the level of the political system. One can, for instance, consider processes in different regions of the world or among developed versus less developed nations. Also such studies allow for systematic analyses of the relations between characteristics of the population in a nation and characteristics of political structures. For instance, studies have been conducted – across nations and across the states of the United States – on the relationship between economic, social, or political characteristics of a population (per capita income, the percentage with advanced education, the percentage voting) and policy outputs.

Data of this sort have some inherent disadvantages though. For one thing, one is limited to those measures that are "available" – that is, those that are contained in published compendiums or that can be coded from newspapers and the like. These may not be the most relevant for one's purposes. From the point of view of the study of participation, this would often mean limitation to data on voting, the political act that, as we shall demonstrate, is probably the least useful for comparative study. In addition, the data on matters such as political attitudes – which may be crucial for the analysis of participation – are not available.

Second, studies based on aggregate data are forced to treat the nation as a unit; the data are aggregated at that level.[1] They allow little penetration into the social unit to deal with internal variation or internal social structure. Lastly, such data are relatively insensitive to the complex contextual variations from nation to nation; little attention can be paid to the nuances of the meaning of variables in different contexts.

Consider an example of such research, Robert Jackman's excellent book on *Political and Social Equality* (1975). It deals with a problem very similar to our own concerns: determining the sources of social and economic equality. More specifically, the book deals with the question of the extent to which political democracy leads to such equality. (We have discussed some of the substantive results in Chapter 1.) Jackman's data come from the World Data Analysis Program at Yale University, which in turn collected them from various published sources. He uses data for sixty nations. His conclusion is quite consistent with the conclusions of our own work: Political democracy does not appear to lead to greater social and economic equality, whether that equality be measured in terms of government programs aimed at fostering equality or in terms of actual income distribution data. There is a positive zero-order relationship between political democracy and equality, but that turns out to be a spurious effect of level of economic development (Jackman, chap. 4). That Jackman's conclusion is consistent with our conclusion is encouraging, and especially so because he uses a quite different set of data and a quite different approach to analysis. Furthermore, Jackman

---

[1] Whenever relationships found at the aggregate level are interpreted at the level of lower units, one runs into the danger of committing an "ecological fallacy." (See for general discussion, Robinson, 1950; Scheuch, 1968; Alker, 1969.) Even for a study whose main focus is on systemic variables, one may have to deal with aggregate level variables and relationships that are not intrinsically "systemic." For instance, the relationship between the level of education and the rate of voter turnout at the aggregate level may be of interest because of the assumed relationship at the individual level; the expectation is that the higher the level of the education for a given individual, the higher will be his probability of voting. In the context of aggregate data analysis, one does not have the option to examine such relationships at the appropriate level. For this reason multivariate controls at the aggregate level can be misleading as long as some of the relationships in the data are intrinsically "individualistic." (For an illustration of this problem on American states, see Kim, Petrocik, and Enockson, 1975.)

has a large enough sample of nations that the nation becomes the unit for his statistical analysis. His technique of analysis consists of regressions run across the sixty nations. If one wants to generalize about nations, he is operating at the right level. Furthermore, because the data are on the level of the nation-state, he can systematically vary macropolitical phenomena such as expenditures on welfare, the nature of electoral laws, and so forth.

On the other hand, because of the limitations of his data, Jackman can only take the analysis so far. He has little explanation for the fact that political democracy is not related to social and economic equality. We believe we can take the analysis further and explain why political democracy does not lead to equality. To do so we focus on within-nation variations. Surveys allow analysis of such variations, something not possible with most aggregate data sets. One of Jackman's crucial dependent variables is a measure of income inequality, measured as intersectoral inequality (i.e., inequalities across sectors of the economy – agriculture, mining, manufacturing, etc.). The measure does not take into account intrasectoral inequalities – within agriculture, and so forth. As we shall discuss, equalities across sectors of society often mask significant inequalities within sectors. Each type of inequality is important in our model of the politics-equality linkage.

More important for our purposes are the measures of political democracy. Jackman used four such measures: (1) the percentage of the voting-age population that votes, (2) the competitiveness of the party/election system, (3) the absence of election irregularities, and (4) the existence of a free press (Jackman, p. 64). These measures illustrate the relative strengths and weaknesses of his approach and our approach. Two of the measures used by Jackman, election irregularities and free press, do not enter into our analysis in any systematic way. Our nations vary in terms of these characteristics, but we have too few nations to allow for systematic comparison on that basis.

We do deal with the nature of party competitiveness as well as, more intensively, with the proportion of the population politically active. For each of these measures Jackman has the advantage of a larger number of nations and more systematic cross-national variation. We have the advantage of greater within-nation variation. As we shall show, equalitarian outcomes do not depend on party competition per se but on the nature of that competition and, in particular, on the social composition of the competing parties. Austria and the United States are both categorized in the highest category of Jackman's competitiveness scale, and both are essentially two-party systems. But the impact on equality of party competition differs from one nation to the other, largely because of the different social composition of the parties.

Even more limited is his measure of citizen participation, that is, the percentage of voting-age population that votes. As we shall indicate, participation is related to socioeconomic equality, but that is not apparent if participation is measured as the aggregate proportion of the voting-age population that votes. For one thing, voting is only one of the activities one can consider from the point of view of the relationship between socioeconomic factors and politics. And in many ways it is an inadequate indicator of the level of political participation within a population (Verba, Nie, and Kim, 1971; and Chapter 3 of this book). More important, it is not the absolute proportion of the population that is active that counts but the differences across social groups in their proportion that is active. An analysis that allows one to consider which population groups take the greatest advantage of participatory opportunities – analysis that requires survey data about varied political activities that can then be analyzed by social grouping – will take us a step beyond the aggregate analysis and allow an explanation of why socioeconomic equality does not increase with increased political democracy. In Chapter 5 we shall spell out the model that incorporates differences in participation rates across groups.

Our purpose here is not to criticize the Jackman approach in order to praise our own. The approaches are complementary and, therefore, the convergence in results is gratifying.

There is an opposite alternative approach to our problem: One could conduct a close configurative case study of the participatory system in one nation or, if one wanted to carry out a particularly close study, in one community. Such studies have many advantages over the analyses of aggregate data or of survey data. Observations can be richer and more varied. The scholar can know the place and people he is studying firsthand; he can take into account the complexities of the particular situation. Studies of this kind are not superficial; they allow the scholar to penetrate deeply into a particular situation. The individuals or communities one studies are treated as fully rounded entities, not as ciphers in a statistical analysis.

On the other hand, such studies present problems of generalization. Often they are unsystematic; the researcher's methods are not easily replicable by others. And the extent to which the particular case is idiosyncratic is often unknown. Under certain circumstances, depth case studies can contribute to generalizable knowledge. Where theory is well developed, one can have a crucial case in which the predictions of a theory or the rival predictions of two theories are tested (Eckstein, 1975).

Again we can consider an example. Sharon Zukin, in *Beyond Marx and Tito: Theory and Practice in Yugoslav Socialism* (1975), deals, as does Jackman, with a topic close to our own concerns: the patterns of stratification in political participation. She is concerned with the ways individuals participate in Yugoslavian political life, the political strata that emerge, and the social composition of these strata. Her research approach could not be more different from ours. Our surveys cover many nations and many respondents within each nation; they are interviewed with relatively structured interviews and their responses are coded for statistical analysis. Zukin examines a smaller number of people more intensively.[2] She selects ten "ordinary" families in Belgrade, families whom she met through acquaintances; she talks extensively with the members of the families and observes their lives. In addition, she visits and observes political meetings in Yugoslavia. The choice of a few families, all in Belgrade, is made on quite reasonable grounds. The small number provides an opportunity for full and intensive study. The fact that they are all Serbs allows Zukin to interview them personally (she speaks the Serbian version of Serbo-Croatian). And the fact that they are all in the same city makes the study feasible within a limited amount of time.

Zukin's own conclusions are, as were Jackman's, quite consistent with our own. She finds a great deal of stratification both in terms of how active citizens are and in terms of the social characteristics of the activists. Participatory opportunities – such as those provided by voters' meetings – are used by those who would otherwise be active. Her description of the kinds of issues raised at these meetings by different types of participants parallels distinctions we make.

But Zukin's description of participation in Yugoslavia is much richer and more immediate than ours. She describes the drama and setting of a voters' meeting – the importance of who sits where, of gesture, of the nuances of interchange. This conveys an understanding of participation in Yugoslavia well beyond that in our lifeless statistics. In addition, Zukin presents extended quotations from those she interviewed, on the meaning to them of political activity. We learn many things not apparent in our data. Her respondents, for instance, have a clear understanding of the difference between form and substance in participation, a subtle distinction we cannot draw.

That which makes the Zukin study so rich also creates its limitations. One learns much about ten Serbian families in Belgrade. But how far can one generalize from such a small group? Zukin presents a convincing case for the choice of Serbia and, within Serbia, of Belgrade. But, as she points out, Belgrade and Serbia differ substantially from other parts of Yugoslavia (Zukin, pp. 272–3). And, of course, the ten families form no

---

[2] For Zukin, the choice of the intensive approach is not merely a choice among alternative research strategies, as we think it to be. Rather, it appears to express a fundamental orientation to research that is in opposition to "imperialistic, quantitative social science," which she considers to be wrongheaded in political, human, and methodological terms (pp. 267 ff.)

systematic sample from which one could begin to generalize. Nor are Zukin's research techniques easily replicable. Her study, like her respondents, is unique.

Our purpose is not to present the case for one technique over the other, nor even the case for our technique over either that of Jackman or Zukin. Nor have we done justice to the two approaches; there are many variations of each approach and approaches that combine characteristics of each. But the polar approaches allow us to place our approach into context. The comparative-survey strategy has some of the advantages of each approach and some of the disadvantages. Cross-cultural survey studies can cover a range of nations. In this way they partially avoid the problem of the limited-case study in that one has a firmer basis for generalization to other cases. But, unlike the aggregate-data studies, one is still limited to a few nations and they may be atypical. Cross-cultural survey studies penetrate fairly deeply into the individual nations from which samples are drawn. They can pay attention to internal variations. They can be used to measure a wide range of phenomena unavailable in aggregate-data studies – in our case they can tap a wide range of participatory activities as well as attitudes related to participation. Surveys, nevertheless, remain superficial instruments compared with depth case studies: Questioning is stereotyped; it does not probe the nuances of individual meanings; inadequate attention is paid to context and the complexities of the situation.

It is clear that no single research approach is correct. For the set of questions we have, comparative surveys offer, we believe, the best answers. Part of our study involves the systematic analysis of the relationships among individual characteristics, in particular the relation of individual resources and motivation to political activity. Such analysis can be conducted with data from one nation. Cross-national survey data allow us to study such processes within different institutional settings to observe how institutional constraints affect participation.

The answers possible with our technique are far from complete. We shall discuss some complex internal patterns in each of the nations, but these will by no means encompass the totality of the participatory systems in any single case. Our goal is to locate some "main effects" of certain variables on the participatory systems in these nations, not to deal with all aspects of participation. We think that these main effects are important enough so that the "superficiality" of the approach is warranted.

On comparability

Our studies, as we have noted, are of a very heterogeneous set of nations. As an inevitable consequence, as well as by design, the research procedures differed from nation to nation. Some heterogeneity is inevitable when languages differ, the training of interviewers differs, and the social and cultural characteristics of the interviewer-respondent interaction differ as well. But the organization of our study introduced more heterogeneity in the study design than that which was inevitable due to the variety of research settings. The individual teams carried out studies that were parallel but not identical in each nation. Under such circumstances, what warrant have we to assume that our studies are indeed comparable?

Multinational surveys are useful for understanding political processes because of their multicontextual nature – that is, because the nation varies. But it is just this multicontextuality that makes such surveys difficult and that poses the question of how comparable they really are. The sources of noncomparability have been analyzed by various authors and do not need repetition here (Verba, 1969; Scheuch, 1968; Przeworski and Teune, 1970). The analyses demonstrate that the results of comparative survey research are always subject to challenges to their validity and the challenges are never fully answerable. We may find a "similarity" or a "difference" between two societies. The similarity or difference may be in the proportions of a sample responding in particular ways, in the relations among variables in the two societies, in group differences within societies. Thus in the study of political participation we may find difference or similarity between two societies in the proportions who vote, in the relationship between media exposure and voting, or in male-female differences in voting turnout. Or we might find more complicated difference or similarity in the patterning among measures – different factors emerging in a factor analysis, different multivariate relations between independent and dependent variables.

Such similarities and differences are always subject to challenge that they are not "real," that that which seems similar is not really similar, that that which seems different is not really different. Assume for a moment that one has a satisfactory sample in two societies and that some difference between the societies in the response to an item or a pattern of relationships is clearly statistically significant. The finding is still subject to the challenge that the difference is invalid because the measurements in the two societal contexts are not comparable. And this in turn may be because of some systematic difference in measurement technique between the two contexts or because one is measuring something different in each society. Since cross-cultural survey research is nonexperimental, any difference between the two societies is subject to the challenge of an alternative hypothesis: that the "treatment" of the two societies was different and that the differences found are artifacts of the research design (Campbell and Stanley, 1967). And these alternative hypotheses apply not only to the relations among variables within nations but (even more so) to simple findings of differences in responses between nations. The survey finding that organizational membership rates are greater in one country than another (Almond and Verba, 1963, and Chapter 6 in this book) is immediately subject to the challenge that the difference found between the two nations is not a difference in organizational membership rate at all. Rather, it may reflect a difference in the stimulus presented respondents in the two countries, that is, a translation difference perhaps, or any one of a hundred differences in the administration of the survey. Or the argument can be made that organizational systems are so different between the two societies that one has not successfully measured the same thing in each society. The statement that the rates are different, therefore, has no meaning.

Such challenges are not limited to cross-cultural research. Survey research always studies multiple groups – localities, classes, ethnic groups, men and women. As long as the criteria for experimental design are not met – and they never are – any group difference is subject to challenges of the kind just described. The same survey question in the same language can mean different things to different types of respondents. But survey research carried on in different social settings, and in particular when those settings are societies or nations, makes these problems more explicit. One more easily ignores dialect differences within a single language area and assumes, perhaps without validity, that one is dealing with the same interview across the entire sample. One cannot ignore the language problem in cross-cultural research. More important, the fact that the study is carried on in different contexts increases the number of plausible alternative hypotheses that we might call methodological – that is, those alternative hypotheses that explain a difference or similarity as a by-product of the research design. Systematic differences in research instruments and processes between societies and cultures are inevitable and severe – language being the foremost. (And one can add a further reason why rival hypotheses are more likely to require consideration in cross-cultural research: There are more rival "hypothesizors"; in other words, specialists in one society or the other are uneasy about too facile comparison and are ready to suggest such plausible alternatives.)

Consider some results of our comparative studies in political participation. We asked respondents about their political activity. Some activities were asked about in all seven countries. We asked about voting, about contacts with various kinds of officials, about certain kinds of group activities (these activities and their significance are discussed in the next chapter). We find some similarities and some differences across nations in the proportion active as well as similarities and differences in the relation among these acts and in the relation between the acts and other variables. How do we know whether differences and similarities are real or perhaps merely the result of our research technique? To be sure that the results are not a by-product of the research techniques, we would have to be certain that individuals in each country received the same "treatment" – that they were asked the same questions in the same way. But since there were different interviewers interviewing in different languages, this criterion is not met. And the most powerful technique for eliminating these contaminating effects – random assignment to the alternative treatments – is not possible. If Indians, Americans, and Austrians could be randomly given Hindi, English, and German interviews, assigned randomly to situations in which caste relations between interviewer and respondent were relevant and others in which they were not, and so forth, one would have greater confidence that the differences reported in political activities were not an outcome of the research design but a "real" difference across the three countries. But, of course, the situation is just the contrary – the treatments differ and they differ systematically across the line one is trying to make the basis of the comparison. Interviews are conducted in English in the United States, in German in Austria, and in Hindi in India (as well as in a number of other languages). Caste is important in India, but not in the United States. Perhaps the words used to ask about a particular activity in English are evaluatively neutral, whereas in one of the other languages the nearest approximation connotes something reprehensible. This might affect the frequency of positive response as well as the relations of such positive responses to other variables.

Even if we assume our result is not the artifact of our instruments, what warrant have we to assume that political acts – even when they have the same name such as voting or contacting an official – are equivalent across nations? Are votes equivalent acts in one-party, two-party, and multiparty systems; in circumstances where eligibility to vote is an easy status to achieve and where it is hard to achieve? Can contacts be compared where the techniques of contacting may differ (in some nations by mail, in others in person), where the officials contacted differ, and where the subject matter of the contacts differs from nation to nation? In short, can we meaningfully compare acts that may appear on the face of it similar but that are embedded in complexly different political systems?

This latter problem cannot be cured by making the stimulus equivalent from nation to nation. Even if one could achieve equivalence – and the argument suggests that it is impossible to achieve stimulus equivalence in any complete sense of the word – the questions asked are inevitably about different things, that is, about activities within different social systems.

To take this argument to its extreme is to take a profoundly anticomparative position: Everything is unique, hence noncomparable; hence generalizations about social matters are impossible. (See the discussion in Zelditch, 1971.) We do not take this position. But the sense in which everything is, as we all know, unique is worth explicating because it helps us understand what we can and cannot do in comparative analyses such as those we undertake in this book.

Let us consider how we try to bypass these problems.

Functional equivalence. As do other comparativists, we seek functional equivalence, not face or full equivalence. The face similarity of items for comparison is trivial and, for reasons just spelled out, potentially misleading. What is important is the functional equivalence of items.

There is, we must admit, more reference in the literature to the importance of functional equivalence than there are clear definitions of what exactly a functional equivalent is. In functional analysis, the term functional equivalence refers to the fact that the same function may be performed by alternative institutions or in alternative ways (Merton, 1957). In the looser sense in which it is used in relation to comparative research it refers to the fact that the same variable may be indexed by a variety of items, and different items may be the most appropriate indicators in different settings. Wealth in one society may be best indexed by monetary income, in another by ownership of cattle; aggression, by verbal behavior among some groups and by physical violence among others; political participation by one set of activities in one place, by another set elsewhere.

What this means is that in order to achieve functional equivalence one must begin with fairly general dimensions (and, better, fairly general hypotheses or theories). Before one compares voting rates, one ought to consider the underlying dimensions for which voting is relevant. This in turn means considering the underlying theory of politics (or some aspect of politics) for which the study of voting is relevant.

The fact that we are searching for functional equivalents makes clear that we are not looking for full equivalence, that is, for measures that are equivalent in all respects. What is important is that the measures be equivalent in those respects that are relevant to the problem at hand. In Chapter 3 and Appendix A we shall try to demonstrate this kind of equivalence for certain modes of political activity across our seven nations. The modes of activity do not consist of identical acts across nations – in some cases a particular mode of activity is indexed by one set of activities in one nation, another set in another. Or even when the specific activity that indexes a mode of activity is, on the face of it, the same across nations (as in the voting mode), our only claim is that the vote in all nations shares certain significant characteristics; characteristics defined by our abstract dimensions of political activity. It is, for instance, an act requiring little initiative in each of the nations – for reasons we discuss in Chapter 3 and Appendix A. In other respects voting differs from nation to nation. One goal of our analysis of voting is to explicate these differences. But it will only be meaningful to explicate these differences after we have established that voting is in certain respects similar. In short, to establish that measures of some phenomenon such as political participation are functionally equivalent, one must start at a level more abstract than the specific item. The specific items are equivalent only within a framework provided by the more abstract dimensions.

This approach has implications for a variety of aspects of research design. Once one accepts the fact that complete equivalence is not possible and that functional equivalence is all that one can achieve, the problems of translation are eased. One does not seek literal translation, since the goal of exact equivalence is unattainable. Translations can be much freer. (See Verba, 1971, for a discussion of our approach to translation.)

This still means, however, that the determination that one item is a functional equivalent of another is by the fiat of the researcher. Consider two types of political activity: voting and citizen-initiated contacts. Within our scheme of participatory modes, votes are equivalent from nation to nation because in each nation the vote is (among other things) an "easy" act – by which we mean that the act requires less initiative than other acts because the occasion for the vote is presented to the individual (by periodic elections). Similarly, citizen-initiated contacts are considered to be equivalent across nations because they are (among other things) acts in relation to which the individual can "choose the agenda" – by which we mean that he decides whom to contact and on what subject (compared with, say, voting, on which he does not choose the election issues).

Can we go beyond the assertion (based to be sure on quite reasonable inferences from our general knowledge) that these acts have the characteristics they are assumed to have? Two ways of doing so are the use of open-ended questions to see whether these types of political activity mean to the respondents what the researchers think they mean and analysis of the way in which multiple items measuring alternative modes of political activity cluster together.

Open questions. "Closed" questions are those in which the respondent is asked to choose among preselected response alternatives. "Open" questions are ones in which the respondent can freely give what answer he wants. Open questions are expensive and time consuming – they take up much time in an interview and are costly to code. But they may be particularly useful in cross-cultural research. One challenge to the comparability of similar-sounding items cross-culturally is that the cultural meaning of an item may be quite different from one society to another. This makes the use of open questions without rigidly fixed response categories somewhat more attractive than they might be in single-culture research. The openness of the responses provides the researcher with a body of material out of which one can more easily locate lack of equivalence than one can in the response to a fixed-choice question. The open responses more easily reveal linguistic differences than fixed responses, and by reading responses one can gain (or lose) confidence that the question was about the same subject.

Such open questions were used in relation to citizen contacts – a crucial kind of political activity in our scheme of activities. We asked a set of closed questions about contacts on several governmental levels – whether the respondent had ever contacted a governmental official on some problem. These were followed by open questions about the position held by the official, and the subject matter (the problem) of the contact. Thus, for each contact, we have not merely an affirmative answer that a contact was made, but a textured set of responses describing the details of the contact. The latter material is useful for two purposes. It increases our confidence that the contacts mentioned in fact took place and that we are recording more than a random selection among fixed alternatives. (It is, however, less certain on this basis that the contacts *not* mentioned *did not* take place. But we also asked a follow-up question on reasons for not contacting, the answers to which give us some sense of the extent to which those who report no contacts did, indeed, not contact.) And the open material about the contacts tells us something of the extent to which these acts are indeed equivalent across countries as we expect them to be.

The open question about which officials were contacted verified that these contacts were with government officials (as we intended them to be). The open question on the subject matter of the contact verified that these were demand-making contacts (as we intended them to be). Respondents were not reporting visits to an official to express their support for his policies or to pass the time of day (which would not have been the kind of contact in which we were interested) but to articulate some problem they wanted solved. Furthermore, the open question allowed us to make some theoretically important distinctions among types of contact – to be discussed more fully in the next chapter.

Open-ended responses were used in some countries and not in others when we wanted assurance that we were obtaining "real" answers, that is, something that was in the respondent's head before we came along and asked questions rather than responses that were merely the artifact of our questions. In most countries we asked closed questions about party affiliation: Was the respondent a supporter of Party A, Party B, or what? We did not believe that we were contaminating responses by mentioning party names in Austria or the United States, since they were so well known already. In India, where the populace is more heavily illiterate and where knowledge of parties and political matters was more problematic, we asked the respondent whether he supported any political party, and then asked "Which one?" Respondents were classified as party supporters only when they mentioned the name of a party without prompting. This is a small difference in question wording but one that gives us greater confidence that those respondents who are classified as party supporters understood our question and were responding appropriately to it. (For an extended analysis, see Field, 1972.) This of course does not eliminate a number of other ways in which party support might have a different meaning in India. The Indian who volunteers that he supports the Congress Party may not support it at all – he may say so because he thinks that is what the interviewer wants to hear, because that is the only party name with which he is familiar, or because he fears trouble if he says anything else. Our open-ended form eliminates only one possible inequivalence between nations – ignorance in one nation of what the word "party" means and ignorance of the names of parties. It brings us closer to confidence that we have something equivalent across the nations, but it does not establish full confidence.

Multiple indicators and scales. Scaling and clustering techniques are another way of establishing the equivalence of items and dimensions across nations. If items fall into the same dimensional space across the nations, that is evidence that the dimension (and the items that tap them) have some cross-cultural validity. Such analyses are common in single-nation research. The problem is compounded, however, across cultures. Suppose one uses a different set of items in each nation because the different items seem the best measures of the same dimension. If the items in each country cluster together, this indicates that the set of items in each country measures some dimension. But what is the warrant for considering the dimension to be the same in each country? A useful – though partial – solution is suggested by Przeworski and Teune, whereby cross-culturally equivalent scales are constructed out of sets of items some of which are "identical" whereas others are country specific (Przeworski and Teune, 1966; Teune, 1968). In a sense, the equivalence of the scale depends on the fact that there are in each nation items that are, on the face, identical; the internal consistency of the scale depends on the interrelation among the items in each country; and the relevance of the scale to each country depends on the adjustment of the items that derive from the country-specific measures.

Our work on participation uses a similar approach (independently arrived at). In each country, a wide range of questions was asked about specific acts of participation; the acts were assumed to be specific examples of the alternative modes of participation. In each country there

were similar items of participation presumed to tap each type of participation and some different ones as well – since each nation provides its
citizens with a different available repertory of participatory acts. The
questionnaire items were then subjected to a factor analysis – one that
produced in each of the four countries a fairly close match to the
structure we expected among the participatory items: Factors associated
with each of the hypothesized modes of participation were produced.
The four factors are the "same" in each country in that the identical
items are patterned the same way, and the additional country-specific
items are loaded on what is clearly the most appropriate factor given
their face meaning. We shall present this analysis in the next chapter.

The specific items that form the parallel factors are not the same
across all the nations. This is important methodologically. We have
stressed the value of a research design involving heterogeneous nations:
If one finds a similar structure of participatory acts across such a varied
set of nations, it is some warrant for believing that we are tapping
universal dimensions of political activity that are indeed comparable.
But the similarity of structure does not emerge on its own in each
nation. The similarity is found in the analysis of the results from research
studies in each of the nations, and these research studies are not independent one from the other. They are all designed by the same collaborating group with the same purpose in mind.

The similarity in factor structure (or other similarities) could be an
artifact of the similarity in the origin of the research. However, the fact
that the research instruments are different – they contain different
items, in different order, with different format – makes it less likely that
the resulting structure is merely an artifact. In Appendix A we shall give
some specific examples to support our contention that the results we
find are not artifactual. Here we simply want to make the point (a point
with some significance for cross-cultural research design) that under
certain circumstances the fact that different research designs are applied
in different countries may result in an increase in comparability rather
than a decrease.[3]

The absolute and the relative

In most cases, our analysis involves relative rather than absolute
measures. Relative measures are more useful for our purposes and, we
believe, more reliable. We avoid some of the problems of establishing
equivalence by avoiding direct cross-national comparisons of marginal
results. Comparisons of the proportions reporting that they contacted

---

[3] In addition, we shall cite independent evidence from other studies in other
contexts on the dimensions of participation.

an official or of the proportions expressing one or another political attitude are most susceptible to the challenge that they are invalid. The marginal responses to a question are sensitive to question wording, question order, and the way in which the interview is administered. This creates problems of comparability cross-nationally, since nuances of question wording, the structure of the questionnaire, the relationship of the interviewer to the respondent, and so forth, will all differ system-atically across national boundaries. The comparability of marginals de-pends on the equivalence of the stimulus; and such equivalence is hard to achieve in cross-cultural research.

In Chapter 3 we shall present data on the proportions in each nation that have been active in various ways. The data are presented there because they are the raw material for our analysis of the structure of participation. They also have some intrinsic interest. We do not argue that the comparison of the proportion active is meaningless. They rep-resent as good data as exist on the subject. Our point is that the extent to which questions were equivalent from nation to nation cannot be precisely established. The more "straightforward" the question and the more the question is about an unambiguous subject, the more valid are the data. Many of our questions are straightforward and deal with relatively unambiguous subjects. We have greater confidence in the comparability of questions about past behavior than we have in questions about respondents' attitudes on political matters – whether, for instance, they are "efficacious" or not, "alienated" or not. But since the question itself produces its own response pattern, there is no way to know how much of that response pattern is an artifact of the particular question characteristics. When considering the data on rates of political activity in the several nations, the reader should be warned of the uncertainty of their meaning. (For an extended discussion, see Kim, Nie, and Verba, 1974.)

Whereas it is difficult to compare the absolute amount of activity across nations, we can more meaningfully compare the relationship between political activity and other characteristics. Our main dependent variable in this book is not the level of political activity but the relation-ship of political activity to social class. Other dependent variables involve the relationship of political activity to other social characteristics. In other words, we do not try to explain why citizens in one country are more active than others (or why subgroups of citizens in one country are more active than similar subgroups in other countries – why, for instance, farmers in one nation are more active than farmers in another). Rather, we try to explain why the relationship between, say, education and participation is greater in one nation than another, or why the farm sector of a society outparticipates the industrial sector in some societies but not in others.

In making such comparisons, we use measures that are relative to the population within each society. Our measures of participation and socioeconomic level (two of our basic measures) are standardized within each society; the most participant citizens in each of the nations are defined as such relative to the activity rates of others in their nation. Since we are interested in processes within nations, this approach seems reasonable.[4]

System similarities and system differences: validating comparisons through data analysis

In addition to the approaches just spelled out to the validation of our comparisons, we also believe that the cross-national validity of our analysis can be demonstrated by the analysis itself. Since this sounds somewhat circular, let us explain what we mean.

We face a dual problem in our analyses of participation. On the one hand, we seek to confirm some pan-cultural generalizations about the processes that bring people into political life. This means that we seek uniformities in the relations among variables across nations. On the other hand, we want to explain some differences we find across nations in the outcome of these processes; differences in what kinds of people wind up as political activists. The problem is: Why should there be different outcomes if the processes are the same? Our answer is that processes on the individual level are the same, but institutions (which differ from nation to nation) intervene in these processes to produce different outcomes. We describe this model more fully in Chapter 5 and test it in the subsequent chapters. We mention it here because our concern with both similarities and differences across nations is related to the question of the validity of our comparisons.

The similarities and differences across the nations are interlinked with each other both substantively and methodologically. Substantively, the similarities we find on the individual level across nations provide us some warrant for believing that we are dealing with similar processes in each nation and that, when we observe differences that result from the

---

[4] This is not to argue that absolute differences may not be as important as well, though they are hard to measure. See, for example, the comparison between blacks in the United States and Harijans in India (Verba, Ahmed, and Bhatt, 1971). Black Americans were found to be in a similar position relative to white Americans that Harijans occupied in relation to caste Hindus. This resulted in some similar patterns of political behavior. But the absolute position of the Harijans was substantially below that of the blacks in terms of the level of education or income. This too had an impact on political behavior resulting in some significant differences between the two disadvantaged groups.

way in which institutions intervene in these processes, we are observing real differences.

Methodologically, similarities and differences across the nations can each cause problems, though the particular pattern of similarities and differences we find helps resolve some of these problems. As we have pointed out, the fact that we have conducted our study in a very heterogeneous set of nations increases the believability of cross-national similarities but makes cross-national differences uninterpretable. If we find differences among nations, they can be the artifactual result of any one of a myriad of differences in the conduct of the research across nations. If, for instance, the relationship between socioeconomic level and campaign activity differs from nation to nation (as we shall show it does), such a difference could be real or it could be the artifact of differences in the conduct of the research. For instance, the relatively strong relationship found in some nations might be an artifact of response errors in those societies – respondents who are more sophisticated (that is, have higher levels of education) might believe that the interviewer wants to hear that they are participants and therefore give him what they believe he wants. The result is an artifactual correlation of socioeconomic level and political activity. Or the relatively weak relationship found in other nations might be an artifact of processing errors. Random errors – interviewer errors in recording answers, coding and keypunch errors, and so on – would reduce the relationship between socioeconomic level and campaign activity. Again this would be an artifact of the research design. Since the rate and nature of errors may differ systematically across nations, the difference observed could be explained in those terms. (For a fuller discussion, see Verba, 1971.)

Cross-national similarities, we have argued, fare somewhat better in the heterogeneous nation design. The multiplicity of differences among the nations – both in substantive terms and in terms of the conduct of research – reduces the likelihood that one will find similarities. If similarities are found, they are more credible. But this can be overstated. The nations are heterogeneous; the research designs less so. Though the research procedures differed from nation to nation, they are nevertheless products of a joint research project and are similar in intent. Similarities across the nation could be artifacts of the application of a similar set of research procedures in each case.

We believe that the similarities and differences that we find are mutually validating; the similarities validate the differences and vice versa. By this we mean to say more than that there are some similarities and differences among nations and that each shows that the other is not inevitable. Rather, the similarities and differences we find are particularly useful for several reasons.

For one thing, we find similarities in quite complex, embedded patterns of relationships. The more complex the pattern and the more embedded the relationship, the less likely is it that one has an artifact of research design. Thus we are concerned with similarities in relations among variables, not in results to particular questions. See, for instance, the discussion of the cross-national similarity in the relationship between socioeconomic level and psychological involvement in politics in Chapter 4. An example of a more complex embedded similarity is presented in Chapter 7. There we show that in all of the nations for which we have relevant data, the participation gap between those higher and those lower on our socioeconomic scale (i.e., the correlation between socioeconomic level and participation) for difficult political acts such as campaigning or communal activity is greater among those affiliated with institutions than among those unaffiliated; on the other hand, the participation gap between those high and low on the socioeconomic scale is not greater among the institutionally affiliated when it comes to an easier political act such as voting. The substantive meaning of this similarity will become clearer in Chapter 7. Here we simply note the embeddedness of this comparison. We find a similarity in the complex interaction among socioeconomic level, type of political activity, and partisan affiliation. Few rival hypotheses as to how our research techniques could create similarity across the nations – through interviewer cheating, response biases on the part of respondents, loaded questions on our part, and so on – would predict the particular pattern we observe. Systematic measurement error might lead to similar results in each nation in terms of the participatory characteristics of partisans rather than nonpartisans, or of haves rather than have-nots. But it is hard to imagine a systematic error that would create the particular differences between campaign activity and voting that we find.

Secondly, the particular similarities and differences that we find are predicted similarities and differences. According to our model of the forces that lead to participation, we expect certain relationships to be similar from nation to nation (that between socioeconomic level and psychological involvement in politics is an example); and we expect certain relationships to be different (that between socioeconomic level and voting is an example).

Within the framework of the predicted similarities, the differences among nations receive more credibility. For one thing, they are unlikely to be artifacts of differences across the nations in research techniques. Most of the differences in conduct of the research that might produce the differences in results would also have undercut the similarities that we find. One reason why a relationship in some nations might be lower than in others (as is the case, for instance, with the relationship between socioeconomic level and campaign activity) is that in some nations there might be more random error in the data (because of respondent or interviewer or processing errors). Such random error would, however, affect all relationships in the data. But they do not. In other relationships we find strong correlations uniformly across all nations. Under the circumstances, the hypothesis that the cross-national difference is artifactual is less credible.

Lastly, just as our similarities are predicted, so are our differences. In this way, the data become self-validating because of the fact that they match our expectations. In short, the similarities and differences we find are not the result of ransacking computer output, but they are findings our general model predicts.

A word on our use of theory is in order. The study of participation is not yet an area in which deductive theory is well developed; we do not use such a theory, nor do we attempt to estimate precise parameters for the model of participation we propose. Our work is more primitive and exploratory. We are more interested in specifying the correct variables than in estimating their precise relationship to other variables.

But we are not engaged in barefoot empiricism. We have expectations as to the patterns we should find. In Chapter 3 and Appendix A, for instance, we present a factor analysis of modes of political activity in each of the nations. Our purpose there is not to see what emerges from this technique, but to determine whether the specific factors we predict on the basis of logical analysis of political acts do emerge. Similarly, in Chapter 5 we spell out a model of the ways in which we expect the different modes of political activity to interrelate with socioeconomic and institutional forces. In Chapter 7 we apply data to this model.

The previous discussion is somewhat vague and abstract. To make it more precise would be to spell out our theory of participation and to apply it to the data. This is the task of the rest of the book.

3

The modes of democratic participation

"Political participation" is a term having many meanings. It is applied to the activity of ordinary citizens and to the activity of political leaders. It is used to refer to many different kinds of activity: voting, campaign contributions, marching in May Day or Patriots' Day parades. A term so broad can lose its usefulness. We must begin, therefore, by defining and delimiting the meaning of political participation. It is not our purpose to present *the* definition of participation. We simply wish to clarify how we shall be using the term. This is the crucial first step in our analysis. The rest of this book shall be devoted to describing who participates in what way, and to explaining why they do so. But we first must understand what it is we are explaining. For this purpose, it is not enough to define participation; we must also discuss how to measure it, since our analysis requires that we be able to say *how* active a particular individual or group is.

The problem of defining and measuring political participation is compounded by the cross-national nature of our work. We shall be comparing participation across a heterogeneous set of nations. Is there something called political participation that can be meaningfully compared across these nations? And can we measure such activity in ways that are comparable enough to allow parallel analyses in each of the nations? Before we proceed, we must face these issues.

What is political participation?

By political participation, we refer to those legal activities by private citizens that are more or less directly aimed at influencing the selection of governmental personnel and/or the actions they take. Though this is a rough definition, it is adequate for delimiting our sphere of interest. It indicates that we are basically interested in *political* participation, that is, in acts that aim at influencing *governmental* decisions. Ours is a broad conception. We are interested in a wide variety of ways in which citizens participate in relation to varied issues. Many studies of participation focus on the vote. Sometimes by choice, sometimes by default (because other data are not available), voting turnout

46

is used as the measure of citizen participation. This is usually the case when one is comparing rates of participation across a large number of units such as the American states (Sharkansky and Hofferbert, 1969), across nations (Needler, 1968; McCrone and Cnudde, 1967), or over time (Burnham, 1965). Voting, however, is but one way in which citizens participate. Political participation does not take place only at election time, nor is participation at election time necessarily the most effective means of citizen influence. Though elections are a major means of citizen control over government officials, they are rather blunt instruments of control. For the individual or for particular groups of citizens, the most important political activities may be those in the between-elections period, when citizens try to influence government decisions in relation to specific problems that concern them. Our definition, therefore, encompasses electoral and nonelectoral behavior.

On the other hand, our conception of political participation is narrower than some. For one thing, we focus on the activities of private citizens – on those citizens who are not acting in roles in which they are professionally involved in politics. (In professional roles we include government offficials, party officials, as well as professional lobbyists.) Furthermore, we focus on acts that aim at *influencing* the government – either by affecting the *choice* of government personnel or by affecting the *choices made by* government personnel. We shall not deal with what can be called "ceremonial" or "support" participation, whereby citizens "take part" by expressing support for the government, marching in parades, working hard in developmental projects, participating in youth groups organized by the government, or voting in ceremonial elections. The distinction is important especially in an era when so much attention is focused on the political mobilization of citizens in the "support" sense. This is what is meant by participation in many of the developing societies of the world and often in the developed as well (Weiner, 1971; Townsend, 1967; Nettle, 1967, for discussions). In contrast, the kind of participation in which we are interested – perhaps it should be labeled democratic participation – works the other way: It emphasizes a flow of influence upward from the masses; and, above all, it does not involve support for a preexisting unified national interest but is part of a process by which the national interest or interests are created.

Our focus is narrower than some in another way. We are interested in participatory *activities*. We do not include in our definition of participation, as some have, attitudes toward participation – sense of efficacy or civic norms. (See Almond and Verba, 1963; Alford and Scoble, 1968; Matthews and Prothro, 1962; Berelson, Lazarsfeld, and McPhee, 1954. The latter use interest in politics as the sole means of participation beyond the vote.) Measures of psychological involvement in politics are crucial to our argument, as we shall see, but they will be used as a source of participation and for comparison with participation, not as measures of participation.

In addition, we limit our attention largely to participation vis-à-vis the government. The argument has been made that effective participation depends upon opportunities to participate in other spheres – family, school, voluntary associations, the workplace. A participatory polity may rest on a participatory society (Almond and Verba, 1963; Eckstein, 1961). We do not quarrel with this assumption. But we shall not attempt to describe and explain patterns of participation outside those that are more narrowly *political* – that is, aimed at affecting the government.

One last limitation in our focus is our concern with activities "within the system" – with "regular" and legal ways of influencing politics. This eliminates from our span of concern a wide range of acts – protests, riots, assassinations, all kinds of civil violence – through which private citizens might try to influence the government. This is not to argue that the latter is insignificant or unworthy of study. It is simply another topic. The activities with which we deal represent a set distinctive enough in origin and impact to merit separate consideration.

Our conception of political participation is clearly broad enough to apply to the set of nations with which we shall deal. In each there are legitimate channels by which citizens can attempt to influence government policy or the choice of government personnel. But the mere fact that we can identify "political participation" in each of the nations does not mean that we have solved the problem of comparability. For one thing, the nations differ in the extent of the rights of political participation that are available. Several provide guarantees of the full panoply of political rights: the right to vote in meaningful elections, the right to join and form political associations, the right to petition the government, coupled with the auxiliary rights of free speech, a free press, and free assembly. Austria, Japan, the Netherlands, and the United States fall within the category of nations that provide the full range of these rights. But even among these countries there are variations in terms of restrictions on political activity. Japan, for instance, has a rather restrictive campaign law barring activities such as house to house canvassing, signature campaigns, the distribution and display of campaign paraphernalia such as buttons or posters, and a wide range of activities that might "raise ardor" (Curtis, 1971, pp. 214 ff). This makes it difficult to compare campaign activity in Japan with that in other countries where such activities are not proscribed.

The converse problem exists in relation to the Netherlands. Until 1970 one form of political activity – voting – was required in the Netherlands. Our study was conducted after the repeal of that law, and we were able to ask about voting participation in two postrepeal elections. But there is little doubt that the law boosted voting turnout when in effect (Irwin, 1974), and there may be a residual effect raising voting rates above their "natural" level without such a law. Since ours is a study of citizen activity, not of the legal restrictions on (or requirements for) such activity, differences across nations in what is permitted or what is required compound our problems of comparability.

Similar problems exist in relation to our other three nations. In India, the central government has from time to time suspended certain political rights in states it considers troubled, and democracy went through a two-year hiatus in the mid-1970s for the entire nation. At the time of our field work in 1966–67, however, India could certainly be listed with the preceding four nations as a nation providing opportunities for the full range of political activities. In Nigeria, on the other hand, there was a fairly thorough suspension of such rights under military rule about the time of our field work, and such rights have not yet been fully restored. Our field work in Nigeria had been planned before but took place shortly after the suspension of political rights by a military regime. (The field work took place in the summer of 1966.) Our questions, however, were about political activities prior to this suspension. This creates problems of comparability. First, the suspension of political rights under the military regime may have inhibited respondents from mentioning past exercise of such rights. We cannot measure this directly, but the reports of political activity in our survey are sufficiently high to suggest that there was no serious inhibition. The second problem is more directly measurable. Due to the unsettled political situation at the time of our field work, we could not ask certain questions about party affiliation or activity in elections. Thus our data files are blank in relation to an important type of political activity, a fact that will limit certain of our analyses of Nigeria.

The situation in Yugoslavia is even more complicated, since it is a "democracy of a different sort." In terms of the full panoply of political rights, one would have to say that they are neither fully denied nor fully available. The franchise is universalized, and there are often contests for particular elective positions. But organized opposition via competing parties is barred. Speech and publication critical of the government is allowed, though only up to a point, and that point changes from time to time. At the time of our field work, in 1971, controls were somewhat more lax than in recent years. The Yugoslavian system provides, on the other hand, a wide range of alternative political institutions – local councils, workers' councils, and the like – that foster high rates of citizen participation.

These differences in institutional structure make comparisons of political activity across nations difficult. The problem is compounded by other differences across the nations. Opportunities to engage in particular kinds of activity may be inhibited by social and economic conditions as well. One cannot follow politics in the mass media where those media are not well established. One cannot put a bumper sticker on one's car if one does not own a car. In short, our seven nations differ substantially in the opportunities provided for various kinds of political activity.

Furthermore, even if the opportunities to engage in some kind of activity were equal (i.e., if it were legal to put a bumper sticker on one's car and car ownership was equal across two nations), citizens in one nation might have the habit of participating in that way whereas those in another might not. But the citizens in the latter country might be active in other ways – perhaps they display posters. To compare the activity in one nation with that in another one would have to tap the full range of political activities in each nation, establish that bumper stickers and window posters are somehow equivalent (and therefore worth comparing), and decide whether a single bumper sticker is worth a single window poster.

Thus though our concept of political participation is broad enough so that one can locate some such participation in each of the nations, there are a number of complexities in establishing the equivalence of such participation. The legal opportunities to be active may vary and the kinds of activities that citizens choose to engage in out of those that are legal may also vary substantially from nation to nation. How then can we compare participation?

Our answer is that one can compare participation in some respects, not in others. The qualifications listed previously make it difficult to compare the amount of political activity in one nation with that in another. To do so, one would have to know that one had asked about the "right" set of acts in each nation, that is, that one had not asked about an act common in country A but not in B while neglecting a common act in B. Though we have tried to cast our net wide and ask about a wide variety of political activities in each nation (some acts that were common across nations, others that were asked about in only one or a few countries), we cannot be sure that we have covered all relevant acts. If we had asked about a different set of political acts we might have received quite different results about the amount of activity in one place or another (on this general issue see Kim, Nie, and Verba, 1974).

However, our main interest is not in determining whether there is more activity in one nation than in another. We are interested in comparing across nations in terms of the internal distribution of activity within each and in terms of the forces that shape that internal distribution. As we have pointed out in Chapter 1, our main concern is with the relationship between equality of political activity and equality in social and economic terms. This type of comparison eases somewhat the task of locating equivalent measures of political activity. We do not need to know whether Austrians are more active than Japanese, but rather whether there is more or less difference between relevant groups of Austrians than there is among equivalent groups of Japanese – on the basis of the questions asked in each nation. If we ask about a fairly wide range of political acts we should be able to carry out parallel internal analyses.[1]

Our concern with differences within nations also eases the problem of differences across nations in the types of political activities that are legal. What is crucial to our analysis is, as we have said, that all of these nations provide whatever rights they do provide on a *universal* basis – to all adult citizens, with no sex, income, occupational, racial, ethnic, religious, or other limitations. Our concern is not with the opportunities offered to participate but with the differential use that is made of such opportunities by different groups of citizens. As long as whatever opportunities there are are universalized in each of the nations, we can compare the internal differences in the use of these opportunities.[2]

The modes of political participation

We have considered the question of the comparability of political participation from nation to nation as though there were some single and unified set of activities called political participation. In fact, we do not believe this to be the case. There are many ways in which citizens can be active in attempting to influence the government. By this we do not mean merely that alternative activities are available – one can write a letter to a representative, vote, or join a community action group, and so on. Rather, we mean that there are alternative *modes of activity:* that is, sets of activities that differ systematically in how they relate the individual to his government. The explication of these differences among the modes of political activity is important to our argument both substantively and methodologically. It is substantively important because, as we shall see, the processes by which individuals come to be political activists differ from one mode of political activity to another as do the

[1] One problem would arise if we were to ask about acts in one nation that were more likely to be limited to one social group while asking in another country about acts available to a wider set of groups. For instance, if we ask about contributions of money to political parties in one nation but about political discussion in another, we would likely find a greater difference between rich and poor in the former country than in the latter. We avoid this by asking about activities in each country that vary substantially in terms of the resources needed.

[2] The major exception to the universalization of political rights among our seven nations is found in northern Nigeria, where women were not enfranchised. But, as explained in the previous chapter, our analysis is limited to southern Nigeria (known at the time of our study as the western, the midwestern, and the eastern regions).

consequences of the alternative modes of activity. To ignore these differences is to misunderstand some important characteristics of participatory systems. A consideration of alternative modes of political activity is important methodologically as well. If we can locate similar modes of activity in each of the nations, we shall have gone a long way in establishing the equivalence of political participation across nations.

Our stress on the multidimensionality of political participation differs from the emphasis in much of the earlier literature on political activity. In that literature (Milbrath, 1965; Lane, 1959) political participation was considered to be a unidimensional phenomenon. The main distinction across political actors was the extent of their "activeness" – essentially how much effort they put into political participation. Individuals ranged from activists who took a full role in political life, through spectators who observed but did not take part, to apathetic citizens who neither took part nor cared about public matters. We do not deny that this is an important distinction; "effort" is one of our major dimensions of political activity. In fact political participation is both uni- and multidimensional. There is an underlying "activeness" dimension along which citizens can be arrayed; at the same time one can make finer distinctions among the activists in terms of the modes of activity in which they engage.

Our work on the modes of political activity has been reported elsewhere (Verba, Nie, and Kim, 1971; Verba and Nie, 1972; Verba, et al., 1973). The modes we have located appear with remarkable regularity in a number of follow-up studies by others, the similarity being more convincing because of the heterogeneity of the measures used in these studies. We present a synopsis of our analyses of the modes of participation in Appendix A as well as a summary of the follow-up work. Here, we shall simply summarize some results as they affect our argument.

Our approach has been as follows: In each of the nations we asked about a variety of specific political acts. We asked about voting in several types of elections, about a variety of ways in which citizens can take part in election campaigns, about various kinds of group-based activities within the local community, about attempts by the individual to contact officials in his community or outside of his community on various kinds of problems. In some instances we asked about the same kind of act in all the nations; in some instances we asked about different acts in different nations. The surveys therefore tell us whether the respondent has engaged in one or more of the activities about which we inquired. Using these specific acts, we looked for "modes of activity," that is, clusters of acts that customarily go together – in other words, a citizen who performs one act from a particular mode will be likely to perform other acts from the same mode.

We expected certain acts to go together because they were similar on some more abstract dimensions of participation. The dimensions were: (1) the type of influence that was exerted by the act (whether it conveyed information about the actors' preferences and/or applied pressure for compliance); (2) the scope of the outcome (whether the act was aimed at affecting a broad social outcome or a narrower particularized outcome); (3) the degree of conflict with others involved in the activity; (4) the amount of effort and initiative required for the act; and (5) the amount of cooperation with others entailed by the act.

Our analyses of the various specific acts in which individuals engaged went through several stages. (See Verba and Nie, 1972; Verba, Nie, and Kim, 1971; Verba et al., 1973; and Appendix A.) Factor analyses of the various political acts produced modes of activity that were similar across the nations and consistent with our dimensions of activity. The four modes that emerged were:

Voting. Voting is the most frequent citizen activity. It exerts influence over leaders through generalized pressure, but it communicates little information about voter preferences to leaders. The scope of the outcome is very broad, affecting all citizens. This combination of low information about citizen preferences and high pressure on leaders with broad outcomes is what gives voting its unique characteristic as a blunt but powerful instrument of control over the government. Voting involves the citizen in conflict, since the electoral situation is by definition a conflictual one – at least if the election is competitive. The voting act, on the other hand, is an individual act. And voting differs from other political acts in that it requires relatively little initiative. The occasion for voting is presented to the citizen in the form of regular elections; he does not have to create the occasion. These characteristics of voting are fairly obvious, but they are useful, for they highlight some contrast with other modes of citizen activity.

Campaign activity. The next regular mode of citizen activity is, like voting, in the electoral process. It is participation in election campaigns. It is a significant mode of action, for through it the citizen can increase his influence over the election outcome beyond the one vote allocated to him. Like the vote it exerts a lot of pressure on leaders, and for the same reason. But it can communicate more information about the participants' preferences because campaign activists are a more clearly identifiable group with whom candidates may be in close contact. Campaign activity, like voting, produces collective outcomes. Unlike voting, it requires cooperation among citizens. It involves the citizen in conflictual situations. And more initiative is required of the citizen than in relation to the vote; campaign activity is clearly a more difficult political act than mere voting.

3 *Communal activity.* This mode of activity combines two types of activity: individual contacts by citizens with government officials where the subject of that contact is some general social issue, and cooperative, nonpartisan activities involving group or organizational attempts to deal with some social issue. Such activity is outside of the regular electoral process. It conveys a great deal of information to leaders. The amount of pressure depends on the influence of the participating individual or group. The goal is some social outcome. Though some such activity may be conflictual, much communal activity involves little overt conflict. (See Appendix A.) The amount of cooperation with others varies depending on whether we are dealing with individual or group communal activity.

4 *Particularized contacts.* Our last mode of activity involves the citizen as individual (or perhaps with a few family members) contacting a government official on a particularized problem – that is, one limited to himself or his family. Such activity combines high information but usually little pressure. It entails little conflict among social groups and little cooperation with others. But it does require a great deal of initiative.

The characteristics of these four modes of activity in relation to the dimensions of participation are listed in Table 3–1. A factor analysis of the specific political acts on our questionnaire was carried out in each nation and produced results consistent with these four modes. Where alternative modes were found, they were due to specific differences across the nations in participatory institutions or in the information that we could obtain. The alternative patterns were consistent with our overall logic. Deviations were found in Nigeria and Yugoslavia. In the first country we had been unable to ask questions about campaign activity. Our analysis, naturally, produced no such mode. In Yugoslavia, the absence of competitive elections removed the major distinction that separates communal and campaign activity in the other nations – the conflictual nature of campaigning. Items from our communal activity set and items that would have formed a separate campaign dimension elsewhere (working for the nomination of a candidate, for instance) formed a single mode we label "regular" political activity. In addition, we found that functional self-management activities (workers' councils and the like) formed a separate mode.

The fact that we find a structure of participatory acts consistent with our expectations – and, above all, that we find similar structures across our heterogeneous set of nations – is crucial to our argument. From a methodological point of view it provides some evidence for the cross-national equivalence of political participation. Further, the existence of a similar structure of political acts across nations provides us with the raw material to construct comparable scales of political activity to use in our analysis. Substantively, the differences among the modes are im-

Table 3–1. *The dimensions of political activity and modes of activity*

Mode of activity	Type of influence	Scope of outcome	Conflict	Initiative required	Cooperate with others
Voting	High pressure/low information	Collective	Conflictual	Little	Little
Campaign activity	High pressure/low to high information	Collective	Conflictual	Some	Some or much
Communal activity	Low to high pressure/high information	Collective	Maybe yes/maybe no	Some or much	Some or much
Contacting officials on personal matters	Low pressure/high information	Particular	Nonconflictual	Much	Little

portant as well. Our main concern in this volume is with the processes by which individuals become politically active. As we shall see, the processes differ across the acts.

We shall, in this book, focus on the three modes of activity that involve public outcomes. Particularized contacting, though an important mode of activity, does not have the systematic relationship to institutions and to social conflict that would make it relevant to our current analysis. The three modes of activity that involve public outcomes – voting, campaigning, and communal activity – differ in ways that are relevant to our model of political mobilization based on the interaction of individual and group-based forces. Some modes of activity should be more suscep-tible to individual forces, others to group-based forces. The character-istics of the modes that lead us to expect this are the ease of the act (how much effort and initiative are required) and the amount of group conflict entailed. Those acts that require a lot of initiative and effort on the part of the individual ought to be less amenable to mobilization through group-based institutional forces. Individual socioeconomic re-sources ought to play a larger role. On the other hand, those acts that involve conflict across social groups should be acts that group-based institutions would be highly motivated to mobilize insofar as they need support in their conflict with others. As we saw on Table 3–1, voting is an act that requires little effort or initiative, yet involves conflict with contending groups. This suggests that voting will be an act least affected by individual socioeconomic resources and most affected by institutional mobilization. It should be easy to mobilize, and institutions should be motivated to carry out such mobilization. Communal activity is different. It requires individual effort and initiative but the amount of conflict involved is uncertain. We would, therefore, expect communal activity to be susceptible to the influence of individual socioeconomic resources, and we are unsure about how much it is likely to be affected by insti-tutional mobilization. Campaign activity falls in between. It requires initiative and effort and therefore ought to depend on the socioeconomic resources held by the individual, but it is also a conflictual act that institutions would want to mobilize. We should find it affected by both individual and group-based forces.

As we analyze the processes by which individuals come to be politically active, we shall have to consider these differences among the modes of activity. The differences allow a richer analysis of the processes by which individuals come to be politically active. As we shall show, there is no single process operating in a society. Different processes operate for different acts. Furthermore, the differences among the acts in their relation to individual and group-based forces provide an opportunity to disentangle these two types of forces in our analysis.

How active citizens are

Before beginning our analysis of the process by which individuals come to be politically active, we shall present the raw material for that analysis: the series of questions we asked about political activities. The set of questions varies somewhat from country to country. Some questions were asked in all countries; some questions were asked in only one or a few countries. Even where a question was the "same" across nations, there was still substantial variation in question wording. Our goal was not literal translation but translation that tried to get at equivalent activities in each case. The result is a heterogeneous set of measures across the various nations but measures that fall into our hypothesized modes of activity. This heterogeneity is, we believe, an advantage for our analysis. The fact that we found a similar structure of participatory acts across nations based on analysis of somewhat different measures (see Appendix A) increases our conviction that we have found a "real" clustering of political activities rather than a clustering that is an artifact of the measures used.

The questions asked were mostly closed questions – asking whether an individual had engaged in some activity and, in most cases, how frequently. One distinction among political acts, however, is based on the coding of open-ended questions: the distinction between contacting an official on a particularized problem (limited to the individual or his family) and contacting an official on some matter affecting some broader public – the community, region, or nation. Respondents were asked a series of questions about contacting officials at various government levels. In each case a follow-up question asked about the subject matter of the contact. The responses to this latter question were then coded after the interview into responses that referred to the individual's own problems or those of his family versus those that dealt with a broader social reference.

Table 3–2 contains the responses we received to our participation questions. The items are grouped into the various modes of activity. In Table 3–3 we present data for self-management activities in Yugoslavia – activities without parallel elsewhere. The data in Tables 3–2 and 3–3 form the basis for the analysis that will follow. They also have intrinsic interest in terms of what they tell us about the amount of activity in the several nations. Such direct comparisons across nations of the proportions who are active in one way or another are not, as we have suggested, very reliable. (For a more extended discussion of this problem see Kim, Nie, and Verba, 1974; Verba, 1971). In the first place, frequencies such as those reported in Tables 3–2 and 3–3 are quite dependent on the techniques used to elicit the information. Secondly, the meaningfulness

Table 3–2. *Political participation in seven countries: percent who say yes or perform act regularly (for question wording see Appendix B)*

	Austria	India	Japan	Netherlands	Nigeria	United States	Yugoslavia
Voting							
Vote in national election (1)	96	59	72	—	66	72[a]	—
Vote in national election (2)	—	—	—	—	—	71[b]	—
Vote in provincial elections	94	—	—	77	—	—	—
Vote in local elections	93	42	—	78	59	47	—
Vote regularly	—	—	—	—	—	—	88
Take part in campaign activities							
Persuade others for a candidate	33	—	—	11	—	28	—
Ever worked for a party	10	25	25	—	—	26	45[a]
Attended political meetings or rallies	27	14	50	9	—	19	—
Given money in a campaign	—	21	—	6	—	13	—
Member of a political club or organization	28	6	4	13	—	8	9[e]
Display or distribute campaign posters or leaflets	—	—	—	10	—	—	—
Communal activities							
Active member of organization engaged in solving community problems	9	7	11	15	28	32	—
Worked through group on a community problem	—	18	15	16	32	30	57
Helped form local group to deal with a community problem	—	5	5	24	24	14	—

Contacted local official with others	6	—	—	—	10[c]	—	—
Contacted extralocal official with others	3	—	—	—	—	—	—
Worked through a group on an extralocal problem	—	—	11	9	—	—	11[f]
Contacted local official with social referent	5	4	11	7	2	14	—
Contacted extralocal official with social referent	3	2	5	12	3	11	—
Particularized contacts							
Local official on personal matter	16	12	7	38	2	7	20[f]
Extralocal official on personal matter	10	6	3	10	1	6	—

[a] Presidential vote in 1964. [b] Presidential vote in 1960. [c] Sent or joined delegation to contact. [d] Attend voters' meetings. [e] Member of an electoral nominating committee. [f] Government level unspecified.

Table 3–3. *Self-management activities: Yugoslavia (for question wording see Appendix B)*

	Percent active
Member of a workers' council	20
Member of a local community council	7
Member of an apartment or house council	6
Member of one or more municipal self-government councils	4

of comparisons of frequencies of political activities depends upon certain assumptions as to the equivalence of these activities within the respective societies. Acts that appear to be similar may differ in their impact on politics. Furthermore, political acts that appear the same may differ in how difficult they are from nation to nation and, therefore, indicate different levels of active involvement. Voting is a prime example. The lower turnout rate in the United States compared with some other countries is probably less due to political passivity among Americans than to differences in the ease of registration (Kelley, Ayres, and Bowen, 1967). Or the social circumstances under which citizens participate may differ, so that an act in one country represents a greater commitment than a similar act elsewhere. Voting is again an example. Voting in India compared with voting in the United States is a much more passive act reflecting the mobilization of citizens by parties and leaders rather than a personal involvement in political matters (Verba, Ahmed, and Bhatt, 1971).

With these qualifications in mind we can, nevertheless, point to a few highlights. Voting rates do vary widely across the countries, with Austria outvoting the others and India lagging somewhat. When it comes to the campaign activities, one finds a fair degree of similarity across nations, with somewhat less activity apparent in the Netherlands. A very high proportion in Japan reports attendance at a political rally (but the extent to which such an item really measures active involvement in the political process is unclear). (See Curtis, 1971, pp. 211 ff.) Otherwise, the figures on activity range from fairly small percentages up to about one-quarter of the sample. The ways in which citizens become involved in partisan activity differ: In Austria and to a lesser extent the Netherlands, citizens are more likely to belong to a political organization than actually work for a candidate or party. In Japan and the United States formal membership is much rarer, but about one-quarter indicates it has worked for a party. The rates of party membership and campaign activity in India, on the other hand, are somewhat smaller. In Nigeria, we have no campaign measures. In Yugoslavia, attendance at voters' meetings is fairly frequent, but activity in nominating a candidate is rare. (These activities are not fully comparable to campaign activity elsewhere.)

The patterns vis-à-vis communal activities offer some interesting contrasts. A number of items of communal activity involve cooperation with one's fellow citizens. This seems most widespread in the United States and Nigeria, with India, the Netherlands, and Japan having some moderate frequency of informal group activity and Austria the least (though in the latter case the comparison is uncertain due to a substantial difference in the measure used). Community action in Yugoslavia is quite frequent, though much of it appears highly mobilized.

Next we can consider those communal activities in which the citizen contacts an official on his own. When it comes to contacts on a social problem, one finds more of this in the United States but relatively little in India, Austria, and Nigeria, with Japan, the Netherlands, and Yugoslavia in between.

Lastly, we can consider the proportion of citizens who report having brought a personal problem to a government official – either within the community or on a higher level. This takes place most frequently in the Netherlands, followed by Austria, Yugoslavia, India, the United States, Japan, and Nigeria.

A few conclusions do emerge clearly from Tables 3–2 and 3–3. One has to do with the diversity of patterns displayed. It is by no means clear how one would rank the nations in terms of frequency of political activity. On voting one finds Austria displaying greatest frequency; on membership in a political organization, Austria leads as well; on cooperative activity, Yugoslavia, Nigeria, and the United States; on contacting on a personal matter, the Netherlands.

Nor does the amount of participation vary clearly with the level of affluence or economic development. India does tend to have fewer participants than the other countries, but Nigerians report a high frequency of participation of certain kinds. If one expands one's view of participation beyond the electoral process, one finds a richer and more variegated pattern of participation than if one sticks to voting and campaign activity.

Voting is the only political act that a large part of the citizenry engages in. No other political act (with the exception of political meetings in Japan or community action in Yugoslavia) is engaged in by more than one-half of the citizens in any country. In India no political act other than voting is engaged in by more than one-fourth of the citizenry. In short, only a minority of citizens takes part in any of the specific acts listed on Table 3–2. Widespread activity – that is, activity engaged in by close to or more than half of the population – that is found largely for those acts that are relatively easy. The main characteristic of voting and attendance at a political rally is that the citizen does not have to take the initiative in choosing when and how to be active. The same can be said for community actions in Yugoslavia that are initiated from above. The occasion for the activity (the particular community project or action) is provided by others.

Lastly, we can consider participation in self-management bodies in Yugoslavia. Such participation is moderately widespread. One out of five reports at some time having been a member of a workers' council. Since such membership is available only to those employed in the "socialist sector" of the economy, the number who have been members is an even larger proportion of those eligible. (See Chapter 11.) Small percentages report membership in other self-management bodies. However, since such membership entails an ongoing commitment rather than a sporadic act, the percentages would appear to reflect fairly high levels of activity.

The conclusion is simple: Citizens in each country have a wide repertory of ways in which they can participate (and, of course, our questions do not exhaust that repertory). In different countries citizens will choose different ways to take part. Such a conclusion hardly contributes to a generalized understanding of political change and development, if by such understanding we mean the formation and testing of general hypotheses about political participation. But it does warn against overly simple generalizations linking political participation to social change without taking into account the wide range of ways in which citizens can and do participate.

4

The puzzle

In *Participation in America* (Verba and Nie, 1972) we dealt with the relationship between socioeconomic status and political activity. We found the relationship to be quite strong and devoted much of that book to explaining why that should be the case. We ended that earlier work with some comparative data. The data showed that the relationship between socioeconomic status and political activity was greater in the United States than in the other nations in the *Civic Culture* study and as great or greater than the relationship in any nation in our cross-national participation study. The data from the nations in our cross-national participation study are repeated in Table 4–1. For each of the seven nations in our cross-national study we report the correlation between a scale measuring the overall political activity of respondents and a similarly standardized scale measuring the individual's socioeconomic resource level. The former scale is based on the various measures of political activity discussed in the previous chapter. The latter scale is based on the individual's educational level and his or her family income. We consider education and income to represent the socioeconomic resources that individuals have available to them. We shall refer to this scale as the SERL (socioeconomic resource level) scale.[1]

The correlations in Table 4–1 show a great deal of variation. In three nations – India, the United States, and Yugoslavia – we find similarly

[1] The analysis that follows rests heavily on the use of several scales of political participation as well as a scale of socioeconomic resource level. On the basis of the factor analysis discussed in the previous chapter and described more fully in Appendix A, we constructed several participation scales in each nation: an overall participation scale and one scale for each of the modes of participation. (In Nigeria there is no campaign mode; in Yugoslavia we combined the campaign and the communal modes into a scale of "regular" political activity.) The scales were standardized to have means of 0 and standard deviations of 100. Thus individuals or groups with negative scores on these scales participate less than the average of the sample as a whole or have a level of socioeconomic resources below average. An individual or a group with a score of 50 on one of the scales would be one-half a standard deviation above the sample average. Appendix B describes the construction of these scales more fully.

✳ Table 4–1. *Correlation of a scale of socioeconomic resources and a scale of overall political participation*

Austria	.12
India	.36
Japan	.12
Netherlands	.23
Nigeria	.22
United States	.35
Yugoslavia	.36

high relationships in the .35 to .36 range. In others the relationship is weaker, ranging from a relationship of .23 and .22 in Nigeria and the Netherlands respectively, down to .12 in both Japan and Austria. The differences are puzzling in two respects. For one thing, the three nations where we find the strong relationship between socioeconomic level and participation are quite varied. It is difficult to see what they have in common that differentiates them from the other nations (if, indeed, it is some common factor that produces the similarity). Furthermore, the data appear to contradict our basic generalization about individual political behavior: Everything else being equal, individuals with higher levels of education and higher levels of income will be more active in politics. Such a generalization predicts relative uniformity across nations in the relationship between socioeconomic level and political activity. It cannot account for the wide divergences that we see; indeed, the divergences contradict the generalization.

We have already sketched out in Chapter 1 our solution to the puzzle: Our hypothesis is that an individual-based process of political mobilization in which citizens convert individual resources based on income and education into political activity would lead to a uniformly strong relationship between our socioeconomic resources scale and political activity across nations were it not for the differential intervening effect of group-based processes in the various nations. Most of the rest of this volume will be devoted to explicating how this comes about. In this chapter, we wish to post the puzzle a bit more clearly by:

1 Seeing whether the differences shown in Table 4–1 are real differences worth an extended attempt at explanation; and
2 Considering more closely the apparent contradiction between the generalization about the correlates of political participation and the data in Table 4–1.

The relationship between socioeconomic level and political activity: a closer look

Before embarking on our attempt to explain why nations differ in the strength of the relationship between socioeconomic resource level and political activity, we should ask whether the difference is a real one and not merely an artifact of our measurement techniques. The correlation coefficients reported in Table 4–1 represent but one of many ways of expressing the relationship between socioeconomic resource level (SERL) and political activity. Let us consider the data from some alternative perspectives. Table 4–2 presents another way of looking at the relationship between our SERL scale and the general scale of political activity described in Appendix B. It does this by showing the mean activity scores for those on various levels of our SERL scale. The SERL scale is divided into six equal-sized groups, from the lowest sixth on the scale on up. Though scores on the scales are not comparable across nations in an absolute sense (individuals with similar scores in different nations may engage in different amounts of activity or have different amounts of socioeconomic resources), the scores are comparable in a relative sense. An individual's score on each scale gives a good indication of how he or she stands relative to others in the same country.

The data presented in Table 4–2 are in one sense not inconsistent with the generalization about the positive relationship between SERL and political participation. In all seven nations there is a positive relationship between the two scales; the higher an individual's socioeconomic

Table 4–2. *Participation and socioeconomic advantage: overall participation scale by six levels of socioeconomic advantage*

Nation	Level of socioeconomic resources						Difference between highest and lowest sixth
	Lowest sixth	2	3	4	5	Highest sixth	
Austria	−20	−4	−4	4	15	14	34
India	−42	−31	−22	6	17	67	109
Japan	−23	−2	−3	4	10	16	39
Netherlands	−23	−13	−18	−13	14	39	62
Nigeria	−42	−30	−4	6	34	33	75
United States	−42	−26	−11	1	14	61	103
Yugoslavia	−45	−33	−14	4	26	58	103

resource level, the higher will be the activity. But the table also makes clear the striking variation across nations in the magnitude of the relationship. In some nations – particularly India, Yugoslavia, and the United States – the relationship is quite strong. About 100 points (one standard deviation) on the political activity scale separates those in the top sixth of the SERL distribution from those in the bottom sixth. In Austria and Japan, as well, the haves are more active than the have-nots, but they differ from each other by only one-third of a standard deviation. And in Nigeria and the Netherlands, the relationship lies in between the two sets of nations.[2]

The comparison across the seven nations in Table 4–2 represents probably the most reliable way in which to make such comparison given that the shapes of the SERL and the participation distributions differ from nation to nation. Table 4–2 tells us the relationship between the extent to which an individual deviates from the average in his nation in terms of SERL and the extent to which he deviates from the average within his nation in terms of political activity. But it may be enlightening to move away from a standardized scale of socioeconomic advantage to give some indication of how concrete groups in each of the societies differ from each other in rate of political activity. This is done in Table 4–3. There we compare the political activity rates of citizens on three educational levels – those with less than secondary school education, those with some secondary school education, and those with some post-secondary education.

---

[2] Such a variation in the strength of relationship might be merely a statistical artifact. It can happen for two different reasons: (1) standardization of scales and (2) the differences in measurement errors from nation to nation. If, for instance, our measure of SERL were more prone to random errors in Austria than in Japan, that would depress the relationship between it and participation. Furthermore, if there is greater variation (in absolute scale) in one country than in another or if there are variations in other unspecified variables affecting participation, correlations can vary from nation to nation, even when the underlying causal relationship is the same from country to country. (For a general discussion, see Blalock, 1964; Schoenberg, 1972; Kim and Mueller, 1976.) We deal with these potential problems in several ways. First of all, we validate our expectation through analysis as discussed in Chapter 2. Secondly, we argue that the standardized variables (standardized by the variance in each country) probably reflect more fundamental and comparable scale than the raw scales, for the reason that advantages in resources are relative advantages with respect to one's fellow citizens. Thirdly, once these scales are standardized for a given nation, we do not rely on standardized coefficients when relationships within subgroups are analyzed. We shall use unstandardized regression coefficients for internal comparison, for instance.

Table 4–3. *Mean participation scores by educational level (absolute education)*

Nation	Primary school or less	Some secondary (includes junior high or technical schools but not apprenticeships)	Some post-secondary	Difference between primary and postsecondary
Austria	−6	12	17	23
India	−14	60	94	108
Japan	−21	2	18	39
Netherlands	−15	4	43	58
Nigeria	−3	18	46	49
United States	−32	−4	49	81
Yugoslavia	−22	27	105	127

The groups are comparable in only the crudest sense. For one thing, the kind of education found at each of the levels varies greatly from nation to nation. Furthermore, the average levels within the apparently similar groups differ. In India, the overwhelming majority in the lowest educational level are illiterates with no education; in nations like Japan or Austria or the United States, almost all respondents have some education. Lastly, the nations differ in the proportions of the population at various educational levels. In Nigeria and India, those with primary education or less are the bulk of the population. In the United States or Japan they are small minorities. All these variations make comparisons using what seem to be similar absolute levels of education less reliable than comparisons using standardized scales.

Despite these caveats, the data in Table 4–3 present a more concrete indication of the cross-national variation in the extent to which the haves outparticipate the have nots. The contrast between Yugoslavia, India, and the United States on the one hand and Austria and Japan on the other remains. In the latter two countries, those with postsecondary education are more active than those with lower levels of education, but the difference is relatively slight compared with the differences seen in the former three countries. That one finds the widest participation disparity between the haves and the have-nots in the same nations – in India, Yugoslavia, and the United States – using this more concrete measure as one did using the standardized scales of SERL suggests that the difference among the nations is not an artifact of our measurement techniques. Furthermore, the fact that Yugoslavia, India, and the United States vary greatly in the distribution of citizens on the educational measure, adds to the credibility of the similarity among them in the relationship between SERL and political activity.[3] One might have argued that the great difference between the top and bottom educational levels in India was due to the fact that the upper educated were such a small and select group – only 5 percent of our sample. But in Yugoslavia the participation gap between the bottom and top education groups is even larger; yet the upper-educated group is 21 percent of the sample. Furthermore, the upper-educated group in Austria is also small as in India; yet the participation gap is much narrower than in India. (And, of course, the difference in the distribution of educational attainments would not affect the kinds of results seen in Table 4–2, where equal-size segments of the population are compared.)

The fact that we see the same cross-national pattern when we separate out the educational component of our SERL measure and relate it to political activity is important for another reason. The generalization about the SERL/participation relationship that we have proposed assumes that socioeconomic resources lead to political activity. The variation across the nations in the strength of that relationship, according to our argument, derives from the intervening effect of institutions within some of the nations. In some countries they reduce the ability of individuals to convert socioeconomic resources into political activity. But it is possible that the causal relationship runs in the other direction: Rather than socioeconomic resources leading to political activity, political activity may be the road to such resources. The political activist may be able to convert that activity into socioeconomic advantage. And the variations across the nations may reflect forces that enhance or inhibit one's ability to do so.

The reverse causal relationship is certainly plausible. And there is no doubt that political activity is often the road to advancement in socio-economic terms. But the educational data support the interpretation of SERL as a resource *for* participation, not a resource gained *from* participation. For most people, education has ended by the time they enter the political arena. Their political activity might get them more income, but it rarely gets them more education. That the differences among the

---

[3] The way in which the scale of participation is standardized makes it impossible for a large group to obtain a very high or low score – since scores represent deviation from the mean. This helps explain some of the differences among the nations in Table 4–3. In India, for instance, the upper-educated group deviates almost one standard deviation from the mean, a fact made possible in part by its small size. (It is 5 percent of the sample.) On the other hand, the lower-educated group, which form 83 percent of the population, scores 14 points below the mean.

In the United States, in contrast, the upper- and lower-educated groups are more balanced in size and deviations above and below are more balanced.

nations remain when one considers only the educational component of SERL reinforces our belief that the difference among the nations in the extent to which individuals can convert socioeconomic resources into political activity is a real one.[4]

Leader recruitment

We have other evidence that the difference we find among nations is not the mere artifact of our particular samples. As part of our research project, we conducted interviews with local leaders in many of the communities in which we interviewed cross-section respondents. As we shall discuss in Chapter 14, the socioeconomic biases found in the mass sample are replicated in the elite sample. As one would expect, local leaders come disproportionately from upper socioeconomic groups in each of the nations. The disproportion, however, is greater where there is a strong SERL/activity relationship within the mass public. Since the leader data come from separate samples of a different population, they offer strong support for the argument that we are dealing with real differences among nations.

This holds for all leaders as well as for that subset that is elected locally. This latter point is important. The leadership samples in each nation were based on occupancy of specific positions in the community. These positions differ from nation to nation. In some cases, the positions included in the sample required high levels of education (such as the head of the local school system) or inevitably involved high income (such

---

[4] It is, of course, possible that the relationship between education and political activity could run in the opposite direction from that which we assume. Individuals could use political influence to obtain more education. Our guess is that there is little of this reflected in the data. A more plausible way in which the causality could run from political activity to education would be across generations. Politically active parents could obtain better educational opportunities for their children. But even if this was the case, the puzzle would remain as to why there is a difference across the nations in the ability of the current generation to convert that education into political activity.

Another possible source of the relationships we find might be an interaction between age and education. In all of the societies we are studying, there has been a recent expansion of educational opportunities so that younger members of the samples are likely to have higher educational levels. In some cases, such as Japan, the change in the availability of higher education has been dramatic. The absence of a relationship between political activity and education found in Japan or other nations might be the result of the fact that young people are higher on the educational scale but are, for a variety of reasons (see Nie, Verba, and Kim, 1974), less likely to be active. However, analysis of the data for separate age groups indicates that this is not the source of the finding.

as the head of the largest local business). This would affect the proportions of local leaders high on our scale. But in each nation we had some local elected officials as part of the local leader sample. In none of the nations is a specific level of income or education requisite for elective office. The differences, therefore, are not mere artifacts of the position sampled.[5]

The data on local leaders are important for several reasons. For one thing, they come from a separate sample of a different population in each of the nations. As such they offer an independent confirmation of the conclusion derived from our cross-section samples that the nations differ from each other in terms of the extent to which citizens with high socioeconomic resource levels are overrepresented in the participant stratum. The difference among the nations that we have reported thus far would appear, therefore, not to be simply an artifact of the way we measure SERL and participation in our mass samples nor differences peculiar to those samples.

Secondly, the data indicate that similar processes may operate in relation to the political activity of the citizenry and the selection of leaders on the local level. In those nations where ordinary citizens appear most able to convert socioeconomic resources into political activity, potential local leaders appear most able to convert such resources into actual leadership positions. Where such resources are less convertible into political activity, they are less convertible into leadership positions. We shall present these data more fully and interpret them in Chapter 14. We cite them here as confirmatory evidence that, indeed, we have a real puzzle.

Political participation versus psychological involvement in politics

As we pointed out in the introduction, we have defined political participation as activity aimed at influencing the government. We have not, as have some others, considered psychological involvement in pol-

[5] Although we have selected a somewhat different set of elites from nation to nation in order to reflect the different nature of each society, we have used a basic selection strategy across the countries. We have tried to include the following types of elites from each country if such categories were available and relevant for the given society: (1) political elites – elected head or appointed head of the local government; (2) heads of major parties; (3) head of educational organization; (4) leader of business organization; (5) newspaper editor or publisher; (6) other relevant leaders such as leader of the dominant caste in India, head of the Cooperative society in Japan, elected council members in the Netherlands, and so on. We use the same cutting points in terms of education and income that we used to determine the top third in the cross-section sample.

itics as a measure of political participation. By psychological involvement we refer to measures such as awareness of politics, interest in politics, information, attention to the media, and so forth. Although psychological involvement in politics and political activity are positively related, they can vary independently. Some individuals may care about political matters but be inactive; others may be active without caring. This allows us to contrast psychological involvement with actual political activity, a contrast that is illuminating to the question as to the reality of the differences across nations in the SERL/activity relationship.

The generalization about the socioeconomic basis of political activity should apply to the basis of psychological involvement in politics as well. Education and income should lead to greater interest in and concern for political matters, just as they lead to greater political activity. Indeed, the former should be the intervening step to the latter. But psychological involvement in politics ought to differ from political activity in that it should be less susceptible to the intervening effects of institutions. Institutions may prevent some people with the appropriate resources and motivation from converting them into political activity. But it is more difficult to prevent the individual from converting resources and motivation into political interest and political concern. In this sense, psychological involvement ought to be less subject to institutional constraints than is political activity.[6]

If we are correct, the relationship between socioeconomic resource level and psychological involvement in politics should approximate the pattern one would find if there were no institutional constraints. Rather than the variation in strength of relationship that one finds between SERL and political activity across the nations, one ought to find more uniformly strong relationships between SERL and political involvement. More particularly, there ought to be no cases where the SERL/involvement relationship falls close to zero as does the SERL/activity relationship. Table 4–4 presents the correlations between our socioeconomic resource scale and a scale of political involvement. The latter is a principal component scale based on responses to a variety of questions

---

[6] This is not to say that institutional affiliation and psychological involvement in politics are unrelated one to another. As we shall see, those with institutional affiliations are more politically involved – because the involved are likely to affiliate with political institutions and because institutions stimulate political involvement. Our argument is that the relationship between socioeconomic resources and psychological involvement in politics ought not to be reduced by the intervening effect of institutional affiliation. Those affiliated with institutions may be more involved, but among both the affiliated and the unaffiliated, the SERL/ involvement relationship ought to remain strong. We shall test this more directly in Chapter 7. Here we consider the simple bivariate relation between SERL and political involvement.

Table 4–4. *Correlation between SERL and political activity and political involvement*

Nation	Correlation of SERL and overall psychological involvement scale	Correlation of SERL and overall participation scale
Austria	.41	.12
India	.62	.36
Japan	.42	.12
Netherlands	.40	.23
Nigeria	.48	.22
United States	.48	.35
Yugoslavia	.52	.36

tapping political involvement: interest in political matters, political information, awareness of community and national problems, attention to politics in the media, and political discussion. It is standardized like our other scales. (For details, see Appendix B.)

In Table 4–4 we also repeat the data from Table 4–1 so that the contrast of political involvement with political activity is made apparent. The correlations between SERL and political involvement are all positive, statistically significant, and relatively strong (for survey data). They are also quite uniform in magnitude from nation to nation. With the exception of the quite high .62 in India, the correlations range from .40 to .52.[7] In contrast, the SERL/participation relationships range, as we have seen, from the moderately strong ones in India, Yugoslavia, and the United States down to .12 in Japan and Austria. There is a clear spread between the first three and the last two nations.

The contrast with the participation data is quite striking. Our interpretation of the SERL/participation correlations was that they varied from nation to nation because of differential institutional intervention. Our hypothesis was that such institutional intervention would be less likely to affect political involvement and therefore one would find more consistently strong relationships across the nations. The data in Table 4–4 support this hypothesis. These data make our puzzle more precise.

[7] The particularly high correlation in India is due to the inclusion of attention to the media in the involvement scale. This is, we believe, more a measure of status than involvement in India, since media attention requires either literacy or access to a radio or T.V. As we shall see (Table 4–5), India resembles the other nations more when the components of the involvement scale are isolated.

In all of the nations, citizens appear to convert socioeconomic resources into political involvement. What, then, prevents citizens in some countries from converting such resources into activity? Our later analysis will try to indicate how institutions intervene in this conversion process.

The modes of activity

The contrast between political involvement and political activity seen in Table 4–4 is consistent with our argument about the intervening role of institutions. We can further test the plausibility of that argument by disaggregating our scale of overall political activity into the several alternative modes of political activity: voting, campaign activity, and communal activity.[8] We compare these with two measures of political involvement, namely, political discussion and political interest. Discussion of politics is an activity, but one that does not fall under our definition of political participation. It has some interesting features relevant to our argument here. Political interest also serves as a useful contrast to our various political participation measures.

As suggested in the previous chapter, the several measures of political activity ought to be distinct in terms of the extent to which they are likely to be susceptible to the intervening effects of institutions. The more a particular kind of activity is susceptible to institutional forces, the more ought there to be variation across the nations in the strength of its relationship to socioeconomic resource level. The more a mode is susceptible to individual forces and insensitive to institutional forces, the more ought the relationship of that mode of activity to SERL be uniform and strong across nations.

Three characteristics of a mode of activity should determine its susceptibility to individual or institutional forces:

1. The less a political act depends on individual-level motivation and resources, the greater will be the effect of institutional constraint. Thus institutions should have greater effect on "easy" political acts.

2. There are some political acts that institutions such as parties and associations are particularly interested in stimulating; others about which they care less. In particular, they may be expected to intervene most strongly in relation to those acts involving conflict with other

---

[8] We have not dealt with particularized contacting in this analysis. Our analysis of that mode of activity indicates that it is so contingent on the specific personal problems faced by citizens that it does not pattern in regular ways across nations in terms of who engages in such activity. (See Verba, 1978.) There are some interesting patterns across subgroups. See, for instance, Verba and Nie (1972, chap. 12), for a comparison of blacks and whites from this perspective, and Verba, Ahmed, and Bhatt (1971, chap. 5), for some differences based on caste in India.

groups that are necessary to maximize their base of support and institutional strength.

_3_ Lastly, there is some political activity that cannot be carried out by the individual alone but that requires an institutional channel. The more this is the case, the more likely is the intervention of parties or voluntary associations to have an effect on the SERL/participation relationship.

In sum, then, for those activities that are easy for institutions to stimulate, which institutions might want to stimulate, and which may depend on institutional channels, one would expect to find greater institutional constraint and, therefore, variation across nations in the SERL/participation relationship. For activities that are more difficult for institutions to stimulate, that they would be unlikely to want to stimulate, and that do not require institutional channels, we would expect institutional constraint to be weaker. For such acts, the individual forces operate without interference. We should find a fairly strong and uniform SERL/participation relationship across nations.

Let us compare the several acts:

_1_ Voting is the act for which we would expect the greatest institutional constraint. It is an act that is easy for institutions to mobilize, since it is least dependent on individual-level motivation and resources. In addition we would expect institutions – particularly political parties – to be motivated to stimulate voting rates. Here we should find parties and associations creating the greatest deviations from the individual SERL/ participation relationship. The result should be heterogeneity in that relationship across the nations.

_2_ We assume that campaign activity ranks just below voting in terms of its susceptibility to institutional constraint. It is likely to depend on institutional channels. Furthermore, institutions, in particular political parties, are likely to be motivated to stimulate it. But, unlike the vote, it is a relatively difficult act that is likely to depend on individual motivation and resources. In this sense, it should be somewhat less susceptible than the vote to institutional constraint.

_3_. Communal activity has a somewhat ambiguous ranking, since there are many forms of communal activity. Like campaigning, it is a difficult act; and that should reduce the effects of institutions. What is less clear is the extent to which communal activity requires institutional channels and the extent to which it is likely to be the subject of direct institutional mobilization. Some of the specific acts that go into our communal mode of activity take place through formal institutions; others involve informal group activities, whereas a third type consists of individual contacts with government officials. Thus some but not all of the acts in the communal mode require institutional channels. In addition, institutions might be motivated to mobilize citizens to this kind of citizen activity. In short, communal activity is likely not to be as constrained as voting and cam-

Table 4–5. *Correlation between socioeconomic advantage and various political acts*

Nation	Political activity			Political involvement	
	Voting scale	Campaign activity scale	Communal activity scale	Political discussion	Political interest
Austria	−.06	.13	.17	.36	.36
India	.00	.33	.30	.42	.35
Japan	.02	.06	.13	.27	.37
Netherlands	.10	.11	.27	.35	.35
Nigeria	.07	—[a]	.23	.38	.33
United States	.24	.29	.27	.36	.40
Yugoslavia	.19		21[b]	—[c]	.43
Range of correlations	.30	.27	.17	.15	.10

[a] No campaign measure in Nigeria.
[b] Campaign plus communal in Yugoslavia.
[c] No discussion measure in Yugoslavia.

paign activity. On the other hand, it ought to show evidence of more constraint than the components of our involvement scale – discussion and interest.

4. Political discussion is not one of our modes of political participation. It is an activity, however, that forms a nice contrast with our participation measures. It lies at the other extreme from voting. It should be relatively immune from institutional constraint. It is a difficult act for parties or associations to stimulate in the absence of the individual-level motivation that derives from education. Second, there is little reason why such institutions would want to stimulate discussion. And, last, discussion is the political act that is least dependent on institutional channels. In this way political discussion is the political activity that should depend most exclusively on the individual resources and motivation that underlie the SERL/participation relationship. Thus we ought to find least deviation from the individual SERL/participation relationship in relation to this act, and the most cross-national uniformity.

5. We also include data on political interest in Table 4–5. This measure is based on answers to questions about the respondent's interest in various kinds of politics. It should be the least subject to institutional constraint.

To summarize our expectations then, for those acts that are less likely to be affected by institutional constraints, the uniform individual forces should work. We expect a strong and uniform SERL/participation relationship across the various nations. Where the mode of activity is more susceptible to institutional constraint, the shape of the SERL/participation relationship becomes more variable across the nations – in some cases we may find a strong relationship, in others a weak one.

Table 4–5 contains the relevant data. The data reported are the correlations of standard scales measuring the various modes of activity with the SERL scale across the seven nations. The data are quite consistent with our expectations. For the various activities we expected that the variation in the SERL/participation relationship would be greatest for voting, least for political discussion. Furthermore, we expected the variation to be least for political interest. And this turns out to be the case. Moreover, we expected to find relatively strong SERL/discussion relationships in all nations, unlike the situation in relation to voting or compaigning, in which cases, some of the relationships are close to zero. The SERL/voting relationship ranges from a low −.06 in Austria to .24 in the United States. In contrast, the SERL/political discussion relationship is relatively strong in all countries and varies from a low of .27 in Japan to a high of .42 in India. When it comes to political discussion, upper-status citizens are more active in all nations, a finding consistent with our individualistic model of the relationship of SERL to that form of activity. As for voting, they are sometimes more active and sometimes less so, a result consistent with our stress on the role of institutional constraints in relation to voting. The political interest data show an even clearer pattern of uniformly strong relationships ranging from a low of .33 in Nigeria to a high of .43 in Yugoslavia. On this measure, India is no longer a special case with an unusually high score. (See footnote 7.)

Campaign activity and communal activity fall somewhere in between voting and the political involvement measures in terms of the degree to which there is cross-national variation in the strength of the SERL/participation relationship.[9] And the difference between these two modes of activity is in the direction we expect. Campaign activity shows wide variation from nation to nation in the extent to which it is correlated with socioeconomic advantage. Communal activity also shows variation in this respect but the variation is not as great. This is consistent with

---

[9] It is clear that what is important to us is not the amount of variation across all of the nations, which may be measured better by the standard deviation than by the range of variation, but the extent to which it is possible for one or more nations to deviate from the hypothesized, universal positive relationship. Because we do not have an exact measure of the hypothesized universal relationship, we use the range of variation as the possible indicator of the extent to which institutions can interfere with that relationship.

our expectation that institutional constraints have less effect on communal activity than on campaign activity.

In short, the variation among the several measures of political activity and involvement in terms of how strongly and how uniformly they relate to socioeconomic advantage across the seven nations is consistent with our argument as to the source of cross-national variation in the relationship of our overall political activity index and socioeconomic advantage. Where individual-level forces are assumed to operate without institutional intervention, one finds a uniformly strong SERL/participation relationship across the nations. Where institutional constraint is assumed to operate, one finds variation across the nations in the SERL/participation relationship. The data are thus consistent with the assumption that the SERL/participation relationship represents a cross-national generalization about individual political behavior. If it were not for the varying patterns of institutional constraint in the several nations, we would not find the cross-national differences in the SERL/participation relationship.

The data in Table 4–5 lead to a substantive change in the way in which we would rank the various nations in terms of the SERL/participation relationship. With respect to our overall scale of participation, the Netherlands had a moderate SERL/participation relationship – between the level of relationship in the United States, India, and Yugoslavia and the level in Austria and Japan. When one disaggregates the overall activity measure, one finds the Netherlands quite like the weak SERL/participation relationship nations – Austria and Japan – with regard to campaign activity but, with respect to communal activity, quite like the strong relationship nations. Furthermore, when it comes to voting, India joins the weak relationship nations.

We shall have to pay attention to these variations when it comes to explaining the differences among the nations. Table 4–5 suggests that we shall have to deal with the varying modes of activity separately. The overall participation index may hide more than it reveals.

The data in Table 4–5 are also relevant to the question of whether the cross-national differences in the SERL/participation relationship are "real" or not. To see how the data relate to this question, we can return to a methodological point about cross-national research made in Chapter 2. A research design involving a very heterogeneous set of nations – such as that used in the present study – is a very powerful design when one is looking for and finds uniformities in the relationship among variables across the nations.[10] The reason is that the variation among the nations in terms of history, culture, level of development, or political

[10] For a general discussion of this and alternative designs, see Przeworski and Teune (1970) and Verba (in Vallier, 1971).

structure works against such uniformities. More important, perhaps, the heterogeneity of instruments and techniques that one is forced to use (one must interview in varied languages, in totally different research settings) also works against the location of such uniformities. Thus to find a uniform set of relationships under such varying conditions gives strong warrant for the belief that it represents a true cross-national generalization.

On the other hand, a research design involving very different nations causes problems when one finds *differences* among the nations in the relationship among some set of variables. Such differences become un-interpretable. They may represent real differences in the way in which variables relate from nation to nation. Or they may simply result from the difference in research method employed in the various nations. Even if one is convinced that the difference across the nations in the way in which one's variables relate is not an artifact of the different research instruments or techniques, one will be at a loss to explain such differences since they could be due to so many factors (Zelditch, in Vallier, 1971).

Consider the variation we have found across nations in the relation of SERL to our scales of voting and campaign activity. We shall spend a great deal of time and effort attempting to explain why the nations differ in the relationship between socioeconomic status and political activity. Because of the heterogeneity of the nations and the consequent heterogeneity in research instrumentation and technique, can one be sure that such differences among the nations are indeed real and not artifacts of differences in research techniques?

If there were more random error in our measures in one nation (because some questions were ambiguously worded in one of the languages or interviewers were less careful in one of the nations, for instance) this might artificially lower the correlation between SERL and political activity in that nation compared with some of the others. Conversely, certain types of systematic error (a cultural tendency for upper-educated citizens in one nation, for instance, to inflate their activity scores to impress an interviewer) might increase the correlations between SERL and activity compared with other nations. Either situation would mean that a cross-national difference in the SERL/participation relationship was an artifact of the research process. Since the standardization of technique across nations is impossible in any full sense, one can never eliminate the hypothesis that such differences are artifactual.

But when the heterogeneity across nations found in relation to voting and campaign activity is juxtaposed against the relative uniformity found for political discussion and interest, the hypothesis that the former differences are artifactual becomes less plausible. The cross-national similarity in the relationship of SERL and the political involvement measures gives one more confidence that the difference in the relationship of SERL to participation is valid. It makes it unlikely that the low SERL/voting and low SERL/campaign activity correlations found in Austria and Japan are due simply to more random error in our measure of SERL in those nations. Such errors would reduce the SERL/political involvement relationships as well. Yet the latter relationships are relatively strong in Austria and Japan. Conversely, it makes it somewhat unlikely that the larger correlations found between SERL and voting or campaign activity in India and the United States are due to a cultural tendency in those nations for upper-educated respondents to try to impress the interviewer with the extent of their political activity. If that were the case, one would expect stronger correlations between SERL and political discussion in those nations compared with the others.[11]

The data in Table 4–5 are useful, therefore, for several reasons. For one thing, they help firm up our belief that what we are explaining (the variation in the SERL/participation relationship) is a real cross-national difference. Secondly, the data in Table 4–5 pose our puzzle more precisely. Nations such as Austria, Japan, and the Netherlands resemble India, the United States, and Yugoslavia in the strength of the SERL/political involvement relationship. In the former nations, individuals convert socioeconomic resources into political involvement. Why then do the former three nations differ from the latter in the extent to which socioeconomic resources can be converted into political participation?

Our explanation of the differences among nations in the SERL/participation relationship has rested on differences in the extent of institutional constraint. But we have not looked directly at the ways in which the institutions in which we are interested – parties and voluntary associations – affect rates of participation across social groups. The data reported are consistent with an institutional constraint explanation, but a fuller confirmation of that explanation will depend on a more direct look at the role of parties and voluntary associations. To that we now turn.

---

[11] Of course, one could argue that there might be a tendency for upper SERL respondents systematically to inflate their political activity but not their political interest. However, whereas the former rival hypothesis of systematic differences among nations in the degree to which more sophisticated upper-status citizens inflate their political activity was quite plausible, the latter hypothesis that there will be such a bias in answering questions about political activity but not about political discussion or involvement is somewhat less plausible. On the obligation to defend one's hypotheses against *plausible* rival ones rather than all rival ones, see Donald T. Campbell (in Rosenthal, 1969).

5

Individual propensities and institutional constraints: a model

We have demonstrated much cross-national variation in the relationship between socioeconomic resources and participation. In some societies socioeconomic resources are converted into political activity at a much higher rate than in others. Our explanation of this variation is based on the interaction of two sets of forces: individual and group-based ones. More specifically we argue that individuals would convert socioeconomic resources and motivation into political activity at a similar rate across nations were it not for the "interference" of group-based forces. The specific set of group-based forces on which we focus is derived from institutions and can take one of two forms: Institutions can mobilize citizens to a level of activity above that which would be predicted by their socioeconomic resource level, or institutions can inhibit political activity so that it is at a level below that which one would predict on the basis of socioeconomic characteristics. Variations in the nature and intensity of institutional interference explain the variation across nations in the participation disparity between the haves and the have-nots.

The data presented in the previous chapter are consistent with this interpretation. For an activity such as political discussion or for psychological involvement in politics in which we would expect little institutional interference we find what our model of individual-based forces would predict: a fairly strong and uniform relationship between socioeconomic resource level and the political dependent variable from nation to nation. In contrast, we find a great deal of cross-national variation in the SERL/participation relationship for those political activities in which we would expect institutional interference. These results are consistent with our assumption that institutions work differently from nation to nation as a result of the particular historical patterns of institutional development in each of the nations. Thus similar processes of mobilization on the individual level produce different results (in terms of the participation disparity between the haves and the have-nots) because they take place within different institutional contexts.

Our evidence for the existence of this dual set of forces has been indirect: the contrast among various measures of political activity and involvement in terms of how they relate to socioeconomic resources. We can now turn to a more direct look at the way in which institutions modify the SERL/participation relationship or (what is the same thing) the way they modify the extent to which there is a participation disparity between the haves and the have-nots.

The two sets of institutions with which we shall deal are political parties and voluntary associations. These two types of institutions are particularly relevant to citizen participation. They represent the major institutional links between the citizen and his government, links by which the preferences of citizens are communicated upward to political leaders. More important from the point of view of our concerns, parties and voluntary associations affect the participation rates of citizens. This may happen in several ways.

1 Institutions may deliberately and explicitly mobilize political activity, as when parties "get out the vote" or mobilize campaign activists.

2 Institutions may expose those affiliated with them to politically relevant stimuli such as discussion about politics or concern for social issues.

3 Institutions may provide opportunities to be active within them and thereby provide skills and expectations that are then generalized to political activity.

4 Lastly, institutions may so control the channels of political activity that such activity is barred (or at least more difficult) for those who have no institutional affiliation.

The important point is that parties and voluntary associations have an *independent* effect on citizen participation rates – independent that is of the resources and motivation associated with the citizen's socioeconomic level. This means that they can modify the individual conversion rates of socioeconomic resources into political activity. In this chapter we shall spell out our model of the way in which institutions affect differences in participation rates across groups. We shall present a number of graphs representing hypothetical relationships among individual socioeconomic characteristics, institutional affiliations, and participation rates. These are discussed in some detail both because they help clarify our argument and because they are the format in which we shall present our data in subsequent chapters.

We begin with several simplifications. We lump together the effects of all institutions in each nation; that is, we consider the overall effect of the institutional *system* on political activity and pay no attention to differences among institutions within each nation. We also ignore, for the present, differences in the way in which institutions affect the different modes of participation. Further we distinguish among citizens only in terms of their socioeconomic level, ignoring their other social characteristics. Once we present the model of institutional interference within this simplified framework, we can complicate it by considering variations among institutions, as well as differences in the ways in which the model operates among types of political activity. We shall also introduce other social characteristics of individuals beyond socioeconomic resource level. For the simplified model we focus on the overall participation disparity across socioeconomic groups. The more complex model will allow us to deal with participation disparities across acts and institutions as well as groups. The approach in this chapter will be replicated in the rest of the book. We shall first fit data to the simplified model and then move to the more complex variations.

The components of the model

Two characteristics of institutions are relevant for us: the strength of institutions in relation to participation, and the distinctiveness of the population base.

The strength of institutions

By this we refer to the extent to which institutions dominate political participation. They can do this in one of two ways: Institutions can dominate participation negatively by controlling and limiting access to channels of activity or positively by mobilizing citizens. We measure the strength of an institutional system in several ways. One measure is the relationship between the extent of institutional affiliation and activity. We assume institutions to be strong in those settings where the affiliated far exceed the unaffiliated in activity. Secondly, we consider the extent to which institutional affiliation replaces individual resources and motivation as the key to activity. Where institutional affiliation is a necessary and/or sufficient condition for activity, institutions are strong. For our purposes, the latter criterion is more important. In addition, one can compare institutional systems in terms of their "scope," that is, how many kinds of activity are affected by institutions. The larger the number of modes of activity that are dependent on institutional affiliation, the stronger are institutions.

These measures of institutional strength leave the causal direction uncertain. We shall, for instance, speak of a "dominant" institutional system in which affiliation appears to be both a necessary and sufficient condition for political activity and in which socioeconomic resources play no role. A dominant institutional system does not imply that party or organizational leaders actively block the activity of those unaffiliated or force the affiliated to participate. In some dominant institutional systems this may be the case. In others, channels of activity may be open only to those with a party affiliation. Those individuals who choose not to affiliate with a party – for whatever reasons – are thereby blocked from participating, but by their own choice. For our purposes, the important point is that in a polity with a strong institutional system one finds little activity among the unaffiliated and much among the affiliated. The consequence in terms of intergroup participation disparities is the same whether parties actively dominate participation or whether the domination is based on citizen choice to affiliate or not.

We are most interested in the relative strength of institutional affiliation and socioeconomic resource level in determining political activity. Institutions are stronger the more they replace socioeconomic resource level as the basis for political participation. This can happen in several ways. Where institutions are strong, the unaffiliated citizen may be "locked out" of political activity. No matter what his socioeconomic level, he is inactive if he does not have the proper institutional affiliation. Institutional affiliation is a *necessary* condition for political activity. For example, where campaign activity requires a party affiliation – unlike the situation in the United States, where there is a tradition of "independent" activity – those without such affiliation will be inactive no matter what socioeconomic resources they possess. Conversely, institutional affiliation may be a *sufficient* condition for activity. Those affiliated with institutions are pulled into political activity no matter what their other social characteristics. An example is the urban machine when it brings out the vote of its adherents no matter what their individual propensities to be active. The more institutional affiliation is necessary or sufficient for political activity, the greater the "strength" of institutions. And of course if both are the case – if institutional affiliation is a necessary *and* sufficient condition for political activity – institutions will be particularly strong.

The distinctiveness of the institution's population base

Strong institutions stimulate those affiliated with them to participate beyond what would otherwise be expected on the basis of their socioeconomic level, and/or inhibit the participation of those not affiliated. Thus the impact of institutional interference on participation disparities among groups depends on *who* is affiliated and *who* is unaffiliated. We can consider this from the point of view of the socioeconomic characteristics of individuals. Institutions may draw their supporters from the lower end of the SERL scale, from the upper end, or perhaps from across the board.[1] The source of their supporters probably de-

[1] Of course, this does not exhaust all possibilities. Institutions may have supporters that come disproportionately from the middle of the scale, or from the middle and upper parts of the scale, or any one of a number of combinations. From the point of view of the participation disparity between those at the top and those at the bottom of the SERL scale, the impact of institutions that draw the middle groups into politics would not differ from those parties that draw citizens into politics from all parts of the SERL scale, whereas those that draw the middle and upper SERL will have an impact like that of institutions that draw supporters from the upper end of the scale. What counts is the average location of the party supporters on the SERL scale.

pends on the historical contingencies of the initiation and development of institutions. It has been suggested, for instance, that parties will develop support bases that reflect the pattern of cleavage in society at the moment when they are founded. These patterns of support then become "frozen" even after that pattern of cleavage has become less salient (Lipset and Rokkan, 1967). The distinctiveness of the support base, in terms of socioeconomic level or in terms of other social characteristics, determines whose participation is affected by political parties.

The strength of institutions

Let us consider the ways in which institutions can modify the individual relationship between socioeconomic level and political activity. In Figure 5–1 we present some alternative patterns of relationship that one would find for differentially strong institutional systems. Along the horizontal axis of the graphs we plot the socioeconomic level of the citizens; on the vertical axis, their rate of political activity. The dotted line in each example is the relationship one would expect if there were no institutional interference and our assumption of the uniform SERL/ participation relationship held. It is a base line from which we measure institutional impact. In addition, we plot some hypothetical lines for those institutionally affiliated and those unaffiliated. If lines slope upward as one moves from left to right, it means that participation increases with socioeconomic level. If the line for the affiliated is higher than the line for the unaffiliated it means that those with institutional affiliation participate more than those without such affiliation. The greater this distance between the lines, the greater the "strength" of the institutional system.

Figure 5–1(a) illustrates a "weak" institutional system. In this example, the three lines – that for the population as a whole under the "individual forces only" assumption, that for the affiliated, and that for the unaffiliated – are overlayed one on the other. In this example, institutional affiliation has no effect; the affiliated are not more active than the unaffiliated and within each group individuals convert socioeconomic resources into political activity at an equal rate. Figure 5–1(b) is an example in which institutional and individual forces each operate in an additive way. The affiliated are more active than the unaffiliated at each socioeconomic level, but the individual effects of socioeconomic level are also felt both among the affiliated and among the unaffiliated. Institutional affiliation adds to socioeconomic resources. The institutional system is strong in that affiliation has an effect on activity level. However, the institutional system is not so strong that it eliminates the ability of the individual to convert socioeconomic resources into political activity.

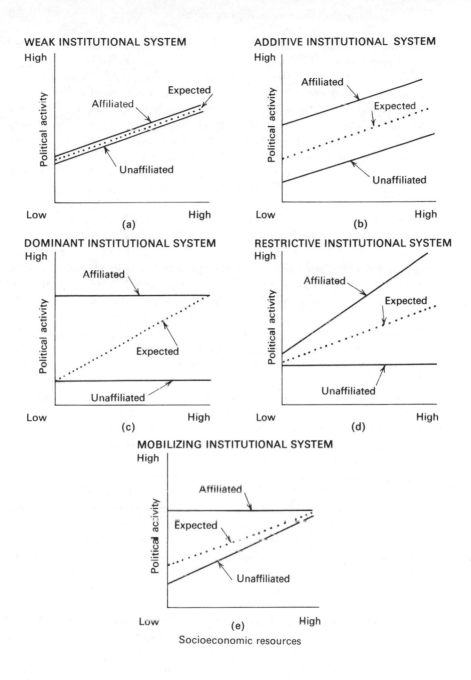

Figure 5-1. Institutional strength and activity: some hypothetical examples.

Among the affiliated, those who are more affluent and better educated are more active, and the same is true among the unaffiliated.

Figure 5–1(c) illustrates the situation in which institutions are fully dominant. Institutional affiliation is both necessary and sufficient for political activity. The affiliated are quite active no matter what their socioeconomic level; those without affiliation are inactive, no matter what their socioeconomic level. In the example in Figure 5–1(c), institutional affiliation overrides any effects of socioeconomic resources. The conversion rate of such resources into political activity is zero: If you are affiliated with a party, you need no such resources; if unaffiliated, you cannot convert them.

Figures 5–1(b) and (c) illustrate another point that is important to our argument. The dotted line tells us what the political activity rate of the individuals at each socioeconomic level would be if there were no institutional interference. The solid lines indicate how institutional affiliation would lead to deviations from the expected activity level. In Figure 5–1(b), where affiliation plays an additive role, the deviations from the expected level are uniform across the entire socioeconomic spectrum: Those with affiliation are more active than expected; those with no affiliation are less active; but how much they over- or underparticipate (compared with expectations) is independent of their own socioeconomic level. In the situation depicted in Figure 5–1(c), the impact of institutional affiliation is not uniform across the socioeconomic spectrum. The largest deviations from expected activity rates are found among the lower-socioeconomic-level affiliated citizens and the upper-socioeconomic-level unaffiliated citizens. The former participate much more than one would expect on the basis of socioeconomic characteristics, whereas the latter participate less. Lower-status unaffiliated citizens and upper-status affiliated citizens, on the other hand, participate at rates closer to their expected levels. This illustrates one way in which institutions, when they are strong, can reduce political inequality across socioeconomic levels. They do this by "locking out" of political activity those affluent citizens who would have been active were it not for their lack of institutional affiliation, and "pulling in" those less affluent affiliated citizens who would otherwise have lacked the socioeconomic resources for activity.

Figures 5–1(d) and (e) illustrate two additional circumstances: Figure 5–1(d) illustrates a "restrictive" institutional system where affiliation is a necessary but not sufficient condition for political activity, and Figure 5–1(e) illustrates a "mobilizing" institutional system where affiliation is a sufficient but not necessary condition. In the restrictive system, those who are unaffiliated are "locked out" of political activity no matter what their socioeconomic resources. Affiliation is the key to activity. But those who are affiliated still convert socioeconomic resources into activity; the have-nots among the affiliated are less active than the haves. Note that in this case, the major impact of institutional forces is felt among the upper-socioeconomic-level unaffiliated citizens who participate well below their expected level.

The situation in (e) of Figure 5–1 is the opposite of that in (d): In a mobilizing institutional system, affiliation is a sufficient but not necessary condition for activity. All those affiliated are active, no matter what their socioeconomic level, but the unaffiliated can convert socioeconomic resources into political activity. In this case, it is the lower-socioeconomic-level affiliated citizens who deviate most from their expected level because of the large boost they receive through their affiliation.

Examples (d) and (e) in Figure 5–1 would suggest quite different institutional systems. In the former case, channels of political participation are open only to those in the institutional system; if one is not affiliated, socioeconomic resources do not lead to activity. But institutions do not mobilize their affiliators equally to political activity; socioeconomic resources play an important role in determining who takes an active part. Institutional interference is felt by those having no institutional affiliation. But the interference is not felt by those who are affiliated. Among them individual resource conversion still takes place.

In the mobilizing case of example (e) in Figure 5–1, institutional interference takes place within the institutional sphere. All those affiliated are activists no matter what their socioeconomic resources. But interference is weaker outside of the institutional sphere. There are opportunities for those without affiliation to convert socioeconomic resources into political activity.

Since we shall often refer to the "lockout" of unaffiliated citizens by the institutional system, it may be useful to explicate more fully what we mean by the term. We refer to the situation where some citizens participate at a level below what one would predict on the basis of their socioeconomic resource level, and where this lower participation level appears to be related to their lack of institutional affiliation. The term "lockout" suggests positive actions on the part of institutions to block the activity of unaffiliated individuals. We do not mean to imply this. Unaffiliated citizens may *lock themselves out* of political activity. Where, for instance, parties dominate the channels of political activity, citizens who find no party attractive enough to affiliate with may withdraw from political activity even though they have the resources and motivation for participation. They are locked out in the sense that they lack the party affiliation needed for participation.

Finally, we must warn the reader that our models are abstract. A nation may not fit neatly into one type of institutional system or another. Further, institutions may operate differently depending upon the specific mode of participation. An institutional system that is best described as restrictive in relation to campaign activity may display a pattern that is either dominant or mobilizing in regard to voting. An institutional system that is weak in relation to difficult acts, such as campaign or communal, may appear closer to the restrictive or mobilizing model in relation to an easier act like voting.

The distinctiveness of the population base of the institutions

In Figure 5–1 we compare the relationship between SERL and participation that one might find among the affiliated and the unaffiliated citizens under varying conditions of institutional strength with an expected relationship that would exist if individual forces operated without institutional interference. The information contained in those graphs, however, is not sufficient to tell us what effect institutions would have on the overall shape of the relationship between SERL and participation – that is, whether they will make participation rates more equal across the socioeconomic levels, less equal, or leave them unchanged. The reason is that much depends upon the social composition of those who are affiliated and those who are unaffiliated with institutions. In a strong institutional system, the activity rate of the affiliated is boosted, that of the unaffiliated reduced. But the impact on intergroup political equality depends on who is affiliated and who is not.

Figure 5–2 offers some illustrative examples. Again, we simplify by characterizing the affiliated and the unaffiliated only in terms of their socioeconomic levels. In addition, we present the average socioeconomic level of the affiliated and the unaffiliated across all institutions. The various graphs in Figure 5–2 take the same form as those in Figure 5–1: Socioeconomic level is plotted on the horizontal axis, participation rates on the vertical. The dotted line represents the expected relationship between SERL and participation in the absence of institutional interference; the solid lines represent the activity rates of the affiliated and unaffiliated in different party systems. But we add two features: On each of the lines representing the affiliated and the unaffiliated we place an x at the point representing their mean socioeconomic level. And we add a dashed line representing the relationship between SERL and participation that would result from the various combinations of institutional strength and socioeconomic composition. The difference between the expected line when only individual forces are operating (the dotted line) and the resultant line when one has taken into account institutional strength and composition (the dashed line) indicates whether institutional interference increases, reduces, or leaves unchanged the participation disparity between the haves and the have-nots.

In Figure 5–2 we present six situations. In three of them the institu-

ADDITIVE INSTITUTIONAL SYSTEMS DOMINANT INSTITUTIONAL SYSTEMS

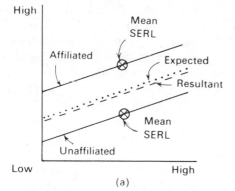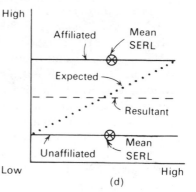

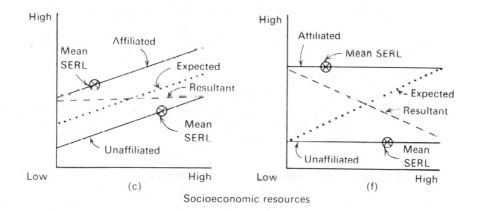

Figure 5-2. Institutional strength and population base: hypothetical examples. (a) no class bias in affiliation; (b) upper-class bias in affiliation; (c) lower-class bias in affiliation; (d) no class bias in affiliation; (e) upper-class bias in affiliation; (f) lower-class bias in affiliation.

tional system plays an additive role in relation to participation; in three it plays a dominant role as a necessary and sufficient condition for participation. For each of these two situations of institutional strength we present three situations of institutional composition: one in which institutional affiliation is unrelated to socioeconomic level (i.e., the affiliated and the unaffiliated have the same mean position on the SERL scale); one in which the affiliated are of higher socioeconomic level than the unaffiliated; and one in which the affiliated are of lower socioeconomic level than the unaffiliated. (We do not illustrate the circumstances where the institutional system is weak, since the composition of the institution in relation to participation is important only where institutions are strong. Nor do we illustrate restrictive or mobilizing institutional systems. Those systems are combinations of the additive and dominant systems.)

Consider the three examples of the additive institutional systems, shown in the top row of Figure 5–2(a). The resulting effect on participation inequality across socioeconomic levels depends on the socioeconomic composition of the affiliated and unaffiliated groups. Where the institutional impact is additive and the affiliated and unaffiliated are equal in mean socioeconomic level – (a) in the figure – the resulting relationship between SERL and participation is identical to the relationship expected in the absence of institutional interference. If, as in Figure 5–2(b), the affiliated come from a higher socioeconomic level than the unaffiliated, the resultant relationship between SERL and participation will be stronger. In this example, the institutional system *increases* political inequality by increasing the participation disparity between the haves and the have-nots. Though institutional affiliation gives an equal boost to the activity rate of the haves and the have-nots, a higher proportion of haves receive that boost since they are overrepresented among the affiliated.

Figure 5–2(c) illustrates the circumstance where the affiliated have a lower average socioeconomic level than do the unaffiliated. In this circumstance, the result is a *decrease* in participatory inequality across social groups. The actual line that results may not be flat as illustrated; it might incline upward or even downward depending on the extent of the difference in socioeconomic composition between the affiliated and the unaffiliated. All that we know for certain is that in a circumstance such as that illustrated in Figure 5–2(c), the inequality of participation between the haves and the have-nots will be less than it would be if only individual forces were at work.

Figure 5–2(d), (e), and (f) illustrate alternative outcomes when the institutional system is dominant over participation. Figure 5–2(d) illustrates the situation when affiliated and unaffiliated citizens do not differ in socioeconomic levels. When that is the case, institutional interference results in greater equality of political activity across the socioeconomic levels. Institutional affiliation is the key to activity, and since affiliation is enjoyed equally by the haves and the have-nots, the result is a reduction or elimination of any participation disparity between them. Figure 5–2(e) is an interesting contrast to Figure 5–2(d). In this illustration, the affiliated have a higher socioeconomic level than the unaffiliated. As in example 5-2(d), institutions dominate channels of participation, locking the unaffiliated out of participation and mobilizing the affiliated to participation without regard for socioeconomic level. In this sense they act to equalize activity rates across social levels. But since socioeconomic level plays a role in determining who becomes affiliated, a larger number of affluent and well-educated citizens take advantage of the participatory boost given by institutions and a larger number of less affluent and less well-educated citizens are kept out of political activity by their lack of party affiliation. The result is a participatory system stratified by socioeconomic level as would be a participatory system in which only individual forces were working. But in this case the stratification takes place through the process of recruitment to institutions.

The last example is in Figure 5–2(f). In this case, institutions recruit affiliators disproportionately from those low on the socioeconomic scale. Since affiliation is necessary and sufficient for political activity, the result is a negative relationship between socioeconomic status and political activity.

The examples given in this chapter deal with the average effects of institutional systems, not the effects of individual institutions. In fact, societies contain various kinds of institutions: In some systems all political parties and political organizations may be similar. But it is more usual to find systems in which institutions differ in their strength, in their population bases, or in both. In all of the nations with which we deal, different institutions appeal to different social groups. Furthermore, they differ in their strength. These variations play an important role in the overall impact that institutions have on the participation disparity among social groups. If a strong middle-class party opposes a strong working-class party, the participation disparity between the haves and the have-nots will be changed less than would be the case if one party were strong and the other weak. If the working-class party is stronger, the have/have-not participation disparity will be reduced; if the middle-class party is stronger, the opposite will happen. As we present our data, we shall encounter various patterns of difference across institutions that we shall have to take into account.

Summary

We have presented a number of examples of the way in which institutional interference could affect the SERL/participation relationship. In subsequent chapters we shall fit data to these models. It may be useful to spell out some expectations as to which of the models will fit the data. The two main variations captured in the model are the strength of institutions and the distinctiveness of their support base. These in turn derive from the historical patterns of institutional development in each nation and, as such, offer no basis for expecting one pattern or another. Whether an institutional system is strong and whether it has a support base that is biased toward the haves or the have-nots or an equal support base is "given" in the model. But we can spell out some expectations as to how these historically determined patterns will work themselves out. This provides us with some hypotheses to test against the data.

To do this we turn back to our distinction among political acts. The expectations are based on the considerations that led us to expect greater institutional interference in relation to some acts than in relation to others.

1. Institutional strength will be greater the fewer the socioeconomic resources needed for the act and the more stake institutions have in dominating the channels of activity. Thus one expects greater institutional strength for voting followed in turn by campaign and communal activity. Institutions should be relatively weak in relation to a quasi activity like political discussion.

2. Strong institutions are more likely to approach a situation of dominance in relation to voting than other acts. Since the closer an institutional system is to a dominant one, the more can it equalize political activity, institutions are more likely to equalize voting than other acts.

3. When it comes to a more difficult political act such as campaigning, institutions may be motivated to control political activity, but individual socioeconomic resources will still play a role. For campaigning, one expects institutional systems to be restrictive rather than mobilizing. We expect institutional interference to "lock out" those who have socioeconomic resources but no institutional affiliation. Their lack of affiliation will prevent them from converting their resources into political activity. We do not, on the other hand, expect institutional interference to reduce the ability of those who are affiliated from converting individual resources into activity. The latter would require a deliberate policy on the part of institutions to mobilize those of their supporters low on the SERL scale and/or inhibit the activity of those higher on the scale. To be sure, institutions might develop deliberate policies of mobilizing one group or another of their supporters. Left parties from time to time favor activists from the lower end of the SERL scale. But such deliberate mobilization from the lower end of the scale is, we believe, relatively rare. Though institutions may try to build or maintain a support base by directing appeals to those low on the SERL scale (a workers' movement deliberately appealing to workers, a peasants' movement to peas-

ants), they are less likely deliberately to favor one group or another when it comes to the issue of which supporters become politically active. In this process, they are more likely to "let nature take its course." And if we are correct in our sociological generalization about the individual-level SERL/participation relationship, this will mean that in all nations (and within all institutions), those among the affiliated higher on the SERL scale will be more active. Thus we would predict that among those affiliated with institutions the individual-level SERL/participation relationship will hold, and those higher on the scale will be more active.

This generalization is useful, since, if correct, it eliminates one of the ways in which institutions could equalize political activity across socio-economic groups. The institutional system in a nation can equalize political activity across social groups through one or a combination of three processes: (1) A strong institutional system can reduce the ability of individuals to convert their personal socioeconomic resources into political activity by "locking out" those who are unaffiliated. And/or, (2), it can mobilize to activity all those who have an institutional affiliation without regard to their personal socioeconomic resources. And/or, (3), it can recruit the affiliated disproportionately from the lower end of the socioeconomic scale. Our expectation is that an institutional system is likely to play an equalizing role via processes (1) or (3): either by locking out those who are unaffiliated or by recruiting supporters from those low on the socioeconomic scale. It is less likely to equalize *within* its support group by process (2): by mobilizing its supporters to activity no matter what their socioeconomic level. Within such support groups, the individual conversion of socioeconomic resources into political activity will take place.

In the following five chapters we shall fit our data into the model presented in this chapter, adding some complications to the model as we go along. In Chapter 6 we present the basic data on the party and organizational systems in the several nations. This forms the raw material for our analysis. In Chapter 7 we fit data into the model outlined in this chapter. In that chapter we also provide a further test of the model by comparing political activity with psychological involvement in politics. In Chapter 8 we complicate the model somewhat by dealing with the impact on participation of political parties from different parts of the political spectrum. In addition, we compare the effects of subjective identification with a political party with the effects of actual party membership. In Chapters 9 and 10 we introduce the most important complication into our model: the nature of the social cleavage system in each society and the way the pattern of social cleavage affects participatory equality. In Chapter 11, we apply the analysis in Chapter 6 through 10 to Yugoslavia, a nation we treat separately (though within the same framework) because of some major institutional differences from the other nations.

6

Parties and organizations

We have explicated a model of the way in which the interaction between individual propensities and institutional affiliation affects the disparity across social groups in political participation. We now want to fit the data from our seven nations into this model. To begin with, however, we wish to sketch some of the differences in the political institutions of our several nations. There are many such differences. The political parties and politically relevant associations in the several nations vary in historical origin. They vary in their internal structure. They vary in the way they are connected to social divisions in their respective societies. To describe these differences fully would require an extended historical account of each of the nations. Our purpose in this chapter is more limited. We want to describe the variation across the nations in some limited and specific characteristics of the institutional systems. The broad, unspecified, historical differences among the institutional systems create the background variation from nation to nation characteristic of our "most different nation" design. Such variation, as we have pointed out, makes the discovery of uniformities more convincing. The specific and measurable variation among the party systems allows us to go several steps further. Such variation, when entered into our model of individual propensities and institutional interference, can be used to explain why similar sociological processes lead to different results. More specifically, certain characteristics of the party and organizational systems will help explain why it is that a similar propensity to convert socioeconomic resources into political activity (which we assume to exist in each nation) leads to a different result in terms of the inequality of political activity across groups.

The specific characteristics we consider are the population base of institutions, the strength of the institutional system in relation to participation, and the degree to which institutions reflect the basic system of social cleavage. In this chapter and the next we present some basic data on the first two characteristics of institutions. We shall consider the relation of institutions to cleavage patterns in Chapters 9 and 10. We begin with parties and then turn to organizations.

The party systems

The party systems in the nations we are studying differ in many ways. In terms of number of parties they range from the one-party dominated system in India (at least when we conducted our study) through the (more or less) two-party systems in Austria, the United States, and Japan (with the Austrian system being the most balanced in terms of size of the two parties and the Japanese characterized by more significant minor parties), to the highly fragmented Dutch system.[1] In terms of our main concern with the way in which affiliation with political parties affects intergroup participation rates, we want to know the number of people who are affiliated with political parties, who they are, and the effects on political activity associated with such affiliation.

[1] In the analysis of parties we shall not deal with Nigeria and shall treat Yugoslavia separately.

Our field research in Nigeria was planned before the military coup of 1966 and was intended to deal with the role of Nigerian parties. However, the military coup took place before our field work. Party activity was then barred. We would have liked to ask about past activity, but the subject was too sensitive. In order that *any* field work be done, it was necessary to remove from our questionnaires certain key questions about the partisan affiliation and activity of the respondents. The researchers in Nigeria did ask one question as to whether the respondent had, in the past, been a strong supporter of any political party. Thirty-seven percent of the sample said yes; 63 percent said no. We had hoped to use this item to distinguish those affiliated with a party from those who were not. But analysis of some data makes it clear that the question did not "work." It was asked too indirectly and covered past behavior, without specifying when. Given the situation at the time, it is likely that many previous party supporters (who may have still had party attachments) denied them. We thus do not have the necessary information for the analysis of party constraints on political activity in Nigeria. We shall return to the Nigerian data in the next section of the chapter, since we do have data on organizational affiliation in Nigeria.

In Yugoslavia, of course, the League of Communists (as the Communist Party there is called) plays a key role. It is not fully comparable as an institution to the parties in the other nations, since it does not exist in a competitive party framework. But as we shall see, it functions quite similarly to parties in the other societies in terms of the impact it has on the participant population. We shall deal with Yugoslavia within the framework of our analysis of the role of parties. But because the differences between the League of Communists and the parties elsewhere are significant and because we have a somewhat different set of dimensions of political activity in Yugoslavia, we shall make our presentation somewhat clearer if we deal with Yugoslavia separately from the other five nations where we have information on party affiliation. Thus in our party analysis we shall compare the five nations and follow with a section on Yugoslavia.

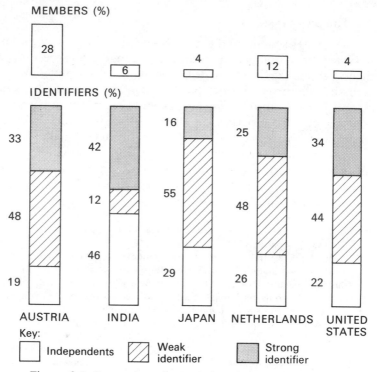

Figure 6-1. Proportion of population: independents, weak and strong party identifiers, and party members.

Party affiliation

Party affiliation can be measured objectively or subjectively. In the former case one uses the respondent's reported formal membership in a party organization. In the latter case one takes as evidence for affiliation the respondent's reported identification with a party. Figure 6–1 contains data for partisanship measured each way. As one can see, the proportion of respondents reporting formal membership varies widely – from a high of 24 percent of the respondents in Austria to rather low figures in the 4 to 7 percent range in the United States, Japan, and India.[2] If we add those who subjectively identify with a party to the members, we find somewhat greater uniformity across nations. In each nation, well over half of the population sampled belongs to or identifies with a political party, the figures running from 69 percent in

[2] The U.S. data on membership came from the University of Michigan Center for Political Studies' 1968 election study. We use the CPS data because our membership question combined party organizations and other political groups.

India to 80 percent in the United States. Among those who identify with but do not belong to a party, more identify weakly than strongly. This holds in all nations except India. In India the bulk of the identifiers identify strongly. Indeed, if we add the party members and strong identifiers, we find India to be the most partisan nation.[3] Japan, in contrast, has the largest group of weak identifiers among those with some party affiliation.

Figure 6–2 provides a more extensive partisan profile for each of the nations. For each of the nations we divide the full sample into those supporting no party and those supporting the various parties. The white space to the left represents the proportion of the sample who report no party identification; the shaded areas to the right the partisans. The partisans are, in turn, divided into those who support each of the parties in the nation (with some smaller parties lumped together when there were few cases). And we divide each of the partisan groups into strong and weak supporters. Again our purpose is not a full characterization of party systems, but a presentation of data that will become part of our subsequent analysis.

The data in Figure 6–2 illustrate the heterogeneity of the party systems with which we are dealing. Austria presents the nearest approximation to a two-party system with relatively equal-sized major parties. The United States and Japan are similar in that one of the two major parties is substantially larger – in terms of number of identifiers – than is the other. Democratic identifiers outnumbered Republican identifiers by about two to one at the time of our study, and there were about one and a half times as many Liberal Democratic supporters in Japan as there were supporters of the next largest party, the Socialist. Minor parties in Japan, particularly the Komei and the Democratic Socialists, also receive significant support (as does the Communist Party – the support for which is likely underestimated in our survey), but they are well below the size of the two major parties. The figure for the Netherlands reflects the wide fragmentation of that multiparty system. No party receives support from as much as 20 percent of our sample, though the Catholic and Labor parties are supported by about 20 percent of those who have a party affiliation. Nor do the data as presented

---

[3] One of the reasons for the lower frequency of reporting of party affiliation in India is the larger proportion of our sample that had difficulty understanding or answering our questions. In this respect, it is important to note that the positive answer that one is affiliated with a political party is unlikely to represent simple uncomprehending acquiescence to the interviewer, a phenomenon that is always possible when one is interviewing relatively uneducated populations. In order to be considered a party supporter, the respondent had to be able to volunteer the name of the party he or she supported. That the respondent named a party provides some confirmation that the question was understood.

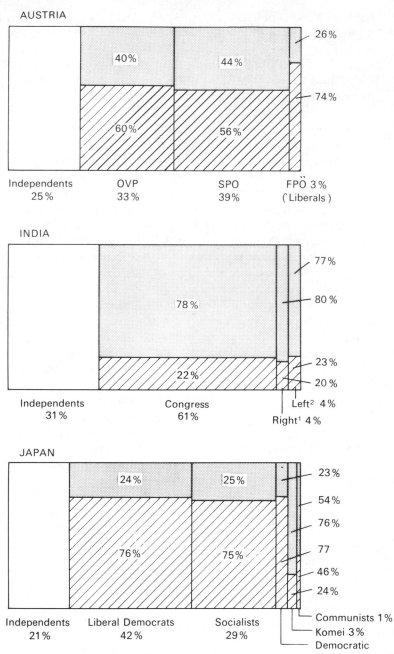

AUSTRIA

| 40% | 44% | 26% |
| 60% | 56% | 74% |

Independents
25%

OVP
33%

SPO
39%

FPÖ 3%
(¨Liberals)

INDIA

	78%	77%
		80%
	22%	23%
		20%

Independents
31%

Congress
61%

Left² 4%
Right¹ 4%

JAPAN

24%	25%	23%
		54%
		76%
76%	75%	77
		46%
		24%

Independents
21%

Liberal Democrats
42%

Socialists
29%

Communists 1%
Komei 3%
Democratic
Socialists 4%

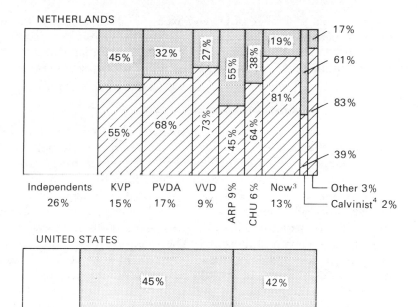

NETHERLANDS

45%	32%	27%	55%	38%	19%		17%
							61%
55%	68%	73%	45%	64%	81%		83%
							39%

| Independents | KVP | PVDA | VVD | ARP 9% | CHU 6% | New[3] | Other 3% |
| 26% | 15% | 17% | 9% | | | 13% | Calvinist[4] 2% |

UNITED STATES

| 45% | 42% |
| 55% | 58% |

| Independents | Democrats | Republicans |
| 30% | 52% | 28% |

Key:

1. Swatantra, Jan Sangh, religious, linguistic, and communal parties.

2. Communist Party of India, Socialist parties.

3. D66, D70, PSP, PPR.

4 SGP, GPV.

☐ Independent   ▨ Weak identifiers   ▦ Strong identifiers

Figure 6-2. Partisan profiles.

encompass the full range of Dutch parties, since we categorize a number of heterogeneous new parties together. India is in sharpest contrast to the Netherlands. At the time of our study, the Indian Congress Party was still unified and relatively dominant in the four states surveyed.

The organizational systems

In addition to affiliation with political parties, we consider the role of membership in private organizations in relation to political activity. Respondents were asked about membership in a variety of kinds of private organizations: work-related organizations such as unions; professional associations or cooperatives; recreational associations; ethnic, caste, or religious ones; community or neighborhood organizations; and so forth.[4] We also wish to distinguish such organizations into those involved in political matters and those not. The ostensible purpose of the organization – as revealed by its name or the type of organization – is of little help for this purpose. All kinds of organizations become politically involved. We, therefore, used as our measure of the degree of political involvement of an organization the respondent's report as to whether regular discussion of political and public affairs took place at meetings of the organization. This is, we believe, a good measure of the degree to which a particular organizational membership is politicized. We shall thus deal with three categories of citizens: (1) those who belong to no organizations, (2) those who are members of one or more nonpolitical organizations, and (3) those who are members of at least one politicized organization.[5]

The data on organizational membership are in Figure 6–3. There is a wider range of variation across the nations in voluntary association membership than is found in relation to party identification: From Japan, where we find 72 percent of the sample indicating some orga-

[4] We use the term "private organizations" rather than "voluntary associations" to stress the fact that the memberships with which we deal are not always strictly voluntary. Union membership or membership in an agricultural organization may be economically necessary. And membership in a religious or an ethnic or a caste association may be an unquestioned concomitant of membership in a social group. Membership in neighborhood associations is also generally expected in Japan. These organizations are subsidized by the local government and perform quasi-governmental functions.

[5] The extent to which the individual is active in an organization is also an important characteristic of his or her membership. (See Verba and Nie, 1972, chap. 11.) We have not used that in the basic measure of organizational affiliation. We want to link organizational affiliation to political activity. It is, therefore, better not to build an activity component into our measure of organizational affiliation.

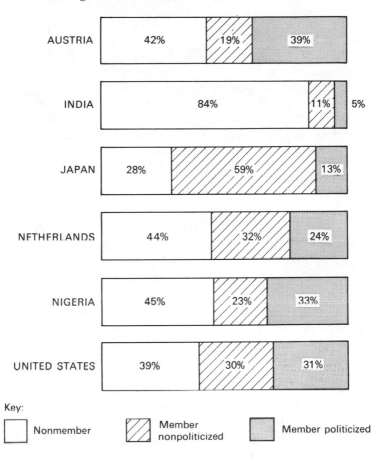

Figure 6-3. Proportion of the population who are nonmembers, members of nonpoliticized organizations, and members of politicized organizations.

nizational membership, to India, which stands out from the other nations in terms of the absence of organizational affiliation – only 16 percent belong to an organization. It is likely that the low frequency of membership reflects the lower level of socioeconomic development in India. The more developed nations in our set have substantially higher and fairly uniform frequencies of membership. On the other hand, the Nigerian data – with rates of membership similar to those in the more developed societies – suggest that a relatively high socioeconomic level is not necessary for development of an organizational system to which many citizens belong. The Nigerian data are strikingly high in terms of the proportion of the respondents who belong to an organization. They are not, however, inconsistent with data from other studies.[6]

The data in Figure 6–3 also indicate the extent to which members of organizations are exposed to political stimuli. The nations vary from Austria, where 39 percent of the sample reports membership in an organization in which political matters are discussed, down to India, where only 5 percent report such politicized memberships. In Japan we found the highest proportion of organizational memberships, but fewer than one in four of the Japanese members reports exposure to political stimuli through his or her membership. In contrast, two out of three of the Austrian members report political exposure. The Austrian sample stands out in this respect, indicating a more politicized organizational system than that found elsewhere. In the other nations the division between politicized and nonpoliticized memberships falls between the Japanese and Austrian figures. In Nigeria politicized memberships predominate over nonpoliticized ones; in the Netherlands and India it is the opposite. In the United States one finds an equal division between the two types.

Table 6–1 provides some further details about the kinds of organizations found in the various nations and the extent to which they provide political stimuli. The types of organizations vary quite widely and the categories listed in the table are in many cases quite heterogeneous. They contain quite a range of specific organizations within the individual nations, and an even more heterogeneous set when one compares them cross-nationally. A more fine-grained analysis is beyond the scope of the present work. These data are presented to give some descriptive material about the kinds of associations with which we shall be dealing.

A few points are worth noting. In the more industrialized societies, trade unions are the largest category, with the exception of Japan, where they are second to neighborhood associations. (In the United States as many respondents are members of school associations as are members of trade unions.) Membership in neighborhood associations is very high in Japan and largely accounts for the overall high proportion of members found in that nation. Otherwise one finds a great deal of variety across the nations.

The data on the proportion of members who report political discussion within the organizations give good indication of the degree to which the associational systems are politicized. We have marked the percentages in such a way as to make it easier to see where extensive politicization is to be found. There is a good deal of political discussion reported

[6] Margaret Peil, in a study of citizen attitudes in several Nigerian cities carried out in 1970–71, found that between 80 and 100 percent of males and only slightly fewer females reported organizational membership (Peil, 1976). See in addition Little (1965).

Table 6–1. *Types of organizations by nations*

	Austria		India		Japan		Netherlands		Nigeria		United States	
	Per-cent mem-bers	Percent of members reporting political discussion	Per-cent mem-bers	Percent of members reporting political discussion	Per-cent mem-bers	Percent of members reporting political discussion	Per-cent mem-bers	Percent of members reporting political discussion	Per-cent mem-bers	Percent of members reporting political discussion	Per-cent mem-bers	Percent of members reporting political discussion
Union organization	25	49	2	41	30	22	24	48			17	42
Cultural organization	3	11	1	45			9	8			9	49
Veterans' organization	4	42									7	54
Sports club	13	25	2	39	14	2	17	20	15	27	12	19
Neighborhood or service club	12	31	2	46	52	9	8	28	25	37	6	63
School association	5	29					9	39			17	52
Religious and ethnic organization	4	29	4	31	10	18	8	44	40	41	8	43
Fraternal organization	4	42					1	64			15	31
Youth organization			1	52			2	49			7	35
Economic organization	9	64	3	41					34	37	11	56
Consumer organization	11	25	7	28			8	35				
Other organization	8	36	1	54	7	12			5	52	7	47

Note: Circled numbers are between 50 and 64 percent; numbers in triangles are between 40 and 49 percent.

within organizations in each of the nations. Japan is somewhat of an exception, however. The rate of political discussion is much lower than in counterpart organizations elsewhere. Note in particular the low frequency of discussion in neighborhood associations. Note as well how much political discussion is reported in organizations with nonpolitical purposes in many of the countries.

The similarity between the United States, the Netherlands, and Austria in terms of the frequency of political discussion within organizations, however, may hide some important differences in the extent to which organizations have direct ties to one or another political party. If characterizations of the Austrian party system in contrast to that in the United States are correct, one would expect more direct partisan ties to organizations in the former country, where the two main parties have traditionally supported a network of affiliated organizations. Unfortunately, we do not have directly comparable data on the degree to which organizations are affiliated with a particular political party or political *tendency* in all of the nations. We do have data on the extent to which individuals in Austria are affiliated with organizations that have party ties. We have parallel data in the Netherlands where respondents were asked to report whether each organization to which they belonged was associated with one or another of the major social "pillars" of Dutch society. These data are presented in Table 6–2. We show the proportion of identifiers with the major parties who are members of organizations that have a link to one or another of the parties (in Austria) or pillars (in the Netherlands).[7]

As one can see from Table 6–2, in Austria those identified with one of the major political parties are quite likely to belong to organizations that are linked to the same party, much more likely than they are to belong to unlinked organizations or to an organization linked to the opposite political camp. Indeed, 58 percent of the organization members who support the Catholic People's Party (ÖVP) belong to organizations with a link to that party. Among the Socialist Party (SPÖ) supporters, the proportion who belong to organizations linked to their political camp rises to 84 percent. If one considers the party members, the figures rise to 72 percent for the People's Party and 86 percent for the Socialist members. Note the paucity of citizens with membership in organizations from both camps. The data make quite clear the extent to which partisan

---

[7] In Austria, the *Lager* linkage of each associational membership was coded by the field supervisors at IFES and is explicitly not survey data reported by respondents. In the Netherlands, on the other hand, respondents were queried about each of their associational memberships so that they reported as to whether that organization was associated with a particular pillar. Given the clarity and parallel nature of the findings in both Austria and the Netherlands, each technique appears to have worked equally well.

Table 6–2. *Percent of party identifiers and members in Austria and the Netherlands, with varying organizational profiles*

Austria	Party affiliation: identifiers (%)		Party affiliation: members (%)	
	Socialist Party	People's Party	Socialist Party	People's Party
Catholic organizations	4	58	3	72
Socialist organizations	84	17	86	9
Both Socialist and Catholic organizations	4	7	5	7
Organizations linked to neither camp	8	17	6	11
	100	99	100	99

Netherlands	Party affiliation: identifiers (%)					Party affiliation: members (%)				
	Labor (PVDA)	Catholic (KVP)	Liberal (VVD)	ARP	CHU	Labor (PVDA)	Catholic (KVP)	Liberal (VVD)	ARP	CHU
Catholic organizations	10	79	14	—	—	—	93	7	—	—
Protestant organizations	13	—	22	33	69	22	—	20	91	96
Both Catholic and Protestant organizations	—	—	1	—	1	—	—	—	—	—
Organizations with no religious affiliation	76	21	64	17	30	78	7	73	9	4
	99	100	101	100	100	100	100	100	100	100

Note: The "Socialist organizations" category in Austria refers to those who belong to at least one organization linked to the Socialist camp and to no Catholic organization. Someone can fall in that category who combines Socialist membership with membership in an "unlinked" organization. The same applies to the "Catholic organizations" category in Austria and to the "Catholic" and "Protestant" organization categories in the Netherlands. Respondents can fall in that category even if they also are affiliated with organizations unlinked to either side. Similarly, those in the "Both" category may, in addition to memberships in organizations from both sides, belong to other unlinked organizations. Respondents in the last category are only members of unlinked organizations.

divisions extend into the organizational life in Austria and the degree to which that society is split by those divisions.

The data for the Netherlands show a similar pattern. There are few organizational affiliations that run counter to the religious orientation of one's party. Consider those who support the Catholic Party (KVP). Among organizational members who identify with the Catholic Party, 79 percent belong to one or more organizations linked to the Catholic sector of society. No one in that group belongs to a Protestant-linked organization. The data are even more striking when one considers members of the Catholic Party: Ninety-three percent are in Catholic-linked organizations, none in Protestant-linked ones. Among supporters of parties from the Protestant sector of Dutch politics, one finds a similar concentration of membership within the Protestant sector. Similarly, supporters of the secular parties (the Labor Party and the Liberals) tend to limit their memberships to nonreligious organizations.

It is unfortunate that we do not have parallel data for organizations in the United States or Japan. We believe the contrast would have been striking.[8] In any case, the data do indicate a strong link between party and organizations in Austria and pillar and organizations in the Netherlands.

Institutional affiliation: a typology

In the following analysis we wish to categorize citizens in terms of the extensiveness of their ties to political institutions. For this purpose we have constructed a typology of institutional affiliation. The typology is based on the subjective affiliation of the respondent with a political party (whether the respondent identifies strongly with a party, weakly, or not at all) and on our measure of organizational affiliation (whether the individual is a member or not and, if a member, is exposed to political stimuli within the organization).

The use of the subjective rather than the objective measure of party affiliation requires some justification. Neither an objective nor a subjective measure is quite right. Formal membership is difficult to use as a basis for distinguishing the affiliated from the unaffiliated because of wide structural differences across nations in requirements for such mem-

---

[8] Indeed, it was the belief that party-linked organizations were so rare in the other nations that led us and our collaborators from those nations to neglect to ask questions that would have demonstrated this to be the case. The research groups in Austria and the Netherlands – who joined in our enterprise only after the work was completed in most of the other nations – were more sensitive to this issue. In retrospect, it would have been good to have explicit data from all of the nations parallel to the Austrian and Dutch data in Table 6–3.

bership. In addition, fewer than one in ten has a formal membership in three of the countries. Subjective identification is more widespread. It is, on the other hand, only an indirect measure of affiliation. It does not necessarily imply contact with a party as an organization; neither does it imply attendance at meetings nor payment of dues. Also, the meaning of party identification may not be stable from nation to nation. Party identification in the United States, where its use as a politically important variable developed, was found to be a long-term commitment for most respondents and a good predictor of the vote. Party identification, however, was not coterminous with a voting decision. One could (and often did) identify with one party and support the candidate of the other party. In other countries, researchers have found that party identification is more closely linked to current voting intention in the mind of the individual. If one changes one's vote intention, one reports a change in identification as well (Butler and Stokes, 1969; Kaase, 1976; and Thomassen, 1976).

Despite these problems with subjective partisan identification, we shall rely on it in our analysis of institutional affiliation. It allows us to consider the impact of party affiliation across all five nations where we have party measures. Though the measure is subjective, it remains appropriate for our model of institutional interference. Institutional interference exists where an individual behaves differently from the way in which he would have behaved in the absence of the relevant political institutions. In relation to parties, this may be due to initiatives on the part of party operatives to mobilize activity or to stifle it.

The impact of institutions on political behavior may, however, be felt in the absence of initiatives on the part of party operatives or contact between the individual and the party. The particular set of parties available may give some individuals an opportunity to express their political beliefs through action and inhibits the ability of others to do so. There are many reasons why an individual might identify with a party: the congruence between his policy preferences and those presented by the party, the fact that the party appears to him to embody some cultural orientations he shares, the fact that his friends and neighbors all identify with the party, the fact his parents did, or the fact that the party has traditionally been identified with a group to which he belongs. Whatever the reason for the identification, however, such identification depends on the availability of an appropriate party. Subjective identification with a party is, in this way, dependent on the institutional structure of society – what parties there are to identify with. If such an identification, in turn, appears to be related to political activity, we can appropriately talk of an institutional impact on participation – even if the impact implies no initiative on the part of a party. The institutional impact is the indirect result of the fact that only certain types of citizens find parties with which they identify. Where such identification is the key to activity, the ability to convert socioeconomic resources into political activity by those citizens who have no party will be inhibited whereas those with a party may be active in the absence of resources otherwise necessary.

These considerations justify, we believe, the use of subjective identification in our measure of institutional affiliation. Furthermore, where, as in Austria and the Netherlands, we have a sufficient number of actual party members, we shall be able to compare the results we have obtained by using the subjective measure, with those we have obtained by using the objective definition of affiliation.

Table 6–3 presents the proportions of respondents found in the various categories of a typology created from our measures of organizational affiliation and party identification. The data are for five nations.[9] Those lowest on our measure of institutional affiliation identify with no party and belong to no organization. Forty-three percent of the Indian sample falls in this category, compared with a much smaller percentage in the other nations. At the other extreme, we have those who are both strong partisans and who belong to at least one organization in which political discussion takes place. Here one finds the largest proportion in Austria (15 percent), with about 10 percent in the United States and the Netherlands. In Japan and India, about 4 percent are in this highly institutionally involved category.

We shall use this typology in order to distinguish those citizens exposed to institutional stimuli from those who are outside of the institutional system. The ninefold typology is, however, awkward to use and contains too many cells with low frequencies. For that reason we have combined the categories into four composite types. The combinations are indicated in the left-hand side of Table 6–4. The four categories are defined as follows:

1 *Nonpoliticals:* These are respondents who either are totally unaffiliated (they report no party identification and no organizational membership) or have only a nonpoliticized organizational membership. Their main characteristic is the low level of institutional attachment and the absence of any political content. They have no party ties, and if they belong to an organization, it is a nonpoliticized one.

2 *Nonmember, weak partisans:* These are individuals who belong to no organization but who report weak identification with a party. They have very little institutional affiliation, but what little they have has a partisan cast to it.

3 *Moderately affiliated:* This is a mixed category made up of those who have either a politicized organizational affiliation coupled with parti-

---

[9] There is no measure of partisan affiliation in Nigeria. We shall use the measure of organizational affiliation (Figure 6–3) as the substitute. We shall treat Yugoslavia separately in Chapter 11.

Table 6-3. Institutional affiliation typology

Institutional affiliation

Party	Organization	Austria (%)	India (%)	Japan (%)	Netherlands (%)	United States (%)
Nonpoliticals						
Independent	Nonmember	10	43	10	15	8
Independent	Nonpoliticized member	4	3	16	7	7
Nonmember weak partisans						
Weak identifier	Nonmember	21	10	14	21	17
Moderately affiliated						
Independent	Politicized member	6	1	2	4	8
Weak identifier	Nonpoliticized member	8	1	32	16	13
Strong identifier	Nonmember	12	31	3	9	14
Strongly affiliated						
Weak identifier	Politicized member	19	1	7	11	13
Strong identifier	Nonpoliticized member	7	7	11	8	10
Strong identifier	Politicized member	14	4	4	9	10

Table 6–4. *Institutional affiliation: combined typology*

Institutional involvement	Austria (%)	India (%)	Japan (%)	Netherlands (%)	United States (%)
Nonpoliticized	14	46	26	22	15
Weak identifiers	21	10	14	21	17
Moderately affiliated	26	33	37	29	34
Strongly affiliated	40	12	22	28	34

    san independence, a strong partisan identification coupled with no organizational membership, or middle positions in relation to both parties and organizations.

  4 *Strongly affiliated:* All the individuals in this category have institutional affiliations with both parties and organizations. They are in the highest category of affiliation in relation to at least one of the institutions. They are either strong identifiers or members of a politicized organization (or both).

    The fourfold typology can be thought to be ranked ordinally in terms of the extent to which individuals are involved with the set of politically relevant institutions in their societies. The lowest two categories on our typology are somewhat ambiguous in their ranking. Some respondents in the nonpolitical category belong to organizations, but they are distinguished by the absence of any political content in their institutional affiliation. They have no partisan leanings. If they belong to an organization, it is one in which political discussion does not take place. Those in the nonmember, weak-partisan category have no memberships, but they do express a political leaning. Thus one group may have some objective organizational membership but has no political bent; the other has no membership, but a subjective identification.

    Table 6–4 presents the proportions that fall in the four categories of this typology. The table gives a good summary of the extent of involvement with political institutions in the several nations. In India close to half of the respondents fall in the lowest category of the typology and more than half fall in the two lower categories. In Austria and the United States only 14 to 15 percent fall in the lowest category and about a third fall in the two lowest categories. If we consider the proportion in the top category in terms of institutional affiliation, Austria stands out. Forty percent of the Austrian sample is in that category in terms of affiliation, with the figures falling down to 12 percent in India.

    These figures are important as basic information about the extent to which the populations in the several nations are affiliated with institutions that are involved in political life. The data provide sketchy profiles of the institutional systems in each nation but profiles that are not inconsistent with more discursive accounts. In Austria we find a quite potent system of political institutions. Many respondents have close party and/or organizational ties. The organizational system in Austria is notable both for the extent to which it is politicized (respondents report political discussions in most organizational settings) and for the close connection between organizations and parties. (See Powell, 1970; Bluhm, 1973; Steiner, 1972.)

In the United States, there is evidence for widespread party identification as well as a great deal of membership in organizations that involve political stimuli. Unlike Austria, however, few respondents actually belong to party organizations. Furthermore, organizations are not as clearly tied to one or the other of the major political parties.[10] (See Verba and Nie, 1972, as well as the voluminous literature on party identification in the United States, e.g., Nie, Verba, and Petrocik, 1976.) In the Netherlands there is much party identification as well as organizational membership. As in Austria, the organizations are closely tied to one or the other of the pillars of Dutch society. However, the organizations do not appear to have the political intensity of the Austrian ones. Though their members report them to be attached to one or the other of the pillars, their members report less frequent political discussion (Lipjhart, 1975; Daalder and Rusk, 1972). In Japan we find widespread but rather low-keyed institutional affiliation; many have partisan ties, but the proportion of partisans having weak ties is quite high. There is much organizational membership, but little involves political stimuli. Many organizational members belong to neighborhood association – organizations in which political discussion is likely to be avoided. (See also Flanagan, 1977.) In India we find few organizational members but quite widespread and strong partisan affiliation. Partisanship appears to have penetrated quite deeply into Indian society (Field, 1978; Kothari, 1970). Lastly, the data for Nigeria indicate that organizational affiliation is not limited to more highly developed nations. As others have found, the organizational system in Nigeria – based on ethnic affiliation – is quite well developed (Peil, 1976). Though we have no direct measure of partisanship in Nigeria, other evidence suggests that it had been widespread and strong before the military coup that preceded our survey (Sklar, 1963).

The data in this chapter are also an important component of our model of the process by which the participant population in a society is shaped, a model that juxtaposes individual and institutional forces. The data in Tables 6–3 and 6–4 indicate the differing proportions in the several nations that are exposed to institutional forces. In the next chapter we shall examine how institutional affiliation affects activity.

---

[10] We do not have a direct measure of this but assume it to be the case. See footnote 7.

7

Individual and institutional forces: the model applied

We now have the raw materials to investigate the way in which individual and institutional forces interact to affect political activity. Individual resources are measured by our socioeconomic resource level scale; institutional forces are indexed by our typology of institutional affiliation. In Chapter 5 we presented five hypothetical institutional systems:

1 *A weak institutional system* in which institutional affiliation has no impact on political activity. The individual SERL/participation relationship is left unmodified.

2 *An additive institutional system* in which institutional affiliation affects activity rates in a way that adds to but does not eliminate the role of individual socioeconomic resources. Those affiliated with institutions are more active than those unaffiliated at each socioeconomic level. But both the affiliated and the unaffiliated can convert socioeconomic resources into political activity.

3 *A dominant institutional system* in which institutional affiliation is both a necessary and a sufficient condition for political activity. If one is affiliated with institutions, one is active, no matter what one's socioeconomic resource level; if one is unaffiliated, one is "locked out" of political activity. Individuals do not convert SERL to political activity.

4 *A restrictive institutional system* in which those who are unaffiliated are "locked out"; they do not convert SERL to activity. But among those with institutional affiliation, individual socioeconomic resources can be converted into political activity.

5 *A mobilizing institutional system* in which those with institutional affiliation are active, no matter what their socioeconomic resource level. Those with no affiliation can still become active by converting socioeconomic resources to activity.

These five institutional systems have been illustrated in Figure 5–1. We shall present data in the same format as those hypothetical figures. On the vertical axis of the figures in this chapter we place our scales of political activity. We shall present data for campaign activity, voting, and communal activity. As our model predicts (and as we have already illustrated), there are important differences in the relative importance of individual and institutional forces for the various acts. The actual institutional system in a society may resemble one of our hypothetical types in relation to one mode of activity and another hypothetical type

112

in relation to another mode. We shall compare these three modes of activity with each other and, in turn, with political discussion and psychological involvement in politics. Political discussion and psychological involvement should show less institutional and more individual impact. Each of these five dependent variables is measured by a scale standardized so that the mean of the population is zero and the standard deviation 100 (see Appendix B). Negative scores on the various scales indicate activity or involvement below the average for the sample as a whole.

Across the horizontal axis of the graphs we place our measure of socioeconomic resources, trichotomized into those in the low, middle, and high thirds of that scale. The relationship between the activity scales and one's position on the socioeconomic resources scale is then plotted for each of the four groups in our typology of institutional affiliation: (1) the nonpoliticals (those with no politicized institutional affiliation); (2) the nonmember weak-party identifiers; (3) the moderately affiliated; and (4) the strongly affiliated. Thus for each of the four types of affiliators we show how the rate of political activity is related to their location on the SERL scale.[1]

On each graph we place a horizontal line at one-fourth of a standard deviation below the mean of the activity and involvement scales (at −25). This we label the "minimal-activity line." Individuals whose scores fall below −25 are those whose activity or involvement is at best quite minimal. On the campaign activity scale, for instance, they would be those who at most attend an occasional political rally. On the voting scale, they would be occasional voters. The minimal-activity line provides a useful benchmark for locating those groups "locked out" of political activity or involvement, that is, a group that falls below the minimal-activity line across all three socioeconomic levels.[2]

---

[1] We have trichotomized the SERL scale and present the mean activity rate for those in each of the thirds of the scale. We present the data in this format in order to make more concrete the activity rates for the various groups. The data could have been presented as a series of regression lines between our SERL and activity scales. The patterns would not differ from those presented in this chapter had the alternative approach been used.

[2] The reader will remember that the acts differ in terms of the proportion of the population that is above or below the mean. For "hard" acts such as campaign activity or communal activity, about two-thirds to three-quarters of the samples fall below the mean; for the easy act of voting, about one-third falls below the mean. (See Appendix B.) This difference makes intuitive sense in terms of our notion of lockout. A group locked out of campaign activity would be one whose members, no matter what their level of socioeconomic resources, do not on average move into the activist minority of the population. A group locked out of voting would be one whose members do not move out of the minority of nonvoters no matter where they are on the SERL scale. This of course does not mean that no

Campaign activity

We begin our analysis with campaign activity. Campaign activity is an activity in relation to which we should expect both individual and institutional effects; the former because campaigning requires individual resources and motivation, the latter because campaigning may require institutional channels or institutions may mobilize campaigners. The data are in Figure 7–1. In one respect the graphs are quite similar in each nation. In all cases, those with strong institutional ties are more active than those with moderate ties, whereas those with moderate ties are more active than the two groups with weaker institutional ties. This holds at all socioeconomic resource levels. The two lower groups on the institutional typology – the weak partisans and the nonpoliticals – are the least active. There is, however, no consistent ranking on activity between the two groups.

The relationship between institutional affiliation and campaign activity indicates that there are no cases of weak institutional systems. That there is an unclear distinction in terms of activity level between the two lowest groups on the institutional affiliation scale reflects the fact that each of these groups can have a weak institutional tie but of a different kind. The weak partisans have no memberships, but a partisan identification. The nonpoliticals may have some memberships, but neither partisan identification nor any politicized memberships. Whether the somewhat greater politicization of the weak partisans or the somewhat greater organizational affiliation of the nonpoliticals would have the greater effect on activity appears to vary from nation to nation.

There is another similarity among the nations that is more relevant for our concerns. In all countries there is a positive slope to the line relating SERL and campaign activity among those with a strong institutional affiliation. Those from the upper third of the SERL scale outparticipate those from the lower third. Institutional affiliation is in no case (with the partial exception of the Netherlands, to which we shall return) a sufficient condition for campaign activity. Among those with institutional affiliation, socioeconomic resources can be converted into political activity. This uniformity across five such varying institutional systems is consistent with our hypothesis that within institutions, individuals would convert socioeconomic resources into political activity.

There remain, however, substantial differences across nations in the

---

member of the group is an activist if the group remains below the zero line all across the SERL spectrum. It means that at no point on the SERL scale does the average activity score of the members of that group at that point exceed zero. A large proportion of the locked out group may be voters, but their voting percentage deviates substantially from the population as a whole.

conversion rate of socioeconomic resources into political activity among those with institutional affiliation. In the Netherlands the relationship between socioeconomic resources and activity rate is not linear for either the strongly affiliated or the moderately affiliated. In each case, those from the top third of the SERL scale outparticipate those from the bottom third, but for the strongly affiliated those in the middle SERL group are the most active, whereas for the moderately affiliated those in the middle group are the least active. Furthermore, the differences across the three SERL levels are much less in the Netherlands than elsewhere. In the Netherlands, institutional affiliation borders on being a sufficient condition for campaign activity.

If we consider those citizens with institutional affiliation in the other four nations, we find variation in the extent to which the haves (i.e., those in the top third of the SERL scale) outparticipate the have-nots (those in the bottom third of the SERL scale). In India a gap of over one standard deviation (108 points in the campaign activity scale) separates the haves from the have-nots among those with strong institutional ties, whereas in the United States the difference is 61 points. In Austria and Japan the gap is smaller (37 and 25 points, respectively).

A greater difference among nations is found when we look at those citizens with weaker institutional affiliation. Among the nonpoliticals – that is, those who are at most affiliated with a nonpoliticized organization and have no party ties–we find clear evidence for a lockout in Austria, Japan, and the Netherlands. In Japan and the Netherlands there is almost no difference in activity level between the haves and the have-nots. The unaffiliated do not convert socioeconomic resources; they are found below the minimal-activity line all across the SERL scale. In Austria the haves outparticipate the have-nots among the nonpoliticals, but even the haves remain well below the minimum level of campaign activity. In addition, one finds a lockout among the weak partisans in Japan and Austria.

The situation in Austria, Japan, and the Netherlands contrasts quite clearly with that in the United States and India. In the latter two countries socioeconomic resources play a role in the participation rate of citizens at all levels of institutional involvement. Those with strong institutional ties convert socioeconomic resources into political activity at a higher rate than in the other three nations. An even sharper contrast is found among the unaffiliated. In the United States and India they have fairly high conversion rates as well. The result is that the upper-status unaffiliated citizens are quite a bit more active than their lower-status counterparts; the former participate in campaign activity well above the minimal-activity line. They are by no means "locked out" of campaign activity by their lack of affiliation.

Our measure of the "strength" of institutions in relation to political

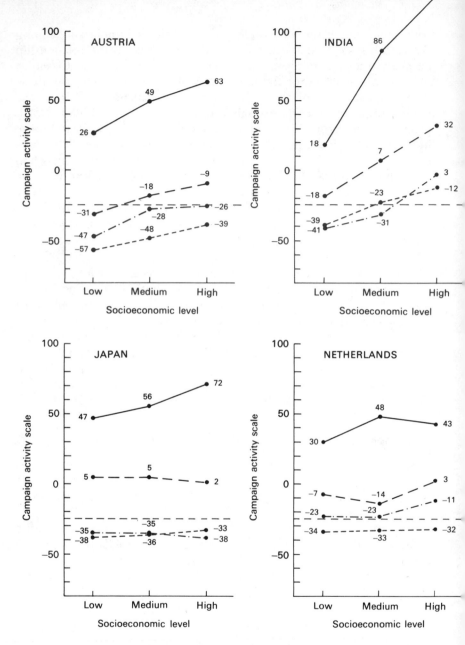

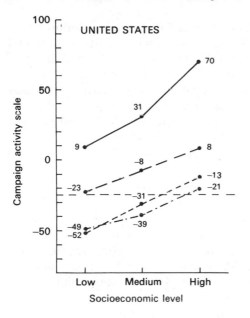

Figure 7-1. Campaign activity by socioeconomic resource level for level of institutional affiliation.

activity has two components: (1) the extent to which the affiliators outparticipate the nonaffiliators; (2) more importantly, the extent to which institutional affiliation replaces individual socioeconomic resources as the key to activity. On the basis of the data in Figure 7–1 we can distinguish among the nations in the strength of institutions over campaign activity. The Netherlands appears to have the strongest institutional system. It borders on being a dominant system: The unaffiliated are locked out; the affiliated almost fully mobilized. In the former group, socioeconomic resources make no difference; in the latter group, they make only a slight difference. Austria and Japan also have strong institutional systems, but the systems are restrictive rather than dominant. The unaffiliated are locked out, but the affiliated can still convert individual resources into activity. In the United States and India one finds a weaker institutional system. In these two nations the institutions have an additive effect on campaign activity. Those with institutional affiliation are more active than those without such affiliation. But affiliation does not completely determine the rate of campaign activity. Among the unaffiliated and among the affiliated, individual socioeconomic resources play a role.

Despite these differences between the two sets of nations in the strength of institutions, there is one important similarity across the nations. In all five cases the slope upward of the participation line is substantially greater for those with strong institutional affiliation than it is for those with no political affiliation. This is of course implicit in the fact that in Austria, Japan, and the Netherlands those who have weak institutional affiliation are locked out of campaign activity no matter what their socioeconomic resource level, whereas SERL plays a role among the affiliated. But it is the case in India and the United States as well. In the last two countries there is a positive relationship between SERL and campaign activity for unaffiliated and affiliated citizens, but the relationship is greater for the strongly affiliated.

Thus although the unaffiliated are not completely locked out of campaign activity in India and the United States, their lack of affiliation appears to reduce their ability to convert their individual socioeconomic resources into activity. Table 7–1 illustrates this by summarizing the data in Figure 7–1. We compare the average campaign activity score for those in the top third of our SERL scale with those in the bottom third. In each nation the participation disparity between those high on the SERL scale and those low on that scale is greater among those with institutional affiliation. The data indicate that in all of the nations there is more inequality in participation within the institutional sphere than outside it.

The data thus make clear the way in which institutions in Austria, Japan, and the Netherlands reduce the participation disparity between the haves and the have-nots. In part, they do this by providing opportunities or stimulation for political activity for those of their affiliators who are low on the SERL scale. But this effect is dampened by the fact that within the institutional sphere the more advantaged affiliators take the lead in political activity. The main impact of institutions is felt among the unaffiliated. The unaffiliated do not convert socioeconomic re-

Table 7–1. *Campaign participation disparity between haves and have-nots outside of and within the institutional sphere*

Nation	Disparity in campaign activity between top and bottom SERL groups among *unaffiliated*	Disparity in campaign activity between top and bottom SERL groups among *strongly affiliated*
Austria	18	37
India	27	108
Japan	5	25
Netherlands	2	13
United States	39	61

sources into campaign activity. This has its greatest impact on upper-status unaffiliated citizens. They participate below the level one would expect given their resources. This, in turn, dampens the overall relationship between SERL and participation that one would find in the absence of institutional interference. Here is an excellent example of the way in which a restrictive institutional system can increase participatory equality.

This does not imply that institutions interfere in an overt way with the propensities toward political activity of those who are unaffiliated but have the socioeconomic resources that would ordinarily lead to activity. Parties and organizations do not block individuals from taking part in campaigns – certainly not in Austria, the Netherlands, or Japan, our three strong party nations. Rather, institutional interference means that those who do not choose to identify with a party or belong to no politically involved organization (for whatever reason, including the simple fact that there may be no party or political organization with whose policies they agree) thereby lose the opportunity to take part in campaigns where campaigns are heavily institutionally dominated. In the United States and in India those who are unaffiliated but have socioeconomic resources can still find opportunities for campaign activity. The argument sounds almost tautological, but it is not. We are not merely arguing that "strong" institutional systems differ from the others in that they leave less room for "independent" political activity. We are arguing that the existence of a strong institutional system has consequences for the equality of political activity across socioeconomic levels.

Voting

Institutional effects ought to be greater in relation to voting than in relation to other activities. In Chapter 5 we discussed why this is to be expected in brief because institutions may actively try to bring out the vote of their supporters and because institutional affiliation provides the motivation to vote. We expect the voting to differ from campaign activity. Socioeconomic resource level should make less difference in relation to voting. Institutions are likely to try to bring out the vote of all SERL levels among their supporters, rather than letting the upper SERL supporters come forward as the most active participants as appears to be the case in relation to campaign activity. Furthermore, if institutions make such an effort, they are more likely to succeed. Voting is an "easier" act, less dependent on the individual socioeconomic resources needed for campaign activity.

The result should be that institutions can more effectively overcome the individual-level effects of SERL participation. And this should happen among those with strong institutional ties; institutional affiliation, that is, may be a sufficient condition for voting. Whether or not affiliation is a necessary condition for voting (whether the unaffiliated are locked out of such activity) is somewhat problematic. The fact that voting is an "easy" act requiring little resources and motivation makes it difficult to tell whether the absence of institutional affiliation will lock out the unaffiliated.

Figure 7–2 presents the data for voting participation in relation to SERL and the levels of institutional affiliation. As with Figure 7–1, we plot the SERL/activity relationship separately for the four types of institutional affiliation. (We include data on Nigeria for which we have a measure of voting activity as well as a measure of organizational – though not party – affiliation.) In all of the nations, with the exception of the United States, institutions are dominant; affiliation appears to be both a necessary and sufficient condition for voting. If one has strong ties to political institutions, one's voting participation is high no matter what one's level of socioeconomic resources. Conversely, if one is not affiliated with any political institution, one's voting participation is low no matter what one's position on the SERL scale. Indeed, a number of the SERL/voting relationships are negative, though only moderately so. Negative relationships appear among those with strong or moderate institutional affiliation in India and among those with moderate affiliation in Austria. In these cases it appears that institutions more effectively mobilize those low on the SERL scale from among the affiliated.

There is a fairly clear contrast between the United States and the other nations in relation to voting. The comparative weakness of institutions in the United States is reflected in the fact that among affiliated and unaffiliated citizens there is a positive relationship between SERL and activity. The unaffiliated are not locked out; those high on socioeconomic resources are above the minimal-activity level in voting activity. Nor is the relationship between SERL and voting eliminated among the affiliated; those higher on the SERL scale are more active. The data also reflect the fact that voting is a more "difficult" act in the United States than elsewhere because of registration and residency requirements (Kelley et al., 1967). Socioeconomic resources play a more important role in relation to difficult acts.

Despite the difference between the United States and the other nations, there is also a great deal of uniformity across all of the nations, especially when one compares the data to those on campaign activity. For one thing, institutions tend to be stronger in relation to voting than campaign activity. In general the presence or absence of institutional affiliation reduces the conversion rate of socioeconomic resources into voting activity more than it reduces the conversion of SERL into campaigning. In Austria, the Netherlands, and Japan we found a positive conversion rate among the strongly affiliated when it came to campaign activity. We find a flat relationship between SERL and voting for this group. In India we found a strong SERL/activity relationship at all institutional levels when it came to campaign activity. We find no relationship or a negative one in relation to voting. Only in the United States does the SERL/voting relationship hold within institutional levels.

With the exception of the United States, then, we find that institutions are dominant over voting activity; they both mobilize the affiliated and restrict the unaffiliated. This differs from the situation in relation to compaign activity, where the strong institutional systems tended to restrict the unaffiliated rather than mobilize the affiliated. The data are quite consistent with our general model of the ways in which institutional affiliation affects the relationship between SERL and activity. When it comes to a difficult act such as campaigning – that is, an act for which individual socioeconomic resources are most relevant – the effect of institutions is felt more strongly among those with no affiliation. The unaffiliated do not convert socioeconomic resources into activity. On the other hand, within the institutional sphere (i.e., among the affiliated) resources do affect activity. The result is a differentiation between the haves and the have nots in activity rate.[3]

This contrasts with the situation for voting. Voting, as we have pointed out, is less dependent on individual socioeconomic resources. Thus the fact of affiliation is sufficient to motivate the individual to vote. The impact of institutions on voting is thus felt among the affiliated as well as the unaffiliated.

The United States deviates from the other nations in that individual socioeconomic resources play a role for both campaign activity and voting at all levels of institutional affiliation. Nevertheless, the United States fits the general pattern of the difference between voting and campaigning. When it comes to campaigning, socioeconomic resources play a more important role among the affiliated than among the unaffiliated as we saw in Table 7–1. When it comes to voting, the opposite is true: Socioeconomic resources play a larger role among the unaffi-

---

[3] Cross-national uniformities of this kind are, we believe, particularly strong evidence that one has isolated a true cross-national generalization in the relationship between institutional structure and political behavior. The very complexity of the uniformity makes it less likely that it is merely the artifact of our research design. Note that we are comparing the impact of institutional affiliation on two different modes of activity, with the relevant impact being not on the rate of activity in the population but on the differential rate of activity across social groups. Such a cross-national uniformity in a complex pattern of relationships within each nation is less susceptible to the challenge that it merely reflects our measurement procedures. This is particularly the case when such a pattern is predicted on the basis of some general considerations as to the differences between the two modes of activity.

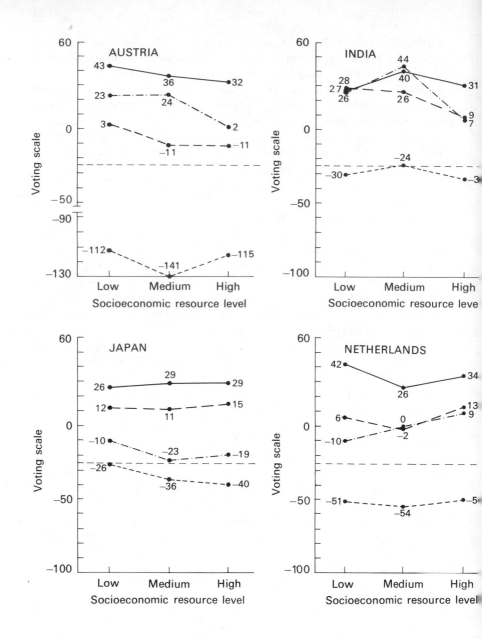

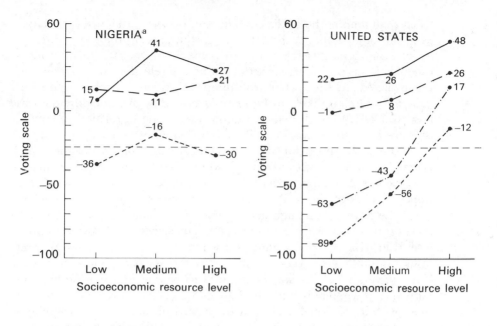

Key: Strong affiliators ———————

Moderate affiliators — — — —

Only weak party tie — · — · — ··

No affiliators — — — — — —

Minimal activity line — — — — —

[a] In Nigeria, strong affiliators refer to members of politicized organizations, moderate affiliators refer to members of nonpoliticized organizations.

Figure 7-2. Voting by socioeconomic resource level for levels of institutional affiliation.

liated than among the affiliated. This can be seen in Figure 7–2. Thus, as in the other nations, the effect of institutions on the more difficult act of campaigning is felt more strongly among the unaffiliated; institutional effects on the easier act of voting are felt more strongly among the affiliated. In sum, when institutions are strong in relation to campaigning, they are likely to be restrictive, if they are not dominant as they usually are not. When institutions are strong in relation to voting, they are likely to be dominant or, if not dominant, mobilizing.

Substantively, this distinction between campaigning and voting is important. It means that even when institutions are strong, those who are mobilized to campaign activity will come disproportionately from the upper reaches of the SERL scale. This happens in all five nations for which we have a campaign activity measure, including those in which the overall relationship between campaign activity and socioeconomic level is low for the population as a whole. On the other hand, strong institutions mobilize voters from across the socioeconomic spectrum. The "universal" relationship between SERL and activity that we hypothesize to exist when only individual forces are operating reappears among those with institutional affiliation for a difficult act like campaigning – even in cases in which the SERL/activity relationship is low for the population as a whole. When it comes to an easier act such as voting, for which individual socioeconomic resources are less important, strong institutions eliminate the SERL/activity relationship.

Communal activity

Figure 7–3 presents the data relating institutional affiliation and communal activity. Our expectations about communal activity are not clear because it is an activity with mixed characteristics. In one sense, we can expect institutional affiliation to relate to communal activity in the same way that such affiliation relates to campaign activity. Both are "difficult" activities dependent on the motivations and resources of the individual. Thus if institutions provide stimulation toward communal activity or offer channels making such activity easier, those from the upper part of the SERL scale are likely to take more advantage of the opportunities. We expect institutions to be weaker in relation to communal activity than in relation to campaign activity. That expectation, however, must be qualified. One would expect institutions to be strong in relation to those communal activities that take place in a group context, less so for those activities that are individual. Thus we expect communal activity to be, on balance, less dominated by institutional affiliation than is campaign activity, all components of which have a group basis.

The data in Figure 7–3 are consistent with our expectation based on the difficulty of communal activity: i.e., that those with higher levels of resources and motivation are likely to take greater advantage of stimulation to activity provided by institutional affiliation. Among those with strong institutional ties there is a substantial positive slope to the SERL/communal activity relationship. Furthermore, the slope for the SERL/communal activity relationship is, in each nation, greater among those with strong institutional ties than among those with weaker ties.

The data are also fairly consistent with our expectations as to how strong institutions are in relation to communal activity or, more specifically, whether institutions are stronger in relation to campaign than to communal activity. The clearest evidence that institutions are stronger in relation to campaign activity is a comparison of the activity level of the strongly affiliated with that of those less closely affiliated with institutions. This is indicated by the distance separating the lines on Figures 7–1 and 7–3. As with campaign activity, those with strong institutional ties are more active than those with weaker ties. But the difference across institutional levels is less for communal than for campaign activity. This is the case in all nations with the exception of India, where campaign and communal activity are equally affected by institutional affiliation. Table 7–2 summarizes the difference between campaign and communal activity in this regard (for those nations where we have both measures). It presents the average distance (i.e., average across socioeconomic levels) on the campaign and communal activity scales between the strongly affiliated and the unaffiliated.

The data on the relative strength of institutions in relation to campaign and communal activity are somewhat mixed when it comes to the issue of the extent to which institutional affiliation reduces the relationship between SERL and activity. If one considers those with strong institutional affiliation, one finds, as we have pointed out, that there is a positive SERL/communal activity relationship in all cases, just as there

Table 7–2. *Average distance on the campaign and communal participation scales between strong affiliators and the unaffiliated (controlling for SERL)*

Nation	Distance between strong affiliators and unaffiliated on *campaign scale*	Distance between strong affiliators and unaffiliated on *communal* scale
Austria	94	46
India	103	104
Japan	94	54
Netherlands	80	62
United States	74	58

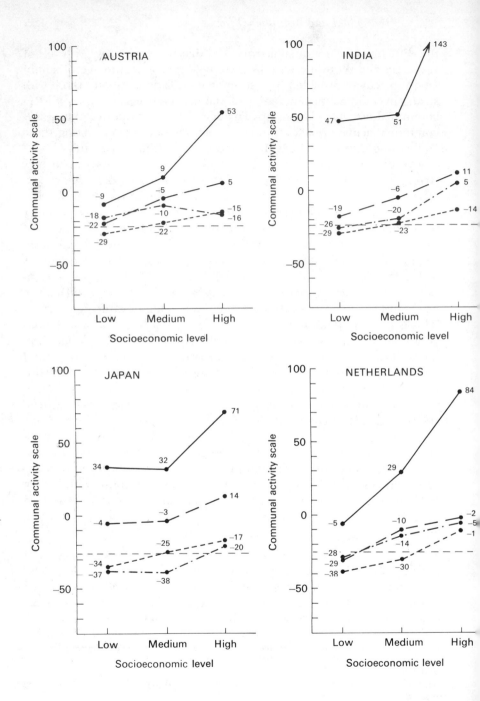

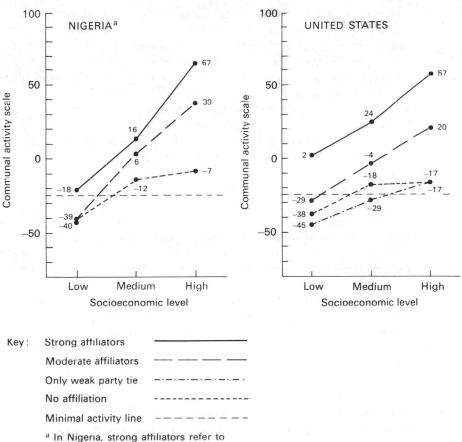

Key :   Strong affiliators
        Moderate affiliators   — — — —
        Only weak party tie   — ·— ·— ·— ·— ·
        No affiliation   - - - - - - - - - -
        Minimal activity line   — — — — — — — —

[a] In Nigeria, strong affiliators refer to
   members of politicized organizations,
   moderate affiliators refer to members
   of nonpoliticized organizations

Figure 7-3. Communal activity by socioeconomic resource level for
level of affiliation.

was with campaign activity. In this sense, institutional affiliation is in no country a sufficient condition for either of these activities. However, among the strongly affiliated, institutions appear to reduce the participation gap between the haves and the have-nots more in relation to campaign than in relation to communal activity. This is seen in Table 7–3. In those nations where the impact of institutions on campaign activity was seen to be the strongest – Austria, Japan, and the Netherlands – the participation disparity between the haves and the have-nots among those with strong institutional affiliation is greater in relation to communal activity than in relation to campaign activity. The difference between the two acts is especially great in the Netherlands, but is substantial in the other two nations. In India and the United States, we found institutions to be weak in relation to campaign activity among the strongly affiliated. They are weak in relation to communal activity as well, though in these cases the data go somewhat against our expectations in that there is a somewhat larger have/have-not participation gap for campaign than communal activity. The differences between the two acts are, however, in the cases of India and the United States quite small. In sum, when we look at the strongly affiliated, we find less institutional interference with the relation between SERL and activity when it comes to communal activity than when it comes to campaign.

The evidence as to the relative strength of institutions across the two modes of activity is less clear when we look at the unaffiliated. In relation to campaign activity we found several instances of lockout, that is, situations in which those with no institutional affiliation could not convert socioeconomic resources into political activity. The result was that even those from the top third of the SERL scale among the unaffiliated had a level of participation below the minimal-activity line. When we compare that situation with the data for communal activity, we find some

Table 7–3. *Campaign and communal participation disparity between haves and have-nots among strongly affiliated*

Nation	Disparity in *campaign* activity between top and bottom SERL groups among strongly affiliated	Disparity in *communal* activity between top and bottom SERL groups among strongly affiliated
Austria	37	62
India	108	96
Japan	25	37
Netherlands	13	89
United States	61	55

evidence that institutions are weaker in relation to communal activity. In two of the nations where we had clear instances of lockout – Japan and the Netherlands – the lockout phenomenon is less pronounced. There is a slight slope to the SERL/communal activity relationship (a participation disparity between the haves and the have-nots of 17 in Japan and 27 points in the Netherlands compared with figures of 5 and 2 points respectively for campaign activity). Furthermore in those two nations the upper status unaffiliated participate at a level above the minimal-activity line when it comes to communal activity.

The data on the Austrian unaffiliated citizens offer less support for the position that institutions are weaker in relation to communal activity than in relation to campaigning. The upper status unaffiliated citizens participate in communal activity above the minimal-activity line, but the slope of the SERL/communal activity relationship is actually less than the SERL/campaign activity slope. The data for the Indian and American unaffiliated citizens also provide little evidence that institutions are weaker in relation to communal activity. In India the SERL/communal activity slope is greater than the slope for campaign activity. In the United States both slopes are the same.

In general the evidence tends to suggest that communal activity is less dominated by institutional affiliation than is campaign activity. The data in Table 7–2 on the relation between institutional affiliation and the two modes of activity, controlling for socioeconomic level, make this clear. The data on the interaction among socioeconomic level, institutional affiliation, and the two modes of activity are less unambiguous, but they tend to support the same conclusion.

The data also seem to reflect differences in the degree to which institutions are the channels for activity within the community. In the Netherlands a large number of "action groups" had emerged by the time of our survey, groups that deliberately were independent of the political parties or established formal organizations. Activity of this kind is outside of institutional control; individual socioeconomic resources play an important role. Such groups are predominantly middle class (Molleman, forthcoming). In Austria and Japan communal activity comes more heavily under the control of formal organizations. In Austria much of the associational life of communities is dominated by party-related organizations or by corporate economic groups, the membership of which is not fully voluntary. The organizations and groups apparently play a major role in community activity (Powell, 1976). In Japan as well, community activity appears to be dependent on organizational affiliation. Data gathered in an urban study in Japan by Ichiro Miyake support this interpretation. He found that four out of five of communal activists report that they were mobilized to that activity through an organizational affiliation, usually through neighborhood associations.

Institutional forces and political equality: a summary

The data in Figures 7–1, 7–2, and 7–3 illustrate the way in which institutional interference affects the conversion of socioeconomic resources into political activity. We shall explore the role of institutions more fully, but it may be useful to summarize some results thus far. Some important uniformities appear in the data. For one thing, we find, as expected, that institutional affiliation has its greatest impact on voting, a weaker impact on campaign activity, and a weaker impact still in relation to communal activity. More significant (and less obvious) is the uniform difference found between voting and campaign activity in terms of where the impact of institutions is felt. When it comes to campaigning, the conversion rate of socioeconomic resources into activity is lower among the unaffiliated than the affiliated; when it comes to voting, the conversion rate is generally low among both the affiliated and the unaffiliated. This difference is predicted by our model, based on the distinction between more or less "difficult" acts – that is, acts requiring more or less socioeconomic resources. An absence of institutional affiliation can prevent individuals from converting resources into activity; but the presence of affiliation does not eliminate the usefulness of resources. When it comes to an easier act such as the vote, the presence of affiliation can bring all those with such affiliation into political activity.

The differences across nations derive from the differing effects of institutions. Where institutions are strong, the segment of the population that has no institutional affiliation is kept out of campaign activity. In the United States, where institutional affiliation is less of a necessity for such activity, the unaffiliated take part in campaigns. The consequences for the participation disparity between the haves and the have-nots is substantial. The haves among the unaffiliated take greater advantage of the participatory opportunities. The data illustrate the way in which the provision of opportunities to participate, in the absence of other forces such as institutional restriction, can result in participatory inequality. Unaffiliated citizens in systems with restrictive institutions are equally inactive no matter what their socioeconomic level. When such citizens have participatory opportunities because institutions are less restrictive, participatory inequality across socioeconomic levels appears.

When it comes to voting, strong institutions also play an equalizing role, but in a somewhat different way. Affiliation becomes a sufficient condition for voting. This is because voting is an easy act and institutions are motivated to mobilize voters. The result is that the affiliated from the lower portion of the socioeconomic scale take part at levels equal to those higher on the scale.

In sum, institutional interference can lead to greater political equality, but it does so somewhat differently for voting and campaign activity.

Institutions have their main impact on different groups for each of the acts. For voting, the major impact is on the lower-status affiliated citizens; for campaigning, the major impact is on the upper-status unaffiliated citizens. Equalization of voting participation takes place by bringing the former into politics; equalization of campaign participation takes place by holding the latter out.

Socioeconomic level and institutional affiliation

There is one further component of our model as spelled out in Chapter 5 that we have not dealt with thus far. As explicated in Chapter 5 (see Figure 5–2 and the discussion associated with it), the impact that institutional affiliation has on the relationship between SERL and political activity depends in part on the socioeconomic composition of those who are affiliated with institutions and those who are not. The situation is simplest in the case where institutions are dominant, where all those who are unaffiliated are locked out and all those who are affiliated are mobilized. The result is not necessarily the absence of any relationship between SERL and activity. If the affiliated and the unaffiliated do not differ in socioeconomic level, the SERL/activity relationship will disappear. But if the affiliated come from the upper reaches of the SERL scale whereas the unaffiliated come from the lower parts of the scale, a positive SERL/activity relationship will result. Individuals may not directly convert socioeconomic resources into activity. Their activity level will depend on whether or not they are affiliated with institutions. But their socioeconomic resources will be related to the extent of their institutional affiliation. In such a case, individual socioeconomic resources work *through* institutional affiliation to affect participation.

The opposite would be the case if, in a dominant institutional system, those affiliated with institutions came disproportionately from the lower parts of the SERL scale. The result would be a negative relationship between SERL and activity. Similar results appear in the mixed systems where institutions are restrictive or mobilizing. Consider the restrictive institutional systems found in several nations in relation to campaign activity. Such systems act to equalize political activity by locking out upper-status unaffiliated citizens. Because of their lack of affiliation, they cannot convert socioeconomic resources into political activity. The degree of equalization deriving from this lockout depends in part on the socioeconomic composition of the unaffiliated citizens. If most are from the top of the SERL scale, the equalizing effect of the lockout of that group will be greater than if most of the unaffiliated come from the bottom of the socioeconomic scale.

Lastly, as illustrated in Figure 5–2, the composition of the various groups of affiliators makes a difference even if the effect on institutions is an additive one. Under such circumstances, institutions give an added boost to the political activity of those affiliated with them. If upper-status citizens are disproportionately found among the affiliated, the boost goes to them, increasing participatory inequality. If lower-status citizens are disproportionately among the affiliated, the boost in activity goes to them and participation is equalized.

In Figure 7–4 we present data on the socioeconomic composition of the various groups of affiliators. The figure repeats the data from Figure 7–1 on the relationship between SERL and campaign activity for each of the four levels of institutional affiliation. But it adds another bit of information. We place at each of the data points on the lines for the four types of affiliators the percentage of the population that falls at that point: for instance, the proportion of the sample that is both strongly affiliated and in the lower third of the SERL scale, the proportion of the strongly affiliated in the middle third of the SERL scale, and so forth. (Note that the numbers on the lines are not, as they usually are, scores on the activity scales; they are proportions of the *total* sample.) By looking at the proportions on any of the lines, one can tell whether that group is disproportionately from the top or the bottom of the SERL scale as well as the size of the group. The strong affiliators in the United States, for instance, come disproportionately from the top third of the SERL scale (the strongly affiliated in the top third of the SERL scale are 15 percent of the sample; the strongly affiliated in the bottom third of the SERL scale are 9 percent of the sample). The effects of the composition of the various groups can be seen at either end of the institutional affiliation scale. Consider those with strong institutional affiliation. In each of the nations this group receives an extra participatory boost from that affiliation. Insofar as this group comes disproportionately from the upper levels of the SERL scale, such a boost increases participatory inequality. This is most clearly illustrated in India. The strongly affiliated receive a large boost through their affiliation. Since the group is heavily skewed in favor of the top categories on SERL, the result is an increase in participatory inequality. On the other hand, the absolute size of the group is important. The strongly affiliated are a relatively small group (only about 12 percent of the sample). This reduces somewhat the effect of institutional affiliation on participatory inequality. A similar skewing of the institutionally affiliated is found in most of the nations – Japan is the exception – but the extent of that skewing is not as great as in India. Insofar as there is such skewing, participatory inequality is increased by the effects of institutions.

The effects of the composition of the various institutional groups is found as well among those with little institutional affiliation. In general, they come somewhat disproportionately from the bottom of the SERL scale. Insofar as that is the case, the equalizing effects of lockout are mitigated. Where there is lockout, those with no institutional affiliation cannot convert their socioeconomic resources into political activity. Insofar as few of the locked out have high levels of resources, the equalizing tendency is reduced somewhat. In no country, however, is the disproportion of lower SERL individuals among those with little institutional affiliation very great. In Austria those with no politicized institutional affiliation come equally from the top and the bottom of the SERL scale. In the other nations the nonpoliticized and/or the weak identifiers contain substantial proportions from the top third of the SERL scale. Insofar as those groups are locked out, participatory equality is increased; the larger the group, the more this is the case.

Political activity versus political involvement: a further test of our model

Let us recapitulate our argument and then subject it to a further test. In Chapter 4 we posed our puzzle: Individuals with higher levels of socioeconomic resources should, according to our cross-cultural generalization, be more politically active; yet there is wide variation across nations in the extent to which socioeconomic resource level correlates with political activity. The puzzle is to explain how the generalization about individual propensities to be politically active can be consistent with data showing such wide cross-national variation in the SERL/participation relationship. The solution to the puzzle requires a distinction between individual and institutional forces: If it were not for institutional interference, individuals would convert their socioeconomic resources into political activity at the same rate in each nation.

We cannot test this modified version of our generalization directly. To do so we would have to isolate individuals from the institutional settings within which they live. We would have to see how individuals would act if there were no institutional constraints. We have tried an indirect test of the generalization. In Chapter 4 we compared the relationships between SERL and various political activities on the one hand with the relationship between SERL and political discussion or psychological involvement in politics on the other. We assumed that in contrast with the situation in relation to political activity, institutions would be less motivated and less able to interfere with the extent to which individuals discuss politics or with the extent to which they are psychologically involved in political matters. If this is the case, the relationship between SERL and discussion or psychological involvement ought to resemble the situation that would obtain in relation to political activity if activity were free from institutional interference. By considering, for instance, the SERL/psychological involvement relationship in a nation where institutions have a strong impact on activity, we should be able to

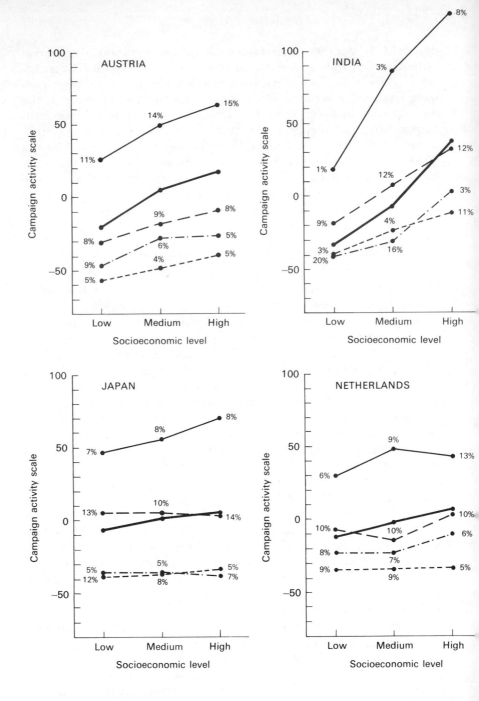

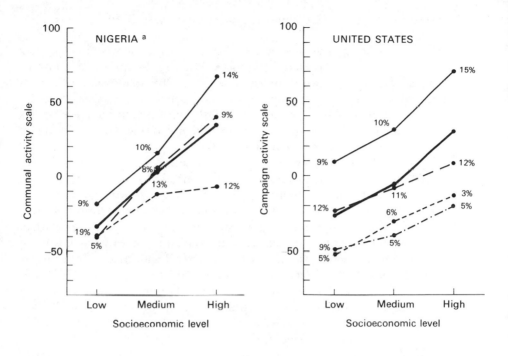

Key: Strong affiliators   ————————
        Moderate affiliators   — — — —
        Only weak party tie   —·—·—·
        No affiliation   — — — — —
        Whole population   ————————

[a] In Nigeria, strong affiliators refer
    to members of politicized orginizations
    and moderate affiliators refer to members
    of nonpoliticized organizations

Figure 7-4. Campaign activity by socioeconomic level for level of
institutional affiliation with percentage of population base.

observe those activity patterns that would exist if institutions were weaker.

When we compared activity with discussion or involvement in Chapter 4, we found the expected differences. Where we expect heavy institutional interference, we found a widespread cross-national variation in the SERL/activity relationship. Campaign activity and voting were the best examples. Where we expected little institutional interference (as with political discussion or psychological involvement in politics), we found greater cross-national uniformity.

In this chapter we have looked more closely at the role of institutional affiliation in relation to various kinds of political activity. The analysis allowed us to specify more precisely the ways in which institutional interference works: In particular we found that where institutional affiliation is a strong force on political activity, institutions are restrictive forces vis-à-vis campaign activity and dominant forces vis-à-vis voting. We can now combine the analysis in Chapter 4 with that in this chapter. Let us look at the relationships between SERL on the one hand and political discussion or involvement on the other among those with varying degrees of institutional affiliation.

If institutions are relatively ineffective in relation to rates of political discussion or involvement, we should find the following: Institutions should be "weak" or at most "additive" in relation to these variables. This means that institutional affiliation should be neither necessary nor sufficient for political interest or discussion. Those who have the resources for political involvement may be inhibited from taking an active role in a campaign if they have no institutional affiliation, but they will not be inhibited from discussing politics or from maintaining an interest in such matters. There should be no lock out of unaffiliated citizens. Similarly, those who have few resources for activity may be mobilized to activity (as we have shown for voting) where institutions are strong. But they will not be turned into involved citizens, nor will discussion be generated.

Data for political discussion are plotted on Figure 7–5, for political involvement on Figure 7–6. The measures of political discussion and political interest have been standardized so as to be similar to the political activity scales – that is, they have a mean of 0 and a standard deviation of 100. The patterns on both Figures 7–5 and 7–6 can be briefly described because they are so strikingly uniform. The pattern for political discussion is similar to that for political interest, and the patterns are similar across the nations. In every case one finds that institutional affiliation has some effect on political discussion or political involvement – that is, the line for the strongly affiliated is above the lines for those with moderate affiliation and the lines for the two least-affiliated groups are below the others. But in no case does institutional affiliation or its absence eliminate the ability of individuals to convert socioeconomic resources into political discussion or involvement.

The cross-national uniformity is compelling. In each nation, for each of the institutional types, there is a positive relationship between socioeconomic resources and political discussion or involvement. And the relationships are quite similar across the various groups. The data in Figures 7–5 and 7–6 can be considered a further elaboration and confirmation of our argument in Chapter 4 that political discussion or psychological involvement in politics can be used to isolate the individual-level relationship between socioeconomic resources and political involvement. In Chapter 4 we found that the data were consistent with that interpretation in that we found a strong SERL/discussion and SERL/involvement relationship that was uniform across the nations. When we look at the SERL/discussion or involvement relationship among groups with varying degrees of institutional affiliation, we find that the individual-level hypothesis continues to hold.

The data in Figures 7–5 and 7–6 form a striking contrast to the similar figures presented for political activities. In several nations – Austria, Japan, the Netherlands – those who had no institutional affiliation were effectively locked out of campaign activity no matter what their level of socioeconomic resources. When it comes to political involvement or discussion, one finds no examples of lockout. Consider those with no political institutional affiliation but with a high level of individual resources. Only in the Netherlands do we find this group below the minimal-activity line for involvement and discussion. In Austria and Japan this group (low on institutional affiliation but high on resources) is well above that line for discussion and involvement, whereas they were well below the line in relation to campaign activity and voting. And in the Netherlands, though the unaffiliated only reach the minimal-activity line in relation to discussion and involvement, their score on those scales is well above the scores achieved by those from the same unaffiliated group with fewer socioeconomic resources. This contrasts with the situation for voting or campaign activity where those high on resources but low on institutional affiliation are no more active than those low on resources and low on institutional affiliation.

In addition, we found examples of groups for whom institutional affiliation was a sufficient condition for voting – that is, groups mobilized to vote no matter what their level of socioeconomic resources. In no nation is strong institutional affiliation a sufficient condition for discussion and involvement.

The data in Figures 7–5 and 7–6 are another and, we believe, more powerful illustration of a point made in Chapter 4 – cross-national differences receive more credence as "real" differences (in contrast to research artifacts) when they can be juxtaposed against cross-national

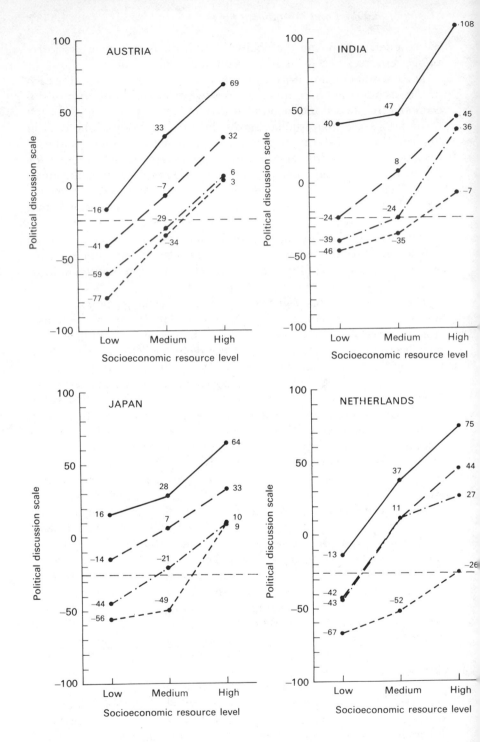

138

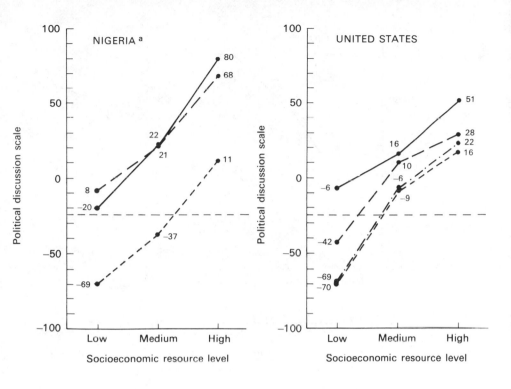

Key: Strong affiliators   ——————
        Moderate affiliators   — — — —
        Only weak party tie   — · — · — ·
        No affiliation   — — — — —
        Minimal-activity line   — — — —

        [a] In Nigeria, strong affiliators refer
        to members of politicized organizations
        and moderate affiliators refer to members
        of nonpoliticized organizations

Figure 7-5. Political discussion by socioeconomic resource level for
levels of institutional affiliation.

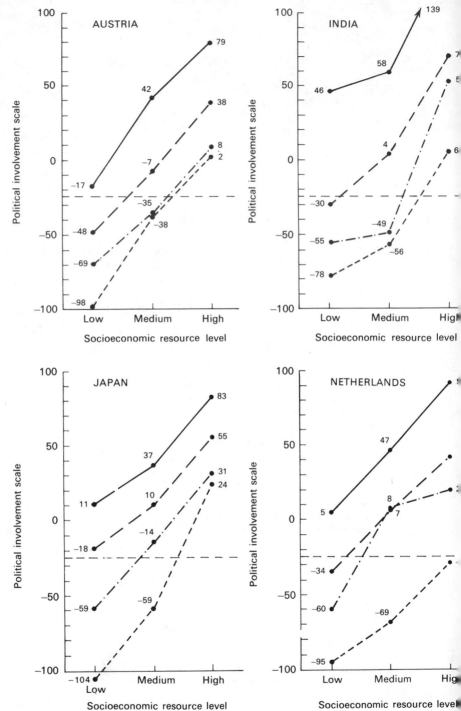

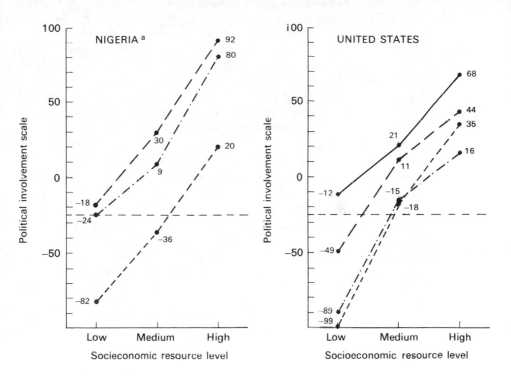

Key: Strong affiliators   ————————

       Moderate affiliators   — — — —

       Only weak party tie   — · — · — ·

       No affiliation   — — — — —

       Minimal activity line   — — — —

[a] In Nigeria, strong affiliators refer
to members of politicized organizations
and moderate affiliators refer to members
of nonpoliticized organizations

Figure 7-6. Political involvement by socioeconomic resource level for
level of affiliation.

141

similarities. The fact that individual-level socioeconomic characteristics relate so uniformly to political discussion and political interest in each of the nations and that it makes little difference to the strength of those relationships whether one considers those with institutional affiliation or those without it adds weight to our assumption that both the differences found among nations and the differences found within nations across different levels of institutional affiliation represent real differences in the interrelationship among SERL, partisanship, and participation. Note, for instance, how the difference between the United States and the other nations found in relation to campaign and voting activity disappears when one considers involvement and discussion.

The United States represents a deviant case when it comes to voting and campaign activity. It is the only nation where positive SERL/activity relationships exist at all levels of institutional affiliation. The deviation from the other nations is, we have argued, due to the fact that institutional constraints are weaker in the United States and individual socioeconomic resources are freer to play a role in determining activity levels. That interpretation receives some support from the similarity of the other nations to the U.S. pattern when it comes to discussion and involvement.

Conclusion

The data on psychological involvement and discussion help confirm our argument that institutional interference with political activity can be an equalizing force across socioeconomic levels. In all nations, the SERL/discussion and the SERL/psychological involvement relationships are strong. Discussion and involvement, in other words, are highly stratified by socioeconomic levels. Those nations where activity is relatively equal across socioeconomic levels resemble the more stratified nations when it comes to these "quasi activities." The reason that discussion and involvement are stratified is that they reflect the effects of individual socioeconomic resources relatively unimpeded by institutional constraints. If political activity were similarly unimpeded across all nations, it would also be similarly stratified.

8
Some variations on our model: parties of the left and right

Our analysis thus far has dealt with the impact of the "institutional system" in each nation on the political behavior and attitudes of individuals. We have distinguished among citizens in terms of their overall level of affiliation with political institutions without regard to the kind of institution with which they are affiliated. A number of distinctions among institutions are possible, however. One such distinction is between political parties and other organizations. In writing this book, our first inclination was to treat these institutions separately; to analyze the relation between partisanship and participation separately from the relation between organizational affiliation and participation. Indeed, an earlier draft of this book contained parallel analyses for each of the institutions. Graphs similar to those in Figures 7–1 through 7–4 were prepared for partisan affiliation and for organizational affiliation separately. The graphs for partisanship allowed us to compare those having strong partisan affiliation with those having weak affiliation and in turn with those having no affiliation. The graphs for organizations allowed us to compare those affiliated with politicized organizations with those having only nonpoliticized affiliations and those, in turn, with the nonmembers. We had expected some differences in the impact of the two types of institutions. Parties, we expected, would have a greater impact on campaign activity and voting than on communal activity; organizations would have a greater impact on communal activity.

There was some tendency in this direction, but less than expected. The lockout of the unaffiliated in relation to voting and campaign activity, that we have reported previously using our combined measure of institutional affiliation, tended to be replicated whether one used a measure of party affiliation or a measure of organizational membership. Communal activity, in turn, was less affected by either type of institutional affiliation, though there was a tendency in several of the nations for organizational affiliation to have a "stronger" impact on communal activity than did partisan affiliation. In general, however, the differences between the two types of institutions were not substantial enough to warrant a full parallel treatment of each. Consider our generalization that the SERL/participation relationship for difficult political acts would

143

be greater among those with institutional affiliation than among those with no such affiliation. The generalization held in almost all cases no matter whether one used partisanship or organizational affiliation as the measure of institutionalization.

Parties of the right and of the left

There is, however, one distinction worth making and for which we shall present some comparative data. We built our measure of institutional affiliation using the strength of partisan affiliation as the measure of an individual's tie to a political party. We did not differentiate among types of party. A distinction among political parties along ideological lines might require modification of our analysis in two ways. The way in which institutions affect participatory inequality depends in part on the socioeconomic characteristics of those citizens affiliated with institutions. Affiliated citizens tend to come from the upper reaches of the SERL scale. When they receive a boost in activity through their affiliation, that boost increases participatory inequality. But our measure of the socioeconomic origins of the affiliator group represents an average across all parties and organizations. It is possible that some parties recruit more heavily from those lower on the socioeconomic scale and, thereby, may contribute more to political equality than do other parties. (If that turns out to be the case, incidentally, it in no way changes the conclusion as to the impact of the institutional system as a whole on participatory inequality. It merely elaborates the process.)

Secondly, the disaggregation of our measure of institutional affiliation to allow consideration of the impact on participation of parties from different parts of the political spectrum will allow us a crucial test of our model. Our general expectation has been that among those with institutional affiliation the process by which one becomes a political activist will tend uniformly to follow our cross-cultural generalization that upper-status citizens will become more active. Our data are consistent with this for campaign and communal activity: In all nations there is a positive SERL/activity relationship for those two acts among the strongly affiliated. The separate consideration of the political parties puts the generalization to a particularly hard test.

One might expect a disproportionate mobilization to political activity of upper-status supporters in more conservative parties. One would, in contrast, ordinarily expect a greater equalizing impact from parties of the left rather than of the right. Left institutions ought to have a more conscious commitment to political equalization and ought, as well, to have supporters from the lower parts of the SERL scale that they will want to mobilize. One would expect that parties of the left (particularly working-class parties with a conscious socialist tradition such as those in

Austria and the Netherlands) would be both more motivated and able to increase the relative rates of participation of the lower socioeconomic strata.

On the other hand, our model suggests that individual socioeconomic resources ought to lead to participation if institutional forces are held constant. This suggests that *within the sphere* of the parties of the left as well as of the right, those with greater individual resources will take a stronger participatory role. This would not occur, according to our model, only if there were a deliberate policy on the part of a party to mobilize the lower socioeconomic strata from among its support group. In the absence of such a policy – and the left parties in the nations we study do not have such policies as far as we can tell – our generalization about the positive SERL/activity relationship should hold in parties of all ideological stripe.

We are not alone in suggesting that participatory channels even in left-oriented political parties will be dominated by those of greater wealth and educational attainment. Robert Michels touches on this theme numerous times in his classic study of political parties. Although his study concentrates on the inevitability of political stratification and the development of bureaucratized leadership even in democratically oriented political parties, he also has a great deal to say about the types of individuals who are most likely to emerge as activists and party leaders. In his discussion of the social analysis of party leadership he states: ". . . pages could be filled with the names of leading socialist politicians sprung from the bourgeoisie, whereas in a single breath we could complete the list of political leaders of truly working class origin . . ." and he concludes, ". . . taken in the mass the poor are powerless and disarmed . . . their intellectual and cultural inferiority makes it impossible for them to see whither the leader is going or to estimate in advance the significance of his action . . ." (Michels, 1968, pp. 231, 369). Moreover, at many points in his book, wherever the characteristics of leadership are discussed, Michels is keenly aware of what he terms the cultural, educational, rhetorical, and organizational superiority of the leaders over the led. It is almost a corollary of the iron law of oligarchy that those who emerge in leadership positions will be of higher socioeconomic position with all of the attendant participatory skills and resources that that implies.

Ideally, our analysis ought to deal with each of the parties in each of the nations. In fact, our samples are often too small to allow us to separate all of the parties. Thus we have at times combined parties into a party "type." The main criterion is the ideological position of the parties. In the United States we simply distinguish between the Republican and Democratic parties. In Austria we make a similar distinction between the ÖVP (the Austrian People's Party) and the SPÖ (the Austrian Socialist Party), ignoring the few supporters of the Communist Party and the FPÖ in our sample. In Japan the left category consists of supporters of the Japanese Socialist and Communist parties. On the right in Japan, we place the supporters of the Liberal Democratic Party.

The situation in the multiparty Netherlands is, as one might expect, more complex. Some have said that the tendency in the Netherlands is a party for each citizen. It does not quite happen that way in real life, but when one takes a sample survey, it is not infrequent that one finds parties with one or two supporters. Furthermore, it is by no means clear that the parties can be arrayed along a single continuum. Therefore, following the suggestions in Daalder and Rusk (1972), we have categorized the Dutch parties into three categories: those of the left, the middle, and the right. The following lists the parties placed in each category:

Left	*Middle*	*Right*
PVDA (Labor Party)	KVP (Catholics)	VVD (Liberals)
D '66 (Democrats '66)	ARP (Anti-Revolutionary)	CHU (Christian-Historicals)
CPN (Communists)		BP (Farmers)
PSP (Pacifists)		DS '70 (Democratic-Socialists '70)
PPR (Radical Party)		GPV (Reformed Party)

In India 88 percent of the party supporters in our sample supported the Congress Party. We can, however, lump together the parties of the left that appear in our sample (various Communist and Socialist parties) and the parties of the right (Swatantra, Jan Sangh) to make some limited comparisons in India as well.

Party support

Table 8–1 presents the party support profiles of the various socioeconomic levels in each of the nations. Table 8–1 tells us whether various SERL groups are more likely to be found supporting one type of party or another. Consider the extent to which the various SERL levels are *strong* supporters of parties of the right or left. In Austria the upper and the lower SERL groups each provide strong supporters for both parties, but there is a clear tendency for lower SERL citizens to be more likely to be strong supporters of the SPÖ, the upper SERL group to be strong supporters of the ÖVP. Among those lower SERL citizens who are strong party supporters, about three out of five give their support to the SPÖ; among the upper SERL strong supporters, about three out of five give their support to the ÖVP. In this respect, the middle SERL group resembles the lower, and indeed the middle SERL group provides the largest proportion of support for the SPÖ.

In Japan, on the other hand, the various SERL groups are not more likely to give strong support to one or the other of the party groupings. Lower SERL citizens are slightly more likely to be strong supporters of the left than are upper SERL citizens, but they are also slightly more likely to be strong supporters of the right parties. Nor is the pattern much different in the Netherlands. The upper SERL groups are more likely than the lower to be strong supporters of the right parties, a little less likely to be strong supporters of the left parties, but the differences are small.

The situation in the Netherlands is, as always, more complex. We consider the three broad groupings of parties as described previously. Upper-status citizens are less likely to be independent and more likely to support the parties of the right. But as high a proportion of the upper-status citizens is found among the left and center supporters as is found among those lower on the SERL scale.

In the United States there is some polarization of party support on the basis of SERL. High SERL citizens are somewhat more likely than low SERL citizens to be strong Republicans (but the highest proportion of strong Republicans is found among the middle SERL citizens). The main difference between the SERL groupings is in the proportion who are strong Democrats. Twenty-nine percent of the lower SERL group are strong Democrats compared with 15 percent among the upper SERL group.

In India the major tendency is for lower-status respondents to be unaffiliated. Most of the support of all socioeconomic levels goes to Congress. The left and the right also receive a higher proportion of upper-status supporters.

The data in Table 8–1 could be misleading if one took them to tell more than they are intended to tell. The major distinction between the supporters of one party or another are not summed up in the dimension of SERL, as we shall see in detail later in Chapters 9 and 10. Characteristics such as religion, race, farm versus nonfarm occupation, distinguish the support bases of the various parties much more sharply. In most of the countries with a strong socialist party, the farm sector, one of the groups lowest on our SERL index, is predominantly affiliated with the conservative party. Austria and Japan are probably the most striking in this regard. Further, as Przeworski nicely points out, most of the socialist parties have attempted in the past fifty years to expand their electoral base by consciously courting middle and upper strata, thus diluting the purely proletarian character of their constituency (Przeworski, 1976).

Table 8–1 merely tells us whether different parties in the five nations

Table 8–1. *Affiliation with parties of the left and right by socioeconomic advantage*

	Austria				India			
	Total	Low SERL	Mid SERL	High SERL	Total	Low SERL	Mid SERL	High SERL
Independents		19%	18%	18%	22%	46%	60%	46%	33%
Right parties								
Weak		24	25	18	27	01	—	—	01
Strong		15	12	14	20	02	01	02	05
Left parties								
Weak		24	26	28	18	01	—	01	01
Strong		18	18	22	13	02	02	02	04
Middle parties					Congress Party			
Weak						11	09	12	11
Strong						38	29	37	46
Total		100%	99%	100%	100%	101%	101%	100%	101%

differ in terms of the SERL groups that support them. This information is important for our analysis. It tells us whether the various party group-ings differ in their potential for modifying the have/have-not partici-pation disparity. The data suggest that in the United States and, to a lesser extent, in Austria, the parties of the left (the Democrats and the SPÖ) have a somewhat greater potential than the parties of the right (the Republicans and the ÖVP) for reducing the participation disparity between the haves and the have-nots, since the former recruit supporters disproportionately from the lower SERL groups. And in India, the main tendency is for affiliation – but not *direction* of affiliation – to be asso-ciated with higher socioeconomic levels. The absence of a clear pattern in the SERL composition of left-versus-right parties provides an answer to one aspect of the questions raised at the beginning of this chapter. Left and right parties are not as different in terms of the socioeconomic level of their adherents as one might expect from party labels or rhetoric. Although there are national differences, it seems fair to say that there is no clear evidence that left parties play a larger role in modifying the SERL-to-participation relationship by recruiting substantially larger numbers from lower-status groups. We do not imply by these findings that left and right parties have relatively undifferentiated social bases. As we shall see in Chapters 9 and 10, both left and right parties recruit lower-status individuals, but they are of different types.

Recruitment patterns for left and right parties represent half of the story. The other major question that must be examined is the compar-

Japan				Netherlands				United States			
Total	Low SERL	Mid SERL	High SERL	Total	Low SERL	Mid SERL	High SERL	Total	Low SERL	Mid SERL	High SERL
28%	33%	28%	22%	28%	33%	32%	19%	22%	17%	23%	27%
30	27	27	36	11	06	09	18	17	12	14	20
11	11	13	10	06	04	03	08	12	11	9	14
23	21	23	26	22	18	23	23	29	31	30	24
08	08	09	06	08	11	06	08	21	29	23	15
				14	15	15	14				
				11	13	12	10				
100%	100%	100%	100%	100%	100%	100%	100%	101%	100%	100%	100%

ative participation rates of haves and have-nots within the left-versus-right parties. Our hypothesis is that dominant-party systems reduce the SERL/participation relationship by locking out nonadherents from all strata in relation to difficult modes of participation, while mobilizing all supporters when it comes to the vote. In other words, dominant institutional systems affect the SERL composition of the participant strata in large part by controlling the behavior of nonadherents. In countries with less dominant institutional systems, nonadherents may or may not participate depending upon their individual motivation and resources. Our general model would further predict, however, that once individuals fall within the institutional fold, parties will have neither the desire nor the ability to control levels of activity. We should find levels of activity substantially correlated with socioeconomic position. Thus all party groupings should be similar among their strong supporters. We expect the more affluent and better educated to be more active in parties of the left as well as in parties of the right. This should be particularly true for difficult acts. When it comes to voting, we expect that parties will deliberately mobilize supporters from all parts of the socioeconomic scale and the more dominant the party system, the more complete will be the mobilization.

Data relevant to this expectation are presented in Figures 8–1 and 8–2. The data are for campaign activity and voting. The figures take the same form as Figures 7–1 and 7–2 which related SERL and activity for the several levels of institutional affiliation. But Figures 8–1 and

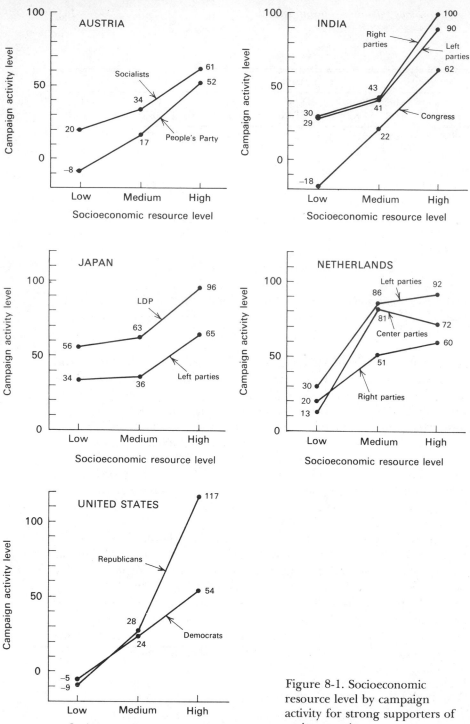

Figure 8-1. Socioeconomic resource level by campaign activity for strong supporters of various parties.

150

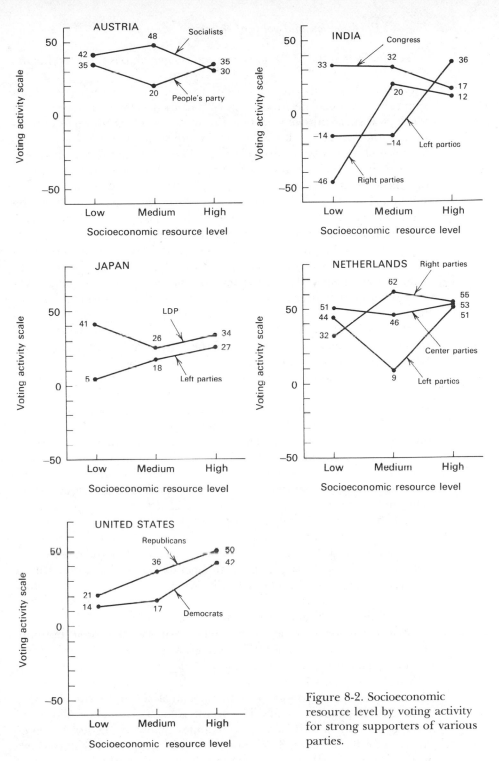

Figure 8-2. Socioeconomic resource level by voting activity for strong supporters of various parties.

8–2 differ in that the SERL/participation relationship is reported for the strong supporters of the various party groupings.

Consider Figure 8–1 for campaign activity. We find our expectations supported. Among the supporters of parties from various parts of the ideological spectrum we find that the upper SERL supporters outparticipate the lower. In all five nations there is an upward slope of the lines for all supporter groups. If we take the difference in activity scores between those high on the SERL scale and those low on that scale as our measure of the strength of the SERL/activity relationship, we find substantial differences in each case – even in those nations where the SERL/campaign activity relationship for the whole population was weak. The data thus support our contention that parties of varying political orientation will behave in the same way; the haves among their supporters are more likely to become activists. The fact that our generalization holds among the supporters of the left party groupings is a confirmation of that generalization under particularly difficult circumstances.

There is some tendency for the SERL/campaign activity relationship to be stronger among supporters of the right than of the left parties, but no very consistent pattern. In Austria, India, and the United States, the haves differ from the have-nots more among the supporters of the right than among the supporters of the left. In Japan, however, there is no difference in this respect between left and right supporters, and in the Netherlands the SERL/campaign activity relationship is stronger among the supporters of the left parties than among those of the right. In any case, the major point is that we find in all of the nations a tendency for the haves among party supporters to outparticipate the have-nots within the support groups of the parties of the right (where one might expect this to happen) as well as among the supporters of the left (where one might have expected the opposite).

The data for voting in Figure 8–2 provide the usual contrast to campaign activity. In the United States there is a positive relationship between SERL and voting among Democrats and Republicans. But in Austria, Japan, and the Netherlands, we find no clear SERL/voting relationship in any party grouping. In these three countries with the more dominant institutional systems, strong adherents to the party vote at relatively high levels no matter what their socioeconomic position. Those without institutional affiliation, as we have seen, are locked out of voting. Again we see a clear case of a dominant institutional system in which institutional involvement is both a necessary and sufficient condition for participation. The present analysis shows that left and right parties play an equally important role in the mobilization and lockout of voting and thus both contribute equally to the dissolution of the relationship between SERL and voting. In the United States, where institutions are much weaker, having only a modest additive impact on voting, individual motivation and resources affect voting rates of both strong Democrats and strong Republicans. Further, because the parties are not dominant, those without party adherents vote at rates even more reflective of their SERL.

The Indian data are particularly interesting. There is a positive SERL/ voting relationship within the support groups of the smaller parties of the left and the right, but a somewhat negative relationship among the supporters of the Congress Party. The data suggest that (at least at the time of the survey) the dominant Congress Party effectively mobilizes voters from across the socioeconomic spectrum whereas the smaller parties depend more heavily on the internalized commitments of their supporters to the party – an internalized commitment more likely to be found among those with higher levels of socioeconomic resources. There is a striking contrast in the voting scale scores between the Congress supporters from the lower third of the SERL scale and the supporters of the other parties from the lower third of the SERL scale. The lower-status Congress supporters score well above the mean for the population as a whole – they are regular voters. The lower-status supporters of the other parties score well below the mean.

In sum, our general findings about the relationship among institutional affiliation, SERL, and activity hold up when one deals with supporters of various political tendencies. Within the institutional sphere – in this case, among strong party supporters – there is a positive SERL/ activity relationship for difficult political acts in each of the nations; and this holds for supporters of left, center, and right parties. This is what our model predicts. Once in the institutional sphere, parties have neither the desire nor perhaps the capability to block the general tendency for those with SERL-based motivations and resources from dominating channels of participation. On the other hand, when it comes to voting, socioeconomic resources play less of a role – except in the United States and among minor parties in India. This too is consistent with our model. Where institutions are dominant, they not only lock out those who are nonadherents but mobilize high rates of turnout for the easier act of voting among all adherents.

By comparing the various party tendencies in the several nations, we have submitted our model to a somewhat harder test; and it has survived. Even within the parties of the left where one might expect ideology to favor participation of those low on the SERL scale, one finds confirmation of our cross-cultural generalization that those with greater socioeconomic resources will be more active.

Party membership and partisan identification

In creating our typology of institutional affiliation we have used subjective identification with a political party as the measure of party affiliation. As we pointed out in Chapter 6, such a definition is useful for a variety of reasons, not the least of which is that it is available across all of the nations. Party membership – a more direct measure of affiliation – cannot easily be used cross-nationally. There are differences across nations in the specific ways in which parties define membership as well as differences in the proportion of members in the population. In most of the nations, less than 10 percent of our samples (see Chapter 6) were party members.

Subjective partisan identification, however, is also problematic as a measure. It has been found to have varied meaning across nations when it comes to its relationship to the voting decision. In the United States, subjective party identification appears to be a long-term commitment that does not necessarily predict the vote. One can remain a Democrat or Republican while voting for the candidate of the opposite party. In other nations one more often shifts identification when one shifts one's vote. (See Budge, Crewe and Farlie, 1976.)

Membership is a better indicator of actual exposure to the party as an institution. We would have preferred to use such a measure had it been feasible. In two of the nations – Austria and the Netherlands – we find a sufficient number of party members to allow us to compare the results one obtains using subjective identification as a criterion of party affiliation with the results one obtains using actual membership. In Austria, 24 percent of our respondents report party membership; in the Netherlands, 12 percent. If the same pattern of results holds when we use the objective measure as is found using the criterion of subjective identification, it will be evidence that our use of a subjective rather than an objective indicator of party attachment causes no distortion. Further, this is a strong test of our model, given that all previous analysis suggests that Austria and the Netherlands are the two countries in our study with the most dominant institutional systems.

We have found that those with strong institutional ties are more politically active than those with weaker ties. We also found that among those with strong institutional ties, there is a positive relationship between socioeconomic resources and political activity–at least, for more difficult acts such as campaigning and communal activity. This holds, we have just seen, for strong supporters of various parties. Those with no institutional affiliation are in some cases locked out of politics. For them, socioeconomic resources are unrelated to activity level. Those within institutions, on the other hand, can convert their socioeconomic resources into political activity. Our cross-cultural generalization about the SERL/activity relationship reemerged within the institutional sphere. Does this pattern hold up when one uses the objective definition of partisan affiliation as it did with the subjective?

Figure 8–3 presents the relevant data for Austria and the Netherlands.

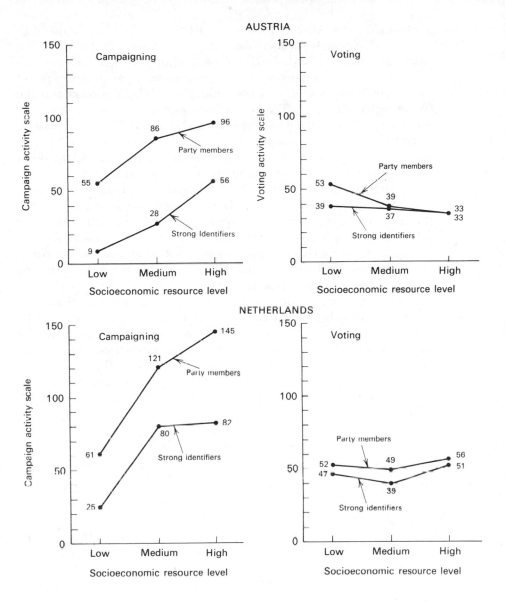

Figure 8 3. Party membership and identification compared: Austria and the Netherlands.

It shows the relationship between SERL and activity for those with partisan affiliation, both where that affiliation is defined subjectively and where that affiliation is defined by membership in a party. The data are quite clear. When it comes to campaign activity, party members are more active than subjective identifiers. This holds in Austria and the Netherlands. But for affiliators defined either way – as members or identifiers – there is a positive relationship between SERL and campaign activity. The generalization that socioeconomic resources make a difference in campaign activity among those with strong institutional ties holds up no matter which of the definitions of party ties is used.[1]

Similarly, we find that the choice of operationalization of partisan affiliation makes no difference in the conclusions one would draw about the SERL /voting activity relationship. In Austria there is a slight negative relationship between SERL and voting when one uses a subjective definition, and a somewhat stronger negative one when one uses an objective definition. In the Netherlands the relationship is essentially flat no matter which definition is used.

In sum, the comparison of the two ways of measuring partisan affiliation indicates that the process of institutional interference with the individual's conversion of socioeconomic resources into political activity works in a similar manner no matter which definition is used. The objectively defined partisans are a more active group than the subjectively defined ones. But using either definition, one finds socioeconomic resources working the same way within the group of institutional affiliators.

[1] The same pattern holds for communal activity.

9

Social segmentation and political equality: expectations

In our analysis thus far we have juxtaposed pan-cultural individual forces against nation-specific institutional ones. If institutions did not "interfere" with the ability of individuals to convert socioeconomic resources into political activity, we argue, there would be a similar pattern of participatory stratification in each nation. The distribution of political activity would closely parallel the distribution of socioeconomic resources. Institutions are important in that they lead individuals to be more or less active in politics than one would predict on the basis of individual socioeconomic resources or individual psychological involvement in political life.

We can now take the argument one step further, to explore the conditions under which institutions play this equalizing role. We have considered the institutional structures of the various nations to be the result of historical processes we do not analyze. The two characteristics of an institution that are relevant to our model – its population base and its "strength" vis-à-vis participation – have been taken as given. We can, however, look more closely at the question of why some institutions play an equalizing role whereas others do not. We seek to answer that question by considering the bases of political and social cleavage in each of these societies. The nature of cleavage in a society and the extent to which that cleavage is reflected in the institutional structures of the society affect the processes by which individuals and groups are mobilized to political activity. As we shall try to demonstrate, political conflict, particularly that structured by the party and organizational systems of a society, can result in increased participatory equality across social strata.

Our analysis of the participatory differences among social groups in the various nations has focused on groups defined by socioeconomic resource level. This simplification was useful in highlighting some similar processes across a heterogeneous set of nations. But differences based on income or educational level are by no means the only socially relevant differences among citizens, nor are they likely to be the most salient set of political differences. Race, religion, ethnic affiliation, and region are characteristics that are important bases of political disputation. The consequence of such divisions is not unrelated to socioeconomic differ-

157

ences. Conflict among groups based on characteristics such as race or religion is likely to be most severe when the groups also differ in socioeconomic terms.

Political sociology has often dealt with the way in which social differences are converted into political differences, usually through the party system, and the way in which these institutionalized differences affect the nature of political conflict in a society (Lipset and Rokkan, 1967; Rose and Urwin, 1969). Our analysis draws on this literature, but our problem is a slightly different one. We are concerned with the impact of cleavage patterns on the process by which individuals and groups become political participants and the resulting representativeness or lack of representativeness of the participant population.

The consideration of alternative patterns of social cleavage is relevant to our concern with the representativeness of the participant population in two ways. In the first place, it is related to the issue of the extent to which the participant population comes disproportionately from those high on the scale of socioeconomic resources. If social characteristics other than socioeconomic resources lead to political activity (by processes we shall shortly spell out), this can modify the participation disparity between the haves and the have-nots that would exist if the individual forces associated with SERL were the only ones at work. If the crucial cleavage in society is race, and this in turn leads particular racial groups to engage in high levels of political activity, the composition of the participant population in both racial terms and socioeconomic terms is likely to be affected. For example, as we have shown in earlier work, racial identification increases the political activity rate of black Americans above that which would be expected on the basis of their socioeconomic characteristics (Verba and Nie, 1972). Since blacks come on average from fairly low on the SERL scale, this tends to reduce somewhat the have/have-not participation disparity in the United States.

Secondly, a participation disparity on the basis of socioeconomic resources is only one of the ways in which the participant population may be unrepresentative of the population as a whole. The activists may be unrepresentative in terms of a variety of other social characteristics – race, religion, and so on. Insofar as such other characteristics are the basis of contention over government policy, such lack of representativeness is politically important.

We begin our analysis of the way in which alternative patterns of social cleavage affect the process of recruitment of the participant population with our pan-cultural generalization that, everything else being equal, individuals with higher incomes and/or higher education will be more politically active. This generalization allows us to locate the "baseline" from which to measure the effects of group-based forces on participation. Insofar as political contention in a society revolves around a particular social characteristic such as race or religion, identification with one or the other contending groups can lead citizens to be more active than they would otherwise be. In the United States, as we have pointed out, race is such a politically salient characteristic. Blacks who have a sense of group consciousness participate more than one would predict on the basis of their level of education or income (Verba and Nie, 1972).

Individual and group-based processes

We can look at this process more generally by comparing an individual-based process, that leads to participation, with a group-based process. By an individual-based process we refer to the fact that individuals are more likely to be politically active the more they possess socioeconomic resources such as education and income. These resources lead to political activity through the intervening effects of certain political motivations – interest and psychological involvement in politics, information about politics, political efficacy, and a sense of obligation to be politically active. These individual resources and motivations are "issue neutral." The resources do not imply any policy preferences; they are general-purpose resources that can be used to pursue any political goal. The motivations are similarly issue neutral; they imply no preferences for one type of political outcome or another. This does not mean that participation on the part of those with higher levels of socioeconomic resources is neutral in terms of the outcome of that participation. Quite the contrary. One of the main themes of this book is that the issue-neutral process by which individuals high on the SERL scale come to participate has nonneutral consequences in terms of whose preferences are represented. But the political outcome – that is, the more effective representation of the interests of the haves – is the indirect effect of the fact that certain individuals are both more capable and more motivated to be active. Their group interests are not the direct motivation of the activity.[1]

We contrast the individual-based process with a group-based process characterized by group-specific motivations and group-specific resources. Group-specific motivations to be politically active have more political content. A group may wish to improve (or prevent the deterioration of) its position. If its members believe that the government is capable of helping them in this, they may become politically active. Their

---

[1] As we shall soon see, socioeconomic characteristics such as education and income can also function as group-specific motivation by creating group interests.

policy preferences provide a specific motivation to political activity, a motivation that is independent of the neutral forces leading to participation on the part of those high on the SERL scale.

Our work on participation in the United States provides an example of such specific motivation in a group at the top of the SERL scale and in a group near the bottom of the scale. We found upper-status Republicans to be the most active group in the United States and traced their high activity rate to a combination of their high socioeconomic status and their commitment to a conservative economic ideology. Their high average level of socioeconomic resources makes them high participants, but their issue commitment leads to a rate of political activity well above the level that one would expect on the basis of their socioeconomic resources. The conservative economic attitudes play a similar role for this group to that played by "group consciousness" among American blacks – to take the group with specific political motivations we found at the lower end of the SERL scale. It represents an issue-specific set of preferences that leads the group to be more active than its SERL characteristics would predict. In the former case it leads an affluent group whose activity would ordinarily be high to be higher yet. In the latter case it leads a relatively disadvantaged group to be more active than it otherwise would be (Verba and Nie, 1972).

The resource that is relevant in the group-based process of political mobilization is organization. Group motivation and organization can vary independently of each other. The members of a group may have a high level of group-specific motivation but be unorganized. Or a well-organized group may have no strongly felt sense of political motivation. Where the two go together, however, one would expect the greatest amount of group-specific political mobilization. The well-organized group whose members are motivated to take part in political life because of interests they want to further is likely to be a group with a particularly high level of political activity. In some cases, group motivations may result in organizations that survive after the motivations have declined somewhat. Lipset and Rokkan (1967) suggest that this has been the case with many political parties. They reflect salient political cleavages at the time of their formation, but they may survive and "freeze" those cleavages even after they have become less salient. In such a case, the organization can still mobilize individuals to political activity even if the individuals no longer share the particular concerns that led to the formation of the group in the first place.

A group-based process of political mobilization is likely to be more potent – that is, to cause greater deviations from the individual SERL/participation relationship – where there is a fairly well structured pattern of cleavage in a society. By "well structured" we mean a pattern of cleavage where the main lines of cleavage are agreed upon by most citizens and where such cleavage is reflected in the institutional structure of the society: That is, parties and organizations have distinctive support bases with each (or most) of the cleavage groups having a party to represent it. Individuals who believe that their interests are in conflict with others in the society will be more likely to act to protect and further their interests when there are institutions that represent those interests. If there is a political party linked to their group (i.e., a party that receives the support of a high proportion of their group and/or depends on that group for a high proportion of its support), it is likely to provide a channel for political activity aimed at expressing the group interest. Where a party or organization has an agrarian base, members of the agrarian sector of society will "benefit" in terms of activity rate; where a party or organization has its base in a particular religious grouping, those who are affiliated with that religion are likely to be more active than others whose religious affiliation is not politically organized. If the cleavage group has no such institution connected to it, the sense of group membership is less likely to be converted into political activity. Furthermore, institutions that are tied to a particular cleavage group will not be mere channels of participation. These institutions will attempt to mobilize those members of their support base who come from that group.

The result of a well-structured cleavage system may be an increase in the equality in political activity across socioeconomic levels. We say that the result *may* be (rather than *will* be) an increase in the equality of participation. Group motivation and organization may appear among those fairly low on the socioeconomic scale. Workers or a disadvantaged ethnic group may develop the self-conscious sense of social conflict and the organizational resources that lead to an increase in their political activity. This in turn will lead to an equalization of political activity across socioeconomic levels. But such self-consciousness and organization may also be developed by businessmen or a relatively affluent ethnic group. Any additional political motivation of such a group will increase the participatory disparity between the haves and the have-nots.

Furthermore, the equality that may be achieved in socioeconomic terms if a have-not group is politically mobilized may lead to inequality in other terms. If a particular ethnic or religious group is politically motivated by a sense of grievance vis-à-vis other groups and has the institutional base to channel and reinforce that motivation, it may become much more active than its socioeconomic level would predict. If that group is on average low on the SERL scale, there will be greater political equality in socioeconomic terms. But this may also result in greater participatory inequality in religious and ethnic terms. In our detailed analyses of the cleavage patterns in each nation and their relationship to participation we shall provide examples of each outcome.

This suggests that position on a socioeconomic hierarchy can form the basis for group-specific political activity. Rather than such a position providing an individual with issue-neutral resources for political activity, it can be the basis of political cleavage between rich and poor or between educational groups. If there is political conflict among identifiable strata, socioeconomic position becomes a group-specific motivation for political activity. The haves and/or the have-nots are motivated to be active in order to further or protect their specific interests.

In our analysis of patterns of cleavage in the various nations, we shall in some cases distinguish groups on the basis of position on a stratification hierarchy – an occupational hierarchy or, in India, a caste hierarchy. We treat these positions somewhat differently than our treatment of the hierarchy measured by our SERL scale. When we use the SERL scale, we place individuals on a continuum of socioeconomic position. When we deal with social segments, we divide the population into discrete categories. There has long been a debate in the literature on stratification as to whether societies are divided into discrete hierarchical classes or whether stratification involves a more gradual hierarchy among individuals with no clear group boundaries. Our SERL measure implies the latter; our use of social cleavage groups implies the former. Each of the approaches to stratification makes sense. When one thinks of stratification in relation to competing groups within a society, the division into discrete groups is appropriate. When one thinks of individual motivation and resources, a less discrete set of categories is appropriate. In this sense, our analysis juxtaposes the two types of stratification in order to see how they jointly affect participation.

Socioeconomic position as the basis for group-specific motivation or organization differs from socioeconomic position as a source of resources for individual activity. As an issue-neutral force, the resources that derive from socioeconomic position boost the participation of the affluent and educated. As a group-specific characteristic, socioeconomic position may increase the activity of those low on the SERL scale or the activity of those high on the scale. As issue-neutral forces, socioeconomic inequalities lead to political inequality. As group-specific forces, they may lead to more or less political equality depending on which groups are mobilized.

Group-specific motivation and organization function very much like the institutional constraints we discussed in relation to political parties and organizations; they modify the effects of the individual forces associated with socioeconomic status. But they do not eliminate such forces. If our model is correct, we should find that social segments with group-specific motivation or organization have average participation rates above what one would predict on the basis of their socioeconomic resource level. Within the segments, however, the usual individual forces associated with SERL should be operative. Thus a party or an organization that has as its social base a segment of society fairly low on the SERL scale (blue-collar workers, blacks in the United States) will have contradictory effects on the SERL/participation relationship. The fact that it pulls into politics a social segment low on that scale will tend to reduce the have/have-not participation disparity. The fact that it particularly mobilizes those members of its social base highest on the SERL scale undercuts somewhat the equalizing effect. However, if a social segment is generally low on the SERL scale, even its most advantaged members may be lower than average in income and education. In this way there will be a "net" increase in participation by those low on the SERL scale even if the individual forces lead the more advantaged members of the segment to be more active.

Patterns of segmentation

To begin, we must locate the relevant cleavage groups in each society. The characteristics that form the basis of political contestation vary. In some nations, political conflict concerns race; in some, class; in some, language; in some, it is a combination of these or other factors. For our purposes we want to locate that division of the society that has the strongest potential impact on political activity. An individual's membership in some social category is likely to have a greater effect on his activity rate the more he self-consciously identifies with the category, the more the category is involved in political contestation, and the more organized is the category.

There are a variety of approaches to the analysis of social cleavage. One of the most promising is that of Lipset and Rokkan (1967), who trace the party systems in contemporary democracies to a series of cleavages that emerged during the national and industrial revolutions. They isolate four cleavage lines: between the central nation-building culture and the peripheral culture; between state and church; between the rural agrarian and urban commercial/industrial interests; and between workers and management within the urban sector. The sequence in which these cleavages become important, the ways in which one cleavage line relates to another, and the way in which political parties institutionalize these patterns of cleavage determine the contemporary cleavage pattern. The last point is important. They note that the current patterns of party support in most contemporary European democracies reflect patterns of cleavage established earlier. At some later time, the difference among groups that led to a cleavage pattern may no longer be as salient, but the fact that the split is institutionalized in political parties means that the cleavage remains significant even though the original reasons for it have faded. This is important to us in our search for the proper segmentation pattern in our societies.

The role of political cleavage is stressed in the recent literature on politically segmented societies, particularly the literature on "consociational" democracies (Lijphart, 1975; McRae, 1974). This literature focuses upon democracies with a high degree of subcultural pluralism based on language or religion or ethnicity or some combination of these attributes. In consociational democracies characterized by a high level of subcultural pluralism various aspects of social life are organized into separate blocs or segments or subcultures. Each of these parts of society has a distinctive set of values and orientations. In such societies, social relations tend to take place within, not between, the separate subcultures. Informal social relations as well as formal organizational life tend to be encapsulated within the subculture. Such subcultural segments of society have a high ratio of internal to external communications. Most important from our point of view, society is organized politically on a segmental basis. Political parties are attached to one or another of the segments. They gather their voting support from the members of the segment; they do not seek support from other parts of society.

Nations with such a pattern of segmentation are of particular interest to us. Two of the prime examples of such nations – Austria and the Netherlands – are in our set of nations. And the pattern of cleavage in such societies approximates what we have called a well-structured cleavage pattern, with, as we shall see, some important consequences for equality of political participation. We are interested in comparing less well structured cleavage with the cleavage found in more clearly segmented societies. As we shall see, it is easier to select the "proper" segmentation in the more clearly segmented than in the less clearly segmented societies.

There are a number of ways in which one might divide up the societies with which we are dealing in terms of social segments. One could use an empirical statistical approach to see what social characteristics best discriminate among citizens in terms of partisan support or, more relevant to our concerns, levels of political activity. Or, one can use as a guide the kinds of characteristics found in the general literature on political cleavages (such as the Lipset-Rokkan scheme) and divide the population into groups based on such characteristics. Or, lastly, one can consult the literature and the specialists on each of the nations in order to find the most useful set of population groups.

None of the techniques yields completely unambiguous results. But, fortunately, the several different techniques yield similar results. The cleavages that the specialists on one or the other nations told us were most relevant, were usually the kinds of cleavage that the general literature suggests are important in any society, and they tended to divide up the society into groups found by empirical analysis to be distinctive in their participation profiles.

We were constrained by another criterion in choosing our groups. We needed groups large enough so that we could carry on internal analysis of their members, and that means that some of the distinctions we make are cruder than might have been desirable.

In presenting the data on segmentation and its impact on participation, we shall change in two ways the approach used heretofore. For one thing, we do not use the same categories in each nation. The social segments used are specific to each nation. Secondly, we shall present country-by-country analyses rather than thematic analyses across all the nations. The reason for the second change is ease of presentation, since the configuration presented for each nation is complex. But the approach remains within the intellectual framework we have been using. The national analyses are parallel and try to deal with the same processes in each case.

The national party systems

We are fortunate that our set of nations includes some that have a segmented political structure and others that do not. Austria and the Netherlands are two of the clearest examples of segmented political systems. From the time of the earliest beginnings of parliamentary democracy in Austria in the 1890s, political life was structured into three major *Lagern* (literally "armed camps"). These groupings were: a Catholic clerical bloc composed of the peasantry and the urban petit bourgeoisie; a Socialist bloc based on the urban working class; and a Pan-German segment drawing strongest support from the commercial and industrial sectors and dedicated to unification with Germany. Engelmann describes these *Lagern* at the birth of the First Republic after World War I. "They were veritable subcultures with their own ideologies, interest groupings, and the manifold ancillary party organizations . . . which provided spiritual guidance, economic representation, and avocational direction" (Engelmann, 1966, p. 262; see also Wandruszka, 1954, and Stiefbold, 1972).

World War II changed the *Lager* system by discrediting the Pan-German segment; the other two camps – the Black and the Red – remained the dominant forces in Austrian society. The Catholic segment finds its party organization in the ÖVP and the Socialist segment in the SPÖ. In some ways the *Lagern* have changed: The ideological differences between them have been muted and they cooperate effectively. Under the system of *Proporz* they cooperated very effectively in dividing up the spoils of government office. Yet most observers agree that Austria remains divided institutionally into segments. Indeed, the *Proporz* system reinforced this division by making affiliation with one or the other of the *Lagern* a necessary condition for access to employment in the large public sector. And though the intensity of hostility between the segments has diminished, *Lagermentalität* (the habit of thinking as a member of one's own camp) remains (Steiner, 1972; Stiefbold, 1974; Engelmann, 1966; Powell, 1970, 1976).

Political and social life in the Netherlands has also been described as being organized subculturally, though the pattern is more complex than that in Austria. Cleavage in the Netherlands is, as in Austria, along religious and socioeconomic lines. But there are more lines. A religious cleavage separates the society into a Catholic, a Calvinist Protestant, and a secular segment. The latter in turn is divided into a liberal segment based on the middle and upper classes and a socialist segment based on the urban work force. As in Austria, social life tends to take place within segments, or *Zuilen* (pillars), and each segment has its own institutional infrastructure: a political party, a separate school system, separate newspapers, and a separate television network (Lijphart, 1975). The separation among the pillars has diminished in recent years with the development of more national institutions such as national media and parties that are outside of and often overtly hostile to "pillarization." Further economic and cultural changes have diminished the intensity of psychological commitment to the pillar system (Lijphart, 1975). Nevertheless, the pillars remain important in structuring Dutch social and political life.

The Austrian and Dutch parties represent their own segments of society; they draw their support from within their own group and do not seek votes across segmental lines. If Austria and the Netherlands are our clearest examples of societies in which social and political life is segmented, the United States is our best example of a society in which this is not the case. The United States is far from a homogeneous society. There are significant class, ethnic, religious, and regional differences. Race represents a sharp cleavage line. But the society is not divided into closed, politically organized subcultures. A separate working class, Socialist subculture, and party never emerged in America, nor have parties emerged to represent the interest of particular ethnic, religious, or racial groups. Black Americans are closely tied to the Democratic Party, but that party is not a party of blacks. Rather, like its Republican counterpart, it is a broad-based coalitional party representing numerous interests and groups. Furthermore, unlike Austria and the Netherlands, where a large part of the institutional structure of society – voluntary associations, the media of communications, and so on – is affiliated with the political parties, the American parties have little social infrastructure associated with them. Lastly, the American parties, unlike the Austrian and the

Dutch, do not limit their electoral activities to an attempt to mobilize those groups already committed to them. Rather, they hunt for voters wherever they can be found – among those with no partisan affiliation and among those identified with the opposition.

The other nations in our set fall less neatly into one or another category, but distinctions can be made as to the extent to which they have party systems that reflect the major cleavage lines within the society.

It is difficult to evaluate the extent to which Japanese parties are tied to particular cleavage groups in Japan because of the absence of clear lines of cleavage. There is no clear religious split in Japan nor any other primordial affiliation of a racial or an ethnic sort (Flanagan and Richardson, 1977, and Richardson, 1976). There is however some resemblance between Austria and Japan. In each nation, a large party with roots in the agrarian sector as well as in the business community stands for more conservative policies economically and for more traditional values socially. In Austria this is the ÖVP; in Japan it is the Liberal Democrats. And the conservative party is counterpoised against a Socialist opposition with support among urban workers (blue and white collar) as well as among intellectuals. Furthermore, the Japanese parties resemble those in Austria and the Netherlands in that they tend to gather in the votes of those already committed to them, rather than hunting broadly for votes by appealing to a wide public. And they do so through an associational infrastructure of candidate support groups. On the other hand, unlike Austria and the Netherlands, where political support is based on subcultural differences, the connection of the Japanese parties to their support groups tends to be based on personal association between candidates and their supporters. Political contests tend to be among groups identified with particular candidates rather than among groups that differ in religion or ideology (Richardson, 1975; Curtis, 1971; and Langdon, 1967).

Our attempt to delineate the social and organizational bases of support in Japan is consistent with the work of Flanagan and Richardson (1977), who urge us to pay particular attention to what they term the "social network bases" of mass politics in Japan:

> the cleavages of religion, region and ethnicity have largely been absent throughout Japan's modern period, or at least since the advent of mass politics. Thus, Japan's political parties have no division along these lines, nor has any Japanese party sought to champion the interest of any one social group defined by such cleavages . . . We have suggested a social network approach as a useful modification to the social cleavage model. Our social network model emphasizes the importance of both formal and organizational networks and informal small group networks in the transmission of voting cues and other influence communication.

The Indian party system – as it existed in 1966 during our field work
there – falls closer to the American party system than to the Austrian or
the Dutch in terms of the characteristics that are of most concern to us.
At the time of our study, the Congress Party was the dominant force.
It had received about 45 percent of the vote in the national elections
from 1952 to 1962. In 1967, shortly after our study, it received 41
percent. Its dominance is understated somewhat by those figures. The
opposition parties were fragmented and none approached the Congress
figures. More important from our perspective, the Congress Party was
broad-based, containing within it most of the social groupings and ideological positions to be found in India. Opposition parties tended to
speak for narrower constituencies – constituencies like the social segments we have discussed in other nations, or a particular state or region.
But the party system bore little resemblance to the party system in
Austria or the Netherlands because the dominant Congress Party usually
encompassed within itself most of the social groups represented by the
opposition parties. It was a system in which a single party of consensus
was surrounded by a series of narrow parties of pressure (Kothari,
1970).

From our perspective such a party system resembles the broad-based
coalitional system in the United States. The dominant tone was set by
the Congress, a party that sought votes from all social groups and
welcomed all groups and all viewpoints under its wing.

We shall not analyze the relation between social segmentation and
party in Nigeria because, as we have pointed out, we were unable to
obtain information on party affiliation at the time of our survey. It may
be worth noting in passing, however, that the Nigerian party system – a
system that came to its end on the eve of our study – resembled that of
the segmented societies, but is a tragic example of a segmented system
that failed. Political parties had been organized on a regional basis,
reflecting the major ethnic divisions of Nigerian society. As in the consociational democracies, accommodation among them was based on mu-
tual guarantees of autonomy to the several regions. The breakdown of
this segmental separation led to the collapse of the Nigerian party system
and, ultimately, to civil war.[2]

Some expectations

We can recapitulate the argument and introduce our data by
presenting some expectations as to the conditions under which the
cleavage pattern in a society will result in a decrease in the stratification

[2] The absence of partisan competition in Yugoslavia makes it impossible to
apply this analysis to that country. We shall treat political participating in
Yugoslavia separately in Chapter 11.

of political activity by socioeconomic level. The explication of the conditions under which political equality is increased represents a further attempt to solve our puzzle: How can we reconcile the cross-cultural generalization that SERL and participation are positively related with the fact of variation in that relationship? The solution to the puzzle, as we have presented it thus far, is that political institutions interfere with the SERL/participation relationship – and do so differentially from nation to nation. The consideration of social segments deals with the question of the conditions under which such institutional interference takes place.

Institutional interference will have a greater effect on the SERL/participation relationship where: (1) there are groups in society with clear cleavage positions, that is, groups that are unambiguously on one side or another of the political conflict lines in the society and that recognize this fact; (2) these groups have close institutional ties. Such ties can be manifested in two different ways: as a high degree of institutional affiliation on the part of the members of the group (a high proportion are affiliated with a party and/or a high proportion are organization members) or as an exclusivity of affiliation. The latter means that the group members have ties with a particular set of institutions. There is either a particular political party or organization to which a high proportion of the members of the group give their support (rather than spreading their support across a large number of institutions), or there is a party or organization that depends heavily on the support of the group (rather than receiving support from a wide range of social segments). The exclusivity of a segment's attachment to a party or to specific organizations is relevant to the segment's participation rate. A party or an organization that depends upon a particular segment for its support – either in the sense of getting a large proportion of its support from that segment or knowing that a large proportion of that group's support will come to it – is likely to direct its political mobilization efforts to such a group. The criterion of mobilization used by the institution will be segmental affiliation, rather than more general socioeconomic resources.

If particular social groups are in an unambiguous cleavage position and are well institutionalized, they ought to overparticipate – that is, participate more than one would predict on the basis of individual resources or motivation of their members. They will do so because of group-specific motivation and institutional mobilization. In such a circumstance, furthermore, those groups that are not unambiguously on one side or the other of the main cleavage lines or that are not well institutionalized are likely to underparticipate. In a society in which some groups have high levels of motivation and organization, those groups without such a group basis for activity may be inhibited from taking part in political life.

The impact of this over- and underparticipation on the equality of political participation across socioeconomic levels depends in turn on the socioeconomic characteristics of the social segments that over- or underparticipate. If the overparticipants come from segments high on the SERL scale, the SERL/participation relationship and the participation disparity will be increased. If the overparticipants come from segments that are on average low on the SERL scale, the SERL/participation relationship and the participation disparity across socioeconomic levels will be lowered. Similarly, the socioeconomic level of the groups that withdrew from politics will determine the effect on the equality of participation across socioeconomic levels. Where upper-status groups dominate politics, the less affluent may withdraw, thereby increasing political inequality. Or conversely those high on the SERL scale may withdraw, thereby increasing equality. The educated and the affluent may deliberately withdraw from political life if political activity is dominated by those lower on the socioeconomic scale. Where, for instance, working-class or lower-status farm groups dominate campaign activities (as is the case in many places with strong mobilizing parties), the middle classes may withdraw from such activity (or concentrate perhaps on forms of campaign activity less obtrusive but more effective).[3]

Participatory types

In the next chapter we shall consider a number of social segments in each of the nations. These segments are characterized by their average level of socioeconomic resources, by the strength of their institutional ties, and by the clarity of their position in the cleavage structure. The combination of characteristics for any segment leads us to expect that the segment will have a particular pattern of political participation. The pattern of political participation of a group will be defined in terms of its score on scales of political activity and on our scale of psychological involvement in politics. The measures of political activity and psychological involvement allow us to locate four types of participatory groups.

Level of political activity	Level of psychological involvement in politics *issue-neutral Motivation*	
	High	Low
High	1. Committed segments	2. Mobilized segments
Low	3. Inhibited segments	4. Apathetic segments

1. Some population segments will be high in issue-neutral motivation

[3] James Q. Wilson's work on political organization suggests one possible reason. One of the main incentives for party activity is the social prestige one can obtain from group affiliation. But where a group is a lower-status one, upper-status citizens can receive no such benefits from affiliation (Wilson, 1975).

as well as in political activity. We can call these *committed* segments. One would expect such segments to be made up of upper socioeconomic citizens. Furthermore, one would expect such segments to have clear positions in a nation's cleavage system and to have close institutional ties.

2. Some segments will have a high level of activity coupled with a low level of issue-neutral motivation. These segments are *mobilized* to political activity. One would expect to find such a combination in groups relatively low on the socioeconomic scale that have a clear cleavage position and strong institutional ties.[4]

3. *Inhibited* segments are the opposite of the mobilized ones. Members of such segments are concerned about political matters but inactive. We use the term "inhibited" to refer both to self-restraint and to externally applied restraint. Those who are interested and involved in political matters but take little active part may choose not to participate for any one of a number of reasons, one likely reason being that they find no party or organization expressing their own preferences. Or such a group may be more directly barred from participation, perhaps by being denied access to formal or informal political channels or to political organizations. For our purposes, what is important is that they care about political life but find that its institutional structure offers them no opportunity to take part. One would expect that inhibited segments would be made up of citizens from the upper reaches of the SERL scale who have an unclear cleavage position and relatively weak institutional ties.

4. Lastly, there are the *apathetic* segments. They are neither concerned nor active. Apathetic segments are likely to consist of citizens from the lower parts of the SERL scale who have neither a clear cleavage position nor strong institutional ties.

---

[4] We use the term "mobilized" in a specially delimited sense in this and Chapters 10 and 12 when we describe a particular segment or group as *mobilized*. In the general literature and elsewhere in the text, we use it in a broader sense; it refers to the general process by which individuals become involved and active in the larger society rather than in the narrow world of village or tribe.

10

Social segmentation and political equality: application

We can now consider the data on social segmentation. We first present the data for the three "weak SERL/participation" nations – Austria, Japan, and the Netherlands – to see whether there are similar patterns in relation to the social segments. For each nation we shall describe the social segments, indicate which ones have strong institutional ties, and compare their rates of political activity with their level of political involvement to see whether they fit into our typology of segments (committed, mobilized, inhibited, and apathetic). We begin with a somewhat more extended analysis of the Austrian data, to illustrate the way in which we treat social segments. We can then move more expeditiously through parallel analyses elsewhere.

Austria

The population segments

Any politically relevant population division in Austria must reflect the existence of the traditional *Lagern*, the "red" and the "black" that have been the basis of Austrian politics for many decades. The significance of this distinction is reflected in an AID "tree analysis" reported by Richard Rose of the social characteristics that best discriminate political party supporters in Austria. The most important characteristic is religiosity, followed by occupation. These are the main characteristics that define the two Austrian camps (Rose, 1974, p. 17; also, Liepelt, 1971). Following this lead, we created our segments on the basis of occupation and religiosity. The sample was first divided into four occupational categories: farmers, blue-collar workers, white-collar workers in the public sector, and "middle class" in the private sector (white-collar workers, business and professional occupations).[1] The distinction between white-collar occupations in the private and public sectors was included because of the quite large number working in the public sector

---

[1] Respondents were classified by their own occupation. Where the respondent was not employed – housewives largely – they were classified by the occupation of the head of household.

Table 10–1. *Population segments: Austria*

Segment	Percent of sample	Average score on SERL scale
Farmers	12	−77
Blue collar, observant Catholic	11	−53
Blue collar, nonreligious	30	−28
Public sector, nonreligious	12	33
Middle class, observant Catholic	9	46
Public sector, observant Catholic	5	48
Middle class, nonreligious	22	64
	101	

(17 percent of our sample fall in the public white-collar category) and because of some distinctive characteristics of their participation. We then divided these groups on the basis of a measure of religiosity. In one category we put those Catholics who report regular church attendance and who consider religion to be important in their lives. In the other category we place all others – Catholics who are low on the measure of religiosity, those who profess no religion, and Protestants. This division is applied to all the occupational segments except farmers, since almost all members of the farm segment were high on the religiosity measures.

The result is the seven population segments listed in Table 10–1. They are ranked by their average scores on the SERL scale. Table 10–1 gives the proportion of the population that falls into each of the groups,[2] and the average score of the group on the socioeconomic resource level scale.[3] The farm group has the lowest average score, with the rankings going up as one moves through the blue-collar to the public white-collar to the private middle-class segments.

The data on the socioeconomic resource level of the various segments suggest where we might find overparticipant citizens. The two groups most unambiguously identified with one of the sides of the traditional Austrian cleavage line are the Catholic farmers and the nonreligious blue-collar workers. Their position as clear political contestants should provide group-specific motivation for greater political activity. Each,

[2] In each country, some respondents were not classifiable, but they were relatively small in number.
[3] The SERL scale has a mean of 0 and a standard deviation of 100 in each nation. Thus a negative number indicates a group with a less than average SERL level, a positive number the opposite. (See Appendix B.)

furthermore, is a group with below-average SERL scores. If one or both groups were to be mobilized to activity levels above what one would predict on the basis of individual characteristics, the result would be greater political equality.

We can also consider the degree to which these various population segments have connections with institutions that might mobilize them. In Table 10–2 we present data on the extent to which members of the various segments are affiliated with politically relevant institutions. The observant Catholics employed in the public sector have the largest proportion of individuals with strong institutional affiliations. The two low-status groups most clearly identified with one or the other political camps – the farm group and the nonreligious blue-collar group – do not have as high levels of institutional affiliation. The farmers, however, are as likely to be affiliated strongly as are the members of several groups much higher on the SERL scale. And the nonreligious blue-collar workers are more likely to be affiliated strongly than the observant blue-collar workers who straddle the two political camps.

More important than the amount of affiliation of a particular segment may be what we have called the exclusivity of its institutional ties: whether a particular segment gives the bulk of its support to a particular set of political institutions or scatters its support.[4] In the former case, there should be a greater institutional impact on the participation of the segment. Where a segment has ties to a party, that party is likely to make a special effort to mobilize the segment's members.

As Table 10–3 indicates, the various Austrian social segments heavily cluster their support in one or the other of the major parties. The most distinctive group is the farm segment: Of those in this segment who support a party, more than nine out of ten identify with the ÖVP. In addition, over 80 percent of the observant Catholic middle class in the private sector are so identified, whereas a similar proportion of the nonreligious blue-collar workers identify with the Socialist Party. The data in Table 10–3 make clear how important is the religious dimension in distinguishing party support; in general, observant Catholics line up with the ÖVP, the nonreligious groups with the SPÖ. The two groups that are in a cross-pressured position between religion and social class are the only groups without a clear partisan bent. Consider the observant blue-collar workers: Their religion pushes them one way, their class identification the other. The result is that they divide their support fairly

---

[4] We shall concentrate on the extent to which segments give the bulk of their support to one party rather than the extent to which a party depends on a segment. The latter depends heavily on the fineness of our segmental division. If we place all Catholics together, we find that the Austrian ÖVP is heavily dependent on them. If we split the Catholics into several segments, we find that no one of them forms the bulk of ÖVP support.

Table 10–2. *Institutional affiliation of population segments: Austria*

Segment	Non-politicized (%)	Weak identifiers (%)	Moderately affiliated (%)	Strongly affiliated (%)	Total (%)
Farmers	10	26	20	45	101
Blue collar, observant Catholic	14	25	31	31	101
Blue collar, nonreligious	12	22	29	38	101
Public sector, nonreligious	14	13	26	48	101
Middle class, observant Catholic	11	22	23	44	100
Public sector, observant Catholic	10	18	15	57	100
Middle class, nonreligious	18	19	26	37	100

Table 10–3. *Party support by population segments (supporters only): Austria*

Segment	Percent of segment supporting each party (supporters only)			Index of partisan bent (%)[a]
	ÖVP	SPÖ	FPÖ	
Farmers	91	6	3	47 (ÖVP)
Blue collar, observant Catholic	47	53		1 (SPÖ)
Blue collar, nonreligious	11	84	4	32 (SPÖ)
Public sector, nonreligious	26	71	2	27 (SPÖ)
Middle class, observant Catholic	83	12	5	39 (ÖVP)
Public sector, observant Catholic	72	25	3	28 (ÖVP)
Middle class, nonreligious	47	44	8	3 (ÖVP)
Total	44	52	4	

[a] The party to which a segment gives its plurality of support is indicated in parentheses.

evenly between the two parties. In a similar manner, the nonreligious middle class in the private sector has a class affiliation that should push them away from the Socialists, but because they are nonreligious they should shy away from the ÖVP. They too divide their identification fairly evenly. (On this topic, see Powell, 1976.)

The extent to which a segment has a distinctive partisan profile is made clearer in the last column of Table 10–3, where we present an "index of partisan bent." This index reflects the extent to which a group deviates from the population as a whole in the support it gives the party to which it gives the plurality of its support. For instance, the farmers give their plurality support to the ÖVP. Ninety-one percent of that segment support the ÖVP compared with 44 percent of the population as a whole. The farmers are, then, 47 percent more supportive of the ÖVP than is the general population. The index is a useful measure, since it takes into account the relative size of the various parties.[5] As one can see, the farmers are most distinctive in their partisan bent, followed by the middle-class Catholics, who also lean to the ÖVP. Nonreligious blue-collar workers are quite distinctive in the opposite direction. The two public-sector groups line up as their religious convictions predict. And the figures for the two cross-pressured groups – the Catholic blue-collar workers and the non-Catholic middle class – show them to have no distinctive partisan bent.

Table 10–4 presents the proportions of the various segments who are actually members of one or the other of the main political parties. The data underline the extent of fragmentation along religious and occupational lines. Blue-collar nonreligious workers are almost never members of the ÖVP; farmers or those in the observant middle class do not

---

[5] The index is simply the difference between the percent of a segment supporting the party to which the segment gives its plurality of support and the percentage in the population as a whole supporting that party. For instance, the figure of 47 percent in the ÖVP direction reported for the farmers in Table 10–3 reflects the fact that 44 percent of Austrians support the ÖVP compared with 91 percent among farmers. If a segment were to give its plurality of support to a party that receives even more support from the population at large, the index would be negative. In such cases the segment will be giving its support *disproportionately* to some other party – even though that other party is not its favored party in the sense of receiving the plurality of the support of that segment. Despite the fact that the segment, in such a case, would be more *distinctive* in its support of the second party, we have decided to use the party to which the segment gives its plurality of support as the base for measuring its "partisan bent" rather than the party to which it gives its most disproportionate support. This eliminates the possibility that we shall find some segment with a high partisan bent score calculated on the basis of its support for one party, when in fact the segment gives more support to another party.

Table 10–4. *Party membership by population segments: Austria*

Segment	Percent of population segment member of party		
	ÖVP	SPÖ	Nonmember
Farmers	44	1	55
Blue collar, observant Catholic	5	7	88
Blue collar, nonreligious	2	24	73
Public sector, nonreligious	6	31	62
Middle class, observant Catholic	22	1	75
Public sector, observant Catholic	27	6	67
Middle class, nonreligious	7	12	80

belong to the SPÖ. The data also highlight the extent to which the agrarian segment of Austrian society is organized within the ÖVP. Similar data are found in Table 10–5, where we indicate the kinds of organizations to which individuals belong. We distinguish among those who belong only to organizations affiliated with the political camp to which their segment is most closely tied, those who belong to some organization tied to the opposite camp, and those who are affiliated with organizations that are tied to neither camp. Among the farmers, 78 percent of those who are organizational members belong to organizations tied to the Black camp and have no affiliation with organizations tied to the opposite camp. Fifteen percent belong to an organization with ties to the opposite camp (our categorization allows them at the same time to have Black affiliations), and 8 percent belong to independent organizations. As one can see, the farm segment and the nonreligious blue-collar segment have the most exclusive organizational ties; about four out of five of the organizational members within these segments belong only to organizations linked to their own political tendency. Other groups have less exclusive ties.

Political activity versus psychological involvement

The preceding data allow us to predict where the various segments will fall in our typology based on psychological involvement and political activity. The farm segment and the nonreligious blue-collar segment are likely candidates for the mobilized type. The two segments – especially the farm segment – are relatively low on the SERL scale. Furthermore, they have a clear cleavage position and strong institutional ties: the farmers with the ÖVP and its affiliated organizations, the nonreligious blue-collar workers with the SPÖ and its affiliated organi-

Table 10–5. *Proportion of population segments belonging to linked or unlinked organizations: Austria*

Segment	Percent of segment belonging to some organization	Type of membership among members		
		Linked memberships[a]	Cross-linked memberships[b]	Memberships in independent organizations[c]
Farmers	49%	78 ("black")	15	8
Blue collar, observant Catholic	41	57 ("red")	31	12
Blue collar, nonreligious	48	83 ("red")	11	7
Public sector, nonreligious	69	58 ("red")	19	23
Middle class, observant Catholic	51	52 ("black")	26	22
Public sector, observant Catholic	62	37 ("black")	35	29
Middle class, nonreligious	47	57 ("red")		16

[a] Belong to at least one organization with ties to the "camp" cited in parentheses, and to no organization linked to the opposite camp. Can also belong to an unlinked organization.
[b] Belong to at least one organization tied to the opposite camp. Can belong to other organizations–linked to own camp and/or unlinked–as well.
[c] Belong only to organizations with no link to either camp.

zations. If our argument is correct, the observant religious blue-collar workers ought to be an apathetic group. They are relatively low on the SERL scale and have weak and divided institutional ties. The two segments made up of workers in the public sector as well as the religious middle-class segment ought to be committed segments. They are high on the SERL scale and have strong institutional ties. Lastly, the nonreligious middle-class group is a prime candidate for an inhibited segment. Though they come from the upper parts of the SERL scale, they divide their institutional allegiance across the political camps.

The relevant data are in Table 10–6. For each of the segments, we present the average score on the campaign activity, the voting activity,

Table 10–6. *Participation and involvement scores by segments: Austria*

Segment	Campaign activity	Voting activity	Psychological involvement
Farmers	6	25	−39
Blue collar, observant Catholic	−27	−9	−40
Blue collar, nonreligious	−7	4	−10
Public sector, nonreligious	33	−1	41
Middle class, observant Catholic	7	−7	18
Public sector, observant Catholic	32	25	45
Middle class, nonreligious	−8	−17	29

and the political involvement scales. Most of the groups fall into the expected category of our typology. The farmers score quite low on the psychological involvement scale but are above the population mean on the scale of campaign activity and are tied for the highest score on the voting scale. They are clearly a mobilized segment. The observant blue-collar workers are an apathetic segment. They have the lowest score of any group on the psychological involvement and campaign activity scales and the second lowest score on the voting scale. The two public-sector segments fit the committed category fairly well; they have high activity and involvement scores (though the nonreligious public segment is only on the population mean on the voting scale). And the nonreligious middle-class group clearly fits our inhibited category; it scores high in psychological involvement but below the population mean on the campaign and voting activity scales.[6]

Two groups, on the other hand, do not fall neatly into the expected categories. We expected the nonreligious blue-collar workers, who form the core of the "red" camp, to be a mobilized group. Their pattern of activity and involvement faintly resembles such a group. They score below the mean in psychological involvement and above the mean in voting activity, and their campaign score is higher than their score on the psychological involvement scale. The differences, however, are not great. Furthermore, their campaign score remains below the population average. The segment is perhaps best characterized as moderately ap-

[6] The low rate of participation of the nonobservant middle class illustrates, we believe, the participatory consequences for a group that has no institutions to represent its views in a society with well-structured cleavage. If the third *Lager* of the Austrian system – the liberal, commercial, and industrial camp – had not been discredited by its Pan-Germanism (Engelmann, 1966), there might have been a party tied to that camp and a higher participation rate for the group.

athetic. It is worth noting, though, that the nonreligious blue-collar segment differs from the religious blue-collar group in the expected direction. The former is more active than its cross-pressured counterpart. Lastly, the religious middle-class group was expected to be a committed group, high both on psychological concern and activity. It scores somewhat above the mean on psychological involvement and campaign activity, but slightly below the mean on voting. It is perhaps best described as a moderately committed group.[7]

The data reveal an important characteristic of participation in Austria. In previous analysis we have focused on the relative equality of campaign participation in Austria. When we compared those high and low on the SERL scale, we found relatively little difference in activity rates. Only 32 points on the campaign activity scale differentiate those in the top third of the SERL scale from those in the bottom third. The differences between those high and low on the SERL scale were about three times as large in the United States and India. But if one looks at the variation in campaign activity rates across the social segments in Austria, one finds fairly wide differences. Sixty points on the campaign activity scale differentiate the most and the least active segments of the Austrian population. For voting, the contrast is more striking. Only 4 points on the voting scale separate the top and bottom thirds on the SERL scale, whereas 42 points separate the most and least active social segments. Though participation may be relatively equal across socioeconomic levels, it is not equal across other social categories.

The profiles of the various segments are summarized in Table 10–7. The table presents the scores of the social segments on the socioeconomic resource scale, their degree of institutional affiliation (the proportion in the strong-affiliator category and the index of partisan bent), as well as their scores on the activity and involvement scales. Several points become clear from the summary. The first is that the ranking of groups on the SERL scale is quite different from the ranking of groups on the political activity scales. The SERL ranking, as expected, is closer to the ranking on psychological involvement in politics. The farm segment is lowest on the SERL scale, but scores above the mean on campaign activity and well above the mean on voting. The highest segment on the SERL scale – the nonreligious middle class – is below the mean on campaign activity and scores the lowest on voting. The key to the reversal of positions of

---

[7] We have not included the data on communal activity, in order to shorten and simplify the presentation. Communal activity is less likely to be affected by the group-specific forces we are dealing with in this chapter. This is most apparent in the mobilized and the withdrawn segments (segments whose level of concern is inconsistent with the level of campaign or voting activity). The farm segment is not as mobilized to communal activity, scoring −3 on the communal scale; and the nonreligious middle-class segment is not as withdrawn, scoring 6 on the communal scale.

Table 10–7. *Summary chart: participant types by segment in Austria*

Segment	Socio-economic level: mean SERL score	Institutional involvement		Participation profile		
		Strong affiliators (%)	Index of partisan bent (%)	Campaign score	Voting score	Involvement score
Farmers	−77	45	47	6	25	−39
Blue collar, observant Catholic	−53	31	1	−27	−9	−40
Blue collar, nonreligious	−28	38	32	−7	4	−10
Public sector, nonreligious	33	48	27	33	−1	41
Middle class, observant Catholic	46	44	39	7	−7	18
Public sector, observant Catholic	48	57	28	32	25	45
Middle class, nonreligious	64	37	3	−8	−17	29

the farm segment and the nonreligious middle-class segment is found in the institutional involvement measures. The farmers, compared with the nonreligious middle class, are somewhat more likely to be in the strong-affiliator category and have a substantially stronger partisan bent. The differences in institutionalization, in turn, are probably the result of the fact that the farmers have a clearer position in the Austrian cleavage system than does the nonreligious middle class. The nonreligious middle-class segment is in a cross-pressured position as are the observant blue-collar workers. Its higher economic status ought to associate it with the black *Lager* and the ÖVP, but the absence of religious commitment most likely makes its attachment to that position less complete.[8]

[8] The nonreligious middle class has no natural political "home" among the Austrian parties. A middle-class liberal party might be such a home, but the Austrian Freedom Party (FPÖ) may have too much of a nationalistic Pan-German orientation (and some contamination in the minds of some from the Nazi era) to be an attractive alternative.

The high participation rate of the public-sector workers is not clearly predictable in terms of our model of social cleavage. We have hesitated to bring in ad hoc explanatory factors to explain perturbations in our data, but in this case it appears appropriate to suggest that such a high participation rate is to be expected in a society in which the allocation of government jobs has traditionally taken place through the political parties. A public-sector position is usually a party position, and that clearly implies a high level of campaign activity.

The data are fairly consistent with our model of the process by which attachment to one of the poles of political contestation reduces the SERL/participation relationship in Austria. Where a group is clearly identified with a particular political position (in the Austrian case, being unambiguously a member of one or the other *Lager*) and where a party exists to which that group is closely tied, that group is likely to participate more than one would expect on the basis of its issue-neutral motivation and socioeconomic resources. The motivation associated with defending its political position against the opposing one as well as the special pull from institutions will raise its activity rates. This is clearly the case with the farm segment. It is less the case with the nonreligious blue-collar workers, though they outparticipate their observant counterparts by a substantial amount. If a segment does not fall clearly in one or the other of the camps – as the observant blue-collar workers and the nonreligious middle class do not – its activity rates are depressed.

This has consequences for political equality. If a mobilized group comes from fairly low on the SERL scale (as do the Austrian farmers), or an inhibited group comes from high on the SERL scale (as does the nonreligious middle class), this reduces the extent to which the haves would outparticipate the have-nots if only the individual issue-neutral motivations and resources associated with socioeconomic level were operating.

The Netherlands

The population segments

If Austria is an example of a democratic society bifurcated into two contending political groupings, the Netherlands is a society divided into a multiplicity of separate pillars, or *Zuilen*. And the multiplicity of social pillars is matched by a multiplicity of parties, representing both the main social divisions as well as numerous variations on the main themes that divide Dutch society. Indeed, the parties are one of the mainstays of the social division in the Netherlands.

We have divided our social segments in the Netherlands along the major religious fault lines of Dutch society. This is consistent with the results of Rose's AID analysis, which finds religion to be the main distinguishing force in Dutch politics (Rose, 1974; Lijphart, 1975; Daalder and Rusk, 1972). To begin with, one can distinguish the three main spiritual families: the secular, the Catholic, and the Protestant. In addition we divide the Protestants into two groups: the Calvinist adherents of the strict Orthodox Reformed Church on the one hand and the adherents of the Dutch Reformed Church combined with other Protestants on the other hand. (In subsequent discussion we shall refer to the latter group as Dutch Reformed.) The secular segment is, in turn, divided on the basis of occupation into a high- and a low-status group – a distinction parallel to the division between the socialist and liberal groups.

As in the case of Austria, where we divided a population almost entirely Catholic in the nominal sense into those who were and those who were not observant, we have divided the religious segments of Dutch society on the basis of their degree of observance – based on a measure of frequency of church attendance and the importance of religion in their lives. Among the adherents of the Orthodox Calvinist Church we found almost none who could be characterized as nonobservant, and have not used that distinction for that group. But we do divide the other Protestants and the Catholics into observant and nonobservant groups.

The resulting seven groups include five that clearly fall into one or the other of the three large subcultures: (1) the observant Catholics represent the Catholic pillar; (2) the Orthodox Calvinists and observant Dutch Reform adherents form the Protestant pillar; and (3) the two secular groups form the secular or general pillar. Two segments are more ambiguously placed: the nonobservant Catholics and Protestants. Their religious identification ought to place them in their respective religious subcultures, but their lack of religious observance may indicate a weak commitment to subcultural divisions.

The resulting social segments are listed in Table 10-8, along with their size and average level on the SERL scale. One important point ought to be noted in relation to the SERL scale. The divisions in Dutch society are based more on "spiritual family" than on class or on the mixture of class and religion found in Austria. The result is that there is less variation across the segments in terms of socioeconomic level than in Austria (compare Tables 10-1 and 10-8). The exceptions are the two secular segments, which we deliberately divide on the basis of socioeconomic level, and the observant Protestants (non-Calvinists), who have a relatively low SERL score. But even in these cases, the variation is not as great as in Austria.

Table 10-9 indicates which of the segments have the strongest institutional ties. The Orthodox Calvinists stand out; fully half are in the strongly affiliated category and only 8 percent in the nonpoliticized

Table 10–8. *Population segments: Netherlands*

Segment	Percent of sample	Average score on SERL scale
Low-status secular	19	−32
Observant Dutch Reformed and other Protestants	8	−31
Nonobservant Dutch Reformed and other Protestants	12	−8
Orthodox Calvinists	11	−7
Nonobservant Catholic	19	−4
Observant Catholic	14	0
High-status secular	17	60
	100	

Table 10–9. *Institutional affiliation of population segments: Netherlands*

Segment	Non-politicized (%)	Weak identifiers (%)	Moderately affiliated (%)	Strongly affiliated (%)	Total (%)
Low-status secular	28	24	29	19	100
Observant Dutch Reformed and other Protestants	21	23	21	36	101
Nonobservant Dutch Reformed and other Protestants	17	18	34	31	100
Orthodox Calvinists	8	12	30	51	101
Nonobservant Catholics	32	17	28	23	100
Observant Catholics	20	23	32	25	100
High-status secular	20	26	28	26	100

category. For the other groups, the patterns are not as clear. The observant Protestants are, after the Orthodox Calvinists, the most likely to be in the strongly affiliated category. They are more likely to be in this category than are the nonobservant Protestants, but they are also more likely than their nonobservant counterparts to be in the category of the nonpoliticized. High-status seculars and observant Catholics have, on the average, stronger institutional ties than do low-status seculars and nonobservant Catholics.

The data on the amount of institutional affiliation may not be as useful as the data on the direction and exclusivity of that affiliation. Let us turn to that. Table 10–10 presents information on the direction of party support of the various population segments. The close connection of some of the segments with a certain party is quite clearly indicated. The two segments with the most exclusive party ties are the observant Catholics and the Orthodox Reformed adherents; 82 percent of the party supporters in the former group support the Catholic Party; 76 percent of the party supporters among the Orthodox Calvinists support the Calvinist Anti-Revolutionary Party. The nonobservant Catholics are more divided in their party support, many supporting the new parties or the Labor Party. But about half remain Catholic Party supporters. Among the respondents who adhere to the Dutch Reformed and other Protestant churches, those who are observant give support most frequently to the confessional party, the Christian-Historicals. The nonobservant Protestants are more committed to the Socialists. However, neither of the nonorthodox Protestant groups concentrates its support as much as do the Orthodox Calvinists. The secular groups spread their support across several parties. Low-status seculars are most committed to the Socialists (PVDA) and the newer parties. The upper-status seculars support the Liberals (VVD), the Socialists, as well as the new parties.

The data indicate a varying concentration of support among the population segments in the Netherlands. Some groups concentrate their support very heavily on one party; others spread their support somewhat more. But the best evidence for the existence of sharp social boundaries among party support groups may be the empty spaces in Table 10–10 – that is, the instances where a segment gives no support to a particular party or set of parties. The most obvious instance is the Protestant-Catholic boundary. No one in the three Protestant segments supports the Catholic Party; no Catholic (observant or not) supports any of the Protestant confessional parties. Lastly, the seculars give almost no support to the Protestant or Catholic confessional parties.

When one considers the allocation of party support to the party or set of parties representing the three broad cultures – Catholic, Protestant, and secular – the location of the various segments becomes clearer. The five segments that are clearly within one or another subculture overwhelmingly vote for parties within the subculture. The observant Catholics give almost all support to the Catholic Party, as we have noted. The observant Dutch Reformed adherents and especially the Orthodox Calvinists concentrate their support within the Protestant confessional parties (the former give 61 percent of their support to that those parties,

Table 10–10. Party support by population segments (supporters only): Netherlands

| Segment | Catholic | Secular | | Protestant | | | New | Other | Index of partisan bent |
	KVP (Catholic) (%)	PVDA (Labor) (%)	VVD (People's Party Liberals) (%)	CHU (Christian-Historicals) (%)	ARP (Anti-Revolutionary) (%)	SGP, GPV (Fundamentalist Calvinist) (%)	parties (D '66, DS '70, and others) (%)	(%)	(%)
Low-status secular	5	44	13	3	3		25	6	21 (PVDA)
Observant Dutch Reformed and other Protestants		15	11	44	11	6	8	5	36 (CHU)
Nonobservant Dutch Reformed and other Protestants	1	39	25	15	3		13	4	21 (PVDA)
Orthodox Calvinists				3	76	16	2	2	64 (ARP)
Nonobservant Catholics	46	17	6				27	5	26 (KVP)
Observant Catholics	82	3	3				10	3	62 (KVP)
High-status secular	2	27	34		2		29	5	22 (VVD)

the latter 95 percent). And the two secular segments concentrate their support in the nonconfessional parties, the Labor Party, the Liberals, and the new parties. The low-status seculars give 82 percent of their support to these parties; the upper-status seculars, 90 percent. On the other hand, the two more ambiguous segments – the nonobservant Catholics and the nonobservant Protestants – split their support across the confessional and nonconfessional parties.

The last column of Table 10–10 contains the index of partisan bent, which measures the extent to which a segment gives its "favored" party (i.e., the party to which it gives a plurality) a share of support greater than the share that party gets from the population-at-large. The data show that each segment has a distinctive partisan bent. The largest deviations from the population-at-large are found among the observant Catholics and Orthodox Calvinists, who give the Catholic Party and the Anti-Revolutionary Party 62 and 64 percent more support respectively than the population-at-large gives to these parties. The observant Dutch Reformed supporters also have a quite distinctive partisan bent, giving the Christian-Historical Party 36 percent more of their support than does the population at large. In contrast, the two nonobservant religious segments and the seculars divide their support more. The latter keep their support within the secular camp but split across parties.

The extent to which the Orthodox Calvinists stand out as a segment with strong and exclusive institutional ties is seen in the next two tables: Table 10–11 indicates the proportion of each segment that reports membership in a party; and Table 10–12 shows the proportions that are members of organizations linked to one or the other pillars. The Orthodox Calvinists have the highest proportion who are members of a party and the memberships are all in the ARP or the fundamentalist Calvinist parties. They also have the highest proportion who are members of some organization, and they concentrate that membership in organizations linked to the Protestant pillar. The observant Catholics and the observant Protestants differ from their nonobservant counterparts in their greater frequency of both party and organizational memberships as well as in the concentration of those memberships within their own religious camp. The seculars are less likely than the observant religious segments to be party members, but whatever memberships they have are with nonconfessional parties. The high-status seculars are more likely to be members of an organization than are the low-status seculars, though for each group the memberships cluster in organizations without confessional links.

Political activity versus psychological involvement
The data on the socioeconomic resource level and institutional connections of the various segments suggest where they should fall on

Table 10–11. *Party membership by population segment: Netherlands*

| | Percent of segment member of party | | | | | | | |
| | Catholic | Secular | | Protestant | | | New parties (D '66, DS '70, and others) | Non-member |
Segment	KVP (Catholic)	PVDA (Labor)	VVD (People's Party, Liberals)	CHU (Christian-Historicals)	ARP (Anti-Revolutionary)	SGP, GPV (Fundamentalist Calvinist)		
Low-status secular	[a]	4					1	93
Observant Dutch Reformed and other Protestant		2	1	9	1			84
Nonobservant Dutch Reformed and other Protestant		3						94
Orthodox Calvinists					29	8		63
Nonobservant Catholics	4						1	95
Observant Catholics	16							84
High-status secular		2	5				1	90

[a] Less than 1 percent in all empty spaces.

Table 10–12. *Proportion of population segments belonging to linked and unlinked organizations: Netherlands*

| | Percent of segment belonging to some organization | Of the members, percent with memberships | | |
| | | Linked to Catholic pillar | Linked to Protestant pillar | Mixed or not linked to religious group |
Segment				
Low-status secular	46	9	13	76
Observant Dutch Reformed and other Protestants	66		70	29
Nonobservant Dutch Reformed and other Protestants	63		29	70
Orthodox Calvinists	69		83	17
Nonobservant Catholics	50	64	4	32
Observant Catholics	58	79		21
High-status secular	60	5	10	86

our typology of participant groups. Two segments should fall in the mobilized category. The Calvinists and the observant Dutch Reformed adherents are both below the mean on socioeconomic level and have at the same time high levels of institutional affiliation. The Calvinists, in particular, stand out in terms of the amount of institutional affiliation and its degree of concentration. The observant Catholics might also be a mobilized segment. They are average in socioeconomic level and not particularly distinctive in the strength of their institutional affiliation, but they are similar to the Calvinists in the extent to which they concentrate their partisan support. In contrast, the nonobservant religious groups should fall into our apathetic category. They are a bit below the mean in socioeconomic level and have relatively low levels of institutional connectedness. Their most distinctive characteristic is the absence of a particular partisan bent. The low-status seculars are an even better candidate for the apathetic category; they are quite low on the SERL scale and are low on both measures of institutional connectedness. Lastly, we have the high-status seculars. They have social characteristics that lead us to expect them to be an inhibited segment. They have high socioeconomic status but relatively low institutional affiliation.

The data on the socioeconomic level and institutional affiliation of the segments are summarized in Table 10–13. The participation and psychological involvement scores of the various groups appear in the last data section of the table. They show a moderately good fit to our expectations. Consider the two groups we expected to have a mobilized participation profile. The Calvinists are by far the most active group in campaigning and voting, followed by the observant Dutch Reformed. In each case the activity scores are higher than the involvement scores, especially among the Calvinists. The two groups, however, do not fall as neatly into the mobilized category as do the Austrian farmers, since each group has an above-average psychological involvement score. Overall, these segments appear to fall between our committed and mobilized categories; but they display some characteristics of a mobilized group in that their activity outstrips their issue-neutral involvement, but their involvement scores are above average, placing them close to the committed category.[9]

The observant Catholics present a mixed picture. As voters, they resemble a mobilized group with an average voting score well above their score on the involvement scale. As campaign activists, they seem to be a moderately apathetic group, with activity and involvement scores slightly below average. This mixed pattern is in an interesting way consistent with their pattern of institutional affiliation. The observant Catholics do not have a particularly high amount of institutional affiliation; not many are strongly affiliated with political institutions. But they have a distinctive profile in terms of the direction of party support. This is consistent with an activity pattern that combines a high voting score with a lower campaign activity score. The existence of the clear partisan bent mobilizes them to vote while the relatively low level of more intense institutional involvement is reflected in a moderately low score in campaign activity (a much more difficult type of activity).

The three groups that were expected to be in the apathetic category all have participation and involvement profiles that approximate expectations. The nonobservant Catholics and the low-status seculars are below average on the psychological involvement scale and the two participation scales although the pattern differs somewhat for each. The former are particularly low in voting whereas the latter are low on involvement. The nonobservant Protestants are slightly below the mean in involvement and campaign activity and slightly above in voting. They are, if anything, marginally in the apathetic category.

Lastly, we have the upper-status seculars, a group high in socioeconomic resources and low in institutional connectedness. This is consistent with their activity and involvement profile. They have a political involve-

---

[9] Neither of the two Dutch groups has a SERL score as low as that of the Austrian farmers. They would not, therefore, be expected to have as low involvement scores.

Table 10–13. *A Summary of participant types by segment: Netherlands*

Segment	Socio-economic level: mean SERL score	Institutional involvement		Participation profile		
		Strong affiliators (%)	Index of partisan bent (%)	Campaign score	Voting score	Involvement score
Low-status secular	−32	19	21	−12	−21	−30
Observant Dutch Reformed and other Protestants	−31	36	36	21	23	15
Nonobservant Dutch Reformed and other Protestants	−8	31	21	−7	6	−4
Orthodox Calvinists	−7	51	64	41	38	16
Nonobservant Catholics	−4	23	26	−17	−35	−10
Observant Catholics	0	25	62	−7	23	−2
High-status secular	60	26	22	1	5	46

ment score well above their activity scores. Although the latter scores are at the population average, rather than below average, the contrast with the high scores on the involvement scale makes it appropriate to consider them an inhibited group.

The data for the Netherlands do not fit our expectations as clearly as do the Austrian data. But there are a number of similarities to the rather better fit found in Austria. There are two segments that form a clear pole in the cleavage system in the Netherlands. The Orthodox Calvinists and the observant Dutch Reformed represent the groups most concerned with protecting the integrity of their pillars from the encroachments of Dutch society at large. These two groups are somewhat low on the SERL scale but high in institutional connectedness. This is consistent with their pattern of high activity coupled with somewhat lower psychological involvement in politics. The two Dutch groups differ from the Austrian farmers, however, in that the latter group falls more clearly into the mobilized category, combining high activity with low psychological involvement. The Orthodox Calvinists and the observant Dutch Reformed resemble mobilized segments in that they participate more than one would expect given their low socioeconomic levels. Their participation scores, furthermore, are higher than their psychological involvement scores. But their involvement scores are high for a group relatively low on the SERL scale. It would appear that our fourfold typology of participant groups needs elaboration. Close institutional connection can increase both the political activity and the psychological involvement of a group. In Austria the farm segment appears to be brought into political activity in a passive and an uninvolved way; in the Netherlands the Protestant religious parties mobilize their adherents to levels of activity beyond what one would expect given their socioeconomic characteristics, but they also get them more psychologically involved in political life.

We see a further parallel to the Austrian pattern in the political inhibition of the middle-class secular group, which ranks high on the SERL scale. Here, also, the Austrian pattern is clearer. The Austrian high-status, nonreligious group scored below the population average in activity; the Dutch counterpart scores a bit above average. The difference may lie in the greater availability of parties in the Netherlands suited to the characteristics of this group – especially the liberal VVD and the new secular parties.

In sum, one finds in the Netherlands a situation similar to that in Austria whereby certain segments deviate in their activity rates from their level of issue-neutral concern. Since these deviations are toward more participation from some groups low on the SERL scale and less participation from at least one group high on that scale, the result is an equalizing of participation across socioeconomic levels.

Japan

The population segments

Japan is the third nation we shall consider in the analysis of the role of social segments. Like Austria and the Netherlands, it is a nation with a relatively weak relationship between socioeconomic level and political activity and one in which the impact of institutional constraint is quite strong.

The delineation of the Japanese social segments is not as clear-cut as in the other two nations. As we have indicated, there is no clear religious split in Japan nor any other primordial affiliation of a racial or ethnic kind that would provide an obvious clue as to the proper division of the nation into social segments.[10] The absence of clear subcultural cleavages suggests emphasis on occupational characteristics in Japan. The roots of the Liberal Democratic Party in the agrarian and business sectors of society suggest two population segments based on occupational sector: the farm sector and a segment of independent business, management, and professionals. The latter, of course, contains a wide range of occupations. Among workers in Japan, we wanted to capture a distinction often drawn between the more modern and more traditional sectors of the economy. The former are the larger businesses whose workers tend to be unionized; the latter are smaller family firms. Work relations in the latter are more paternalistic; wages tend to be lower, and the workers are less likely to be unionized (Vogel, 1963; Watanuki, 1967). To capture this distinction we divided workers into those who are unionized and those who are not. Since union affiliation is a major positive characteristic that, we believe, has an important effect on a variety of other characteristics, we have put all union members together – whether blue or white collar (Watanuki, 1967, pp. 454–55). Among the nonunionized workers, on the other hand, we distinguish between blue- and white-collar workers. Lastly, we have placed all those identifying with the religious sect, Soka Gakkai, into a separate segment. Though they are relatively few in number (5 percent of our sample), they represent a group with distinctive political characteristics, resembling to some extent a committed religious group like the Orthodox Calvinists in the Netherlands.

Table 10–14 presents the six population segments, their size, and their average score on the SERL scale, while Table 10–15 presents their institutional affiliation profiles. The various segments are quite distinctive. Three segments are well below the mean on the SERL scale – the farmers, the nonunionized blue-collar workers, and the Soka Gakkai. These three differ, however, in the strength of their institutional affiliation. The Soka Gakkai adherents outstrip all other groups in the proportion having strong institutional affiliation (Table 10–15), whereas the nonunionized blue-collar workers are the next to lowest group in this respect. The farmers are also relatively low in the proportion having strong institutional affiliation. Three groups score well above the mean on the SERL scale, but they also differ substantially in the degree of institutional affiliation. Union members have a relatively high socioeconomic level and are second highest on frequency of strong affiliation. The nonunion white-collar workers present a sharp contrast. They are

---

[10] A good discussion of the cleavages in Japanese society, comparing Japan to the European countries covered by Lipset and Rokkan, is found in Flanagan and Richardson (1977). See also Watanuki (1967).

Table 10–14. *Population segments: Japan*

Segment	Percent of sample	Average score on SERL scale
Farmers	24	−44
Soka Gakkai	5	−35
Nonunion blue collar	13	−30
Union members	18	30
Independent business, professional, managerial	31	35
Nonunion white collar	10	42
	100	

Table 10–15. *Institutional affiliation of population segments: Japan*

Segment	Non-politicized (%)	Weak identifiers (%)	Moderately affiliated (%)	Strongly affiliated (%)	Total (%)
Farmers	30	13	34	22	99
Soka Gakkai	9	4	20	67	100
Nonunion blue collar	28	24	34	14	100
Union members	14	0	48	38	100
Independent business, professional, managerial	25	15	42	19	101
Nonunion white collar	29	29	31	11	100

the highest group on the SERL scale and the lowest in institutional affiliation.[11] The business and professional group has a less clear pattern – high on the SERL scale and moderately low in frequency of strong affiliation.

The segments are also distinct in their degree of commitment to a particular political party. This is seen in Table 10–16. The farm segment

[11] The very low level of institutional affiliation among this upper-status group is striking. It is consistent with the absence of distinctly middle-class organizations in Japan (Flanagan and Richardson, 1977).

Table 10–16. *Party support by population segment (supporters only): Japan*

Segment	Liberal Democrats (%)	Socialists (%)	Democratic Socialists (%)	Communists (%)	Komei (%)	Index of partisan bent (%)
Farmers	72	24	3			19 (LDP)
Soka Gakkai	7	12	3		77	73 (Komei)
Nonunion blue collar	55	41	7			2 (LDP)
Union members	30	61	7	2		24 (Soc)
Independent business, professional, managerial	50	44	3	2		−3 (LDP)
Nonunion white collar	67	26	5	1		14 (LDP)

is quite unified in its commitment to the Liberal Democratic Party. Almost three out of four of the party supporters in that segment support the Liberal Democrats. They are joined in this high level of support by the nonunion white-collar group. Among the workers, we find that the union/nonunion distinction is important. Unionized workers are much more consistently found in the socialist camp. The nonunionized blue-collar workers are more split in their party affiliation, giving the edge to the Liberal Democrats. The Soka Gakkai is the most distinctive, giving the bulk of its support to the Komei (Clean Government) Party.

Table 10–16 also reports the index of partisan bent among the various segments. The Soka Gakkai has the most distinctive profile (as one would expect from a group closely tied to a small party). Farmers and the union members have distinctive partisan profiles – the former supporting the LDP, the latter the Socialist Party. In contrast, the nonunionized blue-collar workers and the independent business and professional groups have the least distinctive partisan bent.

The Japanese farm segment and the Japanese worker segment have an interesting resemblance to the parallel segments in Austria. The farmers in each case are low on the SERL scale and closely tied to the more conservative party. The workers in each case are divided into one group more closely tied to the Socialist Party and another group more ambivalent in its party support. The specific characteristics that distinguish the two parts of the working class differ; in Austria it is religiosity, whereas in Japan it is union membership. But in each case, the division distinguishes between workers who are more "traditional" and those who are less so. The traditional workers are in a more cross-pressured situation vis-á-vis the Socialist Party. In Austria the religious ties of the Catholic workers place them in that ambivalent position, and such workers are less committed in their Socialist support. In Japan, the nonunionized workers are likely to be found in more traditional and smaller firms where there may be patron pressure for support for the Liberal Democrats.

Participation versus psychological involvement

The socioeconomic and institutional profiles of the groups lead us to expect them to fall in one or another of the categories in our typology of participant segments. These profiles along with the activity and political involvement scores are in Table 10–17. Two groups are candidates for our mobilized type. The Soka Gakkai supporters and the farm segment are both low on the SERL scale but high on institutional connectedness, the Soka Gakkai being especially distinctive in this regard. The nonunion white-collar workers and the independent business, professional, and managerial segments are relatively high on the SERL scale and low in institutional connectedness. This leads us to expect

Table 10–17. *A summary of participant types by segment: Japan*

| Segment | Socio-economic level: mean SERL score | Institutional involvement | | Participation profile | | |
		Strong affiliators (%)	Index of partisan bent (%)	Campaign score	Voting score	Involve-ment score
Farmers	−44	22	19	14	10	−51
Soka Gakkai	−35	67	73	34	16	3
Nonunion blue collar	−30	14	2	−18	−11	−7
Union members	30	38	24	16	9	55
Independent business, professional, managerial	35	19	−3	−8	5	12
Nonunion white collar	42	11	14	−29	−21	44

them to fall into the inhibited category. The nonunion blue-collar workers are low on the SERL scale and have low institutional ties. We would
expect them to be apathetic. Lastly, we have the unionized workers who
are high both in socioeconomic level and in institutional connectedness.
They should fall in our committed category.

The groups fit our expectations fairly closely. The two groups we
expect to be mobilized – the farmers and the Soka Gakkai – have participation and involvement profiles consistent with that expectation. Each
group scores higher on the activity scales than on the psychological
involvement scale. The farmers have the lowest score in political involvement but are well above the mean in campaign and voting activity. The
Soka Gakkai adherents have involvement scores close to the mean of
the population but activity scores (especially for campaign activity) well
above the mean. The nonunion white-collar group offers a sharp contrast. It clearly fits into the category of an inhibited social segment, with
a high score on the involvement scale but scores well below the population mean on the activity scales. The other group that combines a high
SERL score with a low level of institutionalization – the independent
business and professional group – also can be categorized as an inhibited
segment, though only to a moderate degree. It scores somewhat above
the mean on the involvement scale and below the mean on campaign
activity. (It is, on the other hand, slightly above the mean on the voting

scale.) The group we expect to be apathetic – the nonunionized blue-collar group – has a moderately apathetic participation and involvement profile. And, lastly, the unionized workers fall, as we would expect them, into the committed category. They are high on the activity and psychological involvement scales. This group, however, does not fit the committed category completely. They score much higher on the psychological involvement scale than on the activity scales. From that perspective they resemble a withdrawn group.

Social segmentation and political activity: a recapitulation

We have considered a variety of social groups in the three nations where we have observed a relatively low SERL/participation relationship. In each nation we have been able to place most of the social segments into our categories of committed, mobilized, inhibited, and apathetic segments. Furthermore, the segments that fall in these categories on the basis of their scores on the participation and psychological involvement in politics scales have in almost all cases the social characteristics that would lead us to expect to find them there. The committed segments tend to be high in socioeconomic level and have close institutional ties; the mobilized segments are low in socioeconomic level and high in institutional connectedness; the inhibited segments are high on the SERL scale but have little institutionalization; and the apathetic segments are low on both socioeconomic resources and institutional ties.

Of particular interest to us is the fact that in each of the nations we find examples of two kinds of segments: (1) mobilized segments from fairly low on the socioeconomic resource scale who participate above the level one might predict given their scores on the political involvement scale, and (2) inhibited segments from the upper parts of the socioeconomic scale who participate below the level one might expect given their level of psychological involvement in politics. The mobilized segments tend to fall in one or another of the competing cleavage groups and to have close ties to the parties and organizations representing their cleavage group. The inhibited segments tend to have less clear ties to a cleavage group or the institutions associated with it. The data fit fairly well the model we have developed of the way in which the social basis of political conflict can affect who becomes a political activist and, in turn, the extent to which there is a wide have/have-not participation disparity. The data are consistent with our speculation about the relationship of equality to political competition. Explicit political conflict may be an important equalizing force. Where there are clearly defined competing groups and the groups are well organized, one is more likely to have political activists recruited on other bases than their socioeconomic resource level. Where such competition is blurred or absent, the individual forces associated with socioeconomic resource level take over, resulting in a greater participation disparity between the haves and the have-nots.

It is, furthermore, worth noting some of the more specific similarities among the three nations – similarities on a level of generality below the rather abstract level on which we have pitched our model. The largest deviation from the individual-level SERL/participation relationship derives from the mobilization of the farm segment by a large, relatively conservative and traditional party as in Austria and Japan or from the mobilization of adherents of a fundamentalist religion as found among the Orthodox Calvinists in the Netherlands and the Soka Gakkai in Japan. The participation and psychological involvement profiles of the farmers in Austria and Japan are quite similar; they score well below the population mean on psychological involvement and somewhat above the mean on activity. The Orthodox Calvinists and Soka Gakkai are similar to each other in having involvement scores near the population mean coupled with substantially higher activity scores. Some weaker evidence of religion-based mobilization is found among the observant Dutch Reformed and the observant Catholics in the Netherlands. The difference between the pattern of mobilization for the farm segments in Austria and Japan on the one hand, and the mobilization pattern for the fundamentalist religious segments in Japan and the Netherlands on the other is intriguing. The activity of the farm groups is accompanied by a very low level of psychological involvement in politics.[12] They appear to be brought to the polls or into campaign activity. The activity of the religious groups is accompanied by greater psychological involvement than is the case among the farmers. The segmental affiliation of the adherents of the fundamentalist religions appears to arouse their political interest and concern as well as making them politically active.

The data on the mobilization of workers is less clear. The worker segments we expect to be mobilized – the nonreligious blue-collar workers in Austria and the unionized workers in Japan – do not fall neatly into a mobilized category. The former group is moderately apathetic, with low involvement and activity scores; the latter is a cross between a committed and an inhibited group, with a high involvement score and an activity score above the mean but below the level of political involvement. However, in each case the distinction between the more and less traditional of the blue-collar workers is in the expected direction. The

[12] This is consistent with the descriptions of campaign organization in Japan (Curtis, 1971).

nonobservant workers in Austria are more active than the observant ones, and the unionized workers in Japan are more active than the nonunion workers.

There is also a parallel among the three nations in the nature of certain middle-class segments. In each case we found a group of relatively high-status citizens with weak institutional ties – the nonreligious middle class in Austria, the high-status seculars in the Netherlands, and the nonunion white-collar and the independent business and professional segments in Japan. In each case the segment is inhibited; it has a relatively low score on the activity scale coupled with a high score on psychological involvement.

The United States

We can apply our analysis of social segmentation to the United States. If our contrast of the United States with the three nations just considered is correct, we should find that membership in some social segment and the accompanying institutional ties make less difference in participation rates than does the possession of socioeconomic resources. In Austria, Japan, and the Netherlands we found social segments whose political activity rate differed from what one would have predicted on the basis of socioeconomic resource level or issue-neutral motivation. If, despite the existence of social cleavage in the United States, the political institutions do not perform a mobilizing function for particular social segments, we should be less able to find mobilized or inhibited segments.

It is somewhat harder to apply an analysis of social segments to a nation in which we believe such segmentation plays little or no role in relation to participation. It is easier to demonstrate that segmentation is important, as we have done in Austria, Japan, and the Netherlands, rather than to demonstrate that it is unimportant. Where social segments are less clearly tied to institutions, one cannot be confident that one has selected the proper set of segments for analysis. The patterns of party affiliation offer less clear cues. Rose's AID analysis, for instance, shows that partisanship in the United States is not as predictable on the basis of social characteristics as it is in most other countries (Rose, 1974, p. 17). If we demonstrate that the process located in Austria, Japan, and the Netherlands does not take place in relation to the social segments we consider in the United States, the possibility remains that we would have found a pattern in the United States similar to that in those three nations had we selected some other set of social segments. In other words, we can demonstrate that social segments play a role in relation to participation rates in weak SERL/participation nations merely by locating a set of population segments for which our model works. We cannot demonstrate that they *do not work* elsewhere by showing that the model does not work for a particular set of segments. Despite the ambiguity this lends to our analysis, we shall look at the United States from the same perspective used in the three nations studied thus far.

The population segments

Any consideration of the salient sociopolitical divisions in the United States must begin at the major faultline that separates black from white. In terms of clear involvement on one side of a political conflict line, of self-consciousness of group membership, of a distinctive pattern of party support, and of activity rates, black Americans represent a most distinctive segment of society. But once one has separated blacks from whites, the issue remains whether one can meaningfully substructure the white population. (The black population is, of course, heterogeneous as well. But considerations of sample size as well as the fairly great political homogeneity of blacks leads us to leave the black segment intact.) There are a number of ways one could divide the white population. Divisions are possible on the basis of social status, occupation, region, religion, ethnicity or place of residence. Some experimentation as to what division makes the most difference in terms of partisan direction and political attitudes led us to divide the white population on the basis of region, religion, and occupation.[13] (These three characteristics are about equally potent in predicting partisanship in the Rose AID analysis.)

Table 10–18 lists these social segments, gives their size, and their average score on the SERL scale. The black social segment scores on the average about one-half of a standard deviation below the population as a whole on the SERL scale, whereas the white groups are quite varied in their scores. Table 10–19 presents the strength of institutional affiliation of the various population segments. The most distinctive groups are the northern white Protestants with white-collar employment, the border South group, and the southern blue-collar workers. The former has the highest frequency of strong affiliators, and the latter two groups have a lower frequency than other groups. Of the four groups that score well below the mean on the SERL scale, three are low on institutionalization. Only one group – the blacks – appears to be a possible mobilized segment on the basis of the data on institutional affiliation. Though they are about average in terms of the proportion showing strong institutional affiliation, they have relatively few members having no politicized affiliation whatsoever. However, their pattern is not very distinctive.

Table 10–20 contains the information on the party attachments of the

---

[13] For a fuller discussion of the choice of groups in the United States, see Petrocik (1976) and Nie, Verba, and Petrocik (1976).

Table 10–18. *Population segments: United States*

Segment	Percent of sample	Average score on SERL scale
Blacks	14	−52
South, blue collar	7	−29
Border South	6	−29
Northern Protestant, blue collar	19	−21
South, white collar	8	6
Catholics	23	7
Northern Protestant, white collar	21	60
Jews	2	86
	100	

Table 10–19. *Institutional affiliation of population segments: United States*

Segment	Non-politicized (%)	Weak identifiers (%)	Moderately affiliated (%)	Strongly affiliated (%)	Total (%)
Blacks	11	19	37	33	100
South, blue collar	17	25	34	25	101
Border South	7	30	38	25	100
Northern Protestant, blue collar	19	17	30	34	100
South, white collar	13	18	35	34	100
Catholics	15	14	36	35	100
Northern Protestant, white collar	14	12	33	41	100
Jews	17	13	37	34	101

various segments. The most distinctive group in terms of party affiliation is the black segment. Ninety-three percent of black partisans are affiliated with the Democratic Party, with only 7 percent identifying with the Republicans. The blue-collar southern whites, the Catholics, and the Jews also tend toward the Democratic Party, the former two groups by over three to one and the Jews by over two to one. The northern white-collar

Table 10–20. *Party support by population segment (supporters only): United States*

Segment	Democrats	Republicans	Index of partisan bent (%)
Blacks	93	7	28 (Dem)
South, blue collar	83	17	18 (Dem)
Border South	49	51	16 (Rep)
Northern Protestant, blue collar	57	43	−8 (Dem) ?
South, white collar	71	29	6 (Dem)
Catholics	77	23	12 (Dem)
Northern Protestant, white collar	39	61	26 (Rep)
Jews	69	31	4 (Dem)

Protestants are heavily Republican, while the blue-collar Protestants and the border South residents are quite divided.

The party support proportions in Table 10–20 do not take into account the tendency of the population as a whole in the Democratic direction. At the time of our survey, sixty-five percent of our party identifiers were Democratic compared with the 35 percent who reported Republican identification. The index of partisan bent takes this into account. In terms of deviation from the population as a whole, the two most distinctive groups are the blacks, who are 28 percent more Democratic than the population norm, and the northern Protestant white-collar workers, who are 26 percent more Republican. Southern blue-collar workers and Catholics also show a decidedly Democratic bent, whereas the border South has a Republican one. The "partisan bent" figures are quite modest in comparison with Austria and the Netherlands, though comparable to those found in Japan. Clearly, the segmentation we have chosen for the United States reflects a less sharp partisan division than does the segmentation in Austria and the Netherlands.

Participation versus psychological involvement

The patterns of socioeconomic resources and institutional ties are summarized in Table 10–21, along with participation and psychological involvement scores for social groups. The participation and psychological involvement patterns for several of the segments are fairly consistent with what one would have predicted on the basis of their

Table 10–21. *A summary of participant types by segments: United States*

Segment	Socio-economic level: mean SERL score	Institutional involvement		Participation profile		
		Strong affiliators (%)	Index of partisan bent (%)	Campaign score	Voting score	Involvement score
Blacks	−52	33	28	−8	−24	−39
South, blue collar	−29	25	18	−19	−41	−7
Border South	−29	25	16	−12	−4	−11
Northern Protestant, blue collar	−21	34	−8	−10	3	−10
South, white collar	6	34	6	2	−7	26
Catholics	7	35	12	1	12	−1
Northern Protestant, white collar	60	41	25	23	25	33
Jews	86	34	4	13	19	42

socioeconomic and institutional characteristics. The northern white-collar Protestants are high on the socioeconomic scale and high in their institutional ties. They are, as we would have predicted, a committed segment, with high political involvement and activity scores. The Jews are similar, but their socioeconomic level (which is the highest of any group) exceeds the level of their institutional ties. Their participation and involvement pattern, which combines high involvement and a somewhat lower activity level, is what one would expect in that situation. Most of the other groups have socioeconomic levels and levels of institutional connectedness that lead us to expect them to be apathetic. The northern white Protestant blue-collar workers and the border South groups have moderately apathetic participation and involvement profiles, whereas the two southern groups can better be characterized as inhibited. The Catholics are close to the population mean in socioeconomic level and have an average level of institutional affiliation. The participation and involvement scores are also average.

Only one group, the blacks, combines low socioeconomic level with a relatively high level of institutional connectedness – the latter manifested as a particularly distinctive partisan direction. This makes them a likely mobilized group. Their participation and involvement profile makes them a cross between an apathetic and a mobilized group. Their campaign activity score is below the mean, and their voting score even more so. But their score on the political involvement scale is even lower.

The data in the United States present a fairly clear contrast with those in the other three nations. In the other nations we found examples of mobilized groups from the bottom of the SERL scale and inhibited groups from the top of the scale. The "over-" and "under-" participation of these groups ("over" and "under" compared with their issue-neutral motivation) tended to reduce the SERL/participation relationship for the population as a whole. In the United States we find that most of the groups with low scores on the SERL scale are apathetic or inhibited. The one exception is the black segment. It comes from the lower reaches of the SERL scale and has strong institutional ties (particularly a high index of partisan bent). Its activity scores are higher than its involvement scores. But it does not overparticipate much. Indeed, unlike groups such as the Austrian farmers, who have activity scores above the population average, the American blacks have below-average campaign and voting activity rates. In short, the group is only moderately mobilized, and, being in any case a small group, the mobilization has little impact on the overall SERL/participation relationship.

We can also note the absence of any upper-status inhibited segments. The group nearest in social characteristics to the middle-class inhibited groups in the other nations is the white-collar northern white Protestant group. But they have a high level of institutionalization, and, as one would predict from a group high on SERL and institutional connectedness, they are a highly participant committed group. The Jews do have a participation and involvement pattern that is a cross between a committed and an inhibited group, though they are, in any case, a very small segment and have little effect on the overall SERL/activity relationship.

In sum, one finds less deviation in the United States from the pattern of participation one would expect on the basis of socioeconomic level. The inhibited groups come from the lower level of the SERL scale. The largest upper-status group is not inhibited. It has close institutional ties and is highly active. The contrast between the United States on the one hand and the other three nations is fairly clear. The strong SERL/activity relationship that appears to characterize participation in the United States results from the absence of other social forces to disrupt that relationship. In other societies the existence of close ties between particular segments and institutions creates alternative motivation and institutional forces that modify the individual-level relationship between socioeconomic resource level and political activity.

Political mobilization and the generality of the SERL/ participation relationship

In each of the four nations whose social segments we have analyzed we located low-status mobilized segments, groups low on the SERL scale that participated at a level above that which their socioeconomic resources or their issue-neutral motivation would predict. In each of the nations these mobilized groups participated at a higher level than other groups farther up on the SERL scale. How does this fact fit with our pan-cultural generalization that, all else being equal, the haves will be more active than the have-nots? According to our model, group-based forces cause deviation from the expected activity rate for particular segments. However, if our argument is correct, within each segment one ought still to find differentiation based on income and education. Figure 10–1 indicates that this is in fact the case. On that figure we plot the relationship between position on the SERL scale and score on the campaign activity scale for the members of the various mobilized segments that we found in each of the nations. The mobilized segments are, in general, more active than one would expect given their socioeconomic characteristics: At each level of the SERL scale members of the mobilized segment are more active than is the average for that SERL level. (The only exception is found among the Austrian farmers from the lower third of the SERL scale, who participate at the level one finds for all Austrians from that third of the scale.) In each of the cases, however, there is a fairly sharp difference in activity scores between those segment members from the lower third of the SERL scale and those from the upper third. The one exception is the Soka Gakkai in Japan. In that instance, supporters from each of the socioeconomic levels are as likely to be active.

The data on the relationship between socioeconomic resource level and campaign activity *within* mobilized segments make clear how institutional systems can affect participation inequality between socioeconomic levels. The institutions mobilize their particular support groups to higher levels of political activity than they would ordinarily reach on the basis of their individual resources and motivation. When the mobilized groups comes on the average from the lower reaches of the SERL scale, this mobilization tends to reverse the usual relationship between socioeconomic level and activity. On the other hand, within the mobilized segment, the individual socioeconomic forces operate. In Austria or Japan, for instance, farmers who are more affluent and more educated are the more active. A parallel situation exists among mobilized religious groups in the Netherlands and among blacks in the United States. Only the Soka Gakkai – probably the most militant and well-organized as well as the newest of the segments we study – mobilizes activists from all

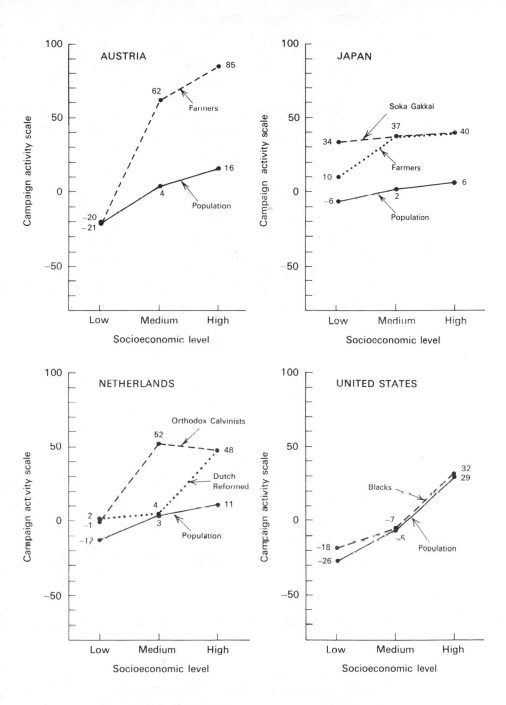

Figure 10-1. The relationship between SERL and campaign activity for mobilized segments.

social levels equally. In short, equality in participation among socioeconomic levels is achieved by the way activists are mobilized *across* social segments. *Within* the segments, the mobilization reflects individual socioeconomic forces.

The data on within-segment variations help round out our picture of the way in which group-specific forces interact with individual forces to modify the extent of the have/have-not participation disparity. The data on institutions in Austria, Japan, and the Netherlands make clear that one of the reasons why we find a relatively weak SERL/participation relationship is that institutional affiliation is a necessary condition for political activity; those with no such affiliation are essentially locked out of campaign activity no matter what their socioeconomic resource level. The data on social segments in these nations add to that picture by telling us something about the particular social groups that find access to political activity via institutions. Certain social segments are closely identified with one or the other of the cleavage groups in each society and, in turn, with institutions that represent that cleavage position. Members of such segments generally receive a boost in political activity through this association. Other groups have less clear ties to one or the other of the cleavage groups, and their activity rate is thereby depressed. The segments that are mobilized to a higher activity rate are relatively low on the SERL scale, whereas those segments whose activity rate is depressed by their lack of clear institutional attachment are at the top of the SERL scale. The relationship between SERL and participation for the population as a whole is thus reduced by deviation of groups from their expected activity levels.

However, the mobilizing institutions work in the opposite direction as well. They also increase the participation disparity between the haves and the have-nots. They do this by drawing into political life those members of "their" social segments who come from the upper reaches of the SERL scale. Mobilizing political institutions thus play a dual role in relation to the have/have-not participation disparity. Their overall effect appears to be to reduce the relationship from what it would be if individual forces were left to act untrammeled. In this sense they play an equalizing role vis-á-vis participation. But they do this by their differential attachment with and recruitment from the various social segments. Within the mobilized social segments the activists tend to come from the haves.

In conclusion, it might be well to refer back to an earlier interpretation of the role of group-based forces. Drawing on analogies from the small-group experimental literature, we suggested that affiliation with one or another of the political conflict groups in a society represents an "issue-specific" motivation to political activity that counteracts effects of the "issue-neutral" motivations and resources with which upper SERL citizens are more generously endowed. This interpretation is consistent with the data on mobilized segments. Those most closely connected with one or the other of the political contention groups are the most active– no matter what their level of SERL. But *within* the various social segments, the more issue-neutral forces associated with SERL reemerge. To be a Catholic farmer when faced with the rest of Austrian society, or a Calvinist faced with Dutch society is to have an identification that can mobilize one's political activity to defend one's interests. But *among* farmers or Calvinists, the group affiliation offers no specific cue, since all segment members share those traits. Under such circumstances, the forces associated with SERL reemerge, and the more affluent and better educated within the segment become more active. Structured political conflict, this suggests, equalizes activity among conflicting groups. It does not necessarily diminish inequalities within the groups.

A note on social segmentation in India

Our model of the role of social segmentation does not easily fit our Indian data. The analysis depends on the relationship between social segments and political institutions in competition with each other. When we conducted our study, the Congress Party was dominant in the states surveyed, and we have too few cases of opposition party supporters to link them to particular social segments. We shall, however, present some data on social segments in India to round out our presentation. The data do touch on our model at various places and where they do, we can test for their conformity to that model. In addition, the data illustrate some interesting political patterns in India.[14]

The social segments

One shudders at the thought of selecting a pattern of social segmentation for a nation as diverse as India. India is certainly not characterized by the clear patterns of segmented pluralism of the European consociational societies. It bears no resemblance to the basic social homogeneity in Japan, and it is many times more heterogeneous than American society. The subcontinent is a myriad of distinctive social groupings and cleavages covering almost every conceivable social dimension. Linguistic distinctions are numerous and important and they often parallel but are not coterminous with ethnic groupings – there are ethnic divisions within linguistic groupings and vice versa. There is a major religious cleavage between Hindu and Moslem, but there are numerous

---

[14] As noted earlier, in Nigeria we have neither measures of partisanship nor of campaign activity. This makes an analysis of "segments" in Nigeria impossible. Yugoslavia will be discussed in the next chapter.

subdivisions, particularly within the former religious group. Region adds to and often reinforces many of these cleavages. Class differences are important and are interwoven in complex ways with the hierarchy of caste. Finally, there is the cleavage between the agrarian and urban sectors. All these social cleavages are potentially important for political attitudes and activities, and we cannot begin to capture them all in our analysis.

We have chosen to rest our segment distinctions on three bases: religion (dividing the population into a Hindu and Muslim grouping), sector of the economy (dividing the population into farm and nonfarm families), and caste (dividing the Hindu portion of the sample into Harijans, low, middle, and high castes).[15] The result is the eight population segments listed in Table 10–22. In that table we also present the other characteristics of the various social segments: their socioeconomic level, their degree of institutional involvement, as well as their participation and psychological involvement profiles.

As one can see, the groups differ widely in their scores on the socioeconomic resources scale. The Harijans fall well below the population average as do the low-caste respondents in the farm sector. Middle-caste farmers as well as the farm and nonfarm Muslim groups also have relatively low scores on the SERL scale. Among the Harijans and the Muslims there is little difference in socioeconomic level between those in the farm sector and those in nonfarm occupations. Among the three levels of caste Hindus, on the other hand, there is a substantial difference between those in the farm sector and those in the nonfarm sector, with the latter having substantially higher socioeconomic levels.

The combination of the SERL scores for each of the segments and the degree of their institutional involvement provides some predictions as to the participant types we are likely to find. Several groups have low scores on the SERL scale and relatively low proportions with strong institutional involvement. This would lead us to expect them to be apathetic, scoring low on both political involvement and political activity. The groups whose socioeconomic and institutional profiles have this characteristic are the two Harijan groups, particularly those in the farm sector, and the nonfarm Muslims. Their participation profiles are fairly consistent with these predictions. All three groups score well below the mean on psychological involvement and have below-average scores on campaign activity. The nonfarm Muslims also have a low score on the voting scale. The nonfarm Harijans score slightly below the mean on voting whereas the farm sector Harijans score somewhat above the

---

[15] For details on this classification, see Bhatt (1975), and Appendix B. Bhatt's book, based on the same data as the present work, deals more fully with the role of caste in relation to participation in India.

Table 10–22. *Summary of participant types by segment: India*

Segment	Percent of sample	Socio-economic level: mean SERL score	Institu-tional involvement Strong affiliators (%)	Participation profile Campaign score	Voting score	Involve-ment score
Harijans, Farm	9	−54	7	−8	13	−35
Harijans, nonfarm	6	−52	10	−11	−5	−30
Low caste, farm	8	−36	13	3	14	−13
Muslim, farm	7	−20	12	0	−19	4
Middle caste, farm	10	−19	12	−13	19	−17
Muslim, nonfarm	9	−15	6	−5	−25	−20
Low caste, nonfarm	10	0	12	−9	16	7
High caste, farm	22	5	16	16	−6	6
Middle caste, nonfarm	5	21	8	−25	23	12
High caste, nonfarm	14	98	13	19	−10	48
	100					

mean. The data suggest that Harijans, particularly in the farm sector, are mobilized to vote though not to engage in more difficult campaign activity.

Three groups score above the mean on the SERL scale: The high-caste respondents in nonfarm occupations score about a full standard deviation above the mean, whereas the middle-caste nonfarm respondents and high-caste farm respondents have SERL scores more moderately above the mean. The degree of institutional affiliation of these three groups varies, with the middle-caste nonfarm respondents having relatively low institutional affiliation, the high-caste farmers having the highest frequency of respondents with strong affiliation, and the high-caste nonfarm respondents falling in between, though closer to, the more strongly affiliated high-caste farmers. The combination of scores on the SERL scale and frequencies of institutional affiliation would suggest that the middle-caste nonfarm respondents would be likely to resemble an inhibited social segment with higher scores on psychological involvement than on activity. This is the case when one compares their score on the scale of psychological involvement in politics with their score for campaign activity. On the other hand, one finds them scoring fairly high on the voting scale. The combination of high frequency of institutional affiliation with a score on the SERL scale only slightly above the mean suggests that the high-caste farmers ought to have a mobilized participation profile. Their participation profile resembles a mobilized one to a slight degree. They score higher on the campaign scale than on the political involvement scale, though their voting score is below the mean. They can probably be placed in a category somewhere between a committed and a mobilized group when it comes to campaigning and a moderately inhibited group when it comes to voting. The high-caste nonfarm respondents have by far the highest scores on the SERL scale. Their frequency of institutional affiliation is moderately high but not nearly as distinctive as their socioeconomic position. This would suggest that they would have a committed participation profile but that the level of psychological involvement would exceed the level of political activity. The data on their participation profile support this expectation. They have the highest score on the psychological involvement scale as well as on the campaign activity scale, but they are most distinctive on the former scale. On the other hand, they score below the population average on voting and can be categorized as an inhibited group in relation to that activity.

The most likely candidates for mobilized groups would be the low-caste farmers and the middle-caste farmers, as well as the Muslim farmers. Each one of these groups has a score on the SERL scale somewhat below the mean and has a level of institutionalization slightly above average. However, in none of these cases is the profile of socioeconomic and institutional resources particularly distinctive. The low-caste farmers show a slightly mobilized pattern in relation to the vote; the middle-caste farmers as well, are mobilized for voting, though they would have to be characterized as apathetic when it comes to campaign activity. The Muslim farmers are roughly average in political involvement and campaign activity scores but below average in voting, a pattern that fits none of our categories easily. Lastly, we have the low-caste nonfarm respondents, who score exactly on the population mean when it comes to socioeconomic level and are close to the population average in institutional involvement. Their participation profile is somewhat confused one, with slightly above-average scores on the psychological involvement scale, above-average scores in voting, and slightly below-average scores on political campaigning. They could be categorized as moderately inhibited in relation to campaigning and committed in relation to voting.

The participation patterns in India are somewhat complex and yield no simple conclusion. Several points, however, ought to be noted. First, a number of the groups fall into the participant type that one would predict based on their socioeconomic levels and their frequency of institutionalization. Those groups that do not neatly fall into one of our participant types also have rather unclear profiles in terms of socioeconomic and institutional characteristics. Secondly, we note the disjunction between voting and campaigning. Several groups are mobilized with respect to voting but not with respect to campaign activity. This is particularly the case for groups in the farm sector, the Harijan farmers, the low-caste farmers, and the middle-caste farmers. This is consistent with other data on the extent to which voting is a mobilized activity in India (Verba, Ahmed, and Bhatt, 1971; Goel, 1975).

Most important from the point of view of our argument about the role of segmentation and institutions in relation to inequality in political participation is the fact that we find no examples of low-status mobilized segments or high-status inhibited segments. The low-status groups that might be mobilized are sometimes mobilized in relation to voting but not in relation to campaign activity. At the other end of the socioeconomic scale we do find one group inhibited in relation to campaign activity – the middle-caste nonfarm respondents. They are, however, a relatively small segment, comprising only 5 percent of our sample. On the other hand, the larger group of high-caste nonfarm respondents with the highest score on the SERL scale also has the highest average score in campaign activity, making it a committed group.

In this respect, the data in India resemble those in the United States. There is little evidence that the political institutions in India contribute substantially to the equalization of political activity through their connection to particular social segments.

Conclusion

The data on India do not, as we have pointed out, fit our model very closely. Nevertheless, the data on India add something to our understanding of the processes of political mobilization in the various nations. One of the most puzzling features of the data with which we began our analysis was the similarity between the United States and India in the strength of the relationship between socioeconomic resource level and political activity.[16] One could hardly imagine nations as different as the United States is from India in terms of level of political

---

[16] Yugoslavia was similar as well. We shall consider it within this framework in the next chapter.

development or in terms of political structure. The unifying feature that distinguishes these two nations from Austria, the Netherlands, and Japan is the absence of what we have called well-structured political cleavage – that is, clearly defined political contestation across well-defined social groups where political institutions are closely linked to the contesting groups. In India and the United States we find that political competition is not well structured. The reason is different in each case: In the United States two catchall parties represent varied social groups; in India a single dominant catchall party represented varying interests in the four states in which we carried on our study. In each case, the absence of structured party competition supported by institutions linked to specific groups allows the individual socioeconomic forces relatively full play. The result is the stronger SERL/participation relationship found in those nations.

11

Party and participation in Yugoslavia

We have, thus far, omitted an analysis of the relationship among institutional affiliation, participation and socioeconomic advantage in Yugoslavia. Because of the important differences between the institutional structure in Yugoslavia and that in the other nations, an attempt to incorporate Yugoslavia into the analysis in the previous chapters would have complicated matters unnecessarily. However, we believe that our model can be applied in Yugoslavia, and we shall attempt to do so here.

The issue of comparability

There has been a long debate in the comparative politics literature as to the comparability of communist and noncommunist systems or the comparability of political parties in the context of competitive party systems and political parties in single-party systems. When posed in a global way, the question of comparability is not very useful. Anything can be compared to anything – as long as one can find some dimension that they have in common. The important question is whether one can *fruitfully* compare parties or systems, and that depends on whether the comparison allows one to raise and/or answer significant general questions about politics. Comparison has to have a purpose; there must be a specific research question.

The issue as to the fruitfulness of a comparison between Yugoslavia and the other nations cannot be answered by considering the overall properties of the systems, but by seeing whether our research question can be meaningfully dealt with in Yugoslavia. This means asking whether we can identify the same type of process in Yugoslavia that we have studied elsewhere – whereby the individual conversion of socioeconomic resources into political activity is affected by institutional constraints. To study such a process in Yugoslavia requires us to identify and measure a similar set of dimensions there as elsewhere. We must locate citizens on a scale of socioeconomic resources, on scales of political activity, and distinguish among them in terms of affiliation with relevant institutions. And these dimensions must be meaningfully comparable to similar dimensions elsewhere.

Locating comparable dimensions

Socioeconomic resources. Is SERL in Yugoslavia comparable to that elsewhere? In Yugoslavia, as in the other societies we have been studying, it is possible to array citizens along a hierarchy of socioeconomic advantage – in terms of their level of education and their level of material well-being. The shape of the education and of the income distributions differ in Yugoslavia from those elsewhere, but no more so than the differences between, say, India and the Netherlands. SERL in Yugoslavia is, furthermore, similar to SERL elsewhere in that higher positions on the scale are generally more desirable than lower ones, and that government policies affecting the distribution of education and income are the subject of controversy.

Political participation. Can political participation in Yugoslavia be compared with that elsewhere? Here our answer is a more qualified yes. If by participation we mean legal citizen activities that are aimed at influencing the decisions and policies of government officials or the selection of such officials, there is no doubt that opportunities for such participation exist in Yugoslavia. Whether such opportunities are more or less extensive than those elsewhere is a complicated question. Yugoslavia offers few opportunities to control officials through electoral mechanisms. Individual election races may be contested, but structured competition among political parties does not exist. On the other hand, Yugoslavia has a wide array of quite meaningful self-government institutions in local communities, the workplace, residential units, and elsewhere, that represent significant channels of participation.

For our purposes, we can beg the issue of the amount of participation that exists in Yugoslavia as well as the tougher question of how responsive officials are to it. As long as there is some meaningful participation (and that there certainly is), our research question of the equality of distribution of that participation is relevant.

Our analysis of participation in the other nations has depended on our ability to discover similar modes of political activity across the nations, a similarity that greatly increases our belief in the cross-national comparability of political activity. Are there similar modes in Yugoslavia? Again the answer is a somewhat qualified yes. In the other nations we found that citizens engaged in different specific political acts, but that it was possible to reduce the individual acts to four comparable modes of activity, as well as to combine these four modes of activity into a more general overall activity index (Verba, Nie and Kim, 1971; and Appendix A). We demonstrated further that a similar analysis applied to the Yugoslavian data produced a somewhat different set of modes. In the other nations we found that political activity could be classified into one of four modes – campaign activity, communal activity, voting, and particularized contacting. But the various acts that went to make up the campaign and communal modes in the other nations appeared to form a single mode in Yugoslavia – a mode we label "regular political activity." And lastly we found that activity within functional self-management bodies (workers' councils, residential unit councils, and the like) formed a separate mode[1] (Verba et al., 1973; and Appendix A).

The specific modes of activity found in Yugoslavia differed somewhat from those found elsewhere, but these differences were predictable on the basis of some general considerations about the ways in which citizens can be active. In particular, the distinction between communal and campaign activity in other nations depended on the fact that the latter was always in a competitive or conflictual setting, whereas the former was not likely to involve conflict or competition. In Yugoslavia, activity within elections does not have this competitive or conflictual basis.[2] Furthermore, the "functional self-management" mode of activity merely reflects the availability in Yugoslavia of a set of institutions (absent elsewhere) that provides a meaningfully different opportunity for citizen activity. In short, the modes of political activity in Yugoslavia differ from those elsewhere. But the differences are predictable by our general model of political participation on the basis of institutional differences in Yugoslavia.

This is very encouraging for the general model of political activity, but it does somewhat complicate the comparison of participation in Yugoslavia with that elsewhere. Some of the analysis in the other nations depended on a comparison between campaign and communal activity. No such comparison is possible in Yugoslavia, where they form a single mode. And there is no direct equivalent of functional self-management activity in the other nations. Yet the fact that the modes of activity in Yugoslavia do form a meaningful structure and one that is, though different from that elsewhere, predictable on the basis of the same model that predicted the different modes in the other nations, gives us some confidence that one is dealing with the same general phenomenon in Yugoslavia.

Institutional constraints. In the other nations we have considered political parties and politically involved organizations as the institutions that can modify the SERL/participation relationship. Our typology of respond-

---

[1] For a full account of this analysis of the modes of participation, see Verba, Nie, and Kim (1971) and Verba, Nie, Barbic, Irwin, Molleman, and Shabad (1973). For a fuller analysis of the stratification pattern associated with participation in Yugoslavia, see Verba and Shabad (1975).
[2] There are often competitive races for individual seats but no general structure of party competition.

ents in terms of the degree of institutional affiliation differs from that in other nations. We consider those who are members of the League of Communists (as the Communist Party of Yugoslavia is called) to have the strongest affiliation; those who are members of the Socialist Alliance (but not of the League) to have moderate affiliation; and those belonging to neither organization to be unaffiliated. The functions of the League of Communists differ substantially from the functions of parties and political institutions in the other nations. The significance of the League has varied in recent Yugoslavian history, but it has generally been assigned a governing role absent from parties in other nations. Furthermore, the League differs from the political parties in our other nations in that it is not part of a system of competitive parties, each trying to outdo the other in the electoral struggle.

Despite these differences, the League is comparable to the parties and political organizations elsewhere from the point of view of the process in which we are interested. The League is a channel for political participation. It mobilizes its members to political activity; members of the League are supposed to be exemplary activists (see Denitch, 1973*b*). Thus it can function in a way similar to institutions in the other nations. The three characteristics of institutions that we found to be important elsewhere – the strength of the party, the distinctiveness of its support base, and the extent to which it mobilizes a distinctive set of supporters to political activity – are applicable to the League.

The equivalent of moderate affiliation elsewhere is membership in the Socialist Alliance (but not the League). The Socialist Alliance is a more broadly based institution; membership is a much more routine matter (it is easier to become a member and it does not require, as does League membership, the recommendation of other members), and membership in the Socialist Alliance does not imply a commitment of time and resources. In this way, it makes sense as a rough equivalent of moderate affiliation elsewhere.

Relevance of comparisons

In sum, then, we can measure phenomena in Yugoslavia similar to those measured elsewhere. The phenomena are not identical, but they are similar enough to make the comparison meaningful.

The problem of comparison is only in part one of the ability to locate similar dimensions along which to array our respondents in Yugoslavia. More important is the issue of whether such an analysis is meaningful for our understanding of Yugoslavian politics and, in turn, for the understanding of political processes more generally. If the problem with which we are dealing was irrelevant in the Yugoslavian context, our analysis would be fruitless. If, for instance, activity within the framework of competitive elections was the only effective means of citizen activity, it would make no sense to apply our model to a system without such elections.

However, participation in competitive elections is not the only mode of effective citizen activity. Yugoslavia has been in the forefront in the innovation of new modes of political activity, particularly functional self-management institutions. Many students of democracy see a possible solution to the problems of participation in the establishment of direct participatory channels in decentralized socioeconomic and political institutions similar to those found in Yugoslavia (Blumberg, 1968; Dahl, 1970; Hunnius, 1973; and Pateman, 1970). Workers' councils, for example, provide direct participatory opportunities within smaller and more proximate units. They give citizens a chance to take part in that aspect of their lives that they understand best and to which a great deal of time is devoted – their work. Therefore, they give all citizens, not only those who are more socially and politically advantaged, a more equitable opportunity to control decisions that affect their everyday life. At least, so argue advocates of participatory democracy and the Yugoslavs (Denitch, 1973a). An analysis of these new modes of activity, from the point of view of our general model of participation, may shed light on how these modes function and how they differ from the more traditional modes of political activity we have studied elsewhere. The differences between Yugoslavia and the other nations are therefore a challenge, but also promise important insights into the institutional innovations attempted there.

There is another reason why our analysis might be useless in Yugoslavia. If leaders in a nation like Yugoslavia were in no way influenced by political activists (either because they used special techniques to find out the preferences of all the citizens, not just the activists, or because they were responsive to no citizens), it would make little sense to pursue our analysis. It would make no difference if the activist population overrepresented the more affluent and better educated. We have no systematic data on the process by which Yugoslavian leaders make policy nor hard data on whose voices they hear (just as we have little hard evidence elsewhere), but we have no reason to believe that they are insensitive to the messages carried via political activity in Yugoslavia (Supek, in Barton et al., 1973). Thus it makes a difference in Yugoslavia, as elsewhere, what the composition of the activist population is.

Institutions, socioeconomic resources, and participation

We have already presented some data on Yugoslavia in Chapter 4–data that help confirm the comparability of participation between Yugoslavia and the other nations. For one thing, we found evidence that the individual forces relating socioeconomic resource level to participation existed in Yugoslavia as elsewhere: The correlation of subjective political interest with SERL was .43 – similar to that in other nations. In addition we found that Yugoslavia was a nation with a fairly strong SERL/participation relationship. In Chapter 4 we showed that the relationship in Yugoslavia is similar to that in India and the United States: the SERL/overall participation relationship in Yugoslavia is .35, in India .38, in the United States .36. The similarity is intriguing, because India, the United States, and Yugoslavia are of course a quite heterogeneous triad of nations. If we can show that they are linked by some similar patterns of institutional constraint, despite the differences in the specific institutions, we shall have provided a quite powerful test of our model.

Party affiliation and socioeconomic advantage

We can begin with some basic data. Table 11–1 provides the proportions of the samples that fall into the three categories of our institutional affiliation scale: Fourteen percent of our sample reports membership in the League of Communists; 40 percent are members of the Socialist Alliance (but not of the League – a citizen who belongs to both is found in the "League" category); and 46 percent have no affiliation.

These data set the stage for our analysis. We can now turn to a more direct look at the way in which institutional affiliation affects the participation disparity between the haves and the have-nots. We can begin by considering the support base for the League and Socialist Alliance. Do those at the top or the bottom of the SERL scale contribute more to the League membership, or do members come proportionately from all SERL levels? Figure 11–1 shows that there is a clear positive relationship between SERL and party affiliation. Those low on the SERL scale are more likely to be unaffiliated (two-thirds are unaffiliated), whereas those high on the SERL scale are much less likely to be in the unaffiliated category (only one-fourth of those in the top third of the SERL distri-

Table 11–1. *"Party affiliation" in Yugoslavia*

Members of League of Communists	14%
Members of Socialist Alliance (but not League)	40%
Nonmembers	46%
	100%

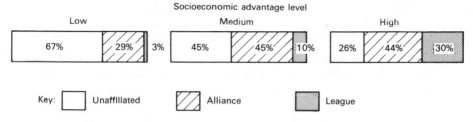

Figure 11-1. Party affiliation and three socioeconomic advantage strata in Yugoslavia.

bution are affiliated with neither the Alliance nor the League). Or let us consider League membership. Only 3 percent of those in the lowest third of the SERL scale report such membership, in contrast with 30 percent of the upper SERL group. To consider the data another way: Seventy-one percent of the League members come from the top one-third of the SERL scale; only 6 percent come from the bottom third.

The data on the stratification of League membership are consistent with data collected by the League (reported in Denitch, 1973*b*, pp. 108–18). In the period following World War II, League membership came heavily from formerly disadvantaged groups. In 1946, 50 percent of League members were peasants; 10 percent had white-collar occupations. More recently, the main criterion for membership has been advanced education; managers and "technical intelligentsia" are greatly overrepresented in the League. By 1968, the League data indicate, the proportion of members with white-collar occupations had risen to 44 percent, and the peasant proportion had fallen to 7 percent (see Denitch, 1973*b*). If affiliation with the League boosts the activity rate of those who are members, it is clear that this boost will go disproportionately to the more affluent and better-educated members.

Pattern of participation and involvement

We can now turn to the interrelationship among socioeconomic resource level, participation, and institutional affiliation. We present these relationships separately for the several modes of activity found in Yugoslavia: "regular" activity (combining campaign and communal activity), voting, and participation in functional self-management bodies. Our analysis of the Yugoslavian data thus far (as well as our experience in the other nations) suggests that the relationship is likely to differ from one mode to another. It is not completely clear what one ought to expect in terms of the relative importance of individual forces and institutional constraints in relation to the several modes of activity. The expectations we had in the other nations are not directly transferable, since the modes of activity differ. One parallel may be found in relation to voting. In the other nations we found that institutional affiliation was a sufficient condition for voting in those cases where institutional systems were strong. This should transfer to Yugoslavia, where institutional affiliation clearly has a strong relationship to activity and voting is an easy act, as it is in the other nations. But in the absence of competitive elections, such an expectation may not be valid. The League would have less need to mobilize its supporters to vote, there being no opposition to defeat.

The "regular" activity also presents a special problem. Where institutions were strong, we found that they were necessary but not sufficient conditions for campaign activity – the unaffiliated citizens were locked out no matter what their SERL level, whereas among the affiliated citizens SERL played a role. For communal activity, SERL played a role at all levels of institutional affiliation; such affiliation was neither necessary nor sufficient. It is hard to know what to expect from the combination of these two modes into "regular" political activity in Yugoslavia. For neither campaign nor communal activity in the other nations was institutional affiliation sufficient to erase differences based on socioeconomic resources. The reason for this, we argued, was that both modes of activity involved "difficult" acts and that individual socioeconomic resources would play a role among those affiliated. This would lead us to expect a similar SERL/activity relationship among the affiliated in Yugoslavia. However, the fact that the lower SERL League members are already such a select group (representing only 3 percent of that stratum) may mean that they represent that minority of the lower socioeconomic group that is well endowed with the motivation and resources that usually accompany higher SERL. Indeed, it may be that the impact of the individualistic forces associated with the higher socioeconomic resource level have their major impact on the recruitment of members to the League.

At the other end of the party affiliation scale – among the unaffiliated – our expectations are not clear either. A lockout of those unaffiliated would certainly not be unexpected, given the strength of the institutional system.

The third mode of activity we shall consider is participation in functional self-management institutions. This mode of activity is one that has not concerned us thus far in our analysis, specific as it is to the Yugoslavian setting. It is not clear what pattern of relationship one might expect among SERL, institutional affiliation, and this kind of activity. On the one hand, one might expect League of Communist dominance over these functional bodies: If League members played their full role as exemplary participants, League membership might be a sufficient condition for participation in such functional bodies; and if the League used these functional bodies as means of extending its control over various public institutions in Yugoslavia, League membership might be a necessary condition for participation in such functional self-management bodies. Under such circumstances individual socioeconomic resources would play no role. On the other hand, such dominance of the League over functional self-management bodies may not take place. There is no formal requirement that members of such self-management bodies be members of the League. Furthermore, such bodies may represent an arena in which individual socioeconomic forces play an important role. This is likely to be the case in connection with the most widespread form of functional self-management – workers' councils. Within enterprises where workers' councils exist, it may be that the more skilled and better-educated workers will become council members – especially if their skills and expertise are related to the technical decisions that are made within such institutions. Functional self-management may, therefore, represent a form of activity where institutional effects (i.e., recruitment through the League of Communists) play a less central role than in relation to other modes of activity. If this is the case, one would expect to find that individuals within the League as well as those outside can convert their individual socioeconomic resources into activity within such functional bodies.

With those somewhat unclear expectations in mind we can consider the data for the various kinds of activity we have measured in Yugoslavia. Data on the interrelationship among socioeconomic resource level, institutional affiliation, and political activity are reported in Figure 11–2. The graphs take the same form as those in Chapter 7 – socioeconomic level is plotted on the horizontal axis, political activity on the vertical, and the data are plotted for those who are League members, those who are Socialist Alliance members (but not in the League), and those who are affiliated with neither institution.

Regular political activity. The first section of the graph plots the data for "regular" political activity – the factor that combines campaign and communal activity in Yugoslavia. For the population as a whole, as we have seen, there is a moderately sharp relationship between socioeconomic status and political activity: the higher the socioeconomic level, the more active one is. However, when one looks at the various population groups differentiated into those affiliated with the League, Alliance members, and those affiliated with neither of these institutions, one finds that such affiliation plays a much bigger role than socioeconomic status. All League members, no matter what their socioeconomic level, are very high in regular political activity. The conversion rate of individual socioeconomic resources into activity is positive – as is seen by the difference between the top and bottom thirds of the SERL scale for League mem-

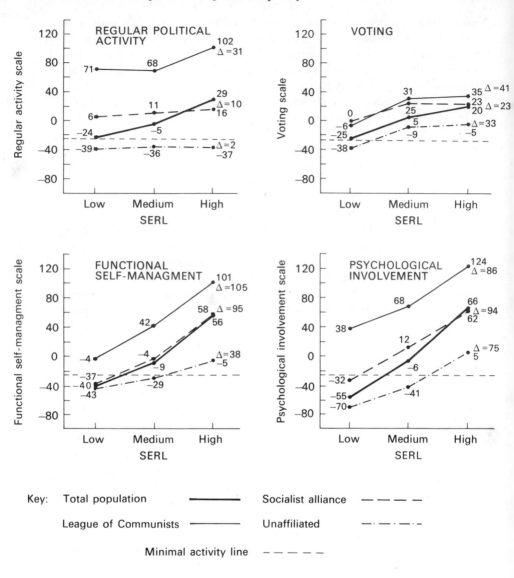

Key: Total population ——————— Socialist alliance — — — —

League of Communists ——————— Unaffiliated — · — · — ·

Minimal activity line — — — — —

Figure 11-2. Institutional affiliation, socioeconomic resource level, and modes of activity in Yugoslavia.

bers–but not much so. Socialist Alliance members are moderately active in regular political activity; they participate at or slightly above the mean level for the population. Socioeconomic resource level, however, plays no role. And those who are affiliated with neither the League nor the Alliance are inactive, no matter what their socioeconomic level. They

participate well below the population mean, and socioeconomic resources make no difference. The data illustrate a dominant institutional
system – affiliation is both a necessary and sufficient condition for very
high levels of regular political activity in Yugoslavia. If one is not a
member of the League, he does not engage in very high levels of activity
no matter what his socioeconomic status may be. If one is affiliated with
neither of the two political institutions, his political activity level is low
no matter what his socioeconomic status. Note, for instance, that the
activity level of League members from the bottom of the SERL scale is
well above that of unaffiliated citizens or Alliance members from the
top of the SERL scale. It is clear that League affiliation represents the
key to a role in "regular" political activity in Yugoslavia.

The data are, however, also consistent with our generalization as to
the "reemergence" of the positive SERL/activity relationship within the
institutional sphere even where institutions are strong mobilizing forces.
We found this in relation to difficult acts such as campaign and communal activity in the other nations. A similar pattern appears in Yugoslavia. Though all League members participate at a high level, there is
a positive relationship between SERL and activity among the League
members, a positive relationship that does not appear among the Alliance members or the unaffiliated. In short, even within a mobilizing
institution such as the League, the individual resources associated with
a high position on the SERL scale play a role in determining who
becomes active. This similarity to the pattern found in other nations
with strong institutional systems gives us greater confidence that we are
studying similar processes within quite different institutional settings.

The data also illustrate how the socioeconomic composition of League
membership affects the inequality of "regular" political activity in Yugoslavia. Note the line for the entire population in Figure 11–2. The
relationship between socioeconomic level and political activity slopes
upward for the population as a whole despite the relative flatness within
each institutional level. The reason for the flatness within institutional
levels is that the presence or absence of League membership erases the
effect of socioeconomic status. But League members, as we have seen,
come disproportionately from those high on the socioeconomic scale,
whereas the unaffiliated come disproportionately from those low on the
socioeconomic scale.

This means that League affiliation plays a dual role in the relationship
between socioeconomic level and political activity. On the one hand, the
fact that all League members are active and all unaffiliated citizens are
inactive (regardless of their socioeconomic status) means that League
membership represents a necessary and an almost sufficient institutional
channel to regular political activity. This reduces the effects of individual
socioeconomic resources and motivations. However, the fact that League

affiliation is so closely associated with socioeconomic level means that the activist population comes disproportionately from those who are more affluent and better educated. The League channels political activity in Yugoslav society, but it draws the haves into those channels.

Voting. The pattern for voting is reported in the next section of Figure 11–2. Several points can be noted. For one thing, institutional affiliation is not necessary for voting. The unaffiliated are less active than others in this respect, but there is some differentiation among them on the basis of socioeconomic level. At the other end of the affiliation scale, we also find some socioeconomic differentiation. Middle- and upper-status Alliance and League members are active as voters, but those in the lower third of the SERL are only at the population average for voting. For voting, then, one can say that affiliation is neither a necessary nor a sufficient condition. In this respect the Yugoslav voting data differ from voting in other nations with strong institutions. This, however, is probably due to the difference between voting in the noncompetitive setting of Yugoslavia and voting where party competition motivates parties to bring out the vote.

Functional self-management. The third section of Figure 11–2 presents parallel data on participation in functional self-management bodies. The pattern is in clear contrast to those found for regular political activity and for voting. Those affiliated with the League are more likely to be active in functional self-management bodies no matter what their socioeconomic level. This is seen in the fact that the line for League members is well above that for the unaffiliated (as well as above that for Alliance members) across all socioeconomic levels. But in contrast with regular political activity, League affiliation is neither necessary nor sufficient for activity in functional self-management bodies. Among those who are League members, among those who are Socialist Alliance members, and among those affiliated with neither institution, socioeconomic level still plays a major role (a fact reflected in the positive slope for each of the lines in Figure 11–2). In other words, the individual resources associated with socioeconomic level play a major role in determining who will become a member of one of the functional self-management bodies.

Some comparison of the graphs for regular activity and functional self-management will make this clear. Consider the League members from the bottom of the socioeconomic scale. When it comes to regular political activity, they participate well above the mean for the population as a whole and well above unaffiliated citizens or Alliance members from the top of the socioeconomic hierarchy. Compare this with the situation in relation to functional self-management. Lower-status League members participate slightly below the mean level for the population as a whole, below the level for upper-status Alliance members, and at the same level as upper-status unaffiliated citizens. League affiliation places the low-status member 108 points above the high-status unaffiliated citizen when it comes to regular political activity. In relation to functional self-management the gap is 2 points. Socioeconomic resources continue to play an important role in connection with functional self-management.

Psychological involvement. Lastly, we can consider the data on psychological involvement in politics. They form the patterns we would expect based on our theoretical assumptions as well as our experience with the other nations. Institutional affiliation is positively related to involvement, but in an additive way. At all levels of institutional affiliation there is a sharp, positive slope to the SERL/involvement relationship. Institutional interference is, in Yugoslavia as elsewhere, relatively weak when it comes to psychological involvement. The data support our cross-national generalization as to the positive SERL/political activity relationships one would find if there was no institutional interference with individual propensities to be active. The fact that we find support for our generalization in a system with an institutional structure as different as is the Yugoslav from those in the other nations adds a great deal of confirmatory weight to the generalization. It also leads us to believe that we are indeed dealing with processes in Yugoslavia comparable to those elsewhere.

Political self-government councils and workers' councils: a refinement of the analysis

The contrast between regular political activity and functional self-management is intriguing because the latter represents the innovative Yugoslavian mode. We can highlight the contrast in several ways. Functional self-management and regular activity differ in an important way over and above the functional character of the former. Citizens are elected to functional self-management bodies and participate in these organizations as an ongoing activity. Most of the specific acts included in regular political activities, in contrast, are more episodic. A better comparison with functional self-management participation might be made with one component of regular activity – participation in self-governing bodies such as community and commune councils. This will isolate the functional aspect of the former. Self-governing community and commune bodies also form part of the self-government system in Yugoslavia. A moderately large proportion of the populace – 9 percent – reports past or present membership in them. One would expect such bodies to be more susceptible to the political criterion of affiliation with the League and less likely to be affected by the technical skills that lead to participation in functional self-management bodies.

Figure 11–3 compares functional self-management with "political self-government" – that is, community and commune self-management. To highlight the distinction between the functional and the political, we use membership in workers' councils as the measure of functional self-management, eliminating from the measure membership in apartment house councils and other functional bodies not connected with the workplace. In the first section of Figure 11–3 we show the relationship between membership in a political self-governing body and socioeconomic resource level for the three levels of institutional affiliation; in the second section we show the relationship between membership in a

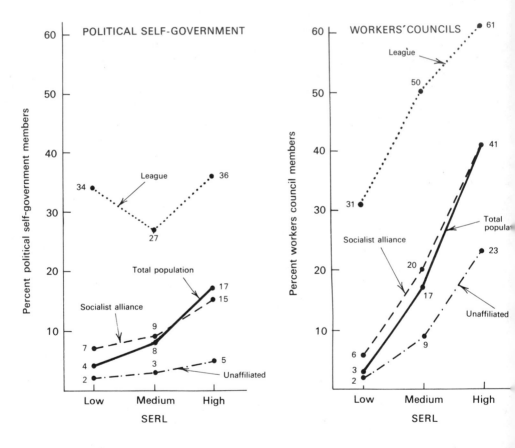

Figure 11-3. Percent members of political or workers' councils by socioeconomic level and party affiliation.

workers' council and SERL for the same institutional levels. The dependent variable in each case (on the vertical axis) is the percentage of the group who are members.

Consider the data for political self-government membership. As with regular political activity, there is a fairly strong relationship between socioeconomic level and participation when we look at the population as a whole (plotted as a solid line). Those high on our socioeconomic scale are four times as likely to be members of self-governing bodies in the political sphere than are those low on the scale. But like regular political activity, affiliation with a political institution, especially with the League, plays a much bigger role than does socioeconomic level. If one is affiliated with the League, one is likely to participate in political self-government councils, regardless of socioeconomic status. If one is unaffiliated, one is unlikely to be a member; and socioeconomic resources do not help much.

The situation differs sharply when it comes to membership in workers' councils. Although a greater proportion of League members than non-League members at each socioeconomic level participate in workers' councils, institutional affiliation does not eliminate the effects of socio-economic resources. There is a difference of 30 percentage points in the frequency of workers' council membership between those League members low on the socioeconomic scale and those high on the scale. Similarly, those who have no affiliation can still convert socioeconomic resources into workers' council activity. There is a sharp difference in membership rates among unaffiliated citizens who are low and those who are high on the socioeconomic scale.[3]

One more comparison between the two parts of Figure 11–3 makes this clear. Consider two opposite types of citizens: the lower-status League member and the upper-status nonmember. The former has the institutional affiliation needed for activity but not the socioeconomic resources. The latter has the socioeconomic resources but not the institutional connection. When it comes to participation in political self-

---

[3] There is one difference between workers' council participation and participation in other kinds of activities. The former is open only to part of the population; to those employed in the "socialist sector" – that is, in those industries, agricultural enterprises, and sociocultural institutions that are publicly rather than privately owned. Workers' council participation is not open to private farmers, private entrepreneurs, or housewives. This, however, does not affect the shape of the relationship among SERL, institutional affiliation, and workers' council membership. If one were to look at the pattern of recruitment of members of workers' councils out of the "eligible" population of the socialist sector alone, one would find a similar pattern of positive relationship between SERL and workers' council membership within each of the institutionally defined groups. For these data, see Verba and Shabad (1975).

government councils, the institutionally connected but socioeconomically disadvantaged citizen greatly outparticipates his opposite number, who is high on socioeconomic resources but unaffiliated with the League. When it comes to workers' councils, the high-status unaffiliated citizen is more likely (if he is an Alliance member) or almost as likely (if he is totally unaffiliated) to be a member of such a council than is the low-status League member.

The differences in the roles played by individual socioeconomic resources and party affiliation in determining who becomes active in regular political activity as compared with workers' councils are nicely summarized in the path diagrams in Figure 11–4. We present both the combined effect of status and party affiliation on the two kinds of activity as well as their independent effects on the two modes of participation. The combined effect of socioeconomic status and party affiliation on regular political activity and on workers' council membership are virtually the same. For regular political activity the multiple r is .42. For participation in workers' councils it is .44. However, when we examine the independent effect of SERL and party affiliation, we get very different patterns. For regular political activity the independent effect of League affiliation is much stronger than that of socioeconomic status. Controlling for the effect of socioeconomic status, the standardized partial beta between party affiliation and regular political activity is a very strong .40. When we control for the effect of League affiliation, the relationship between status and regular political activity is a very slight .05. Let us contrast this with the pattern for membership in workers' councils. Both League affiliation and socioeconomic status have moderately strong independent effects on participation in workers' councils. Of the two, however, it is socioeconomic status that has the larger independent impact on who will become active in workers' self-management.

The data in Figures 11–2, 11–3, and 11–4 tell us a great deal about the role of individual socioeconomic resources and institutional affiliation in relation to the participation modes we have discovered in Yugoslavia. The main route to regular political activity and to participation in political self-government councils appears to be through the League of Communists. Socioeconomic resources play a role, but they do so by increasing the likelihood of affiliation with the League. Without that affiliation there is little activity. Those who are unaffiliated tend not to be active – no matter what their socioeconomic level. The fact that membership in the League eliminates differences in activity rates across various social levels does not mean that socioeconomic resources play no role. Quite the contrary. League membership – the key to regular political activity and to membership on political self-government bodies – is not distributed equally across social groups in Yugoslavia. Rather, it

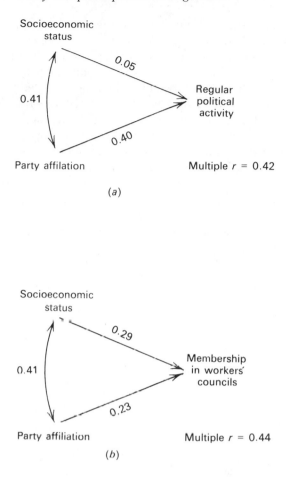

Figure 11-4. Path diagrams of the combined and independent effects of socioeconomic status and party affiliation on participation. (a) "Regular" political activity; (b) membership in workers' councils.

tends to be concentrated fairly heavily in the hands of those in the upper reaches of the socioeconomic resource scale. In sum, affiliation with the League eliminates differences in activity across social levels *among those so affiliated.* But there are sharp social differences between those who become members of the League and those who do not. And because of this, there is in the population as a whole a considerable disparity among social groups in the extent of their participation in regular political activity and in political self-government.

In contrast, the data suggest that there are two alternative paths to participation in workers' councils: political access through the League or access through socioeconomic resources such as technical competence and skill. Of the two, however, socioeconomic resources play a more central role. Because of the importance of socioeconomic level in determining who becomes a member of a workers' council, the role of the League is somewhat diminished. It controls access to workers' council membership to some extent – League members are disproportionately likely to be workers' council members – but it does not dominate access to such activity as much as it dominates access to other forms of political activity. The data are consistent with the interpretation that workers' councils open channels for a more technocratically oriented participation, one based on the skills and expertise believed to be necessary for such activity and less on the political commitments that are implied in affiliation with the League.

Conclusion

We have approached the data for participation in Yugoslavia using the model developed in relation to the other nations – the model whereby individual propensities to convert socioeconomic resources into political activity are modified by the workings of institutions. Though the modes of activity differ somewhat in Yugoslavia, as does the meaning of institutional affiliation, we find that the model "works" in that setting as well. For one thing, we find a pattern of difference between "regular" political activity and psychological involvement in politics that is similar to the pattern found in the other nations. This lends support to our pan-cultural generalizations about the way in which institutional and individual forces will interact across different acts.

In addition, we applied our model to the kind of activity that is unique to Yugoslavia – functional self – management. The analysis reveals that such activity represents an alternative to other political acts. It is a form of activity less dominated by institutional constraints emanating from the League of Communists, and an activity for which individual socioeconomic resources play a more central role.

The analysis is consistent with our contention that the individual and institutional processes of mobilization to political activity can be studied in a society such as Yugoslavia and that similar processes exist on the individual level across nations. The data also help explain why Yugoslavia is linked with the United States and India as a nation having a generally high SERL/participation relationship. The reason for the strong relationship in Yugoslavia, though explicable within the same framework as in the other nations, is somewhat different. In Yugoslavia political institutions are relatively strong. When it comes to regular political activity, the League of Communists is dominant in the sense we have used that term: Membership is both a necessary and sufficient condition for activity. The only deviation from that dominance is the mild positive relationship between individual socioeconomic resources and activity among the League members. The strong relationship between SERL and participation derives from the social composition of League membership. Since that membership is so highly stratified in terms of socioeconomic level, those mobilized to activity through the League are disproportionately from the haves; those locked out because of absence of League membership are disproportionately from the have-nots. The stratification of political activity in Yugoslavia takes place through the League.

12

Men and women: sex-related differences in political activity[1]

Our central concern has been with inequalities in political activity across socioeconomic levels. We have made this type of inequality central to our argument for three reasons. In the first place, socioeconomic stratification is an important force affecting political activity in all nations. Secondly, socioeconomic stratification is often the subject matter of politics; individuals and groups contend over governmental decisions that will affect their socioeconomic positions. Thirdly, socioeconomic differences exist and are measurable in all of our nations. As we have demonstrated, however, there are many other social bases of participatory inequality. The most salient of these may differ from nation to nation. We explored some of these differences in our analysis of social segmentation.

In this chapter we shall consider participatory inequality between men and women. Male/female participatory inequalities share two of the characteristics of socioeconomic inequalities. In all societies for which we have data, sex is related to political activity; men are more active than women. And, of course, in all societies the male/female distinction is measurable. Sex differences differ from socioeconomic differences, however, in that they are less uniformly the subject matter of political contention. In each of the nations, sex-related political issues can be found, but such issues do not form as salient a subject matter of politics as do other issues. Male/female participatory differences are intriguing, nevertheless. Though sex-related issues are less frequently on the political agenda, one reason for their absence may lie in the lesser political role of women. Furthermore, such issues are likely to form a larger part of the political agenda in the future, at least in some, perhaps all, of the nations under study. Lastly, the consideration of such differences allows us to test further our model of the forces that lead to political activity.

The basic difference

Most studies have shown that men are more likely to be politically active than women. (See, for example, Duverger, 1955; Haavio-

---

[1] Goldie Shabad is coauthor of this chapter.

Table 12–1. *Mean activity rates for men and women*

Nation	Overall activity			Voting		
	Men	Women	Difference	Men	Women	Difference
Austria	31	−28	+59	5	− 4	+ 9
India	40	−43	+83	15	−16	+31
Japan	31	−30	+61	9	− 8	+17
Netherlands	17	−20	+37	5	− 7	+12
Nigeria	38	−31	+69	27	−22	+49
United States	9	− 8	+17	6	− 6	+12
Yugoslavia	33	−35	+68	9	−10	+19

Mannila, 1970; and Pickles, 1953.) The disparity in activity grows greater as one moves up from mass political activities such as voting, to more difficult political acts, to occupancy of political office. Such differences between men and women occur in the seven nations we have been studying. Consider the data in Table 12–1. We compare the average scores for men and women on our scale of overall political activity and on our voting scale.[2] In each of the nations men score higher on each of the scales. When it comes to overall political activity, average male scores are about two-thirds of a standard deviation above female scores in five of the nations. The gap is smaller in the Netherlands, where 37 points on the overall participation scale separate men and women. In the United States the gap between men and women (17 points) is smaller still. The data confirm the pervasiveness of the male/female participation gap. But they also indicate that there is substantial variation in the magnitude of that gap.

The data for voting parallel those for overall activity in that men outparticipate women in each of the nations. But there is less of a participatory gap between the sexes in voting than in overall activity. In five of the nations the gap is quite insubstantial – less than 20 points on the voting scale. A difference that small in overall participation appears only in the United States. The data illustrate the way the male/female gap increases as one moves from the relatively easy political act of voting to the more stringent acts contained in our scale of overall political participation.

[2] We shall present data for voting and overall activity in this chapter. We had expected to find a different sex-related participatory pattern for campaign and communal activity. We found, however, no systematic differences between the acts. To simplify the presentation we shall simply distinguish between the easy act of voting and the more difficult acts on our overall activity scale.

Why should there be such a pervasive difference between male and female participation rates? How can we account for the variation in the extent of that difference across the nations? We cannot offer a comprehensive explanation of the differences between men and women. Such an explanation would require more sociological, psychological, and cultural data and theory than we have. (For examples of explanations, see Duverger, 1955; Haavio-Mannila, 1970; Pickles, 1953; Sullerot, 1971; Holter, 1970; Hess and Torney, 1967; and Greenstein, 1965.) Political differences based on sex are one manifestation of a more general role differentiation between men and women. We can, however, offer a more limited explanation of sex-based participatory inequalities by applying our model of the individual and institutional forces that lead to political activity. The variables and attributes that go into that model – socioeconomic resources, institutional affiliation, and the "conversion rates" of individual and institutional resources into activity – are variables and attributes on which we can expect to find male/female differences. Men might be expected to have higher levels of socioeconomic resources and more extensive party and organizational affiliation. In addition, they may be more capable of converting the individual socioeconomic resources and the institutional resource deriving from organizational affiliation into political activity. If we find sex differences in resources and in the ability to convert resources into political activity, we shall have some explanation of the lower levels of political activity among women. Differences in ability to convert resources into activity will be especially interesting. If such differences exist, they would suggest some special inhibition for women when it comes to political matters. It would mean that even when women attain parity in individual and institutional resources, they do not convert their comparable resources into political activity as well as do men.

The analysis involves a limited set of variables. Even if we were to find that a great deal of the participatory difference between men and women can be explained by the fact that women have fewer resources and convert them less effectively, the explanation would only be partial. The differences in resources and in conversion rates might, in turn, be the result of other causes: psychological differences between men and women that make women less "assertive" and therefore less likely to obtain resources and less able to convert them; or (more likely) social norms and institutional patterns that limit access to resources for women and limit as well their ability to convert those resources into political activity.

We cannot with our data probe much beyond the resource and conversion-level explanation. But we shall be able to go one step further and consider two alternative explanations of lower female participation, explanations that go beyond the possession and conversion of resources. One explanation is based on apathy: Women *abstain* from politics because they do not care about political matters. The alternative explanation is that women are *inhibited:* They care about politics but are inhibited from participating because of external restraints or self-restraint. We shall explicate the distinction more fully in the following pages. As we shall see, the distinction between the two explanations is not clear-cut. We shall attempt, nevertheless, to evaluate the relative merit of these two explanations.

Socioeconomic resources

Male/female differences in political activity may simply reflect the fact that women possess fewer socioeconomic resources. However, measuring male/female differences in socioeconomic resource level is difficult. We are concerned with those resources that can be converted into political activity. Thus we want to gauge socioeconomic resources controlled by the individual. It is, however, difficult to know what resources are under individual control and what resources are controlled by other family members. We measure income, for instance, as family income. There are differences across nations as well as differences among families within nations in the extent to which the various family members – in particular husbands and wives – control the financial resources of the family. Our family income measure is, in this way, useless as a measure of the resources available to individual men and women. Disposal of family income for consumption purposes may be under female control. But the use of income in relation to political purposes is, we believe, more likely to be under male domination. Thus a man and a woman who might report the same family income might differ greatly in the extent to which this gave them access to resources available for political purposes.

Because of the ambiguity of the income component of our socioeconomic resource scale, we shall differentiate between men and women in terms of the individual's educational level. This is by no means a perfect solution. It omits an important component of our SERL scale. Furthermore, it does not completely eliminate the problem of the family as the resource-possessing unit. One family member may use the educationally based skills of another as a political resource. In general, though, we assume that educational attainment and the skills and motivation attendant to education inhere in individuals. If women are less well educated than men, we assume they possess fewer socioeconomic resources to convert into political activity.

As Table 12–2 indicates, there are consistent differences between the educational levels of men and women in our samples. Men are more likely than women to be found in the top educational level; men are less likely to be in the bottom group. A finer categorization of the educational levels would reveal even sharper differences (see the footnote to Table

Table 12–2. *Educational level for men and women*

Nation	Educational level	Men (%)	Women (%)	Difference between men and women in low category (men–women)	Difference between men and women in high cateogy (men–women)
Austria	Low	29	59	−30	
	Medium	36	14		
	High	35	27		+ 8
India	Low	52	80	−28	
	Medium	33	17		
	High	16	4		+12
Japan	Low	15	23	− 8	
	Medium	44	40		
	High	42	37		+ 5
Netherlands	Low	31	39	− 8	
	Medium	31	40		
	High	37	22		−19
Nigeria	Low	55	83	−28	
	Medium	32	12		
	High	12	5		+19
United States	Low	31	23	− 8	
	Medium	19	22		
	High	50	55		+ 5
Yugoslavia	Low	35	51	−16	
	Medium	23	26		
	High	42	23		+19

Note: The three educational levels in each nation are defined as follows:

Austria:
(1) grammar school
(2) grammar school plus job apprenticeship
(3) trade school, high school (without diploma), high school, college level
India:
(1) illiterate
(2) literate, some primary school
(3) primary school, and up

Japan:
(1) 0–primary school
(2) junior high school
(3) senior high school, and plus
Netherlands:
(1) basic, elementary school
(2) advanced elementary school
(3) secondary school, and up
Nigeria:
(1) 0–primary school
(2) modern school

Table 12–2 (*note cont.*)

Nigeria:
(3) secondary, technical, postsecondary, seminary, university
United States:
(1) 0–8 years schooling
(2) 9–11 years
(3) 12 years, and plus

Yugoslavia:
(1) no schooling, up to 4 years
primary school
(2) 4–8 years, primary school
(3) occupational school, high
school, technical school, college

12–2 for the definition of the levels). The United States is an exception, where women have a somewhat higher educational profile than men. This is in part a function of the educational categories we use. Women are more likely than men to finish high school, but they fall behind men as one moves to higher educational levels. Aside from the United States, the educational gap appears least in Japan. It is greatest in India and Nigeria. In the latter two countries, most women are in the lowest educational category, and very few make it into the top one. Clearly, insofar as education provides resources and motivation for political activity, men are generally better endowed than women.

In what way is education related to the lower rate of political activity for women? This question is answered in Figures 12–1 and 12–2. The figures present the relationship between educational level and political activity for men and women separately. Figure 12–1 presents data on our overall political activity scale; Figure 12–2 presents data on voting. The data are relevant to two questions. Do men and women at roughly comparable levels of education engage in similar amounts of political activity? The male/female difference at comparable educational levels is indicated by the distance between the lines for the two groups. Secondly, do women convert education into political activity as effectively as men? This is shown by the slope of the line for men and women.

Consider the data for overall political activity. Figure 12–1 makes it clear that in each of the nations, at each level of education, men are more active than women. The differences between the sexes at each educational level are quite substantial. The nations that deviate some-what from this are the United States and, to a lesser extent, the Netherlands. In the former nation, the male/female differences are substan-tially smaller at each educational level than in the other nations.

Let us consider differences in the slope of the education/activity re-lationship.[3] The Δ figures are a useful summary of the slopes of the

---

[3] The measure used is the regression slope between ungrouped education scale and activity scale. This measure supplements the graphs where the finer differences in educational levels between men and women are ignored.

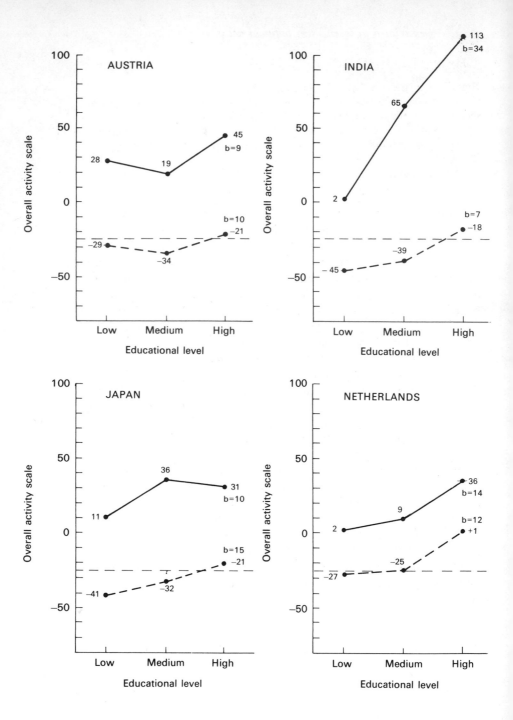

240

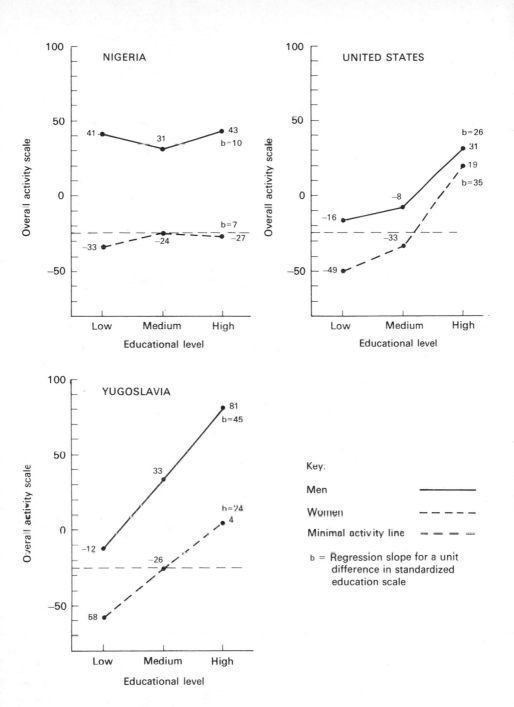

Figure 12–1. Overall activity by educational level for men and women.

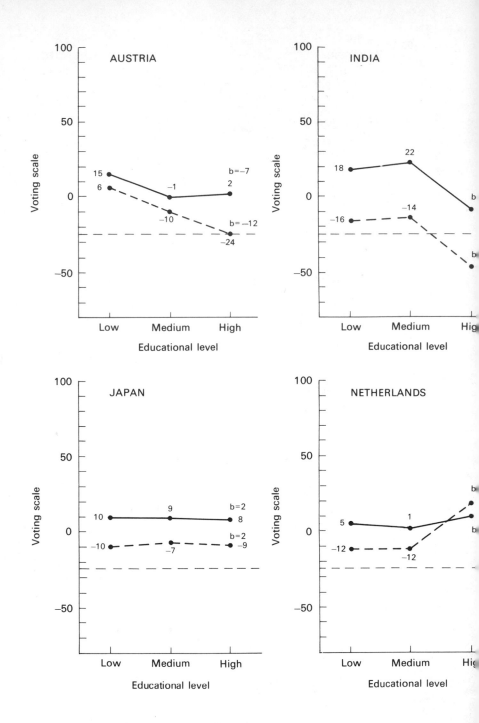

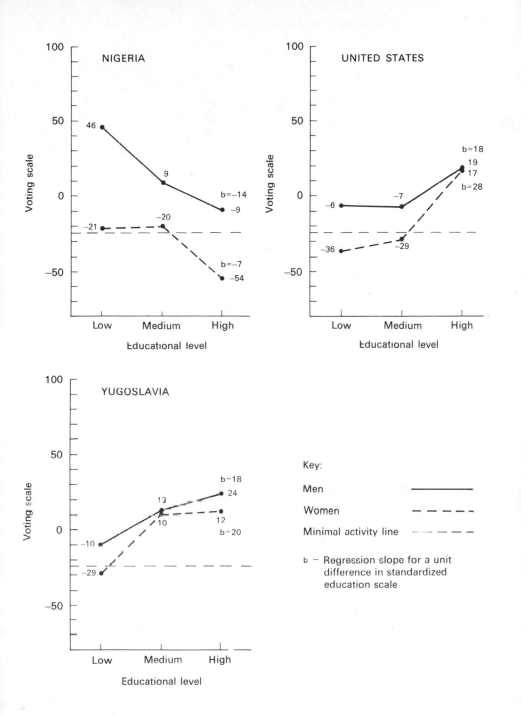

Figure 12–2. Voting activity by educational level for men and women.

relationship. The United States is the only nation in which the slope of the relationship between education and political activity is greater for women than for men. In India and Yugoslavia, the reverse is true; the slope for men is much greater than for women. As one moves up the educational ladder in India and Yugoslavia, one sees a larger increase in male rather than female political activity. The result is that the difference between male and female activity rates is greater in the more educated segment of the society than in the less well educated segment. In the other nations the slope of the relationship of education and activity is similar for men and women.

Figure 12–1 indicates that the educational differences between men and women affect political activity differences in several ways. In the first place, women have less education than men and therefore are less well endowed with the resources necessary for political activity. Secondly, in two out of the seven nations, men have substantially higher conversion rates of education into political activity. In this sense, education benefits women somewhat less than it does men when it comes to activity. Only in the United States do women convert education into activity at a noticeably higher rate. Lastly, and most important, Figure 12–1 indicates that educational differences between men and women are, at best, a partial explanation of the participation gap between the sexes. Even if men and women had similar levels of education and both groups converted education into activity at the same rate (i.e., if the lines in Figure 12–1 were parallel), a participation gap would remain; at every level of education, there is a substantial gap in every nation.

The data in Figure 12–2 show the relationship between education and voting activity for men and women. These data indicate that women are less disadvantaged when it comes to voting. For one thing, the gap in voting participation between men and women at comparable educational levels is much smaller than that between men and women in overall activity. In one instance – among the upper-educated group in the Netherlands – women score higher than men in voting activity; and in several other cases as well they come close to men in that respect. Furthermore, women have no disadvantage in the conversion rate of education into voting activity.

The data are not too encouraging from the point of view of the equalization of political activity between the sexes. One might have expected that the participatory gap between men and women would be diminished in the upper-educated groups, that educated women would be closer to educated men than were less well educated women to less well educated men. This would be the case if women converted education into activity at a greater rate. There are several reasons why we might expect this. For one thing, education might be expected to be more important for women than men in relation to participation – men perhaps possessing other social characteristics such as participation in the labor force that would foster political participation. Furthermore, one would expect that "traditional" values, which tend to support male dominance in most societies, would be less prominent among the educated women than among the less well educated. There is some evidence that education does reduce the gap between the sexes in relation to voting. But voting is an "easy" act on which education has little effect. When it comes to overall activity, education does not reduce the gap. Except in the United States, upper-educated women do not "catch up" to upper-educated men. In most of the nations the participation gap between the sexes is as great at higher education levels as at lower. Indeed, in four out of seven of the nations, as Figure 12–1 shows, women at the highest education level are less active than men at the lowest education level. In the Netherlands, upper-educated women just reach the level of the men in the lowest education group. Only in Yugoslavia and the United States does one find the upper-educated women outparticipating lower-educated men. Even in these nations, women's activity remains below that of men when one compares across similar educational levels.

Differences in the individual-level forces that lead to political activity clearly cannot fully explain male–female differences in activity. The data suggest that women, even were they to have the same level of educational resources, would be less active. Let us then consider the other component of our model – the institutional forces that mobilize groups to political activity.

Institutional forces

Group-based forces are an alternative way in which individuals can be brought to political activity. Groups with particular political interests may develop a self-conscious awareness of these interests, and/or they may develop political organizations. In either case, the role of individual socioeconomic resources becomes less crucial. As we have seen, group-based political mobilization is most likely to take place where there are clear lines of cleavage among political groups and where the various political groupings are organized into political parties or associations. Sex-related differences, however, were not the basis of much explicit political cleavage in any of the seven societies we studied. There is little evidence in our interviews that women see themselves as a group with particular claims on the government.[4] In none of the nations is

---

[4] Our evidence on this is not very complete. We did ask a question in four of the nations about the "main conflicts within the community" and in all of the nations about the main problems the respondent faced as an individual, the main problems facing the community, and the main

there a women's political party, that is, a party organized around sex-role issues or that attempts to mobilize female political activity. There are organizations specifically for women, but such organizations tend to be relatively nonpolitical. We can compare, nonetheless, the institutional resources available to men and women.

Table 12–3 compares men and women in terms of their institutional affiliation. The measure of institutional affiliation is that used in Chapters 6 and 7. In each of the nations, with the exception of the United States, men are more likely to be found in the more active categories of our typology of institutional affiliation, women in the less active categories. The sharpest difference is found in India, where almost no female respondents fell into the "strongly affiliated" category, compared with one out of five males. Two-thirds of the Indian female respondents were in the lowest "nonpoliticized" category. Similar differences, though of lesser magnitude, are found in the other nations. Again, the United States stands out from the other nations in the relative absence of male/female differences. Men are only slightly more likely to be in the strongly affiliated category than women. Thus, in all of the nations except the United States, women are disadvantaged in institutional resources just as they are disadvantaged in educational resources.

Do women "gain" as much as men from whatever institutional affiliation they have? Though women are on the average less likely to be exposed to institutional stimuli, perhaps those who are so exposed will catch up to their male counterparts in political activity. The data in Figure 12–3 are relevant to this point. The figures plot the relationship between the degree of institutional affiliation and the level of overall participation for men and women. In several ways, the data are quite consistent across all of the nations. For one thing, institutional affiliation is associated with increased political activity for both men and women. The lines for each of the sexes slope sharply upward. Men and women who are affiliated with politicized organizations are more likely to be political activists. This makes clear that the lesser frequency of such affiliations among women is a likely source of the male/female partici-

---

problems facing the nation. Such questions were coded in terms of references to different kinds of conflicts or problems. If one looks for references to race problems or race conflicts, for instance, one finds a substantial proportion of American blacks (about two-thirds) who respond to such questions with a racial frame of reference (Verba and Nie, 1972, chap. 10). In none of the nations did we find any noticeable reference to male/female conflicts or to problems involving sex roles. It is possible that we would have found more extensive reference to such differences had we asked about them more directly, or that we would find more frequent reference now, especially in the United States, than we did when our survey was conducted. But there is no reason to suspect that we missed registering female political consciousness in our interviews.

Table 12–3. *Institutional affiliation for men and women*

Affiliation by nation	Men (%)	Women (%)	Difference between men and women in lowest category (men–women)	Difference between men and women in highest category (men–women)
Austria				
Nonpoliticized	11	17	− 6	
Weak identifiers	13	28		
Moderately affiliated	23	28		
Strongly affiliated	54	28		+26
India				
Nonpoliticized	28	65	−37	
Weak identifiers	9	12		
Moderately affiliated	42	23		
Strongly affiliated	21	1		+20
Japan				
Nonpoliticized	18	34	−16	
Weak identifiers	14	15		
Moderately affiliated	41	34		
Strongly affiliated	27	18		+ 9
Netherlands				
Nonpoliticized	16	30	−14	
Weak identifiers	18	24		
Moderately affiliated	32	25		
Strongly affiliated	34	21		+13
Nigeria				
Nonmember	33	55	−22	
Nonpoliticized member	26	19		
Politicized member	40	26		+14
United States				
Nonpoliticized	15	15	0	
Weak identifiers	15	20		
Moderately affiliated	35	34		
Strongly affiliated	36	32		+ 4
Yugoslavia				
Nonmember	36	57	−21	
Alliance member	43	36		
League member	22	7		+15

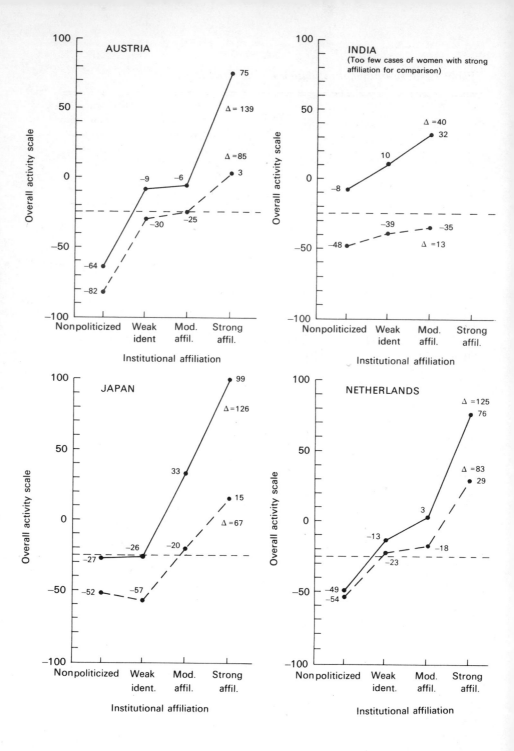

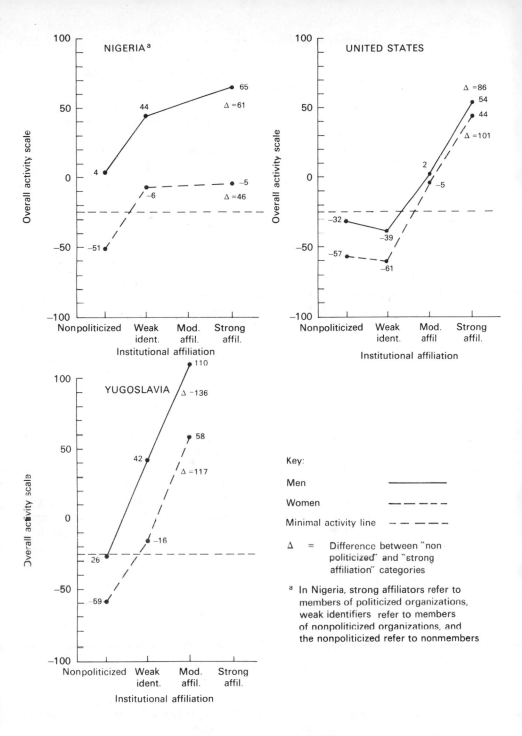

Figure 12–3. Overall activity by institutional affiliation for men and women.

249

pation gap. Secondly, the data in Figure 12–3 make clear that men outparticipate women, even at similar levels of institutional affiliation. Thus even if women are similar to men with respect to the degree of institutional affiliation, they are not as politically active as their male counterparts.

One other quite striking uniformity is found in all of the nations (with the usual exception of the United States): Men "gain" more in political activity through institutional affiliation than do women. This is seen most clearly in a comparison of the scores on the overall activity scale for those in the nonpoliticized category and those in the strongly affiliated category. In each nation the difference between the groups with the most and the least affiliation is greater for men than for women. (See the Δ's in Figure 12–3. We use the difference between the highest and lowest categories of institutional affiliation as our measure of slope or conversion rate.) The result is that women with strong institutional affiliations are further from their male counterparts in activity rate than are women with no political affiliation from their nonpoliticized male counterparts. Institutional affiliation gives men and women a boost in political activity, but it gives a bigger boost to men. In this way the unequalizing effects of institutional affiliation are compounded. Women are less likely to have such affiliation than men. And when they are affiliated, such affiliation has less payoff in terms of increased political activity.

The relationship among sex, institutional affiliation, and voting activity is strikingly different from the relationship with regard to overall political activity (Figure 12–4). Several differences can be seen. For one thing, when one controls for level of institutional affiliation, male/female differences in voting activity become very small. Secondly, the gain in voting activity associated with institutional affiliation is generally as great for women as for men. In India the gain is greater for women than men. Institutional affiliation mobilizes women to vote as effectively as it mobilizes men.

Summary: individual and institutional forces and political activity

Differences between men and women in individual and institutional resources help explain the gap in participation between the sexes. Women appear to be triply disadvantaged when it comes to political activity.

1 They are less well endowed with individual and institutional resources. They are less well educated, and they are less likely to be institutionally affiliated.
2 Individual and institutional resources benefit women less than men

when it comes to political activity. This is most clearly seen in relation to institutional resources. The conversion rate of such resources into political activity is greater for men than for women in six of the seven nations.

3 Over and above differences associated with either the level of resources or the conversion rate of resources into activity, women are less active than men. There appears to be an additional standing difference between the sexes not attributable to the availability of individual and institutional resources nor to their conversion rate into activity.

4 (The foregoing generalizations do not apply to the United States.) The United States differs from the other nations in the relative weakness of male/female differences in participation as well as in the relative absence of differences between the sexes in individual and institutional resources for participation. In addition, women in the United States can convert individual and institutional resources into political activity at a greater rate than can men. Though male/female differences in activity exist in the United States, the striking thing is how moderate are those differences compared with other nations.

5 (The foregoing points refer to male/female differences with regard to overall political activity. Women are not as different from men when it comes to voting.) Their scores on the voting activity scale are closer to those of men than are their scores on the overall activity scale. Furthermore, they convert individual and institutional resources into voting activity as effectively as do men. This is particularly clear in relation to institutional resources.

Women and political activity: apathy or inhibition

Male/female differences in political activity are only partially explained by differences in the individual and institutional resources available to each of the sexes. Even when men and women have comparable levels of individual and institutional resources, female political activity rates remain well below those of their male counterparts. The participatory disadvantage of being female is only partially reduced if resources are equalized. Clearly, such differences in participation have other social and cultural roots. Such pervasive differences in political activity are a manifestation of general patterns of sex-role differentiation found in all societies. They cannot be understood in isolation from the differing roles that men and women have played in economic and social life. Nor can they be understood in isolation from norms as to the appropriate activity for men and women. The data we have available do not allow a full exploration of the social context from which male/female differences arise. We would need information on family structure, on attitudes toward the involvement of women in the work force and in politics, and so forth. But the fact that we have data from several

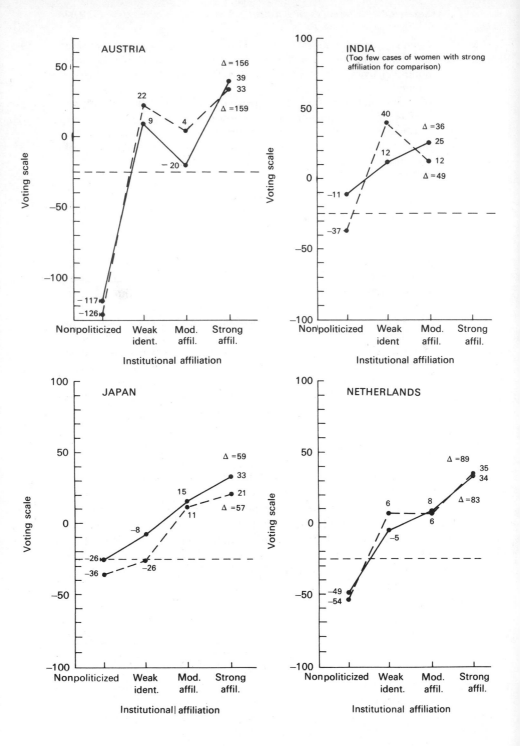

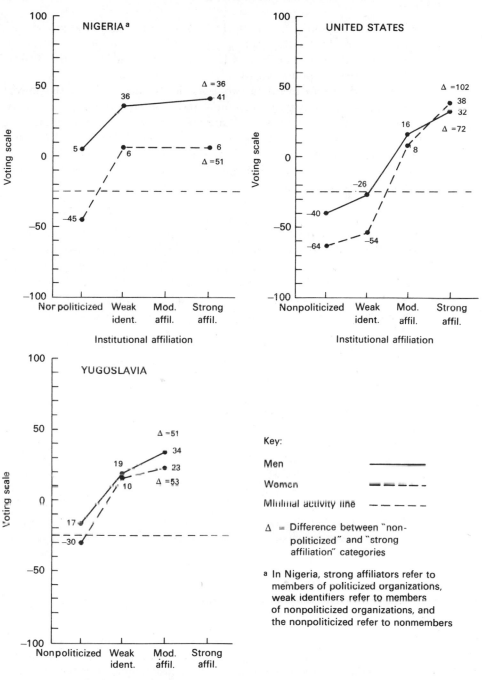

Figure 12–4. Voting activity by institutional affiliation for men and women.

quite diverse nations – and data that, with the partial exception of the United States, reveal the same patterns of sex difference – offers a unique opportunity to probe a little deeper for the source of the differences between the political activities of men and women.

We would like to examine two possible explanations for the lower level of political activity among men and women. One explanation is based on apathy: Women do not care about political matters and, therefore, *abstain* from politics. They concede to men the right to dominate political life. Another explanation is that women are *inhibited* from taking part in political life. Even though they are concerned about political matters, they are not offered the opportunity to take part in politics. The inhibition can be external or internal. Women may be externally restrained from taking part in political life by formal or informal rules barring them from channels of political access or from political organizations. Or they may be externally restrained by social norms against female political activity. Women, however, may accept the social norms against female participation. In such a case the inhibition to political activity derives from self-restraint. We cannot with our data distinguish between lack of participation based on external constraint and lack of participation based on self-restraint. We consider both to be forms of inhibition and different from apathetic abstention. In the case of apathy, women are unconcerned about politics. In the case of inhibition, they care but are held back by rules or norms or lack of opportunity. Apathy and inhibition, though different, can operate at the same time and may jointly explain the male–female differences.

We can test the apathetic-abstention and the inhibition explanation by comparing the level of activity in political life found among women and their level of psychological involvement in political matters. The relation between the extent to which women are psychologically involved in politics – are concerned and informed about politics, attentive to communications about politics – and the extent to which they are politically active ought to help us distinguish between the two alternative explanations of lower activity rates among women. We can think of several tests of the alternative apathetic-abstention and inhibition hypotheses.

1 If women are inhibited from taking part in politics, whereas men are not, one should find a greater disjunction between men and women when it comes to political activity than when it comes to psychological involvement: Women should be less different from men in terms of involvement than in terms of activity.

2 Further evidence would exist that activity is being inhibited if women become more involved psychologically with political matters, as their educational level moves up or their institutional affiliation becomes stronger, but there is less commensurate growth in activity.

3 Lastly, evidence for inhibition on the political activity of women would exist if the relationship between political involvement and political

activity is lower for women than for men. This would indicate that men could convert their psychological involvement in politics into activity more easily than women.

We shall explicate each of these tests more fully in a moment. But it should be noted what the tests mean. To find that women are as involved in politics as men but less active is to suggest that their lower activity rate is not the result of apathy toward political life. This supports the inhibition hypothesis. But inhibition does not, as we have pointed out, necessarily mean external constraints barring women from political life. Inhibition may also derive from women accepting the norm that they ought not to take part in political activity. The fact that women are involved but feel constrained not to act leads to the same end result – exclusion.[5]

If, on the other hand, one finds that women are both inactive and uninvolved, the data would support the apathetic-abstention hypothesis. But one must see what is meant by apathy in this context. Women are not excluded. There is no need to exclude them, since they are not concerned about political matters. The lack of concern, however, may be the result of constraints – social norms as to what it is that women ought to be concerned about or social pressures that stifle expressed political concern. In short, our test of the abstention-versus-inhibition hypotheses is of those hypotheses within a narrow framework. The inhibition hypothesis will be supported if we find women to be involved psychologically but not active, even if the disjunction between involvement and activity is due to a social norm against political activity *accepted by women*. The abstention hypothesis will be supported if women are both inactive and uninvolved at the time of the interview – even if low involvement and activity are the result of some more general social exclusion.

Test 1: male/female differences in political activity compared with male/female differences in psychological involvement in politics.

Our first test of the abstention-versus-inhibition hypothesis is simple and somewhat crude. We ask whether women differ from men more in political activity than in psychological involvement in politics. If women abstain from political life, they ought to be less active than men *and* less concerned. If they are inhibited, they ought to be less active but not less involved. The test is crude because it requires us to compare

---

[5] Withdrawal from politics was evidenced in our "segment" chapter by high psychological involvement coupled with low activity. It is in fact difficult with our data to distinguish between situations in which women attempt to be active but are barred and those in which they anticipate barriers and withdraw. But both of these can be distinguished from apathetic abstention.

levels of political activity with levels of political involvement and there is, of course, no standard metric that allows such comparisons. Yet it is suggestive, if not conclusive, to compare the differences found between men and women on our standardized scales of overall political activity and voting with the differences found between men and women on our standardized scales of political interest and overall psychological involvement in politics. The scales are standardized and calibrated in a comparable way, with a mean of 0 and a standard deviation of 100. Though absolute scores on the scales are not easily comparable, it is reasonable to compare the distance between men and women on the several scales.

The data are in Table 12–4. The data on overall political activity and voting activity repeat data with which we began this chapter. They show the greater distinction between the sexes on overall political activity than on voting. They provide a useful comparison with the more psychological measures in the third and fourth columns. Is the gap between men and women on psychological measures more like the wide gap found on our overall scale of political activity or more like the relatively narrower gap found in connection with the easier act of voting? It is clear from the table that the gap on our scale of political interest and on our scale of overall psychological involvement in politics is more closely comparable to the gap in overall political activity than to the gap in voting. The exception is the United States, where the gap on all the measures is relatively small.

The data are consistent with an abstention hypothesis. Compared with men, women are both inactive and uninvolved. The male/female differences in voting stand out from the others in the table. But voting, we

Table 12–4. *Male/female differences on activity scales and scales of political involvement*

| | Differences between men and women | | | |
| | Activity measures | | Involvement measures | |
Nation	Overall activity scale	Voting scale	Scale of political interest	Overall scale of political involvement
Austria	59	9	74	84
India	83	31	69	96
Japan	61	17	67	67
Netherlands	37	12	46	57
Nigeria	69	49	65	79
United States	17	12	9	17
Yugoslavia	68	19	71	80

have argued, is an easily mobilizable act and one that can be engaged in with little or no motivation or resources. That men and women are over half a standard deviation (and in some cases almost a full standard deviation) apart on the scales that measure overall political activity and psychological involvement in politics suggests that women's closer score to men on voting reflects *mobilized* voting and that women vote with relatively little concern for or involvement in politics.

Test 2: the conversion of resources into psychological involvement versus the conversion of resources into political activity

When it comes to activity, as we have seen, men "gain" more than women from their resources. (See Figures 12–1 and 12–2.) This is especially the case in relation to institutional resources. The gap in political activity between those with strong and those with weak institutional ties is greater among men than among women. Even when women are affiliated with political institutions, that affiliation has less of an impact on their political activity than does comparable affiliation for men.

What impact do individual or institutional resources have on the psychological concern for politics of men and women? If women are less active because of abstention rather than inhibition one would assume a similar pattern for psychological involvement as was found for political activity. As one moves up the educational scale (our measure of individual resources) or up the scale of institutional affiliation (our measure of institutional resources), one should find greater gains in both activity and psychological involvement for men. Increased resources should arouse less activity *and* less involvement among women. If women are inhibited from taking part in politics, one should find similar gains in political involvement for both sexes with increased resources, but less gain for women in activity.

Table 12–5 shows – separately for men and women – the "gains" in psychological involvement associated with higher levels of education and higher levels of institutional affiliation. The gain in political concern deriving from education is regression slope between the psychological involvement scale and the full educational scale. The gain in relation to institutional affiliation is the difference in the score on the psychological involvement scale between those high and low in institutional affiliation. The table also shows the difference between the gains for men and those for women associated with greater individual resources and greater institutional resources. A positive number for those "differences in gain" indicates that male scores on the political concern scale increase more than do female scores as one moves up in level of education or in level of institutional affiliation. Consider first the relationship between education and psychological involvement for men and women. For each

Table 12–5. *Conversion of individual and institutional resources into psychological concern with politics*

| Nation | Difference between political concern scores of highest and lowest *educated* groups for men and women | | | Difference between political concern scores of highest and lowest groups in terms of institutional affiliation, for men and women | | |
	Men	Women	Male/female difference in gain from education	Men	Women	Male/female difference in gain from institutional affiliation
Austria	+71	+75	−4	+71	+60	+11
India[a]	+163	+168	−5	+43	+52	−9
Japan	+101	+131	−30	+94	+82	+12
Netherlands	+79	+83	−4	+138	+99	+39
Nigeria	+103	+123	−20	+51	+77	−26
United States	+103	+100	+3	+50	+68	−18
Yugoslavia	+108	+108	0	+136	+121	+15

[a] Difference between the first and the third categories of institutional affiliation typology. Too few cases of women in top category.

of the sexes, increased education brings increased psychological involvement in politics; and the increases in psychological involvement are of a similar magnitude. In the two cases where there is some substantial difference in the gains for men and women, it is women who benefit more from increased education. In sum, women grow in their level of political involvement about as much as do men (sometimes more) as they move up the educational ladder.

The second section of Table 12–5 presents parallel data for institutional affiliation. Again for each of the sexes there is an increase in psychological involvement in politics as one moves from those with little institutional affiliation to those with strong affiliation. However, there is little clear pattern as to which sex gains the most from institutional affiliation. In four out of seven of the nations, men gain somewhat more. In the other three, women gain more.

The situation becomes clearer when we compare the gains in psychological involvement with the gains in activity associated with increased individual and institutional resources. This is done in Table 12–6. We repeat the difference-in-gain figures from the previous table and put in

Table 12-6. *Male/female differences in conversion rates of education or institutional affiliation into activity or involvement (male advantage over female)*

Nation	Male/female difference in gain from education		Male/female difference in gain from institutional affiliation	
	Overall activity	Psychological involvement	Overall activity	Psychological involvement
Austria	+9	−4	+54	+11
India	+86	−5	+27	−9
Japan	0	−30	+59	+12
Netherlands	+6	−4	+42	+39
Nigeria	−4	−20	+15	−26
United States	−21	+3	−15	−18
Yugoslavia	+19	0	+19	+15

comparable figures for the difference in gain in scores on the overall activity scale. The figures in the first two columns compare the difference-in-gain scores for activity and psychological involvement associated with increases in education; the second two columns compare the difference in gain associated with higher levels of institutional affiliation. (Again, negative numbers indicate that women gain more from resources than men, positive numbers that men gain more.)

Consider the first two columns, which show the effects of education. In four of the nations the level of political activity of men increases more than that of women as one moves up the educational ladder. In three nations women gain more. When it comes to psychological involvement, however, women do better than men: in five nations they gain more than men, and in two nations men gain more than women. The most dramatic contrast between activity and involvement is found in India. As education increases, the gain in activity is much greater for men than women. But women gain a bit more on the political involvement scale than men. Education as a resource appears to help men more than women when it comes to activity; it tends to help women more than men when it comes to psychological involvement in politics.

The data on the effects of education are consistent with an inhibition explanation of women's lower level of political activity. If men convert educational advancement into political activity more effectively than women, it does not seem to be because women remain uninvolved with politics as they move up the educational ladder. Their involvement increases at least as much as that of men (in some cases, more). If they do not then become politically active, it is likely the result of some inhibition rather than apathy.

The data in the third and fourth columns of Table 12–6 show the gains associated with increased institutional affiliation. They are also consistent with an inhibition explanation. When it comes to scores on the political activity scale, men benefit more than women from institutional affiliation in six out of seven of the nations, and the greater gain by men is substantial in many of the cases. When it comes to psychological involvement in politics, the advantages to males are by no means clear. In three out of seven cases, women gain more on the political involvement scale than men; and in the other four nations where men gain more, the differential gain is smaller than the differential gain in political activity. Consider the data for Austria and Japan. Institutional affiliation boosts males over 50 points more than it boosts women on the political activity scale. The differential boost that males get on the psychological involvement scale is one-fifth as great as their differential boost in activity.

When we considered the data on political activity, we concluded that the lower conversion rates of individual and institutional resources into political activity for women suggested internal or external inhibitions on their activity. Even as women gain in resources, they do not gain a commensurate amount of activity. The contrast with the data on political involvement reinforces that interpretation. As women move up in education or as they move into closer affiliation with political institutions, their gain in resources is converted into increases in their interest and psychological involvement in politics as much as men's gain in the resources is converted into involvement – and in many instances, more. Women appear to increase their *inclination* to engage in politics as efficiently as men, but they do not gain as much in terms of opportunity to act upon that inclination.

Test 3: the conversion of psychological involvement into activity

The data comparing political activity and political involvement are inconclusive when it comes to the choice between an inhibition and an abstention explanation of women's lower level of political activity. Our first test revealed that women differ from men in political involvement about as much as they differ from men in political activity, thereby supporting the abstention explanation. Our second test revealed that women do not differ from men in terms of their conversion of resources into political involvement, whereas they do differ in the conversion of resources into political activity. This supports the inhibition explanation. Let us try one more test more directly connected to the question at hand. Women, we have seen, are less involved and less active than men.

Table 12–7. *Relationship of psychological involvement and overall activity: men and women*

Nation	Involvement/ activity relationship[a]		Involvement/ activity relationship, controlling for education and institutional affiliation[a]	
	Men	Women	Men	Women
Austria	.48	.30	.39	.27
India	.64	.14	.52	.13
Japan	.51	.24	.44	.21
Netherlands	.55	.35	.46	.28
Nigeria	.32	.28	.34	.25
United States	.51	.53	.46	.42
Yugoslavia	.62	.45	.48	.33

[a] Unstandardized regression slopes (B's).

As they acquire more education or become affiliated with institutions, their involvement in politics goes up as much as does political involvement among men. But their activity does not increase at the male rate. This suggests that women become politically involved but that involvement does not lead to activity – a result consistent with the inhibition hypothesis. Let us examine this more directly. If the inhibition hypothesis holds, the relationship between political concern and political activity should be larger for men than for women. If women were totally excluded from politics – if there were, for instance, laws against female participation or strong and generally accepted social norms against it – women would be inactive no matter how much they cared about political matters. There would be no relationship between psychological involvement and activity for women, a positive one for men. Table 12–7 shows the regression slopes (B's) between the scale of psychological involvement in politics and the scale of overall political activity for men and for women.[6] The slopes are positive for both men and women. More important, however, in each of the nations (with the exception of the

[6] Note that although we have standarized our scales within each nation, we do not restandardize again; we use unstandardized regression coefficients in order to maintain maximum comparability. See for further discussion of the use of standardized coefficients, Blalock, 1964; Schoenberg, 1972; Kim and Mueller, 1976.

United States) the slopes are steeper for men than for women – often substantially so. The data are clearly consistent with an inhibition hypothesis. It is not that there is complete exclusion; as women become more concerned about politics, their activity goes up. But the fact that male activity varies more closely with involvement indicates that women are in some ways inhibited from taking part in political activity, even when they become politically involved.

In the last two columns of Table 12–7 we present the involvement/activity slopes controlling for education and institutional affiliation. Even after one controls for our measures of individual and institutional resources, one finds that the difference in slopes between men and women remain. Again, the United States is the exception. In the United States the conversion rate of women resembles that of men; for each of the sexes activity rises a similar amount with psychological involvement. In the other nations, women are less likely to convert involvement into activity. The data are consistent with an inhibition hypothesis.

Of the three tests of the rival abstention and inhibition hypotheses, the first one supports the abstension hypothesis, the last supports the inhibition hypothesis, whereas the second supports both. In the first place, although women cannot convert resources into political activity as well as men, they can convert such resources into political involvement about as effectively as men. Secondly, they cannot convert that political involvement into activity as effectively as do men. The first test of the rival hypotheses appears to support the abstention interpretation: Women differ from men as much in terms of political involvement as they do in terms of activity. The first test, however, cannot be taken without qualifications; the low level of psychological involvement with politics among women is, in part, the result of their low level of resources. The apathy hypothesis is supported by some of the data in the second test. The second test shows us that women convert resources into psychological involvement as well as do men; this fact supports the inhibition hypothesis. But at any level of resources, women remain less involved than men. (See footnote 6.) This supports the apathy explanation. The third test, when examined in the light of the second test, clearly indicates that both mechanisms are at work. Women are less involved psychologically than men and remain less involved even when we consider those with similar resource levels. This suggests apathy. On the other hand, they convert additional resources into psychological involvement as well as men, while not converting resources and involvement into political activity. This suggests inhibition. In sum, it appears that increases in individual or institutional resources increase psychological involvement among women more than they do among men. But women start from such a low level of involvement that they never catch up to the male level of political concern.

Granted that both processes are operating, we would like to explore more fully the nature of the inhibition to political activity.

Is it that women are barred from gaining access? Or is it that despite their psychological involvement, they consider politics to be a male activity? One likely explanation of women not becoming as politically active as men, even when they obtain the educational or institutional resources to do so, is that they consider politics to be outside the proper role of women. One would expect this in turn to be part of a more general view about sex roles: According to this view, women belong in the home rather than in the "masculine" world of politics. This suggests taking a closer look at those women who have broken out of the environment of the home and into those areas of activity usually reserved for men. One such group of women are those who are working. Do women who have entered the workplace also enter the political arena? Research in the United States indicates this to be the case (Andersen, 1975).

The most interesting group to compare with men are the educated women who have entered the workplace. For one thing, they have the cognitive resources to "catch up" to male political activity. Furthermore, for educated women, work implies a more positive and voluntary decision to enter the "male" world of employment. Work for lower-status women is often more of an economic necessity than a break with tradition, this being especially the case for those in the agricultural sector.

In Table 12–8 we present the scores on our overall political activity and our overall political involvement scales for those women who are in

Table 12–8. *Political activity and involvement scores for men, women, educated workingwomen*

	Scores on overall activity scale			Scores on overall involvement scale		
Nation[a]	All men	All women	Educated working-women	All men	All women	Educated working-women
Austria	31	−28	−27	44	−40	13
Japan	31	−30	−16	34	−33	26
Netherlands	17	−20	−10	26	−31	23
United States	9	−8	26	9	−28	36
Yugoslavia	33	−35	13	38	−42	35

[a] There were not enough cases of educated workingwomen in Nigeria and India.

our top educational category and who are also working. (We cannot do this for India and Nigeria, where there are too few cases of educated workingwomen.) For purposes of comparison we present similar scores for all women and for all men. As one can see from the activity scores, educated workingwomen are more active than women in general, in most cases substantially so. The one exception is Austria, where there is little difference between women in general and educated working-women. On the other hand, the data also make clear that women who are educated and have entered the workplace do not "catch up" to men in political activity level. In each of the nations, with the exception of the United States, the average score on the political activity scale for educated workingwomen is below the score for all males (and, of course, even farther below the scores for educated workingmen). Only in the United States and Yugoslavia does the score on the activity scale for educated workingwomen go above the mean for the population as a whole. And even in Yugoslavia educated workingwomen are still below the average male score. In sum, even those educated women who enter the workplace do not catch up with the political activity rate of the average male.

The data on psychological involvement form an interesting and useful contrast. Educated workingwomen score well above the population mean on the psychological involvement scale. Indeed, education coupled with employment tends to eliminate the gap between men and women. Educated workingwomen score as well on the political involvement scale as do average men. In Japan, the Netherlands, and Yugoslavia the scores for educated workingwomen on the political involvement scale are only slightly below those of men; in the United States they score above men in political involvement. Only in Austria does a gap remain between men and educated workingwomen. But even in the latter country one finds a substantial contrast between the data for political activity and for political concern. In sum, although increased education and employment status for women do not decrease the male–female gap when it comes to activity, they substantially reduce that gap when it comes to political involvement.[7]

The data illustrate how difficult it is to close the participatory gap between men and women. Even when women achieve education and enter the workplace, they remain less politically active than men. This is not, however, the result of an absence of political concern. Those

[7] Note, however, that educated workingwomen come to score as high as men on the involvement scale but not as high as educated, workingmen. Education and employment bring women up to the average male level, not to the level of males with similar social characteristics. This is evidence for the apathy hypothesis. Women still remain below men of similar status even when they attain education and jobs.

women who have educational resources and have entered the workplace are as psychologically involved in political matters as are men. The data suggest a rather specific inhibition associated with political life. Even when women break from the home to enter the male world of the economy, they are nevertheless inhibited from entering as fully into the political realm.

This interpretation is supported by the data in Table 12–9, where we present the regression slopes between scores on the scale of political involvement and the overall political activity scale for educated working-women. As we saw in Table 12–7, the political involvement/political activity relationships were lower for women than for men in all of the nations but the United States. This appeared to be evidence for some form of inhibition on female political activity. As Table 12–9 shows, this difference between men and women persists even when we consider only educated workingwomen. In Japan, Yugoslavia, and the United States, educated workingwomen have steeper involvement/activity slopes than do women in general, but only in the United States does this relationship come up to the level found for men. In the United States, educated workingwomen "convert" their political involvement into activity better than do men. Elsewhere, a male/female gap remains even when men in general are compared with the special group of women who are both educated and working.

A note on generational differences

The male/female gap in political participation is in all likelihood a reflection of some more general traditional attitudes toward the role

Table 12–9. *Conversion rate of psychological involvement to overall activity: all men, all women, and educated workingwomen (unstandardized regression slopes)*

Nation[a]	All men	All women	Educated working-women
Austria	.48	.30	.28
Japan	.51	.24	.34
Netherlands	.55	.35	.34
United States	.51	.53	.60
Yugoslavia	.62	.45	.50

[a] There were not sufficient cases of educated workingwomen in Nigeria and India.

Table 12–10. *Activity and involvement "gaps" between young men and young women and between older men and older women*

Nation	Political activity		Political involvement	
	Male/female difference for those under 30	Male/female difference for those over 30	Male/female difference for those under 30	Male/female difference for those over 30
Austria	39	64	62	90
India	83	84	102	94
Japan	26	69	39	75
Netherlands	33	38	56	57
Nigeria	58	83	85	88
United States	26	14	28	13
Yugoslavia	37	73	61	85

of women in society. If this is the case, one would expect a diminution of the gap between younger men and women. The relation between age and political activity is, however, quite complex. Younger people are usually less politically active than those in their middle years, and this applies to men as well as women (Nie, Verba, and Kim, 1974). The main explanation of this is a life-cycle one. Young people are less well settled into communities and are more concerned with establishing careers and families. Life-cycle effects, however, may not operate equally for men and women, making a comparison of young men and young women complex if one is seeking for generational effects. The data in Table 12–10 should, therefore, be considered only suggestive. When we compare the participation gap between young men and young women with the gap found between older men and women, we find some evidence that the gap is smaller in the younger age group. This is the case in Austria, Japan, Nigeria, and Yugoslavia. In the Netherlands and India the gap is similar at both age levels, whereas in the United States the gap is somewhat larger at the younger age level. The data on the gap in relation to political concern are similar to those for political activity, with the exception of Nigeria, where the male/female difference is the same at each age level whereas it is smaller in relation to activity in the younger group.

Conclusion

In sum, our data present a persistent pattern of male/female differences in political activity. These differences are only partially explained by differences in the resources that each of the sexes has available to it. Nor is the male/female participation gap explained by female indifference to politics. It is true that women are, on the average, less psychologically involved than men, but that difference is reduced when women are educated and are affiliated with institutions. Among those women who are both educated and employed, the sex gap in psychological involvement in politics is minimal. The concern for politics among women, however, is not converted into political activity. These findings strongly suggest the existence of pervasive inhibiting factors that limit the political role of women. The major exception is found in the United States. Although there is a male/female participation gap in that nation as well as in the others, that gap is strikingly narrow. In the United States, in contrast to the other nations, psychologically involved women convert that involvement into political activity as effectively as do psychologically involved men. For the kind of political activity with which we are dealing, there appears to be little or no exclusion of women in the United States.[8]

The data are ambiguous on the question of the extent to which one might expect some diminution of sex differences in the future. The age differences suggest such a change, but they are difficult to interpret, combining as they do life-cycle and generational effects. The data on education, institutional affiliation, and entrance into the work force indicate that women, as is the case with men, are likely to be more active as they gain education, join organizations, and enter the labor force. Yet even when they match males in this respect, significant differences remain between the sexes in political activity.

The persistence of a sex-based gap in political activity even when one takes into account the various characteristics that foster participation is seen in Table 12–11. This table can serve as a general summary of our data. We present the male–female difference in score on the overall participation scale that remains after we "correct" the scores for the main social and psychological characteristics associated with activity– for level of education (as a surrogate for socioeconomic resources), for the level of institutional affiliation, and for the level of psychological involvement in politics.[9] In other words, the adjusted figures tell us how much

[8] This does not apply to activities higher up on the scale of political participation – the holding of political office, for instance. There do appear to be strong inhibitions against female political activity in the United States once one moves beyond the level of citizen activity with which we are dealing here (Kirkpatrick, 1974, and Gruberg, 1968).

[9] The correction or adjustment was made using regression with dummy variables. Although such techniques do not take into account the interactions among the predictor variables that we have demonstrated, they offer a good approximation to the average difference between male and female and therefore are suitable for the limited purposes at hand.

Table 12–11. *The activity "gap" between men and women, "corrected" for individual and institutional resources and involvement in politics*

Nation	Overall activity		Voting	
	Uncorrected difference	Corrected difference	Uncorrected difference	Corrected difference
Austria	+59	+21	+9	−2
India	+83	+30	+31	+10
Japan	+61	+35	+17	+2
Netherlands	+37	+7	+12	−7
Nigeria	+69	+43	+49	+35
United States	+17	+9	+12	+6
Yugoslavia	+68	+19	+19	−7

residual difference in political activity remains after we take into account the differences in individual and institutional resources between men and women as well as differences in their psychological involvement in politics. In each nation the adjusted differences are substantially less than the raw differences (the latter are repeated in Table 12–11 from Table 12–1). Much of the participation gap between men and women is explained by the characteristics that go into our model. But in each nation a gap remains, and a rather substantial gap at that (with the exception of the United States and the Netherlands). The data indicate that being female – even if one has the same educational level, as much affiliation with political institutions, and as much concern about political matters – implies a lower rate of political activity.

Table 12–11 also contains parallel data on voting. When it comes to voting, the sex-based participation gap does appear to be bridged when one corrects for our various predictor variables. Only in Nigeria does a gap remain. Otherwise, women having similar circumstances educationally and institutionally, and having similar levels of political concern, turn out at the polls as regularly as men. To repeat a theme we have often stressed, this illustrates the strengths and weaknesses of voting as a political act. It is an easy act and an easily mobilized act. This is one reason why we find less sex difference. The vote is the great equalizing political act. At the same time, the very characteristics that make voting turnout relatively equal across groups may make the vote a less significant political act, representing as it does the political behavior of many individuals *mobilized* to political activity.

13

The community context of participation

The seven nations studied in this volume are, as we have often stressed, a very heterogeneous set. The variation among the nations is paralleled by variation within each nation. We have dealt with such internal variation in our comparison across socioeconomic levels, across segments of each society, and between men and women. In each case, though, the nation itself – or the parts of the nation from which we sampled – has been considered the political or territorial unit within which the processes of political mobilization take place. The seven nations are, however, not single, undifferentiated political units. Within each nation there is regional variation as well as variation between urban and rural areas. We shall not deal with regional variation in this book. The omission is, we believe, serious but necessary if we are to handle the complex set of data generated by seven different nations. Analyses of data within individual regions of those nations having the greatest regional heterogeneity – India, Nigeria, and Yugoslavia – indicate that, in general, the pattern of relationships we find for each nation as a whole holds within each region. Fuller consideration of regional differences, however, will have to be conducted elsewhere.[1]

We shall, in this chapter, deal with another territorial division within the various societies, a division that can be dealt with more systematically in a volume of this kind – the comparison of urban with rural communities. The comparison will allow us to examine the relationship between community characteristics and political participation, and also allow us further to test our general model of the way in which individual and institutional forces interact.

In a previous work on participation in the United States (Verba and Nie, 1972, chap. 13) we contrasted two models of the relationship between community characteristics and political activity. One we called the mobilization model, the other the decline-of-community model. The

---

[1] Regional variation is dealt with in some of the individual nation studies based on these data. For India, see Bhatt (1975); for Nigeria, see Igbozurike (1976), and Himmelstrand, Imohiosen, and Igbozurike (forthcoming); for Yugoslavia, see Barbic et al. (1973), Barbic (1975), Verba and Shabad (1975), and Shabad (1976).

former predicts more political activity in urban centers than in smaller, more rural communities; the latter predicts the opposite. We were puzzled by the existence of these two models side by side, but even more so by the fact that there were empirical studies supporting each of the positions. (The term "mobilization" is used here as in much of the literature on political development to refer to a general process by which individuals become involved and active in the larger society rather than in the narrow worlds of village or family. The use of the term differs from our use elsewhere when we refer to "mobilized segments.")

The mobilization model

This model predicts more political activity in urban than in rural settings. The following quotation summarizes the argument well.

> Persons close to the center occupy an environmental position which naturally links them into the communications network involved in policy decisions for the society. They receive from and send more communications to other persons near the center. They have a higher rate of social interaction, and they are more active in groups than persons on the periphery. This central position increases the likelihood that they will develop personality traits, beliefs and attitudes which facilitate participation in politics. There are many more political stimuli in their environment, and this increases the number of opportunities for them to participate. . .
>
> One of the most thoroughly substantiated propositions in all of social science is that *persons near the center of the society are more likely to participate in politics than persons near the periphery.* . . Persons near the center receive more stimuli enticing them to participate, and they receive more support from their peers when they do participate. [Milbrath, 1965, pp. 113–114.]

Twenty-eight studies are cited by Milbrath to support this point.[2]

The decline-of-community model

In *Participation in America,* we summarized the alternative model as follows:

> This alternative model predicts the decline of participation as one moves from the smallness and intimacy of town or village to the massive impersonality of the city. In the small town, the community is a manageable size. Citizens can know the ropes of politics, know

---

[2] The mobilization model is largely associated with the work of scholars interested in modernization and political development. See Karl Deutsch's now classic article (1961). A major statement of the theme is in Lerner (1958).

whom to contact, know each other so that they can form political groups. In the larger units, politics is more complicated, impersonal, and distant. In addition, "modernization" shatters political units. What were once relatively independent communities – providing the individual with the social, economic, political, and cultural services that he needs – become small towns in a mass society. Such communities no longer have clear economic borders as citizens begin to commute to work. They have more permeable social boundaries as recreational and educational facilities move out of the community, and they cease to be well-bounded political units as local services become more dependent on outside governmental authorities.

All these changes, according to the decline-of-community model, should reduce the level of participation within the community. For one thing, the government of the local community loses its importance. Local participation becomes less and less meaningful. Furthermore, the attention of individuals becomes more diffuse. They no longer concentrate upon their local community. Rather, they are exposed to a wider political realm where meaningful participation is much more difficult because of its larger size and greater complexity. [Verba and Nie, 1972, p. 231][3]

Just as there are studies supporting the mobilization model, there are a number that find more activity (in particular, higher voting turnout) in smaller communities (Charlot and Charlot, 1961; Faul, 1960; Lancelot, 1968; Kesselman, 1966; Tarrow, 1971; Burnham, 1965; Richardson, 1973), as well as studies that find little difference between the two types (Nie, Powell, and Prewitt, 1969; Neubauer, 1967; McCrone and Cnudde, 1967; and Goel, 1975). Dahl and Tufte (1973), in the most comprehensive analysis of the relationship between size and democracy, summarize the literature on the relationship between community size and voting as follows: "Within countries, among local units of the same legal type, there is no general relationship between turnout and unit size. Thus in some democratic systems, election turnouts are somewhat higher in smaller than in larger municipalities. In others, it is the reverse. In still others, there appears to be no relationship between size and turnout" (p. 61). They analyze a Swedish study that finds more political discussion and interest in relatively small communities, but lament the absence of data on activities other than the voting turnout. We shall, in this chapter, present data on various activities. The data will also make clear, we hope, why there are such contradictory findings especially in relation to voting.

---

[3] The argument is found in various places, particularly in many contemporary works that call for greater decentralization. One of the strongest advocates of this position was Cole (1921 and 1920). For an excellent statement on the relationship of size to participation, see Dahl (1967).

There are, we argued in our earlier work, three reasons for the two distinct models and the somewhat contradictory findings. The first reason lies in the inadequacy of the indicators often used to distinguish communities from one another. Sheer size of community can place in the same category small isolated towns and small suburbs of large cities. These differ in the stimulation to political activity they offer. If one distinguishes urban places from rural ones or the big city from the small town, one must be careful to take into account the degree to which the small political unit is isolated from the stimuli of the big city. In our work on participation in the United States we developed a complex measure that combined the size of a community with its degree of isolation from major urban centers as well as its degree of "boundedness" – how autonomous the community was in terms of economic life, communications, and political decision making. In this volume, we shall use a much simpler measure of community type – a rural/urban dichotomy. The measure divides the population into those living in or close to relatively large urban centers and those living in smaller communities somewhat separated from major urban centers. The distinction, though cruder than the measure used in *Participation in America*, captures the major distinction we want to make. By dichotomizing in terms of size as well as distance from a large city, we capture the basic dimensions of size and isolation and avoid the problem of categorizing the small suburb of the metropolis into the rural area or small-town category. Because of variations in the data gathered, the cutting point between urban and rural differs somewhat from nation to nation. Since we are interested in the direction of relationships, this should pose little problem. Table 13–1 gives the proportions of the population in each nation falling into each category. The differences across the nations reflect both the differing degrees of urbanization as well as the differing cutting points.

Table 13–1. *Proportion of sample in rural and urban areas*

Nation	Rural (%)	Urban (%)
Austria	53	47
India	82	18
Japan	30	70
Netherlands	21	79
Nigeria	76	24
United States	22	78
Yugoslavia	40	60

Table 13–2. *Mean socioeconomic resource level in rural and urban areas*

Nation	Mean SERL score	
	Rural	Urban
Austria	−35	40
India	−21	95
Japan	−27	12
Netherlands	−24	6
Nigeria	−21	68
United States	−23	7
Yugoslavia	−19	13

The second reason for the conflicting nature of the findings as to the relationship between community size and political activity lies in the failure to distinguish individual from environmental forces. Small towns and big cities are different sociopolitical environments; they are also inhabited by different kinds of people. In particular, urban areas are more likely to have a higher proportion of residents from the upper reaches of our scale of socioeconomic resources. (See Table 13–2, which compares the mean SERL level in rural and urban areas.) Such resources, as we have shown, facilitate participation by individuals. There is no reason to believe that such resources are any more or less effective in one type of community than another. In order to isolate the effect on participation of the sociopolitical environment provided by the community, we must separate out the effects of the socioeconomic characteristics of the individuals living in the communities. We shall do this in the following analysis by "correcting" the participation rates in rural and urban areas for the socioeconomic resource level of the inhabitants.[4]

A third reason for the ambiguity of analyses of urban/rural participation differences lies in the failure to distinguish among modes of political activity. As we have shown, an overall measure of participation often masks some sharp differences among the political acts. Because the two alternative models usually do not distinguish one mode of participation from another, they do not provide clear predictions about the different modes. One expectation is clear, however: If the decline-of-community model holds, it should hold most strongly for communal activity. This mode of participation, unlike activity in the electoral proc-

[4] The corrected or participation scores reported in Figures 13–1 through 13–4 are obtained by adjusting for differences in the SERL levels through regression in which both the dummy variable representing the rural-urban dichotomy and the SERL variable are included as independent variables.

ess, requires informal cooperation among citizens (or, at least, that is one important way citizens engage in communal activity), something that should be easier in the smaller and more well defined communities farther from urban areas. Furthermore, even those acts that fall in the communal mode but do not require cooperation among citizens – individual contacting a local official on some community problem – ought to be easier in smaller communities, where local officials are likely to be more accessible. In sum, communal activity ought to be the mode of activity most susceptible to influence from community characteristics. If the decline-of-community model holds, communal activity ought to be higher in rural than in urban areas, particularly after one has corrected for the socioeconomic characteristics of the individuals living in such communities.

It is less clear how the type of community ought to relate to voting or campaign activity or psychological involvement in politics. Our analysis of the relation of individual and institutional forces to political activity and involvement can, however, help us develop some expectations. Psychological involvement, we have argued, depends heavily on individual socioeconomic resources and is less susceptible to institutional constraints from parties or organizations. The mobilization and the decline-of-community models differ in what they would predict for psychological involvement. The mobilization model predicts more involvement in urban than rural areas, even after the effects of individual socioeconomic position have been controlled. The kinds of stimulation provided in urban areas should, according to the mobilization model, result in increased political activity. Such stimulation should affect involvement as well. The decline-of-community model has less to say about psychological involvement. The major factors dealt with in the decline-of-community model – the difficulty of cooperation, the difficulty of access, and so forth – make *activity* difficult. They have a less clear connection to involvement. Therefore, the decline-of-community model predicts that involvement would be little affected by community type and more the result of individual socioeconomic characteristics. If the decline-of-community model holds, we would expect higher levels of psychological involvement in urban than in rural areas because of the difference between the two types of place in the individual socioeconomic characteristics of the inhabitants. If we correct for these characteristics, however, we should find little difference between the two types of place. If the mobilization model holds, we should find greater involvement in urban than in rural areas even after we correct for socioeconomic level.

Voting and campaign activity are, as we have seen, jointly affected by individual socioeconomic resources and by institutional constraints. This provides no cross-national prediction of the effect of community type. Whether participation is higher in rural than in urban areas would depend on where political institutions are most effective in mobilizing campaign activity and voting. As we have seen, political parties appear particularly effective in mobilizing a rural population in several of the nations. If this is the case, rural activity ought to exceed urban activity, not because of the nature of the community but because of the effectiveness of the organizational infrastructure in rural areas.

In sum, our expectations from the two models are clear and opposite in relation to communal activity and psychological involvement. If the decline-of-community model holds, we expect communal activity to be affected by community characteristics. When we correct for individual socioeconomic level, we expect to find more communal activity in rural than in urban areas. If the mobilization model holds, communal activity should be higher in urban areas. The decline-of-community model predicts that psychological involvement ought to respond to individual forces rather than community ones. It should be high in urban areas, but once we correct for individual characteristics, the urban/rural difference ought to diminish. The mobilization model predicts a community effect on involvement. It should be higher in urban areas. As for voting and campaign activity, the two models offer less guidance. These acts ought to be contingent on the institutional structures in each nation and less contingent on the nature of the community.

In *Participation in America* we concluded that the decline-of-community model – which predicts higher communal activity in smaller places than in big cities – appeared consistent with the data. That was, however, a test of the model in only one nation. If a similar pattern appears in our seven very different nations, we shall have a powerful confirmation of that previous generalization.

Communal activity

Figure 13–1 presents data on the relationship between community size and communal activity for each of the seven nations. The solid line represents unadjusted scores, the dashed line scores adjusted for socioeconomic resource level. The data fit the decline-of-community model nicely. In five out of seven of the nations, there is a higher average level of communal activity in rural than in urban communities even before one has adjusted for socioeconomic level. In each of these cases the correction for the socioeconomic characteristics of the inhabitants increases the rural advantage in communal activity. In two of the nations, India and the Netherlands, there is almost no difference between rural and urban areas on the unadjusted data. When one adjusts for socioeconomic characteristics, however, a clear pattern of rural participatory advantage appears. Thus in all seven nations one finds communal activity more prevalent in smaller rural places than in urban

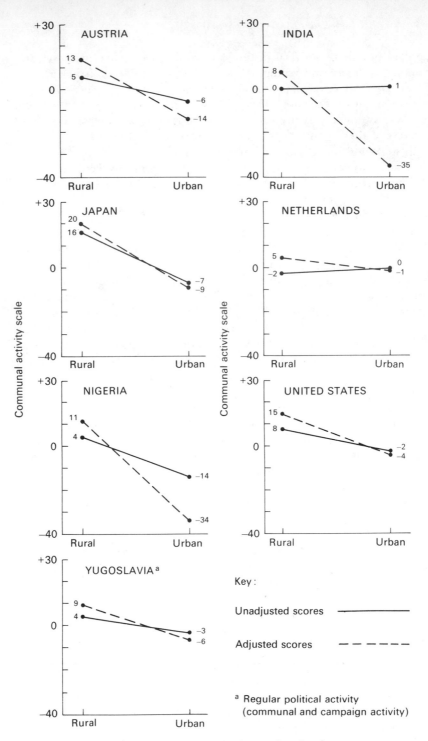

Figure 13–1. Communal activity in rural and urban areas.

places once one has adjusted for the resource level of the individuals living in such places.

It is interesting, furthermore, that the difference in amount of communal participation between rural and urban areas is greatest in those societies where the urban/rural division represents the sharpest distinction in terms of social environment. In the two less developed nations of our seven, India and Nigeria, urban environments are sharply different from rural ones. This is reflected in the sharp urban/rural distinction in average level on the SERL scale (Table 13–2). It is also reflected in the difference in the communal activity scores. The adjusted difference in the communal activity scores between the two types of community is close to half a standard deviation (43 and 45 points respectively). On the other hand, the rural/urban difference in communal activity is least in the Netherlands, a society in which distance between communities is small and in which a generally high population density might be expected to diminish the social significance of the urban/rural distinction.

Such a uniform finding across the seven nations is, we believe, powerful support for the argument that political activity – at least that kind of activity that involves dealing with the problems of the local community in cooperation with one's fellow citizens or as an individual in face-to-face contact with a government official – is fostered in small communities and becomes more difficult as the scale of community grows.

Psychological involvement in politics

Let us consider psychological involvement in politics. The alternative models provide clear and opposite expectations. The extent to which citizens are concerned about political matters is, we have argued, a function of their individual socioeconomic level. The decline-of-community model would predict that if there appears to be more involvement in urban areas, this should be largely a function of the higher average SERL level found in urban places. The mobilization model would predict more urban involvement even after a correction for the average SERL level. The urban citizen, whatever his or her social characteristics, would be expected to be exposed to many more stimuli – to the mass media, to different types of people, to a wider world – all of which should boost political involvement. Figure 13–2 presents the relationship between scores on the scale of psychological involvement and the rural/urban distinction. The data are quite uniform across the nations. When one considers the unadjusted data, one finds a clear difference between urban and rural places. There are higher psychological involvement scores in the former than in the latter. The differences are particularly striking in those nations where there is a sharp rural/urban

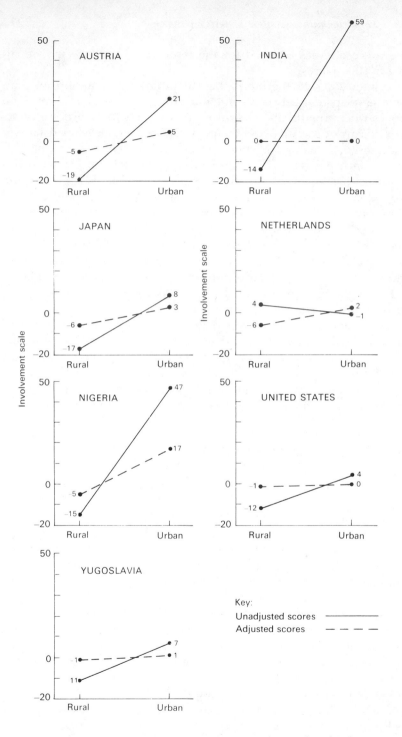

Figure 13–2. Psychological involvement in rural and urban areas.

gap in the average socioeconomic level of the inhabitants – India, Nigeria, and to a lesser extent Austria.

When, however, one adjusts for socioeconomic level, one finds the differences substantially diminished. In four nations – India, the Netherlands, the United States, and Yugoslavia – almost no difference between urban and rural areas remains once one has corrected for individual characteristics. The situation in India is particularly dramatic; the "correction" for individual socioeconomic level reduces the rural/urban gap in psychological involvement from a 73-point advantage for urban areas to no difference between the two types of community. The data on India qualify substantially the notion of the urban environment as a stimulating one. Whether one becomes interested and involved in politics depends most heavily on one's own socioeconomic resources, not on what the city in contrast to the village offers. The educated and affluent rural citizen is no less involved in politics than his urban counterpart; the poor, uneducated urban dweller is no more involved in politics than his rural counterpart.

In Nigeria and, to a lesser extent, Austria and Japan, an urban advantage in involvement remains after one has corrected for socioeconomic resource level. This difference, after adjustments are made for SERL, supports a mobilization interpretation. It may reflect the greater stimulation of the urban areas as one would expect from the mobilization model. However, even in these cases, the correction for socioeconomic level greatly diminishes the urban/rural difference. The data are, we believe, more consistent with our expectation that psychological involvement in politics is relatively independent of the nature of the community, as the decline-of-community model would predict. As we have previously seen, psychological involvement in politics is relatively little constrained by institutional forces. It is apparently also relatively little constrained by the sociopolitical environment.

In sum, the residual advantage in involvement that one finds in urban places in three of the nations would appear to lend support to the mobilization model – that is, that urban environments provide greater stimulation to political activity and involvement. We believe, however, that the data in Figure 13–2 are, in general, more compatible with a decline-of-community model. The decline-of-community model makes no prediction about the degree to which individuals will care about political matters. It deals with factors that would facilitate or inhibit political *activity* – the ease to access to officials, the ability to mobilize friends and neighbors. The mobilization model deals with factors that would have an impact both on activity and psychological involvement – the stimulating environment of the city, the exposure to the media, and so forth. The data in Figure 13–2, despite the support they give to the stimulating quality of the city in Nigeria, Austria, and Japan, appear to

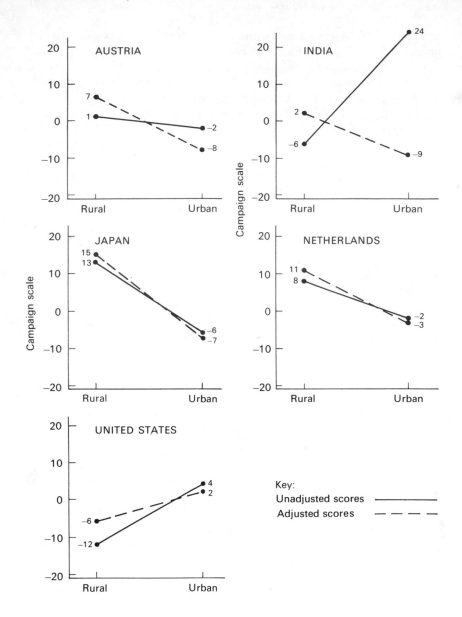

Figure 13–3. Campaign activity in rural and urban areas.

support an argument consistent with the decline-of-community model: Involvement is not a function of the nature of the community, but rather a function of the individual social and economic characteristics of the kinds of people who live there.

Campaign activity

Parallel data for campaign activity are contained in Figure 13–3. Again the data fit our expectations. The pattern varies across the nations in ways that are consistent with our earlier discussion of the role of political institutions in mobilizing certain social segments. Where political organizations have a strong mobilizing effect in the agrarian sector – as in Austria and Japan – or where, as in the Netherlands, mobilization on the basis of religion brings into politics a group that is disproportionately from smaller towns rather than major cities, campaign activity is higher in rural than in urban areas. This is seen in the uncorrected scores and is accentuated in the corrected scores. (See Figure 13–3.) In India as well, the greater potency of political parties in rural areas is seen in the rural advantage in campaign activity found in the corrected scores. There is in India more campaign activity in urban areas, but that is a function of the much higher socioeconomic level of urban residents. Once one has corrected for SERL, one finds more rural than urban activity. Only in the United States does one find an urban advantage in campaign activity, and an advantage that is diminished but not eliminated by a correction for individual socioeconomic resource level.

Voting

As we have indicated, studies of voting turnout and community size have produced conflicting results. Our data on voting also show a great deal of cross-national variation. (See Figure 13–4.) The variation, however, is fairly consistent with the institutional variations we have been discussing. In general, voting seems to be higher in rural areas, especially in cases where political organizations mobilize a rural segment. Only in Yugoslavia (and on the uncorrected data in Nigeria) do we find higher levels of urban than rural voting. The Yugoslavian data are consistent with the mobilizing role played by the League of Communists and the Socialist Alliance in relation to the vote, these two political institutions having a firmer base in the urban industrial sector of society than in the rural. Lastly, we can note that the correction for socioeconomic level makes relatively little difference in those nations where the SERL/voting relationship is low.

The data on campaign activity and voting suggest that these types of

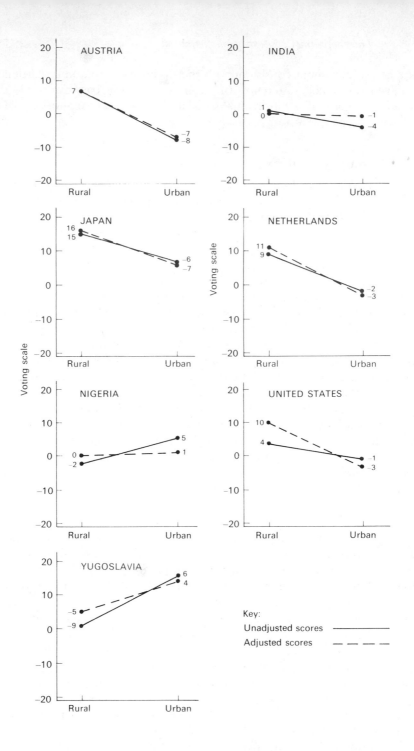

Figure 13–4. Voting activity in rural and urban areas.

activity are not affected in a systematic way by the nature of the community within which they take place. Rather, they depend on the particular configuration of political organizations in each nation. If a relation between the urban/rural distinction and political activity exists, it is a result of the fact that such institutional affiliation is greater in one area than in the other. We can test this interpretation more directly by carrying our correction procedure one step further. We can correct activity rates in rural and urban areas for both the socioeconomic level of the inhabitants and for the extent to which they are affiliated with political organizations. The corrected activity scores should show little difference between the two types of community once we have adjusted for differences in both individual and institutional forces.

Table 13–3 presents these data for campaign activity and voting.[5] We present the difference in campaign activity scores and voting scores between rural and urban areas first adjusting for SERL and second adjusting for both SERL and the extent of institutional affiliation.[6] The data offer some support for our position, though by no means conclusive support. When we consider campaign activity, we find that the urban/rural differences are diminished by the addition of a correction for institutional affiliation in each of the nations. But in only two nations – India and the Netherlands – is the reduction more than a trivial amount. When it comes to voting, one finds a noticeable reduction in the rural/urban difference in Austria and the Netherlands when institutional affiliation is controlled. In the other nations the addition of an institutional control has little effect on the rural/urban participation gap. The one exception is Nigeria, where adjusting for institutional affiliation creates an urban advantage in voting turnout. The data in Table 13–3 support our argument in several cases; in others they do not.

Conclusion

In general, our data support a decline-of-community interpretation of the impact of community size on political activity. This is most clearly seen in the data on communal activity. Such activity is uniformly

---

[5] We do not present data for communal activity and psychological involvement. As we have shown, these are less affected by institutional constraints. We have looked at these data and find that an additional control for institutional affiliation requires no change in the conclusions based on Figures 13–1 and 13–2.

[6] The uncorrected score is the simple regression slope for the urban/rural dichotomy; the first corrected score is the corresponding partial regression slope after the SERL variable is included in the regression; likewise, the final corrected difference is the partial regression slope after both SERL and the dummy variables representing the institutional affiliation are included in the regression equation.

Table 13–3. *Rural/urban difference in campaign and voting activity: adjusting for SERL and institutional affiliation*

Nation	Campaign activity		Voting activity	
	Urban/rural (adjusting for SERL)	Urban/rural (adjusting for SERL and institutional level)	Urban/rural (adjusting for SERL)	Urban/rural (adjusting for SERL and institutional level)
Austria	-15^a	-13	-13	-5
India	-11	-5	-1	0
Japan	-22	-20	-23	-22
Netherlands	-14	-2	-14	-5
Nigeria	—	—	1	9
United States	8	7	-13	-13
Yugoslavia	—	—	9	8

[a] A minus sign indicates that the rural participation rate is higher than the urban rate.

lower in urban than in rural places – especially when one takes into account the socioeconomic resource level of the inhabitants of the two types of places. The data on psychological involvement offer some support for the mobilization model (in the fact that political involvement is higher in urban areas in three nations even after one has corrected for individual socioeconomic level). But, we believe, they offer greater support for the decline-of-community model, a model more compatible than is the mobilization model with the main findings in relation to psychological involvement – that such involvement is largely a function of individual socioeconomic resources and less a function of the nature of the community.

Campaign activity and voting fit neither model of community effects very well. These activities appear to be more responsive to the particular configuration of political institutions in each nation. The data on this latter point are not as unambiguous as are the data on communal activity and psychological involvement. But the data seem clearly to point to the conclusion that activities within the electoral process are, compared with communal activity, less dependent on the nature of the community.

Those who expect a loss of participatory opportunities to accompany the decline of the small community will find support for that position in our data. Such support is especially convincing because of the uniformity of our results across a heterogeneous set of nations. Perhaps the loss of such opportunities can be compensated for by the creation of alternative small units within which participation can flourish – in neighborhoods, in the workplace. That is a subject beyond the scope of this book. Or perhaps the decline in participatory opportunities that accompanies urbanization will be compensated for by an increase in the average level of socioeconomic resources that individuals possess. We find some such compensation in the higher SERL scores in urban areas. This can, however, produce tensions. Urbanization appears to be accompanied by a higher level of socioeconomic resources and, as a result, a higher level of psychological involvement in politics. But the higher SERL and involvement in urban areas are accompanied by diminishing opportunities to participate. One would expect more and more urban dwellers who are "withdrawn" from political life – that is, who are interested and concerned but who, because of the lack of opportunities, are inactive.

14

Stratification and politics: some consequences

Our main concern in this book has been with the way in which individual characteristics interact with institutional and social ones to affect political behavior. In this chapter we shall consider some of the consequences of the different patterns of political mobilization that we have found. We began the book with our cross-cultural generalization about the relationship between socioeconomic resource level and political activity. In subsequent chapters we showed how that relationship was modified by institutions. Whereas some citizens were mobilized to a level of political activity beyond that which one would predict on the basis of individual resources, the participation of others was depressed. The extent to which institutions "interfere" with individual propensities to be politically active was, in turn, related to the patterns of social conflict in each society. As we showed in our analysis of the patterns of social segmentation, institutions most effectively change the shape of the relationship between individual socioeconomic resources and activity where there is "well-structured" conflict among social groups. The differential impact of individual socioeconomic resources and membership in a politically mobilized social segment creates variation across nations in who becomes an activist.

First let us summarize the consequences of the interaction between political institutions and individual resources as they are revealed in resultant political inequality among significant social groups. In Tables 14–1, 14–2, and 14–3 we present the relationships between participation and the three major social distinctions on which we have focused – socioeconomic resource level, sex, and social segment: Table 14–1 deals with campaign activity, Table 14–2 with communal activity, and Table 14–3 with voting. Each figure is a partial standardized regression coefficient (beta) between the independent variable and the measure of activity with the other two variables in the equation. It indicates the impact of each social characteristic, controlling for the others. (We also present the multiple r for the three variables.) The data offer a useful summary of the varied effects we have considered in this book – illustrating some cross-national uniformities (particularly in the differences among the modes of activity in that which correlates with them)

Table 14–1. *Inequality among social groups in campaign activity*

| | | | Social | |
Nation[a]	SERL	Sex	segment	Multiple r
Austria	.06[b]	.35	.16	.40
India	.29	.26	.09	.43
Japan	.05	.29	.21	.34
Netherlands	.12	.13	.14	.23
United States	.28	.05	.05	.30

[a] Campaign scale is not available for Nigeria and Yugoslavia.
[b] These are partial betas obtained from MCA analysis.

Table 14–2. *Inequality among social groups in communal activity*

| | | | Social | |
Nation	SERL	Sex	segment	Multiple r
Austria	.13[b]	.14	.09	.23
India	.30	.25	.15	.43
Japan	.12	.24	.18	.31
Netherlands	.29	.10	.07	.32
Nigeria	.20	.20	.19	.36
United States	.26	.07	.11	.30
Yugoslavia[a]	.10	.39	.13	.44

[a] "Regular" political activity.
[b] These are partial betas obtained from MCA analysis.

Table 14–3. *Inequality among social groups in voting*

| | | | Social | |
Nation	SERL	Sex	segment	Multiple r
Austria	.03[a]	.05	.13	.15
India	.05	.18	.15	.23
Japan	.00	.10	.12	.15
Netherlands	.08	.04	.25	.26
Nigeria	.02	.13	.39	.43
United States	.20	.06	.14	.27
Yugoslavia	.15	.08	.08	.23

[a] These are partial betas obtained from MCA analysis.

as well as some cross-national differences reflecting the different social processes we have been exploring.

Consider Table 14–1 on campaign activity. The data show the wide cross-national variation we have come to expect in relation to this act. In two nations, the United States and India, SERL plays a major role, but it has little impact elsewhere. Furthermore, where SERL has little impact, we see that membership in one of the social segments makes a greater difference in activity. This is clearest, in that respect, in Japan and Austria, which contrast sharply with the United States and India. In Japan and Austria the social group to which one belongs (and, as we have seen, the strength of the institutions associated with the group) plays a major role in determining who is active. In the Netherlands we see both individual SERL and segmental membership playing a role. In three of the nations sex makes a substantial difference in who becomes a campaign activist. It makes less difference in the Netherlands and almost none in the United States.

The data on communal activity are in Table 14–2. In terms of the SERL/activity relationship, there is more cross-national uniformity, with positive relations in each nation – though there is still quite a range across the nations. Sex plays a significant role in most places. Note in particular its importance in Yugoslavia (for which we report data on "regular" political activity). The social segment data present a mixed picture. Since communal activity is tied to the local community, segmental membership is likely to play a varying role from place to place.

Voting offers a contrast to the other modes of behavior. Socioeconomic resources play almost no role – with the exception of the United States and, to a lesser extent, Yugoslavia. The table highlights the distinctive character of voting in the United States – the fact that it is an act affected by the resources and motivation of the individual rather than by institutional affiliation. The reasons lie probably in the fact that voting in the United States is a difficult political act, compared with voting in many other nations. Registration is more difficult (even more so when we conducted our research). Elections are not held on weekends, and so on. Furthermore, it also reflects the weakness of institutions in relation to this particular act. Sex differences in relation to voting are relatively weak compared with sex differences on other acts. As indicated in Chapter 12, women are more likely to be mobilized to the easy act of voting than to other acts. And segmental differences are in almost all cases moderate. They are high in Nigeria, reflecting the regional segments we use.

The data in Tables 14–1, 14–2, and 14–3 illustrate the varying ways in which social groups come to be more active than others: In most nations men are more active than women (though the difference is slight in terms of voting turnout); in several nations the haves outparticipate the have-nots by a substantial amount; and in each nation particular social segments are more active than others. The complex processes by which individual and group-based forces interact to determine who becomes politically active produce a great deal of diversity among the nations. (See Kim, Nie, and Verba, 1974, for a slightly different conceptualization of political inequality.)

Does such a variation in the pattern and degree of inequality make much difference in terms of political consequences? The question is by no means easy to answer. We have better data on who becomes a political activist than we have on the impact of political activity on government decision makers. If differential rates of activity are to have an effect on what the government does – and in our instrumental view of participation, such differences are what would make participation important – several conditions would have to be met.

1 The groups that were active would have to deviate from the population as a whole in ways that were politically relevant. They would have to represent particular interests or particular preferences. (The only exception to this would be if one was dealing only with particularistic benefits. Then whoever participated would benefit even if they matched the population in social characteristics and in preferences.)

2 The government must pay some attention to the public. If leaders are totally autonomous in their decision making, it does not matter who is politically active.

We cannot in this volume look at the latter condition. We shall not attempt to measure the impact on governmental decision makers of the preferences of the populace.[1] But we can consider several aspects of the first question: the extent to which the activist population forms a distinct social group with distinct preferences. We can also consider the implications of the processes of political mobilization for the process of recruitment to political office – to see whether the patterns of "bias" in the activist population are replicated among those who are in political office.

Socioeconomic level and the recruitment of activists and leaders

The processes of political mobilization we have described in this book create participant populations that are more or less representative of the population at large. There is no single objective measure of the degree to which a participant population is representative. It all de-

---

[1] We attempted such linkage analysis in our work in the United States (Verba and Nie, 1972, chap. 17–19). The complexities of such multilevel analyses in a number of countries has prevented us from replicating that analysis in this volume.

pends upon the criterion of representativeness. As we have shown, political mobilization processes that lead to representativeness in terms of socioeconomic level result in unrepresentativeness in terms of social segments. To deal with the question of the representativeness of the activist population, we shall return to our focus on socioeconomic level. This means we shall not encompass all the possible differences between the populace at large and the activist populace. But we shall illustrate the consequences of the differing participatory process in terms of a major social distinction that is everywhere of political relevance.

As we pointed out in our earlier discussion of the modes of political participation, different kinds of political activity can be carried out by different people, with different effects. Our consideration of the differences in the process by which people come to vote and the process by which they are mobilized to more difficult political activities, such as campaigning and communal activity, makes clear that the resultant participant population will have different compositions if we consider the voters in contrast to, say, those who take a more advanced role in political campaigns. Each of the activist populations is important. In the following sections we shall compare the population as a whole with the population of voting activists and the population of campaign activists. In addition, we shall look at the population of "concerned" citizens: those who are psychologically involved in politics even if they are not necessarily active. A consideration of the latter group will let us see what the activist population would look like if psychological involvement in politics were freely converted into political activity.

Socioeconomic level and the activist population

If individual socioeconomic forces alone were operating, our analysis predicts that we would find a similar pattern in each nation: overrepresentation of the haves in the activist population and a concomitant underrepresentation of the have-nots. Institutional interference, as we have shown, may reduce that inequality somewhat (although at the price perhaps of introducing inequalities among other social groups). Let us begin by considering the extent to which the activists in each of the nations are representative of the various socioeconomic levels.

The data are presented in Figure 14–1. For each of the nations we present the socioeconomic composition of the population as a whole, the politically interested population, the voting population, and the campaign activist population.[2] Each circle diagram represents one of these

---

[2] The criterion for activism is a score above the population mean on the standardized participation scale. The shapes of these scales differ, so that a different proportion is above the mean on each scale. In general, a smaller

"populations." The circles are divided in such a way as to reflect the proportion of that population coming from the top third, the middle third, and the lower third of our socioeconomic resources scale. The whole population is, of course, made up of one-third from each of the three socioeconomic levels (give or take a small amount because of cutting-point problems). The other populations, however, can be more or less representative of the population as a whole. If they are representative in socioeconomic terms, they too will have a socioeconomic composition of equal thirds.

The data show some uniformities and some differences across nations. The first uniformity to note is in relation to the politically concerned. As one would expect from the cross-national uniformity in the relation of political concern to our scale of socioeconomic resources, there is, in each nation, a fairly similar degree of overrepresentation of the haves among the interested portion of the population. Between about 40 and 50 percent of the interested come from the upper third of the socioeconomic scale, the overrepresentation being greatest in India (52 percent coming from the top third) and least in Yugoslavia (41 percent).

The interested are, of course, not necessarily politically active. Indeed, it has been one of the main themes of this book that there can be a major disjunction between political involvement in a psychological sense and active participation in political life – a disjunction that results from institutional interference with individual motivation and resources. The data on the politically interested portion of the citizenry illustrate the shape that the participant population would take if there were no institutional interference. In each of the nations the haves would form about twice as large a proportion of the activists as would the have-nots, despite the fact that the haves and the have-nots form equal proportions of the population as a whole.

The voting population in each nation presents a fairly sharp contrast to the interested population. Here again we find uniformity across most of the nations. The uniformity, however, is that the voting population is fairly representative of the population as a whole. The exception is the United States. There, as we have seen, individual socioeconomic resources play an important role in determining who votes. The result is a skewing of the voting population in the direction of the haves. But

---

proportion falls in the activist category on the scales measuring a difficult act such as campaigning, than on voting. Campaigning scores can range fairly high, whereas there is a lower ceiling on how active an individual is in voting. Furthermore, nonvoters deviate more from the population than do noncampaigners and, given our standarization procedures, receive lower scores on the voting scale than do noncampaigners on the campaign scale. The result is that the mean on the voting scale tends to be below the median, but the mean tends to be above the median on the other scales.

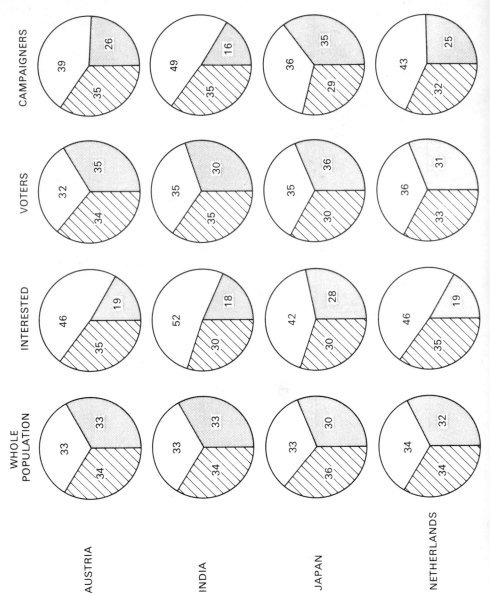

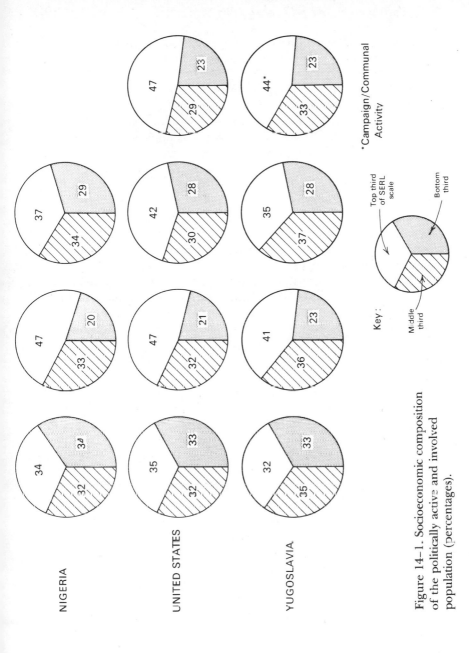

Figure 14-1. Socioeconomic composition
of the politically active and involved
population (percentages).

NIGERIA

UNITED STATES

YUGOSLAVIA

*Campaign/Communal
Activity

Key:

Top third
of SERL
scale

Middle
third

Bottom
third

even in the United States the overrepresentation of the haves among the voters is not as great as their overrepresentation in the politically concerned population.

The data highlight the representative function of voting. Because voting is an easy act, socioeconomic resources are not terribly important in determining who votes. They are not necessary for voting. But neither are they sufficient. Just as it is easy to vote, it is apparently easy to stay away from the voting booth, even if one is interested and involved in politics. Institutional affiliation plays a more important role. Since parties can mobilize voters from all parts of the socioeconomic hierarchy and are motivated to do so, the result is a voting population roughly representative of the population as a whole. The disjunction between political involvement and voting – a disjunction that means that there are many unconcerned voters as well as many concerned nonvoters – makes voting more representative.

The population of campaigners, as is expected, shows the most variation from nation to nation. Where individual socioeconomic forces play a major role in determining who becomes an activist in campaigns, the campaign population has a profile similar to that of the interested population. This is the case in India and the United States. Where institutions play a more important role, one finds a more representative group of campaign activists. This is most clearly the case in Japan, followed by Austria and the Netherlands. In Japan the campaigners are similar in composition to the voters but quite different from the interested portion of the population. In the United States and India the campaigners resemble the interested portion of the population in social composition but are different from the voters. In Austria and the Netherlands the campaigners are between the voters and the interested in the extent to which they are a representative group.

The data for communal activists are easy to summarize. The pattern for communalists resembles that for the politically interested. In all nations there is an overrepresentation of the haves among the communalists, and there is little cross-national variation compared with that found in connection with voting or campaign activity.

The data in Figure 14–1 illustrate the consequences of the alternative ways in which individuals can be mobilized to political activity. The process differs across nations and within nations between political acts. Where socioeconomic resources play a role with little institutional constraint, one finds a pattern of overrepresentation of the haves in each nation. We have no example of an activity immune from institutional interference, but the data on the politically interested population illustrate this circumstance. Where there is institutional constraint and where socioeconomic resources are of little relevance in relation to a political act – as with the easy act of voting – the activist population is likely to be relatively representative of the population as a whole. Where socioeconomic resources are relevant for an act – as with the more difficult campaign activities – and where institutional constraint operates, one finds the greatest variation across nations in the composition of the activist population, a variation that depends on the mix of individual and institutional forces in each nation.

The data we have presented illustrate the consequences of the alternative ways in which individuals can be mobilized to political activity. The society in which institutional constraints are weak and in which individuals are "free" to follow their own inclinations toward political activity and to convert their personal resources into such activity is likely to be a society in which political activity is highly stratified in social and economic terms. Where institutions are more powerful, the result is less certain; much depends on the ties that institutions have to various segments of the society and the way they recruit activists from those segments. Strong institutional constraints can result in an activist population more egalitarian in terms of socioeconomic resources but unrepresentative in other ways. The data in Tables 14-1, 14-2, and 14-3, as well as Chapter 10, illustrate the variety of patterns one can have in terms of segmental over- and underrepresentation. Since political leaders, if they respond to the preferences of the citizenry, are likely to be aware of and responsive to the preferences of the active portion of the population, differences such as those we have described in the composition of the activist populations are likely to have an important effect on political decisions by determining what messages are received by the government.

Local leadership and socioeconomic stratification

We can test the impact of these alternative processes of political mobilization on the government in another way: by considering the relationship between such processes and the kinds of people recruited into leadership positions within the society. As part of our cross-national research on political activity we conducted interviews with a sample of local leaders in the communities from which we took our sample of ordinary respondents. The leaders were selected on the basis of position, with the positions varying somewhat from nation to nation. The positions selected included leaders from government and politics as well as from certain private institutions – such as the leading businessman in the community or the head of the largest voluntary association. Within each community the leaders do not form a sample; rather, we tried to select the single occupant of a particular position – head of local government, head of educational institution, and so forth. Although the communities are a sample of communities in each nation, the leadership sample was

not obtained from the larger communities. Thus the leadership interviews should be considered a sample of local leadership in each nation,
excluding the larger cities.

The local leadership survey allows us to test whether the processes we
have been observing by which citizens become activists also affect the
likelihood that certain kinds of citizens will move up into the ranks of
local leadership. Our hypothesis is simply that whatever process leads to
membership in the activist portion of the population will in turn lead to
membership in the local leadership group. The activist portion of the
population is likely to be the pool from which local leaders are selected.
This should certainly be the case for locally elected leaders. In addition,
the processes of selection into the activist pool are likely to be replicated
for selection out of that pool into the leadership cadre. If individual
socioeconomic resources and motivation are convertible into political
activity, they ought also to be convertible into access to political leadership positions. Where, on the other hand, institutional constraints affect
who becomes an activist, such constraints are likely also to affect who
becomes a local leader.

In short, if the process of political mobilization in a society is such as
to produce an activist population that deviates from the population as
a whole in a particular way, a similar process should produce a group
of local political leaders that deviates from the population in a similar
way – only more so.

The use of our local leadership sample to test this hypothesis is
important because it can offer independent confirmation of the differences among our nations. The patterns of group over- and underrepresentation that we have just described using our samples of citizens
do not provide independent confirmation that the processes we assume
to be operating are in fact operating. The reason is, of course, that the
same data have been used to analyze the process by which people come
to be active and to describe the resultant activist population. The leadership sample thus serves two purposes. It allows an independent test
that the processes we have located in the cross-section sample are in fact
general social processes within the several nations. And it serves to
illustrate the consequences of such processes in terms of the composition
of the local leadership cadres in the several nations.

Table 14–4 compares the results of our analysis of the cross-section
data file with some data on local political leaders. In Table 14–4 we
repeat some data from Chapter 4 on the correlation between SERL and
participation found in our cross-section interviews. The measure of
participation is our overall activity scale. We rank the nations in terms
of the strength of the SERL/participation relationship in the cross-section
data. Next to it we place some data from our leader interviews: the
proportions of our sample of local leaders who on the basis of their

Table 14–4. *The SERL/activity relationship and local leadership recruitment*

Nation	Correlation of SERL and overall activity (cross-section sample)	Proportion of the local leadership sample coming from the top 1/3 of the SERL scale (%)
India	.36	91
Yugoslavia	.36	88
United States	.35	88
Netherlands	.23	75
Nigeria	.22	97
Japan	.12	69
Austria	.11	70

socioeconomic characteristics would fall in the top third of our SERL scale (the top third being determined on the basis of the cross-section sample). The figures are a good indication of the extent to which local leaders come disproportionately from that segment of the society that is more advantaged in socioeconomic terms.

As one might expect, local leaders come disproportionately from the upper socioeconomic group in all of the seven nations. If they came proportionately from each SERL level, one would find 33 percent of the leaders coming from the top third of the socioeconomic advantage scale. In fact, the proportion is much higher in each nation. But what is most striking is that the ranking of the nations in terms of the extent to which the local leaders come disproportionately from the haves is almost identical with the ranking of the SERL/participation relationship within the cross section. Note in particular the contrast in terms of leader background between the countries where the correlation between SERL and political activity is strongest (India, Yugoslavia, and the United States) and the countries where that relationship was found to be quite a bit weaker (Japan and Austria). The two sets of nations differ in the same way in terms of the extent to which local leaders come from the top socioeconomic group. In the former three nations about nine out of ten local leaders come from the top third of the socioeconomic scale. In the latter two nations the figure is closer to two out of three. The Netherlands falls in between the two sets of nations, as one would predict from the SERL/activity relationship.

The one nation that is out of place in this pattern is Nigeria. There we find a moderate SERL/participation relationship in the cross section,

Table 14–5. *The SERL/campaign activity relationship and local elected leadership recruitment*

Nation[a]	Correlation of SERL and campaign activity (cross-section sample)	Proportion of local *elected* officials coming from the top 1/3 of the SERL scale (%)
India	.33	95
United States	.29	83
Yugoslavia	.21[b]	88
Netherlands	.11	69
Austria	.10	71
Japan	.07	63

[a] Campaign scale not available in Nigeria.
[b] Campaign/communal activity.

but Nigeria is similar to India in terms of the proportion of local leaders who come from the top third of the SERL distribution. However, given the shape of the SERL distribution in a nation like Nigeria – where less than ten percent of our sample has an education level beyond that of primary school – it is understandable that almost all local leaders would come from the top third of our SERL distribution.

The data in Table 14–4 are for all local leaders, and that lends some uncertainty to our results. The leadership samples in each nation were based on occupancy of specific positions in the community, positions that differ from nation to nation. In some cases the positions included in the sample require high levels of education (such as head of the local school system) or are likely to imply high income (like head of the largest local business). This would affect the proportions of local leaders high on our socioeconomic resources scale.

Table 14–5 may, therefore, offer a clearer test of our hypothesis. There we present data on local *elected* officals. This in part eliminates the problem associated with the variation in leadership positions used in the several nations. In none of the nations is there a specific income or education requirement for elective position. Therefore, differences among the nations cannot be artifacts of the positions chosen within the local communities. We compare the proportion of local elected officials coming from the top third of the SERL scale with the strength of the relationship between SERL and campaign activity. Our assumption is that campaign activity is more relevant to the election of local officials than is communal activity or our more general activity measure. The results are quite similar to those for all local leaders. The ranking of nations in terms of the SERL/campaign activity relationship is closely parallel to the ranking of nations in terms of the overrepresentation of the haves among local elected officials.

An interesting confirmation of our expectations is seen in the data on the Netherlands. When it comes to the correlation between SERL and overall political activity, the Netherlands was in between India, the United States, and Yugoslavia on the one hand and Austria and Japan on the other. Similarly, the proportion of all Dutch local leaders coming from the top of the SERL scale fell between the proportions in those two sets of nations. When we consider campaign activity, we find the SERL/activity correlation in the Netherlands down near that of Austria. And the Netherlands resembles Austria in the proportion of local elected officials coming from that part of the scale.

The data appear to reflect differences across nations in the characteristics that are relevant for selection to local office. The more political activity is stratified by socioeconomic level in the population at large, the more does access to local office appear similarly stratified. But the meaning of the data are uncertain in one important respect. Socioeconomic resources may facilitate access to office, but officeholding may also be the key to socioeconomic resources. The officeholders' higher scores on the SERL scale may reflect the benefits of office rather than the conditions that got them into office. In Table 14–6 we attempt to correct for this by omitting the income components of our SERL measure and focusing on educational attainment. Occupancy of a local office may lead to higher income, but it is unlikely to lead to higher educational attainment, the latter usually being completed before a job is taken.

We present data on local elected officials in Table 14–6. The educational relationships are not comparable for the nonelected elites because of the variation across the nations in the nonelected positions that formed the basis of selection: Some require advanced education, others do not. The elected positions have no formal educational prerequisites. Column 1 of Table 14–6 presents the proportions of the whole population having "advanced" education. The criterion for advanced education varies from nation to nation (see the footnote to Table 14–6). In each case we tried to find that educational division that isolated the top decile of the educational distribution. In column 2 we present the proportion of the local elected officials who have a similar level of advanced education, and in column 3 we present a measure of the overrepresentation of those having advanced education among the local leaders (the ratio of the proportions in column 2 to the proportions in column 1).

The data are quite consistent with those already reported. In the nations having a weak SERL/participation relationship we find the least

Table 14–6. *The overrepresentation of the educated among local elected leaders*

Nation	Proportion of population with "advanced" education (%)[a]	Proportion of local elected leaders with "advanced" education (%)	Overrepresentation of those with "advanced" education in the local elected leadership
Austria	8	19	2.4
India	10	73	7.3
Japan	10	19	1.9
Netherlands	16	29	1.8
Nigeria	8	32	4.0
United States	9	32	3.6
Yugoslavia	7	44	6.3

[a] The definition of "advanced" education varies from nation to nation depending upon the educational distribution in each nation. The criteria follow: Austria, completed secondary school (Gymnasium); India, some postprimary education; Japan, some postsecondary education (junior college, college, university); Netherlands, some completed postsecondary education (teachers' college, university, etc.); Nigeria, some secondary school; United States, completed college; Yugoslavia, some college or university.

overrepresentation of the educated elite among the local elected leaders. Austria, Japan, and the Netherlands are quite similar in this respect. The nations with a strong SERL/participation relationship – India, the United States, and Yugoslavia – show a higher degree of overrepresentation of the educated elite among local leaders. The level of socioeconomic development of the nation seems to play a role as well, as witnessed in the overrepresentation scores in India and Nigeria. But the data take the general shape we would expect if the processes we have observed on the mass level were operating to determine who was selected into leadership positions.

In sum, we find that in those nations where ordinary citizens appear most able to convert socioeconomic resources into political activity, citizens appear most able to convert such resources into local leadership positions. Where such resources are less convertible into political activity, they are less convertible into leadership positions. This confirms the fact that processes we have found isolated within the population at large appear to have consequences. The greater the disproportion of upper-status citizens in the participant stratum of the population, the greater the disproportion of upper-status citizens among the local leaders. The same processes that lead to the differences among nations in the SERL/ participation relationship in the mass public appear to lead to differences in the degree to which the haves are recruited into local leadership positions.

Participation and the communication of preferences

Participation is important to us as an instrumental act, indeed as the key instrumental political act by citizens in a democracy. Through participation citizens convey to political leaders their needs, problems, and preferences and place pressure on such leaders to act in ways that are responsive. The "biases" in the social composition of the participant population that we have described will have significant consequences when those who are active differ from the rest of the population in their needs and preferences. The fact that the participants in a society are but a minority of the population creates the *potential* that the participant few will communicate to political leaders a set of preferences that are quite different from those of the populace as a whole. This is more likely to be the case the less representative the activist population is in demographic terms. On the other hand, it is possible that the activists will have preferences like those of the less active members of the population (and in this sense can represent them via their activity).

In a sense, we are asking whether it would make a difference if political leaders paid attention to the activists rather than to the populace as a whole. The answer of some other studies is that the political activists are far from being a representative body in terms of preferences. Studies show that letter writers on public matters are not representative of the preferences of the populace as a whole. Letter writers tend to fall in the more extreme categories of a liberalism–conservatism scale, with a tendency to be on the conservative side (Converse, Clausen, and Miller, 1965). The citizens who wrote letters to government officials, political candidates, and newspapers on the Vietnam War tended to have a distribution of preferences that was somewhat more polarized (i.e., either hawkish or dovish and less middle of the road) than the populace as a whole, while tilting somewhat in a hawkish direction (Verba and Brody, 1970). In a similar manner Ranney (1972) has shown that voters in primary elections are by no means representative of all the voters. In addition, the mode of political activity makes a difference in terms of the preferences of those who engage in it. While letter writers on the Vietnam War were somewhat more hawkish than the populace as a whole, those who took part in demonstrations were more dovish (Verba and Brody, 1970). The point is simple: Political leaders who read public preferences by observing the views of the activists saw something different from what they would have seen had they conducted a poll of the public as whole; and what they saw depended on the mode of activity to which they were sensitive.

Do the activists in the various nations we have been studying differ from the population as a whole in their needs and preferences? And do any differences that exist parallel the differences across the nations in the sociological characteristics of the activists? Just as there is no definitive way in which one can determine how representative in a sociological sense is the activist population (because of the alternative criteria on the basis of which one could measure representativeness), so is there no definitive way to determine the representativeness of the activist population in terms of needs and preferences. It would depend on the issue or problem area on which one focused.

Given our own concern with participatory differences in terms of socioeconomic level, it may be best to focus on the representativeness of the activist population in terms of needs associated with socioeconomic level. If the participant population is biased in favor of the haves, one would expect that the needs and preferences of the activist group would be biased in a similar manner. In each of the nations, respondents were asked about the most important needs and problems they faced in their daily lives. The question is a good one on the basis of which to compare the more active with the less active. Specific political issues differ from nation to nation, and many issues have no clear relationship to socioeconomic level. Furthermore, the various strata of the population – particularly in terms of education – differ in the extent to which they have or can articulate views on matters of public policy. But almost all respondents can report their own needs and problems. The main justification for participation in a democracy is, as Lord Lindsay put it, that

Table 14–7. *Proportion mentioning a subsistence need by level of activity*

| Nation | Participation level (%)[a] | | | |
	Inactives	Middle majority	Actives	Population
Austria	24	29	32	29
India	68	63	49	61
Japan	32	35	27	33
Netherlands	31	23	16	23
Nigeria	51	34	44	39
United States	21	19	13	19

[a] Inactives: lowest sixth of overall participation scale. Actives: highest sixth of overall participation scale. Middle: rest of sample.

only the wearer of the shoe knows if it pinched. We asked our respondents about that which they and only they know – the needs in their own
lives.

Table 14–7 reports the proportion in each nation who answered in
response to this question that they had a problem that could be considered to be a basic subsistence need – a need in relation to adequate food,
clothing, or shelter. The figures are not directly comparable across the
nations. The interviewing conventions differed from nation to nation in
terms of how many answers were elicited, and administration of the
question differed in that a varying number of needs and problems were
recorded and coded. Furthermore, there are some differences in the
specific problems that were coded under the rubric of basic subsistence
needs. Thus the absolute frequency of mentions of such problems cannot be compared across the nations. However, the questioning and
coding procedures were carried out consistently within the nations, and
the comparison across groups is valid. The latter is, in any case, that in
which we are interested.[3]

In Table 14–7 we report the proportions mentioning a subsistence
problem for three groups: First, we have the inactives, who fall into the
lowest sixth of our participation scale. In most countries these are individuals who engage in no political activity or, at most, an occasional
easy act such as voting or attendance at a political rally. Second, we have
the actives, who fall in the top sixth of our overall activity scale. These
are individuals who engage in fairly varied and frequent political activity.
And third, we have the middle majority, the middle two-thirds of our
activity scale who are neither totally outside of the participatory universe
nor completely within it.

The data show much cross-national variation in the extent to which
the actives and the inactives are similar in the frequency with which they
report subsistence problems. Furthermore, the differences in this regard
parallel the differences across the nations in the extent to which the
haves are overrepresented in the participant population. In Japan and
Austria, where the correlation between SERL and the overall activity
scale is the weakest, one finds the least tendency for subsistence needs
to be underrepresented among those who are most active. Indeed, in
Austria such needs are more frequently expressed by the actives than
by the inactives. In the other nations one finds the actives less likely than
the inactives to have such needs and problems. In the United States and
India, where political activity is most clearly stratified by socioeconomic
level, there is a clear gap between those active in political life and those

---

[3] Though this question was asked in Yugoslavia, the coding procedures used
were such that we cannot isolate the subsistence problems from a range of
other problems. We have unfortunately had to leave Yugoslavia out of this
analysis.

inactive in the likelihood that they face subsistence problems in their own lives. Political leaders paying attention to the participant population would underestimate the extent to which such needs existed. In the Netherlands there is a particularly sharp gap, though the SERL/overall activity relationship was only moderate. In Nigeria, where there also was a moderate SERL/participation relationship, one also finds a "distortion" of citizen needs expressed through the participatory system, with the inactives more likely to have basic needs than the activist portion of the population.

We can elaborate this process somewhat by considering the varying modes of political activity in those nations where we have measures of all three modes. The modes differ, as we have seen, in the extent to which those who engage in them are representative of the population as a whole. Voting is, in general, the most representative political act in SERL terms, communal activity the least, with campaign activity somewhere in between depending upon the type and degree of institutional interference. There were, however, cross-national variations in relation to the modes of activity. One of the most noticeable was the positive SERL/voting relationship in the United States. Another was the difference between the SERL/campaign activity and the SERL/communal activity relationships in the Netherlands; the former being relatively low as in Austria and Japan, the latter being more substantial. These differences in representativeness among the modes of activity are reflected in the data in Table 14–8. There we show the proportions reporting a subsistence need among those who are active in each of the modes of activity compared with those who are not active in that mode.[4]

The data for the different modes of activity show some interesting variations from the patterns found in the previous table, in which we considered our overall measure of political activity. For one thing, we find differences in several of the nations between communal and campaign activists. In Austria and the Netherlands, communal activists underrepresent those with subsistence needs compared with those who are inactive in communal participation. In Austria they do so by a slight degree; in the Netherlands by a more substantial degree. In contrast the campaign activists in each of these nations represent those with subsistence needs more effectively; in the Netherlands the campaign activists represent such needs as well as the campaign nonactivists; in Austria the campaign activists are more likely to mention subsistence needs. The data reflect, we believe, the dominant role of political institutions in these nations in mobilizing citizens to political activity from across the socioeconomic spectrum, a mobilization that has a greater

[4] The criterion for membership in the activist group is the same as that reported in footnote 2.

Table 14–8. *Proportion mentioning a subsistence need by mode of activity and activity level*

Nation	Campaigning (%)		Communal activity (%)		Voting (%)	
	Inactive	Active	Inactive	Active	Inactive	Active
Austria	25	33	29	24	28	29
India	65	53	64	53	63	60
Japan	35	31	35	28	34	32
Netherlands	23	24	27	18	27	21
Nigeria	—	—[a]	39	39	42	37
United States	20	18	20	18	22	18

[a] No campaign activity measure.

impact on campaign participation than on communal participation. In Japan as well there is a bias against those with subsistence needs among communal activists and among campaign activists but more bias among communal activists. In the United States and India, the pattern for the two acts is essentially the same, each act showing some bias against those mentioning subsistence needs.

The data on voting show that the voting activists represent subsistence needs about as well as do those who do not vote in three nations: Austria, India, and Japan. In each case, the voting activists represent such needs a touch more effectively than do the activists in the other two modes. The United States differs. Voting activists are somewhat less representative of those with subsistence needs than are the activists in the other two modes. This is consistent with the existence in the United States of a positive SERL/voting relationship. Lastly, we find that voters in the Netherlands are less likely to have subsistence needs than are nonvoters. They are less representative of those with such needs than is the case with campaign activists. We are uncertain why this is the case.

Though the magnitude of differences is sometimes small, the data in Tables 14–7 and 14–8 suggest that the composition of the activist populations has a potential for political consequences. Those who are active have different needs and interests from those who are inactive. The democratic function of participation is to communicate the preferences of the population. The results would differ depending upon which process of mobilization to political activity was in operation. The biases in the participatory process are not without significant political effect.

We cannot be certain how great the effect is. There are a number of considerations on the basis of which one might argue that the socioeconomic biases in the participant population we uncover are not as significant as we suggest. For one thing, though there is a skewing of the activist population in favor of the haves when it comes to more difficult political acts, the voting populations in each of the nations show a great deal of socioeconomic representativeness. Voting is, in addition, the act in which the largest number of citizens engage. It is the most basic way in which citizens control political leaders – through the mechanism of periodic elections. However, though voters are representative of the population as a whole – or more representative than other activists – the vote conveys less information to political leaders than do other activities. Voting is a blunt act; the voter is limited to a small number of choices, none of which necessarily expresses his or her views on what is most salient. Though the voters can speak for the populace as a whole better than can other activists, they do not speak as effectively because of the limited information-carrying capability of the vote. In contrast, communal activity – which tends to be most stratified by socioeconomic level – conveys much more information, consisting as it does of contacts with government officials and activity on specific community problems through informal and formal groups. Thus, though the biases in the participant population are not as great in relation to some acts as to others, they are greatest in relation to those acts that can most effectively communicate citizen preferences.

Another argument against the significance of the differences between the actives and the inactives in the needs and problems they face is that political leaders are not limited to participatory mechanisms to find out about the problems of the populace. They can, as we did, conduct surveys or use other techniques of information gathering. They do not have to depend on the participants to come to them with their needs and preferences. Leaders do use varying information-gathering techniques and are by no means dependent on citizen participation. But this is true in democracies and nondemocracies. The special feature of democracies is that citizens have the right to express such views, and political leaders, whose futures depend upon the public, are under pressure to respond. A biased participatory system can be balanced by many other information-gathering techniques on the part of leaders, but it would be a sign of democratic malfunctioning if these replaced participatory mechanisms as the main means of communication from citizen to the government.

A last argument against the significance of bias in the participant population would be that activity reflects needs and preferences, whereas inactivity is the result of satisfaction. Those who take no part in public life, so the argument would go, have no reason to – they are satisfied and have no demands they wish to place on the government. If their views are left out, there is no distortion of the preferences in the population.

But our example of the difference between the actives and the inactives ought to refute this argument. The inactives are by no means satisfied; they are more likely to face severe needs in their day-to-day lives. If they are not active, it is not because there is nothing to be active about but, we believe, because of their low level of socioeconomic resources. Their shoes pinch, but they have neither the resources nor the motivation to complain.

This book has taken us through a number of intricate data analyses. Some readers may have found these tedious at times. But the analyses are, we believe, relevant for some of the major themes in democratic politics: themes of citizen control over leaders, of equality, of social conflict.

In our earlier work on the United States we speculated about an apparent paradox: that social class was at once so unimportant and so important in American politics. On the one hand, the United States is a society in which social class is not an important ingredient of political competition: The American working class has never manifested a strong sense of class consciousness as has the working class in other nations, nor are political parties specifically organized around a particular social class. At the same time, the class basis of political activity is very strong – the participant population is heavily biased in the direction of those who are more affluent and better educated – more so than in other nations. (See Verba and Nie, 1972, chap. 15.) Our explanation of this seeming contradiction was that the very absence of class as a basis of politics in an ideational or organizational sense meant that class would play a key role in relation to individual political activity. In the absence of *explicit* contestation on the basis of social class the haves in society came to play an inordinate role in political life.

The analysis in this volume confirms what could be only speculation when based on a single country. We find that where there is explicit contestation among social groups and where that contestation is reflected in the institutional structure of politics, the implicit class bias in political activity can be diminished. We were able to demonstrate this by looking at a variety of nations, some of which have patterns of political contestation equivalent to that which we speculated was missing in the United States. But the analysis in this volume puts the matter in a more general framework. Political conflict in a society does not have to be about social stratification. It can be about religion or race, or it can be an urban–rural conflict, or a conflict between traditional and modern values (as is to some extent the conflict in Japan). Such conflict can, nevertheless, have consequences for the stratification of political activity, especially when the conflicting groups differ in their position on the socioeconomic scale. What counts is that there be some explicit basis for the mobilization of citizens to counteract the implicit bias built into a participatory system on the individual level.

The analysis in this book also illustrates some major dilemmas in democratic politics. If one of the criteria for successful democratic functioning is relative equality of political activity, access, and influence, our volume indicates how difficult it is to achieve such equality. The "natural" tendency for certain citizens to take greater advantage of participatory opportunities must be overcome. Nor can this advantage be overcome without some costs. One cost involves the other forms of inequality that may replace inequality on the basis of socioeconomic resources. The mobilization of the agrarian sector in Japan or Austria tends to flatten the relationship between socioeconomic resource level and political activity. It creates political equality in socioeconomic terms, but it produces a system in which agrarian interests may have a disproportionate share of influence.

In addition, if the have-nots become active through party and organizational channels, this may have an effect on the "quality" of the participant population. In such systems we find a higher proportion of the participant population who fall into our "mobilized" category – they are active, but they do not have commensurate levels of political interest or information. They are an activist population more open to manipulation – as is indeed implicit in the fact that they have been mobilized to political activity by others rather than on the basis of their own interest and initiative.

Lastly, the analysis indicates that there may be a contradiction between political equality and political harmony. Political equality between haves and have-nots, so our analyses suggest, is fostered by explicit group conflict. Political equality is greater where conflicting interests are explicit and political organizations are based on such conflict, where they perhaps even exacerbate and exploit the conflict. Where there are strong political institutions with clear connections to particular population groups – where the parties do not attempt to catch all citizens but to mobilize their own support groups – political equality may increase, but so does conflict. The United States is the society in our group (of those that have competitive politics) that has moved furthest from a system in which clearly defined conflicting groups faced each other across a party divide. Evidence from earlier times in the history of the U.S. party system indicates that it may once have resembled the Dutch or the Austrian system. Political contestation in the late nineteenth century had more of a religious basis; parties mobilized their own supporters rather than competing for voters from most segments of society (Jensen, 1971; Kleppner, 1970). If Burnham is correct, the American party system then resembled the European systems. It was a system "likely to produce intense party identification, highly stable party voting, and very high levels of political participation . . ." (Burnham, 1974, p. 1020).

Such party systems, as we suggest, produce political equality among groups. Whether the cost in terms of political conflict is worth it is not a question we can answer. In any case, such party systems appear to be on the wane. The U.S. party system moved away from the European model around the turn of the century and has been moving even further away in recent years with the continuing erosion of partisanship and the rise in a politics of "individuation" – whereby individuals with no party ties or weak party ties interact directly with the political system through the media rather than through the intermediary channels of political parties. (See Nie, Verba, and Petrocik, 1976, for a discussion.)

At the same time, the European parties are following suit. In Austria and the Netherlands, traditional commitments to a particular social segment and to the party associated with it are eroding. Traditional voting patterns are weakening, as the pillars in the Netherlands or the *Lagern* in Austria lose their significance. In Japan as well the ties of traditional groups to the Liberal Democratic Party through personal loyalty have begun to erode. Much of this change comes through the universal solvent of the mass media, particularly television, which replaces political organization as the source of information and motivation to be politically active. In addition, new modes of activity outside of the electoral process – action groups, citizen movements – have grown in importance. All this makes political systems more "open." Voters will more freely choose among candidates; they are less likely to be mobilized to political activity on the basis of habitual ties to a social group, a political party, or to some other political organization. Civic groups are not limited to traditional channels or to the issues that come up in elections. The result may, however, be less rather than more political equality.

The modes of participation

In Chapter 3 we presented the results of our analysis of the modes of participation as well as the data on the questions that went into that analysis. The results represent the last step in a long analysis. The four modes we reported in Chapter 3 were not the four we originally expected – though they are close. In this appendix we present the logic of our analysis of these modes and the evolution of our empirical analysis. As indicated in Chapter 3, we asked about a variety of political acts in our surveys. In order to understand why we expect certain acts to cluster together into distinctive modes of activity we must first move to a more abstract level. Before considering the specific acts about which we asked respondents, we can consider some more abstract dimensions of participation. By moving to a more abstract level, we can indicate why specific acts of participation that may differ from nation to nation would, nevertheless, be functionally equivalent – that is, relate the individual actor to the government in a similar way.

Some dimensions of participation

The type of influence exerted
Citizen activities can affect the behavior of governmental leaders in two ways: They can communicate information about the preferences of citizens and/or they can apply pressure on political leaders to conform to these preferences. They do the latter by threatening a leader with some loss or promising some reward – such as a gain or loss of votes. Some political activities communicate a lot of information about citizen preferences, others less. Some put the government under greater pressure, others less. Our first distinction among kinds of political activity is in terms of type of influence exerted: via information, pressure, or both.

The scope of the outcome
Most political science analysis has focused on government policies that have a collective impact and that affect the entire society or large segments of it. The outcome of an election affects all citizens, voter and nonvoter alike. A tax reform bill or a governmental decision on foreign policy has a collective impact on all citizens. It has been argued that this is the essence of govern-

310

mental activity – that the outcome of such activity cannot be decomposed (Olson, 1965; Coleman, 1971). But governments do not make decisions only about broad social policies. Often they produce outcomes that will affect only a particular citizen or his immediate family. The government issues a zoning variance to an individual so that he may enlarge his home, provides a license, grants an exemption from the army because of family hardship, provides a job, offers agricultural assistance, or agrees to provide a better water supply to a given home. Any particular instance of such an act has little effect on the collectivity, but such day-to-day decisions may have an intense impact on the individual or his family. And the impact may depend on the citizen's knowledge, skill, and activity – that is, on the effectiveness of his participation.

Thus, rather than thinking of all governmental activity as having a collective impact, one might distinguish among such activities in terms of their scope – that is, the number of citizens affected. This is clearly a problem of degree and not a simple dichotomy. But though the extreme of a fully collective or fully particularized outcome is never reached, the distinction between governmental actions in terms of the degree to which they have collective or particularized impact is useful if we want to understand the ways in which citizen participation affects those actions. Citizens relate to their government as participants vis-à-vis broad policy decisions, but they also relate vis-à-vis the smaller more narrow actions of the government. A full understanding of the ways in which the citizen can participate requires that we consider him as a participant in relation to the large collective outcomes (as we do consider him when we look at him as a voter in elections). But it is also important to consider him in relation to the narrower governmental actions – as when he attempts to influence some governmental decision specifically relevant to his own life. Thus an important dimension of participation has to do with whether the participatory act is intended to and can in fact influence a particularized outcome, a collective outcome, or both.

The conflict dimension

Political participation inevitably raises questions of the generation and reconciliation of conflict in a society. Insofar as governmental benefits are limited, activity by one group to obtain something for itself may injure the interests of others. But one can make distinctions among participatory activities in terms of the extent to which conflict with others is involved. Some political activities are engaged in against other participants: One set of participants tries to gain some beneficial outcome at the expense of another. In other cases, participants seek some beneficial outcome under circumstances where there are no "counterparticipants"; their gain does not imply clear losses for others. Citizens do not always participate in order to defeat some alternative proposal set forth by an opposed group. Often citizens work to mobilize resources, to bring the apathetic over to active support, to move inert institutions in order to accomplish some goal to which there is little if any opposition.

Again, the distinction is not a clear dichotomy. No benefit for an individual or a group is costless for others. But participatory situations clearly differ in the extent to which the situation is a zero-sum conflict with winners and losers rather than an attempt by one group to influence policy with no clear opposition.

It is likely that the conflict dimension is related to the scope of the potential outcome. The wider the impact of the outcome, the more likely is it that there will be opposing groups active in relation to it. If the governmental outcome that the participants seek has a narrow impact, having a noticeable effect on the participants alone and affecting others only indirectly, this increases the likelihood that the participatory situation would involve just one set of participants attempting to achieve one particular policy outcome.

The cooperative dimension

The conflict dimension refers to the extent to which individuals are opposed by counterparticipants. The cooperative dimension refers to the extent to which they work along with others. Do they act as individuals or collectively with others? This is, of course, a fundamental political dimension. The individual facing the government is in unequal combat – especially if he has any but the most particularized goals in mind. Effective political action often depends upon the ability of citizens to work collaboratively. This dimension also relates to the potential outcome. The more particularized the outcome, the less likely is it that there will be a large cooperating group of citizens active in relation to it. Why should others cooperate with me if the benefit comes largely to me?

Initiative required

This dimension is similar to the criterion for differentiating political acts that has been the usual one within the literature: How "difficult" is the act? We are interested in the amount of time and effort needed for an act of participation, but more so in how much initiative is needed by the individual in choosing when and how to act.

The dimensions and modes of activity

These distinctions among types of political acts, when combined in different ways, produce what one can consider alternative systems by which the citizenry influences the government. Most analysis of politics has involved the study of those situations in which large groups of collaborating citizens oppose each other in relation to some outcome affecting the entire collectivity – party competition for control over governmental offices is the prototype, but this also describes other clashes over major governmental policies that affect many citizens. Some political acts, however, are at the other extreme. The citizen may act alone, the outcome may affect only him, and he may not be directly opposed by any other citizen.

The usefulness of these dimensions can be seen when we consider some of the actual ways in which citizens can be active. The dimensions help distinguish among these ways.

Voting

Voting is the most frequent citizen activity. It exerts influence over leaders through pressure: Leaders adjust their policies in order to gain votes, and of course the vote determines who holds elective office. But it communicates little information about voter preferences to leaders. The act itself conveys no explicit information. The information implicit in the fact that votes go to one candidate rather than another is inadequate to express the specific preferences of the citizen – since the election is unlikely to turn on those issues that are most salient to him. The scope of the outcome is very broad, affecting all citizens. This combination of low information about citizen preferences and high pressure on leaders with broad outcomes is what gives voting its unique characteristic as a blunt but powerful instrument of control over the government.

On the other dimensions: Voting does involve the citizen in conflict, since the electoral situation is by definition a conflictual one – at least if the election is competitive. The voting act, on the other hand, is an individual act. And voting differs from other political acts in that it requires relatively little initiative. The occasion for voting is presented to the citizen in the form of regular elections; he does not have to create the occasion.

These characteristics of voting are fairly obvious, but they are useful, for they highlight some contrast with other modes of citizen activity.

Campaign activity

The next regular mode of citizen activity is, like voting, in the electoral process. It is participation in election campaigns. It is a significant mode of action, for through it the citizen can increase his influence over the election outcome beyond the one vote allocated to him. Like the vote, it exerts a lot of pressure on leaders, and for the same reason. But it can communicate more information about the participants' preferences because campaign activists are a more clearly identifiable group with whom candidates may be in close contact. Campaign activity, like voting, produces collective outcomes. Unlike voting, it requires cooperation among citizens. It involves the citizen in conflictual situations. And more initiative is required of the citizen than in relation to the vote; campaign activity is clearly a more difficult political act than mere voting.

Citizen-initiated contacts

As pointed out, much of the study of participation focuses on activities in the electoral process. But between-election activity counts as well. To find other means of participation, we might consider first that kind of activity most different from the electoral situation. The vote represents a massive involvement of most citizens at scheduled times. Both voting and campaign activity take place in response to elections whose content and timing are set for the citizen, and in which the substantive issues are controlled by candidates and officials. At the other extreme are those instances in which individuals with particular concerns in mind initiate contacts with government officials about these concerns. Here we have the individual vis-à-vis the government – or some small segment of the government. He determines the timing, target, and substance of the act of participation. This type of participation – which we call citizen-initiated contacts–represents a third type of political activity.

Citizen-initiated contacts have one distinctive characteristic when considered from the point of view of the dimensions of participation – in particular in relation to the "scope of the outcome" dimension. Only this mode of participation can reasonably be expected to result in a particularized benefit. The individual participant takes the initiative in contacting a government official, and, most important, he "chooses the agenda" of the act of participation; he decides what to contact about. The "choosing of the agenda" by the citizen-contractor – something that is possible for contacting activity only – is crucial for two reasons. It ensures that the subject matter of the participatory act is salient and important to the individual, and it makes possible particularization of the subject matter to the individual. Under such circumstances, he may still contact about some general social problem – he may write his national representative about foreign policy, or he may complain to a local govermental official about some general failure in performance – but he may also contact about some particular problem affecting only himself or his family. Contacting, as our discussion implies, communicates a lot of information about the preferences of the citizen, but it probably exerts little pressure coming as it does from a single citizen.

The potential-outcome dimension is most crucial for distinguishing citizen-initiated contacts from other acts. On the conflict dimension, we assume that such contacts do not usually involve direct conflict with other citizens. The situation in relation to the cooperative dimension is unclear. Citizens can contact officials by themselves or others can join them. We assume that citizens who contact on a particularized problem will tend to do so alone. Lastly, since the individual chooses the occasion to participate, as well as the subject matter and the official to contact, such activity requires quite a bit of initiative on the part of the contactor.

Cooperative activity
Finally, we can mention another regularly utilized mode of participation outside of the electoral process. This fourth type of activity involves group or organizational activity by citizens to deal with social and political

problems. In this case the individual does not act alone as he does in citizen-initiated contacts, but rather joins with others to influence the actions of government. However, like citizen-initiated contacts and unlike electoral participation, cooperative group activity is initiated by private citizens and may take place at any time and in relation to any type of issue or problem of concern to the group. It may involve activity within formal organizations as well as informal cooperation among citizens.

Cooperative activity is significant because it can combine information about citizen preferences (since citizens come together to work on a particular issue) with pressure (since leaders are more likely to respond to a number of citizens than to a lone contractor). As for the scope of the outcome: When a citizen cooperates with others – either in informal groups or in formal organizations – it reduces the likelihood that the political activity will have as its goal some benefit particularized to him alone. Why would others cooperate with him if that was all there was in it for them? Thus cooperative activity is more likely to be relevant to outcomes of a somewhat collective nature – though the outcome may affect a group in the society rather than the entire collectivity. It is somewhat less clear whether such cooperative activity is likely to take place in a situation of conflict with other groups – it is probably more likely to involve conflict than do citizen-initiated contacts, since the stakes are usually higher, but less likely than in the electoral situation.

Cooperative activity, of course, involves cooperation with others. But some community issues can divide groups into nonpartisan, but conflictual camps. Lastly, cooperative activity probably requires some initiative – though the amount of such initiative would depend on whether the individual helped form such a cooperative group or just joined it. We have explicated the differences among various modes of political activity at greater length elsewhere (see Verba and Nie, 1972, chaps. 3 and 7).

The difference among the modes of activity is summarized in Table A–1. On that table we separate citizen-initiated contacts into two kinds – those aimed at influencing a broad social issue, as when a citizen complains to a government official on some general problem, and those aimed at obtaining some particularized benefit from the government. We do this because these two types of citizen contacting differ significantly on the dimensions of the scope of the outcome and the extent to which they involve cooperation with others. As we shall see, they differ empirically as well.

With these considerations in mind, we carried out a factor analysis of the participatory acts in each nation. It is important to be clear what we did not do. We did not look to see what clustering of activities emerge from a factor analysis of our participation data. Rather, we looked to see whether the clustering we expected to find based on our analysis of the dimensions of participation was indeed found. If we found similar patterns in each nation, it would confirm our model and also suggest that we really were comparing a comparable phenomenon.

Table A–1. *The dimensions of political activity and modes of activity*

Mode of activity	Type of influence	Scope of outcome	Conflict	Initiative required	Cooperate with others
Voting	High pressure/low information	Collective	Conflictual	Little	Little
Campaign activity	High pressure/low to high information	Collective	Conflictual	Some	Some or a lot
Cooperative activity	Low to high pressure/high information	Collective	Maybe yes/maybe no	Some or a lot	A lot
Contacting officials on social issues	Low pressure/high information	Collective	Usually nonconflictual	A lot	Perhaps some
Contacting officials on personal matters	Low pressure/high information	Particular	Nonconflictual	A lot	Little

A factor analysis of the political acts

With the expectations based on our discussion of the dimensions of political activity in mind, we performed a factor analysis on the various political acts reported in Tables 3–2 and 3–3. Our analysis went through several stages. (For a fuller discussion, see Verba, Nie, and Kim, 1971; Verba and Nie, 1972, chap. 4; and Kim, Nie, and Verba, 1977. The second work contains a replication of the factor analysis using Guttman-Lingoes Smallest Space Analysis, and the third work contains factor analysis using tetrachorics and some justification for using correlation coefficients even for items that are dichotomous.) We first performed the analysis on the political acts coded in such a way that no distinction was drawn between contacts on a personal matter and contacts on a broader issue. The result was a relatively clear pattern that distinguished four modes close to those we had anticipated: voting, campaign activity, co-operative activity, and citizen contacting. (See Verba, Nie and Kim, 1971, pp. 23–26.) The analysis did leave some puzzles, however. Contacting did not stand out as a separate mode of activity as clearly as did the other modes. The correlations among the contacting items were not as strong as those among the items in the other modes of activity, and the contrast between the contacting and the cooperative modes of activity was not as sharp as those between other pairs of modes.

This led us to incorporate the dimension of the scope of the outcome more directly into our analysis. We used our open-ended follow-up question on the subject matter of the contact to separate contacts into the two types mentioned previously – particularized and social. Factor analyses were then repeated on the participation items with that distinction incorporated.

Tables A–2 through A–6 report the results of this analysis for Austria, India, Japan, the Netherlands, and the United States. We shall deal with the other two nations separately because of the different measures available in each. Since we expected the various factors to be distinct but not uncorrelated, we used an oblique rotation that allows the factors representing each dimension to be correlated with each other – a fact that will be useful to us later. The result in each of the nations is strikingly similar to that in the others. In each country we find four clear factors. Two of them are consistent with the expectations spelled out in the previous section. Campaign activity forms a clear cluster of activity in each nation, with all the campaign acts loading strongly on that factor whereas other acts do not.[1] Voting is similarly a distinctive factor.

The next two factors are somewhat different from the modes specified by our original distinction between cooperative activities and citizen-initiated contacts. The group-based cooperative activities have high loadings on the third factor, and contacts with a social referent also display large loadings on this

---

[1] The factors are listed in the same order in each country, but they did not necessarily emerge in that order.

Table A–2. *Direct oblimin rotated pattern matrix of the participation variables including both forms of contacting: United States*

Variable	Campaign activity	Voting	Communal activity	Personalized contacts
Persuade others how to vote	.54	.05	.11	−.03
Ever worked for a party	.79	−.02	−.00	.02
Attended political meetings or rallies	.79	−.01	−.05	.08
Contribute money to candidate	.74	.01	−.16	.04
Member of a political club or organization	.80	−.09	−.09	−.00
Vote 1964	−.02	.91	−.02	−.01
Vote 1960	−.02	.90	−.03	−.02
Frequency of local vote	.05	.81	.04	.02
Work with others on community problem	−.05	.04	.75	.06
Helped form local group	−.09	−.08	.77	.10
Active member of organization engaged in solving community problems	.12	.05	.56	.01
Contact a local official on a social problem	.08	−.02	.60	.19
Contact an extralocal official on a social problem	.11	.03	.44	−.31
Contact a local official on a personal problem	.01	.02	−.02	.70
Contact an extralocal official on a personal problem	.03	−.01	.08	.70

factor. In all cases the loadings for both types of acts are above .4 and in most cases well above that. Contacts on a social matter link up with cooperative activities, indicating that these quite different types of concrete act nevertheless form an identifiable activity cluster – those who do one *are more likely to do the other.* The two measures of contacts with a particularized referent load strongly and by themselves on Factor 4.

Particular attention should be paid to the data on Austria in Table A–6. They represent a tougher test of the similarity of structure among the participation items, since the questionnaire was much different and questions were asked about quite different ways of cooperating with one's fellow citizens. Furthermore, the distinction between particularized and more general contacting was based on a closed question – in contrast with the open questions used elsewhere. The pattern found is, however, quite similar. The same four factors are clearly identifiable. The measures of personalized contacting form a factor by themselves, whereas the measures of informal cooperative activity load with contacts on a social problem as in the other nations to form a single

Table A–3. *Direct oblimin rotated pattern matrix of the participation variables including both forms of contacting: Japan*

Variable	Campaign activity	Voting	Communal activity	Personalized contacts
Ever worked for a party	.76	.07	−.01	.01
Attended political meetings or rallies	.62	.32	−.01	.04
Member of a political club or organization	.64	−.24	−.09	.25
Vote in national elections	.05	.90	.00	−.02
Worked with others on community problem	.09	−.03	.66	−.00
Helped form local group	.04	−.07	.64	.06
Active member of organization engaged in solving community problems	−.26	.13	.75	.17
Contact a local official on a social problem	.34	−.09	.51	−.29
Contact an extralocal official on a social problem	.34	−.20	.41	−.26
Contact a local official on a personal problem	.04	.04	.06	.73
Contact an extralocal official on a personal problem	.09	.09	.04	.72

factor. The voting and campaign activity factors are also clear. The one variation is that activity through organized groups to try to deal with community problems loads with the items on campaign participation rather than, as in India, Japan, and the United States, with the non-partisan activities. The cause of this particular difference is fairly clear. Formal organizations in Austria are quite likely to have affiliations with one of the two partisan *Lagern;* and, in tapping organized activity, we are tapping closeness to political parties as well.

In each of these five nations, thus, we now find four modes of participation or activity clusters, each loading on its own factor: (1) campaign activity, (2) voting, (3) cooperative participation plus social contacts, and (4) contacts about particularized issues. Factors three and four are different from the previous expectations. For the sake of convenience we labeled the third factor "communal activity"; the fourth, "particularized contacting."

From one perspective, these four modes of activity appear less clear than the first fourfold distinction, for now two different kinds of act load on a single factor, and a single kind of act – contacting – loads on two separate factors. However, from a theoretical perspective, these activity clusters are clearer than before and consistent with our argument concerning the importance of the potential outcome of a political act. Insofar as different acts are

Table A–4. *Direct oblimin rotated pattern matrix of the participation variables including both forms of contacting: India*

Variable	Campaign activity	Voting	Communal activity	Personalized contacts
Ever worked for a party	.50	.00	.22	.08
Attended political meetings or rallies	.38	.05	.32	.20
Contribute money	.61	.02	−.07	.17
Member of a political club or organization	.77	−.00	.00	.00
National voting	.03	.92	.00	.01
Local voting	−.02	.94	−.01	−.02
Work with others on community problem	−.13	.07	.51	.41
Helped form local group	−.18	.00	.66	.26
Active member of organization engaged in solving community problems	.03	−.04	.59	.17
Contact a local official on a social problem	.08	−.01	.70	−.21
Contact an extralocal official on a social problem	.12	−.03	.70	−.28
Contact a local official on a personal problem	.08	.00	−.06	.73
Contact an extralocal official on a personal problem	.05	−.05	−.02	.70

used to influence a similar type of issue, we find that the acts cluster together. By the same token, when the same concrete act (e.g., contacting) is utilized in reference to different types of issues, we find that they load on separate factors. This is precisely the basis for our earlier theoretical distinction among various modes of activity. Contacts on a general issue and particularized contacts are similar types of activity in certain respects, but that similarity seems less important than the difference entailed in the different goal orientation.[2]

Thus the progression of our ideas on political participation may be sum-

[2] In our original analyses of these data we concluded that the two types of contact were similar in that both were carried out by the individual on his or her own. Social contacts, we argued, linked up with the cooperative acts because of their similarity in goals (Verba, Nie, and Kim, 1971). In the three surveys we conducted after our preliminary analysis of data from the United States, Japan, India, and Nigeria, we included a follow-up question to our questions on contacting. We asked whether the respondent had been joined by others when he contacted. Contacting on a personal matter does appear usually to be an individual activity, as the following table shows, but a quite high proportion of contacts on a social issue involved activity along with others. Thus citizen-initiated contacts on a social issue

Table A–5. *Direct oblimin rotated factor pattern of participation variables: Netherlands*

Variable	Campaign activity	Voting	Communal activity	Personalized contacts
Displayed or distributed campaign posters or leaflets	.77	−.01	−.06	−.06
Persuade others to vote for a certain party	.54	−.01	−.01	.15
Attend an election rally	.73	−.02	−.08	.06
Give money to a political party for election activities	.75	−.03	.03	−.11
Member of a political party	.61	.12	.01	.00
Voted in municipal elections	.04	.88	−.04	−.08
Vote in provincial elections	.00	.88	.02	.01
Contact a local official on a social problem	.03	−.01	.81	.05
Contact an extralocal official on a social problem	.02	−.05	.79	.09
Active member in an organization that takes part in community affairs	−.01	.17	.48	.15
Worked in an informal group on some community matter	−.01	.01	.58	.11
Worked in an informal group on some extralocal problem	.14	.06	.51	−.11
Contacted a local official on a personal or family matter	.03	−.06	−.09	.74
Contacted an extralocal official on a personal or family matter	.01	.00	.09	.70

marized as follows: Our initial conception (see Table A–7) led us to anticipate four modes of participation – voting, campaigning, cooperative activities, and citizen-initiated contacts. However, a closer look at the data suggested that citizen-initiated contacts differ depending upon the potential outcome of the political act. The personalized contacts were found to be distinct from other acts of political participation. Furthermore, the new factor analysis containing

---

are likely to be cooperative activities, which is another reason they load on the same factor as the group activities.

	Yugo-slavia	Austria	Nether-lands
Proportion of those who contact on a personal matter who contact alone	90%	84%	73%
Proportion of those who contact on a social problem who contact alone	30%	39%	44%

Table A–6. *Direct oblimin rotated pattern matrix of the participation variables including both forms of contacting: Austria*

Variable	Campaign activity	Voting	Communal activity	Personalized contacts
Persuade others how to vote	.64	−.01	.04	.04
Ever worked for a party	.78	−.03	.02	−.06
Attended political meetings and rallies	.72	.06	−.04	.10
Member of a party	.81	.03	−.02	−.01
Active member in organizations engaged in solving community problems	.40	−.08	.14	.06
Vote in national elections	.03	.85	−.01	.03
Vote in provincial elections	.01	.90	.02	.00
Vote in local elections	.03	.92	.00	−.02
Contact a local official on a social problem	.19	−.03	.71	−.11
Contact an extralocal official on a social problem	−.06	.03	.83	−.11
Contact a local official with others	.22	−.06	.58	.19
Contact an extralocal official with others	−.19	.02	.72	.17
Contact a local official on a personal or family problem	.02	−.00	−.03	.78
Contact an extralocal official on a personal or family problem	−.05	.00	.06	.79

the distinction between personalized and social contacts revealed a clustering of two dimensions – cooperative acts and contacts on social matters – which we label a "communal activity" dimension.

Nigeria

We present the data on Nigeria separately because of the absence of items on campaign activity. As we have pointed out, the political situation did not allow us to ask such questions. We were able, however, to ask about voting, about cooperative group activities, and about contacts of both a social and personal kind. The results of a parallel factor analysis in Nigeria are presented in Table A–8. There were in Nigeria no measures of involvement in political campaigns, but the results in Nigeria are fully consistent with those elsewhere. In the absence of campaign activities, we find that the four factors are voting, cooperative activity, contacts on a social matter, and particularized contacting. The difference from the results in the other nations is the separation of the "communal" factor into its two components of cooperative activity and contacting on a social matter. These are, however, the four factors one would expect to find given our original analysis and given the absence of a campaign

Table A–7. *Schematic representation of conceptualization process*

Initial conception	Refinement	Empirical clustering
1. Campaigning ⟶	1. Campaigning ⟶	1. Campaigning
2. Voting ⟶	2. Voting ⟶	2. Voting
3. Cooperative acts ⟶	3. Cooperative acts ⟶	3. Communal acts
4. Citizen-initiated contacts ⟶	4. Contacts on social issues ⟶	4. Personalized contacts
	5. Personalized contacts ⟶	

activity factor. The Nigerian results bring back the "cooperative" dimension that is somewhat obscured by the communal activity factor in the other nations.[3]

Yugoslavia

The data on Yugoslavia also require separate consideration in the light of some substantial differences in the participatory system in that country. The structures within which one can participate in politics differ substantially from those in the previous nations studied. The two major differences, it appears to us, are the different role of elections and the existence in Yugoslavia of a wide range of self-government institutions in functionally specific areas like the workplace or the residential unit, which offer opportunities for kinds of participation not found in the other nations. This leads us to expect some differences in the structure of participation:

1. We distinguished between electoral and nonelectoral modes of activity in terms of the extent to which these activities involve the participant in conflict with other groups in the society. Campaign activity and voting involve the citizen in a partisan struggle of one party against another. Communal activity, on the other hand, does not necessarily involve participants and counterparticipants. But, in Yugoslavia, with a noncompetitive party system, this distinction ought not to be so clear. And this should blur the distinction between communal and campaign activity.[4]

2. The existence of official institutions for participation in the workplace

---

[3] Lawrence Rose, in a study of data on participation of several Norwegian communities, performed a similar factor analysis. He found factors similar to ours. He then rotated for five factors. The distinction that emerges when one solves for five factors is exactly that found in Nigeria – a distinction between cooperative activities and social contacting (Rose, 1976).

[4] Specific positions are often contested in Yugoslavia; there are, that is, often alternative candidates, if not alternative parties. But there is little evidence that this involves the structured pattern of opposition found where there are competitive parties.

Table A–8. *Direct oblimin rotated pattern matrix of the participation variables including both forms of contacting: Nigeria*

Variable	Voting	Cooperative activity	Social contacts	Personalized contacts
National voting	.93	.01	.03	−.00
Local voting	.94	−.02	−.04	−.01
Worked with others on a community problem	.01	.83	−.01	−.04
Formed a group	−.03	.86	.01	−.03
Active member in organization involved in community problem	.05	.55	.01	.25
Contact a local official on a social problem	−.01	−.05	.78	−.04
Contact extralocal official on a social problem	−.03	.02	.73	.01
Sent delegation to contact	.09	.11	.58	.06
Contact a local official on a personal or family problem	.01	−.07	.06	.77
Contact extralocal official on a personal or family problem	−.02	.05	−.07	.75

(workers' councils) and in other spheres (apartment house councils, for instance) should create an alternative mode of activity not found elsewhere.

On the other hand, there are important ways in which the structure of participation in Yugoslavia ought to be similar to that elsewhere. For one thing, the distinction between political activity aimed at influencing a general social outcome and activity aimed at influencing an outcome particularized to the individual participant is as valid in Yugoslavia as elsewhere. As we have argued, particularized contacting is the only means by which citizens can seek such outcomes. Thus this mode of activity should be distinctive in Yugoslavia as well. In addition, though the system of elections is quite different in Yugoslavia from elsewhere, in one respect voting is distinguished from other acts in a similar manner across all the countries including Yugoslavia. It remains the "easiest" political activity. In this respect, one ought to find similarity as well.

In short, our general argument about the structure of participation leads us to expect certain similarities in Yugoslavia to the structures elsewhere. But the Yugoslav political system provides such a radically different set of participatory opportunities that we expect some significant differences in the modes of participation.

Tables 3–2 and 3–3 listed the political acts about which we asked in Yugoslavia as well as the proportions of the sample who responded positively to the questions. We asked about ten different acts in Yugoslavia. In Yugoslavia, because of the differences in the structure of political life, we asked a somewhat different set of questions about political activity. Some are closely parallel to questions asked elsewhere. We asked about the regularity of the voting and whether the individual had ever contacted an official about a personal or family problem. These are quite similar items to those asked in other countries to tap voting and particularized contacting. We also asked whether respondents had contacted an official on a social problem or worked with others in various community actions. These are quite similar to the nonconflictual community activities that have fallen into our communal mode of activity elsewhere.

Given the structure of elections in Yugoslavia, it is more difficult to find items that might be expected to fall into a campaign mode of activity. But we did ask about activity in the nomination process for candidates. These nominating activities included attending voters' meetings where candidates are nominated, and serving on a nominating committee. These activities are like campaign activity in other nations in that they involve activity in the electoral process beyond the casting of the vote. Lastly, we asked a series of questions about activity within self-government units.

As pointed out earlier, the fact that campaign activity in Yugoslavia does not involve one party in competition with another led us to expect a blurring of the distinctiveness of the factors found in other nations. And the addition of an alternative set of activities – those associated with self-government institutions – should further change the pattern compared with that found elsewhere. On the other hand, the distinctions between voting and other acts (voting being easier than other acts) and between particularized contacting and other acts (the former allowing one to deal with personal and family problems) should remain.

The results of our factor analysis are reported in Table A-9.

The results differ from those found in the other six nations. Factor 1 combines what we have called communal activity in other nations (cooperative activity and contacting on a community matter) with activity in the electoral process (attendance at voters' meetings and membership in a nominating committee), as well as two of the self-government items (membership on the local community council and membership on some other municipal self-governing council).

The set is at first glance quite mixed. But, in fact, it fits quite neatly into our categorization of activities based on the dimensions of participation: the scope of the outcome, the extent to which the activity involves conflict, and the extent to which the activity requires initiative. All the activities in Factor 1 have the same characteristics: They deal with broad community goals rather than narrow personal ones; they involve little conflict; and they require some initiative. These are exactly the characteristics of the acts we have placed within the communal activity mode elsewhere – that is, the acts of contacting an official on a social matter and working in cooperative projects in the community. In Yugoslavia these characteristics also apply to the items that tap involvement in the electoral process (voters' meetings and nomination committees), since these

Table A–9. *Direct oblimin rotated factor pattern of participation variables:*
Yugoslavia

Variable	Communal activity	Self-manage-ment	Particularized contact	Voting
Attend voters' meetings	.70	.07	.14	.22
Member of an electoral nominating committee	.68	.07	.11	−.03
Worked with a local group in some community action	.68	−.11	.19	.17
Contacted an official about a community problem	.65	−.09	−.32	.01
Member of a local community council	.54	.25	.07	−.15
Member of a municipal self-government council	.57	.22	−.18	−.11
Member of a workers' council	.17	.69	−.01	.11
Member of an apartment or house council	−.12	.85	.02	.11
Contacted an official about a personal or family problem	.08	.00	.92	−.04
Votes regularly	.01	.10	−.06	.96

are not within the framework of a competitive election system. And the two self-government activities, involving as they do service on community self-government institutions, fit these characterizations as well. In short, the specific items on the factor differ quite a bit from those that formed a "communal" factor elsewhere. But from the more general point of view of the dimensions of participation, this factor would appear to be a clear functional equivalent of what we have called communal activity elsewhere.

The second factor combines two items measuring activity in self-governing bodies: membership on a workers' council and membership on a council in one's housing unit. This is a factor for which we have no equivalent elsewhere – indeed, the activities are such that they do not exist elsewhere. They are like communal activities in that they require initiative and probably do not involve explicitly structured conflict. But they differ in that they deal with problems narrower in scope than those associated with communal activities. They are limited to the affairs of one's workplace or dwelling place. They are not, however, as narrow as the subject matter of particularized contacts. We can label this a "self-management" factor.

Factor 3 is quite clear, having particularized contacting as its sole item that loads strongly. The general distinction between that kind of activity and other activities – in terms of the fact that particularized contacting was the only activity in which the scope of the outcome was limited to the specific problems of the citizen and his family – holds in Yugoslavia, as elsewhere.

And Factor 4 is also clear. Voting loads strongly on it, and nothing else does. Clearly, voting, distinguished in Yugoslavia as it is elsewhere by the fact that it is the political act requiring least initiative, stands out there as it does in the other six nations studied.

In sum, the factor analysis fits closely our overall set of dimensions of political activity and is by no means inconsistent with the activity patterns elsewhere. A communal mode of activity is clearly identifiable, as are voting and particularized contacting. Where Yugoslavia differs from the other nations is in the absence of elections competitive across political parties. Thus campaign activity – characterized in other nations by the fact that it brings the citizen into a structure of competition with other groups – is not found to be a separate mode of activity. Acts that might have fallen into that factor fall into the communal factor – as one would expect, since communal and campaign activity are distinguished in other nations solely by the extent to which they involve the citizen in conflict.

Instead of a campaign activity mode, which we do not find in Yugoslavia, we find a separate factor on which are loaded two items that reflect the participatory innovations instituted in Yugoslavia – participation in self-management bodies within such functionally specific areas as the workplace and the housing unit. The self-governing bodies on the community level are not novelties in the same sense as workers' or house councils. These community bodies are equivalent to local government units elsewhere and fall into the communal activity mode, where focus is on community-wide problems. But the self-government bodies within the functionally specialized areas of the workplace and the residential unit are innovations. And the separate factor may be taken as a good indication that, in fact, the Yugoslavs have created a distinctive mode of activity not found elsewhere.

In sum, then, the factor analyses in the seven nations produce, we believe, a strikingly parallel set of results. That structures of participation so similar could be found in societies as diverse deserves special emphasis. The diversity of the nations increases the credibility of the findings. The fact that quite different measures of some of the activities were used in the various nations adds to our belief in the validity of the modes that emerge. The studies differed in myriad ways from nation to nation – in language, in the format of the interviews, and so forth. Somewhat paradoxically, these differences make the similarity in results more convincing.

Furthermore, the fact that the modes of participation are consistent with our a priori expectations as to what kind of activity should go with what other kind, supports our contention that we can validly compare political participation across the very mixed set of nations we have. Where there are differences in the structures of participation that emerge from our analysis, the differences are predictable on the basis of our theoretical dimensions of political activity.

The relations among the factors

We can learn more about the structure of participation by considering the relations among the participation factors. What we are interested in is the extent to which the various modes of political activity are related to some common underlying dimension of "activism" and, if such an underlying dimension can be discerned, which modes of activity are most clearly related to it. The relation among the four modes of activity emerges in a higher-order factor solution for the modes of participation. In Table A–10 we present for each country the first higher-order factor – a factor that can be taken as the best measure of that which is common among the four participatory modes.

The data in Table A–10 offer some interesting similarities coupled with some differences across the nations. In the five nations having identical factor structures, campaign and communal activity are most closely related to the common dimension underlying the several modes. And in all of the nations, voting and contacting on a particularized problem are less well related to that underlying dimension. This result is particularly interesting in the light of the fact that one of the modes of activity (campaigning) that is closely related to this underlying activism dimension is within the electoral sphere; another (communal activity) is outside of it. But there are two characteristics that these two modes of activity have in common (as our previous discussion made clear): Each is a difficult act requiring some initiative, and each is focused on some general social outcome that transcends the narrow problems of the individual.

Table A–10. *Higher-order factor loadings for seven countries*

	Higher-order factors				
Lower-level oblique factor	Austria	India	Japan	Netherlands	United States
Campaign	.56	.58	.65	.78	.81
Communal activity	.45	.57	.66	.73	.66
Voting	.14	.23	.30	.52	.41
Personalized contacts	.23	.40	.16	.25	.09

Nigeria		Yugoslavia	
Lower-level oblique factor	Higher-order factor	Lower-level oblique factor	Higher-order factor
Cooperative activity	.59	Communal/campaign activity	.79
Contacts with a social referent	.39	Self-management	.68
Voting	.28	Voting	.54
Personalized contacts	.14	Personalized contacts	.29

Particularized contact, with the exception of India, is quite weakly related to the general participation dimension, whereas the situation in regards to voting is more mixed. In some cases voting forms part of the general participation dimension; in others it does not. The situation in relation to particularized contacting is consistent with our argument that it is not a "political" act in the ordinary sense of the term – it deals with no questions of a broad social nature. The situation in relation to voting – whereby it is closely related to the general dimension of participation in some cases and not in others – is somewhat more complicated but also fairly consistent with our model. Since voting is an "easy" act requiring little motivation, there can be much variation across nations in the *processes* by which people come to vote. In some cases, they may vote on the basis of their own internalized motivation (in which case the vote does measure some underlying commitment to political activity). In other cases, they may vote because they are mobilized to do so (in which case, the vote gives no indication of the individual's political commitment). As previously shown the process by which citizens come to vote is highly dependent on the kinds of institutions that mobilize citizens to political life in the various nations.

The higher-order factor analyses for Nigeria and Yugoslavia are consistent with these results – despite the different set of lower order factors. In both cases, particularized contact has the weakest relation to the general participation factor, and voting the next weakest. In Nigeria cooperative activity is most closely related to the general higher-order factor; in Yugoslavia it is the factor containing the communal and campaign activities.

The analyses highlight the importance of distinguishing among modes of political activity. Particularized contacting, though an interesting and important mode of political activity, stands off from the other activities. That someone is active in this way predicts little about that individual's other political activity. The main reason for the special character of particularized contacting is, we believe, its narrow focus on the particular problems of the individual and his family. Other modes of activity involve the individual in general social issues, resulting in outcomes that transcend the narrow interests of the individual. Particularized contacting is a kind of "parochial" participation involving no such outcome.

Voting also is somewhat separate from the political activities – campaign activity and communal activity – that appear to form the core of the general dimension of political participation. Voting is distinctive in that it is an easy political act, not necessarily requiring initiative on the part of the actor.

Elsewhere (see Verba, Nie, and Kim, 1971) we have shown that these differences among the modes of political activity are paralleled by differences in the way in which these modes of activity relate to certain political orientations. What is most relevant to our analysis here is the fact that particularized contact is generally unrelated to measures of general political interest and involvement. Citizens can participate in this way without any general concern with political matters. On the other hand, participation in communal and campaign activity was closely related to psychological involvement in politics. Lastly, voting was related to psychological involvement in some nations, but not in others.

The pattern in which the four modes of activity are related to each other parallels the pattern of relations of the modes to psychological involvement. Campaign and communal activities formed the core of a participation syndrome in each nation in that they were most closely related to the general participation factor; they are also most closely related to a scale of psychological involvement in political matters. Particularized contact was unrelated to the other acts except in India, and it is unrelated to psychological involvement, except in India. Voting was in most cases relatively weakly related to the other acts – especially in India and Austria – and also to psychological involvement. This is especially the case in Austria and India, where there is no relationship.

What this suggests is that those modes of participation that are closest to a more general participant syndrome are also held together by the fact that they depend on (or at least are accompanied by) a general psychological concern with political matters. This finding is consistent with the conclusions of Almond and Verba, as well as with those of Inkeles on the existence of a participant syndrome of political activities and civic involvement (Almond and Verba, 1963; Inkeles, 1969). But the data also suggest that there are important modes of activity that may fall outside this syndrome, activity for which there is little accompanying general political motivation.

Conclusion

We have explicated the difference among the several modes of political activity at some length. As we suggested earlier, it is both methodologically and substantively important to make these distinctions. The methodological reason is that our ability to locate a similar structure of participatory acts across our mixed set of nations is strong evidence that there is some parallel phenomenon called political participation that can be validly compared from nation to nation.[5] The fact that similar modes of activity emerge warrants, we believe, the conclusion that such comparison will be valid.

---

[5] For an argument on the usefulness of similarity in factor structure for establishing equivalence in cross-national research, see Przeworski and Teune (1970). The similarity of structure under conditions of such diversity is what is most striking. But the wary reader probably realizes the great limitation on this statement. Though the seven nations studied are quite diverse, the structure does not "emerge" unaided from these nations. It emerges from the application of certain research operations in each of the countries – research operations carried out by collaborative researchers. Thus the data represent far less than perfect independent tests of the existence of similar structure.

There are a number of ways in which the similarity of the structures might be the artifact of the research design – the clustering could reflect response set on the questionnaire or particularities of questionnaire

The substantive reason for making these distinctions among modes of political activity is that they are indeed alternative ways in which citizens take part in political life. As we have seen, the processes of political mobilization by which citizens come to be politically active differ significantly from one mode to the other.

The modes of democratic participation – research by others

Since the publication of our earlier research on the dimensions of citizen participation (Verba, Nie, Kim, 1971; Verba and Nie, 1972), a number of other students of participation have attempted to replicate and extend the search for the dimensions of participation in a wide variety of countries and contexts. We feel it would be most useful to review the findings of some of these studies here, for they add significantly to the weight of our own analysis and suggest the existence of an important set of cross-cultural uniformities in political behavior.

Survey studies from Costa Rica to Norway, employing different sets of specific participation items and asked in a wide range of question formats, all confirm the following generalizations:

1. Citizen participation everywhere appears to be a multidimensional rather than unidimensional phenomenon. Although there is substantial variation in the degree to which different modes of activity correlate with each other, there is always considerable evidence for some specialization of activity – underlining the thesis that different modes of activity carry different kinds of messages and are generally understood by the citizenry to be more or less potent for different types of needs and problems. Thus the existence of the important means-end rationality in the character of instrumental participation appears confirmed.

2. Wherever societies permit a full range of citizen participation, including participation in competitive elections, the basic distinctions between electoral and nonelectoral participation, as well as the distinctiveness of voting, clearly emerge in the dimensional analysis. Furthermore, there appears everywhere

---

format. Such artifacts are difficult to eliminate completely, and they remain plausible rival hypotheses for what we have found. Attempts were made to avoid such problems. The items that load together are based on measures from quite different parts of the questionnaire. The behavior of the two types of contact – the consistent linking of social contacts with cooperative activity while personalized contacts remain on their own factor – is particularly convincing that we have more than mere artifact. The division of contacting between personalized and social contacting was done by coders, coding open-ended answers. Perusal of many such answers indicates that they were indeed picking up a real difference. And there is little methodological artifact that one can imagine causing personalized contacts to load by themselves while social contacts consistently merge with cooperative activity.

several modes of nonelectoral participation that invariably include some form of citizen-initiated contacting or petitioning as well as some form of communal or cooperative participation characterized by either or both formal or informal joining together of citizens to solve community and/or neighborhood problems.

Several factors add to the cumulative impact of these studies. Those engaged in spatial analysis must always be concerned about the artificial creation of factors due to common question wording, coding formats, item grouping, and ordering. We attempted, insofar as possible, to deal effectively with these issues

Table A–11. *Dimensions of participation (factor pattern matrix): Canada*

	Voting	Communal activities	Campaigning	Protest
Times voted	$-.89^a(-.89)^b$	.00	-.03	.05
Voted in last national election	-.93(-.93)	-.08	-.08	.02
Voted in last prov. election	-.75(-.74)	.07	.04	.01
Voted in last municipal election	-.61(-.59)	.11	.10	.03
Take petition around	.08	-.39(.40)	-.06	.07
Go to meeting in government office	.03	-.46(.48)	.11	.19
Go to political official with problem	.04	-.34(.36)	-.16	.04
Go to neighborhood meeting	.01	-.71(.69)	.00	-.12
Talk to friends about a candidate	-.21	-.12	.55(.62)	-.16
Give money in an election campaign	.03	.09	.42(.38)	.13
Attend election rallies	-.00	.07	.48(.57)	-.22
Work in a political campaign	-.01	-.04	.66(.65)	-.01
Participate in an authorized protest rally or march	-.01	-.23	-.07	.55
Disobey an unjust law	-.00	.02	.03	.26
Participate in a non-authorized protest rally or march	-.02	-.07	-.14	.50
Eigenvalue (and explained variance) after rotation	3.51(57.9%)	1.36(22.5%)	.71(11.8%)	.48(7.9%)

^{a} Factor loadings are the result of a principal axis factor analysis with an oblique rotation. The four factors accounted for 56% of the variance before rotation. Due to listwise deletion of variables, the N for this and the following tables is 817. ^{b} Loadings in parenthesis are the variable loadings in the factor pattern solution when protest variables are omitted.
Source: Excerpted from Welch (1975), p. 577.

Table A–12. *Intercorrelations of participation
dimensions*[a]

	Campaigning	Communal	Protest
Voting	.28[b]	.34[b]	−.18[b]
Campaigning	—	.35[b]	.30[b]
Communal	—	—	.18[b]

[a] All correlations are Pearson's r.   [b] Significant at .001.
Source: Excerpted from Welch (1975), p. 577.

in our own seven-nation study. We are, however, a single group of scholars
with a developed hypothesis. Each of the following studies have been conducted by different researchers unrelated to our group, with varying research
objectives. More important, each has used a different set of specific participation items, different, that is, from both our set and from each other. Further,
the items also differ in coding categories, general formats, and question ordering. Together they constitute an impressive verification of the basic findings.

These basic findings are apparent in each of the following studies. Susan
Welch, in "Dimensions of Political Participation in a Canadian Sample," *Canadian Journal of Political Science* (December 1975): 553–9, employing data
from a survey of 850 respondents in Toronto, has found four basic modes of
activity. She used fifteen participation items to question respondents on all
aspects of their participation about which we asked, except for particularized
contacting. In addition, Welch included questions on protest participation.
Tables A–11 and A–12 nicely summarize her findings.

When the protest items are excluded, three separate modes of participation
are located: voting, communal activities, and campaigning. When the protest
measures are included, these form a fourth distinctive factor, quite independent of the traditional three modes. Further, the pattern of correlation among
the three modes of activity that overlap with ours is consistent with the patterns
found in a number of countries included in our study. In the Netherlands,
the one country in our study where we collected data on protest activity, our
findings parallel Welch's. Unfortunately, her study does not contain questions
on particularized contacting and thus can neither confirm nor refute either
the existence or distinctiveness of this mode of activity.

In another study, "Political Participation in Norway: Patterns of Citizen
Behavior in Two Norwegian Municipalities" (unpublished Ph.D. dissertation,
Stanford University, 1976), Lawrence Rose attempted to replicate many aspects
of the cross-national participation study. He carried out a detailed dimensional
analysis of the modes of participation. The 415 respondents interviewed in
this study are from two Norwegian municipalities that, when combined, Rose

argues, may be taken as typical of the social context and characteristics of the Norwegian citizenry.

Table A–13 presents the rotated pattern matrix from Rose's Norwegian data. Although the specific items differ somewhat from those we have used, the similarity of outcome is striking and does not go unnoticed by the author himself:

The results, like those obtained by Verba and his fellow investigators,

Table A–13. *Oblique rotated pattern matrix for fifteen participatory acts: Norway*

Variable	Campaign activity	Voting	Communal activity	Particularized contacting
Persuade others how to vote	.587	−.018	.169	.236
Take part in campaign work and attend election meetings/rallies	.729	−.018	.102	−.087
Contribute money to a political party	.736	.038	−.030	.079
Hold membership in political organizations	.790	.027	−.104	−.136
Voted in 1969 national election	−.024	.891	.040	−.041
Voted in 1967 local election	−.008	.889	−.008	.019
Voting regularity in both local and national elections	.036	.842	−.019	−.002
Cooperate with others in solving important problems	−.066	−.015	.679	.104
Start a movement (form a group) with others concerning important problems	−.052	.097	.756	.083
Take part in organizations interested in social problems	.191	.015	.608	−.055
Take up important problems in organizations or party groups	.144	.022	.684	.223
Contact local officials – social referent	.004	−.052	.609	−.139
Contact extralocal officials – social referent	−.019	−.003	.564	−.120
Contact local officials – particularized referent	.005	.001	−.050	.772
Contact extralocal officials – particularized referent	−.024	−.008	.009	.736

	Campaign	Vote	Communal	Particularized contacting
Campaign	—			
Voting	.17	—		
Communal	.34	.08	—	
Particularized contacting	.05	.06	.06	—

Source: Excerpted from Rose (1976), chap. 5.

reveal a remarkably clean pattern in which the four modes of political activity are clearly distinguished, as hypothesized. . . . The fact that the arguments of Verba and his associates receive further crossnational validation from this replication with Norwegian data . . . is highly significant. . . . [T]he results for the Norwegian case conform quite closely to the general pattern found to pertain in several other countries and provide additional support for the contention that political participation exhibits a certain structural similarity on a crossnational basis. (p. 11)

In a subsequent refinement in which he added a greater number of participation items, Rose has found some tendency for the communal-contacting items, where individuals act alone, to separate from those forms of communal participation that have the common elements of joining with others. This is not surprising to us, and we have in fact seen some strains in this direction in our own data but have never had enough independent questions in these areas to carry out a full-blown analysis.

In the next study, using a national sample of some 1,434 heads of families from 109 communities in Costa Rica, John A. Booth, in "A Replication: Modes of Political Participation in Costa Rica," *Western Political Quarterly* (December 1976): 627–33, has found remarkable similarities in the modes of democratic participation. His summary (and the data presented in Table A–14) is as convincing as anything we could say.

Table A–14. *Varimax rotated factor matrix: Costa Rica*

	Factors					
Variable	I	II	III	IV	V	VI
Party membership	.95	.12	.06	.08	.11	.04
Party attendance	.93	.15	.09	.08	.16	.04
Party leadership	.93	.15	.09	.08	.10	.03
Talk local politics	.15	.06	.09	.19	.85	.01
Talk national politics	.18	.21	.12	−.02	.83	.07
Vote 1970	.08	.11	.01	.02	.06	.98
Contact municipal executive	.07	.02	.42	.39	.20	.08
Contact municipal councilman	.04	.04	.52	.41	.07	.06
Contact police	.01	.10	.66	−.06	.03	−.10
Contact natl. assembly deputy	.20	.05	.51	.21	.13	.11
Contact President	−.01	.07	.72	.07	.00	.01
Contact other official	.06	.01	.58	.01	.04	.00
No. community improvement projects	.07	.12	.03	.79	−.04	−.06
No. group memberships	.39	.58	.16	.43	.22	.07
No. community improvement groups	.08	.26	.14	.64	.17	.06
Overall group attendance	.14	.91	.08	.14	.13	.06
Overall group leadership	.15	.90	.10	.15	.08	.05

Source: Excerpted from Booth (1976), p. 632.

The data are completely independent from the crossnational study conducted by Verba, Nie and company. As such they provide an excellent opportunity to replicate their findings on the modes of participation in yet another social and cultural context. . . .(p. 628)

Four of these six modes of participation resemble those found by the Verba-Nie team: voting behavior, political party activity (most like their campaign activity), organizational activism (similar to their communal activity factor), and contacting public officials. Our contacting indicator does not differentiate between social and personal goals, prohibiting exploration of how these types of contacting would relate to each other and to the group behavior phenomenon. However, that such similar modes of participation emerge from an independent survey and different operational methods in yet another cultural context – a small Central American Republic – further corroborates their conclusion that these are general, cross-cultural participatory syndromes. (pp.630–31)

That two modes of participation emerge here which were not isolated in the Verba-Nie studies is the result of differences in the input variables. Political communication phenomena, not included in the Cross-National Program analyses, were utilized here. Furthermore, that study used no measure directly comparable to the community improvement group or project participation indices. (pp. 631–32)

The parallel nature of the findings is perhaps even closer than Booth states. We have specifically excluded discussions of politics from our definition of participation, for such discussions are not prima facie evidence of an attempt to influence a governmental outcome, or the selection of leadership who make such decisions. Further, in our larger cross-national context, we did not feel that general organizational membership necessarily constituted political activity, although we do recognize that in some settings this may be the case.

The next study we wish to mention is that by James W. White, which was prepared for delivery at the annual meeting of the American Political Science Association in 1975. It is primarily aimed at a more detailed analysis of the relationship between social status and political participation. White has examined the modes of participation for a sample of 762 respondents of voting age in Tokyo.

Once again, we have variations in the specific measures used to measure each of the modes of activity, and once again we have striking uniformity in the pattern matrix and in the correlations among the rotated factors. The data in Table A–15 virtually speak for themselves.

In a highly contextual study of in-migrant or squatters' settlements in Lima, Peru, Henry Dietz – in "Some Modes of Participation in an Authoritarian Regime," University of Texas, Austin (which was prepared for delivery at the annual meeting of the American Political Science Association in 1975) – analyzes the modes of participation among the residents of these newborn com-

Table A–15. *Oblique rotated factor pattern of participation variables: Tokyo*

Variable	Campaign activity	Voting	Communal activity	Particularized contacting
Attended rally	-.44	.18	.17	- 19
Supported candidate	.55	-.04	.09	.42
Put up posters	.71	.03	.00	-.10
Leafletted	.78	-.05	.06	-.20
Held meeting	.62	-.01	-.10	-.11
Drove sound truck	.53	.02	.22	.23
Member of political organization	.35	.05	-.21	.06
Votes in national elections	.05	.80	.10	.03
Votes in local elections	.00	.79	.03	.13
Voted in 1969 national election	-.03	.76	-.05	-.11
Voted in 1971 local election	-.04	.69	-.02	-.08
Member of neighborhood association	.04	.02	-.62	.32
Worked with others on local problem	-.09	-.01	-.60	.03
Contacted official on local problem	.24	.01	-.58	-.35
Contacted official on personal problem	-.06	-.02	-.13	.77

Correlations among factors	Campaign activity	Voting	Communal activity	Particularized contacting
Campaign activity	—	.17	-.13	.12
Voting		—	-.11	.06
Communal activity			—	-.01
Particularized contacting				—

Source: Excerpted from White (1975), p. 7.

munities. Although the nature of the regime prohibits investigation of electoral behavior, a number of types of citizen activity are permitted and frequently performed by the residents. Although both the formal and informal structures or channels of participation have a character of their own, Dietz's dimensional analysis nevertheless corroborates our analysis in two important ways. First, he clearly demonstrates specialization by type of participation while making a strong case for these distinctions on the basis of the kinds of problems with which each deals best. Second, even in such a highly localized and distinctive setting, the personalized contacting and the communal modes of participation clearly emerge.

And, finally, we come to another study prepared for delivery at the annual meeting of the American Political Science Association in 1975. Maureen Fielder, R.S.N.M., in "The Participation of Women in American Politics," attempts to describe different levels of participation among men and women

Table A–16. *Participation variables: oblimin rotated factor solutions: the 1972 CPS dataset and the 1972 Virginia Slims Poll*[a]

Variable	Factor 1 Voting	Factor 2 Campaign activity	Factor 3 Communicating activity	Factor 4 Communal activity
A. The 1972 CPS Dataset:				
Voted in 1968 pres. election				0.06
Voted in 1972 pres. election	0.56	−0.05	−0.01	−0.06
Frequency of pres. voting	0.91	0.03	−0.07	0.07
Congressional voting – 1972	0.61	−0.04	0.10	−0.01
# propositions voted on	0.90	0.02	−0.09	−0.01
Persuade otrs. how to vote	0.63	0.10	0.07	−0.07
Attend polit. mtg. or rally	0.12	0.35	0.15	−0.01
Work for pty, or candidate	0.02	0.60	−0.02	0.10
Use button or bumper stkr.	−0.02	0.52	−0.02	−0.11
Contribute $ to pty, or cand.	0.01	0.57	0.01	0.02
Activity: political clubs	0.02	0.50	0.08	0.18
Letters to public officials	−0.04	0.39	−0.05	0.03
Letters to the editor	0.05	−0.01	0.69	0.03
Activity: nghbrhd. assns.	−0.04	0.02	0.48	0.39
Activity: char.-soc. wlfr. org.	0.02	−0.01	−0.01	0.42
Activity: civic groups	0.00	0.04	0.02	0.40
	0.04	0.01	0.04	1.1
Eigenvalue	3.9	1.9	1.3	1.1
B. The 1972 Virginia Slims Poll:				
Congressional voting – 1970	0.84	−0.00	−0.02	
Voted in 1968 pres. election	0.82	0.04	−0.06	
Registered to vote?	0.77	−0.05	0.06	
Attend political rallies	0.11	0.48	0.08	
Contribute money to politics	0.13	0.44	0.07	
Canvass door-to-door	0.03	0.62	0.11	
Organize rallies	−0.03	0.59	−0.05	
Raise money	−0.05	0.66	0.02	
Paying campaign job	−0.03	0.33	−0.05	
Volunteer campaign job	−0.05	0.59	0.16	
Canvass voters by phone	0.05	0.60	0.06	
General political activity	0.06	0.13	0.45	
Membership: political clubs	−0.07	−0.01	0.70	
Membership: citizens' groups	0.02	0.01	0.35	
Eigenvalue	2.13	4.27	1.00	

[a] The above are oblimin (oblique) solutions with a delta value of zero and Kaiser normalization. "Factor 2" in the Virginia Slims solution was actually the first factor to appear; they are listed this way for comparability with the the CPS factors.

Source: Excerpted from Fielder (1975), p. 6.

in the United States, and to replicate our analysis on the 1972 CPS data set and the 1972 Virginia Slims Poll. These data are presented in Table A–16. The CPS data parallel ours very closely. However, the questions on citizen-initiated contacts contain no information as to whether the referent of the contact is social or particularized. Given the factor pattern, we would suspect that a large number of these contacts were about particular issues. If this is the case, changing Fielder's label from "communicating activity" to "particularized contacting" would indicate a pattern virtually identical to that which we found in the 1967 data. The data from the Virginia Slims Poll, though they contain items from far fewer areas, once again confirm our basic findings.

APPENDIX B

Construction of scales

Indices of political participation

This appendix describes the various measures of participation and other related indices used in this book. In Table 3–1 we listed marginals for the participation variables in each nation. In Table B–1 of this appendix we present the original questions, arranged according to the order of the items in Table 3–1. Note that some of the participation items in Table 3–1 were constructed from a combination of questions.

The participation scales derive from the factor analysis of participation items, the results of which were reported in Appendix A. However, instead of using factor analysis as a means of constructing scales, we have used it as a heuristic means of identifying items that represent the four respective modes of participation, which we had anticipated on the basis of our theoretical analysis of participation. Since our initial expectations of the existence of four modes were confirmed by the data, and the factor structures were in general relatively simple (i.e., few items were loaded on more than one factor), we decided to construct a principal component scale for each mode. In a strict sense, therefore, our scales are not factors scores, but principal component scales.

More specifically, a principal component scale for each mode is created by refactoring sets of variables belonging to that mode and adding the standardized items with the optimal weight provided by the principal component analysis. The resulting scale is readjusted to have a mean equal to 0, and a standard deviation equal to 100. Therefore, a person with a 100 on a particular scale is 1 standard deviation above the average participation in the population; a scale score of −100 would mean that he is 1 standard deviation below the average. In constructing component scales, however, we have not used every item loading highly on a given factor in order to eliminate obvious autocorrelations in our analysis. For instance, we use as the key independent variable, party identification and organizational affiliation. Consequently "membership in political clubs" was eliminated from the campaign scale, and "being active in organizations dealing with community problems" was eliminated from the communal activity scale. The items included, and the optimal weights in constructing this scale are presented in Tables B–1 and B–2. For example, the voting scale in Austria was constructed according to the following equation:

$$\text{Voting Scale} = .34755 \ (Z_1) + .35177 \ (Z_2) + .34924 \ (Z_3)$$

340

I VOTING

I.A *Vote in national elections (1)*

Austria – What party did you vote for in the national elections of March 1966?

India, Japan, Nigeria – How often have you voted in the national elections – have you voted every time, most of the time, or rarely?

United States – Can you tell me how you voted in the 1964 presidential election – did you vote for Johnson or Goldwater, or perhaps you did not vote?

I.B *Vote in national elections (2)*

United States – And how about 1960 – can you tell me how you voted in the presidential election – did you vote for Kennedy or Nixon, or perhaps you did not vote?

I.C *Vote in provincial elections*

Austria – What party did you vote for in the last provincial election?

Netherlands – Did you vote in the elections for provincial estates in March 1970?

I.D *Vote in local elections*

Austria – What party did you vote for in the last community election (City Council)?

India – How often have you voted in Panchayat/Municipal elections – have you voted every time, most of the time, or rarely?

Netherlands – Did you vote in the municipal elections held June 1970?

Nigeria, United States – What about local elections. Did you try to vote in all of those? Did you sometimes miss one? Or did you rarely vote?

II CAMPAIGN PARTICIPATION

II.A *Persuade others for candidate*

Austria – During an election campaign, how often do you talk with other people about which party a person should support?

Netherlands – In the past four years we had three elections. I would like to know whether you displayed certain activities in connection with one or more of these elections. Did you try to persuade others to vote for a certain party?

United States – During an election, do you ever try to show people why they should vote for one of the parties or candidates?

II.B *Work for party*

Austria – Have you ever worked for a party in an election campaign in the past three years, such as distributing leaflets or playing an active role in campaign rallies?

India – Have you ever engaged in any activity during a political campaign to elect some candidate? What kinds of activities?

Japan – Have you ever engaged in any activity during elections campaigns? You may include any experience such as speaking for a candidate, displaying posters, working for a candidate's office, and so on.

United States – Have you ever done (other) work for one of the parties or candidates in most elections, some elections, only a few, or have you every done such work?

II.C *Attended political rallies*

Austria, India, Japan – Have you ever attended a political meeting or rally during an election or at any other time?

Netherlands – Did you attend an election meeting or an election panel?

United States – In the past three or four years have you attended any political meetings or rallies?

II.D *Given money in campaign*

India, Netherlands, United States – Have you ever given money for a political cause?

II.E *Member of political organization*

Austria – Here is a list of organizations [respondent is shown a list of names of political organizations]. In which of the listed organizations are you yourself a member?

India – Are you a member of a political party? Which one?

Japan – We would like to ask you about an organization or union of which you may be a member. Do you belong to any political organizations?

Netherlands – Are you a paying member of a political party?

United States – Now we would like to know something about the groups and organizations to which individuals belong – here is a list of various kinds of organizations [respondent is shown a list of names]. What about political groups such as Democratic or Republican clubs, or political action groups?

II.F *Display posters or leaflets*

Netherlands – Did you put up an election poster or placard? Did you distribute leaflets for a party?

III **COMMUNAL ACTIVITIES**

III.A *Active member of organization for community problems*

Austria – Here is a list of organizations [respondent is shown a list of names]. In which of the listed organizations are you yourself a member? Does the organization attempt to take part in public affairs here in the community? Are you an active participant?

India, Nigeria, United States – Have you ever worked or cooperated with others in this village/town to try to solve some of the problems of this village/town?

Japan – We would like to ask you about an organization or union of which you may be a member. Do you belong to any organization such as the neighborhood society, youth organization, *Kenjin-kai*, and so forth?

Netherlands – Now I should like to ask some questions about associations of which you might be a member, that is, real associations, having a board, meeting sometimes, and to which you pay your subscription regularly. (Sequence of questions are not included here).

III.B *Worked through group on community problem*

India, Nigeria, United States – Have you ever worked or cooperated with others in this community to try to solve some of the community problems?

Japan – Experience of cooperative activity

Netherlands – Have you ever actively done your best for a matter of import for your community? For what activity did you work with others at that time?

III.C *Form local group for community problems*

India, Japan, Nigeria, United States – Have you ever taken part in forming a new group or organization to try to solve some community problem?

Netherlands – Were you one of the leaders in working with others in the community?

III.D *Contacted local officials with others*

Austria – Here is a list of persons of some standing in organization or otherwise in the community [respondent is given a list of names]. Could you tell me if you have approached any of them in the past two years with some sort of request or proposal for yourself or on the behalf of others? Did other people in your community join you in your request?

III.E *Contact extralocal officials with others*

Austria – At any time in the last two years have you approached a member of the national legislature or of the national ministry personally or in writing with a suggestion or request? Did other people in the community join you in this request?

III.F *Working through group on extralocal problem*

Netherlands – Have you ever cooperated with others to do something about a problem that has national importance?

III.G *Contacted local officials with social referent*

Austria – (Same as III.D) (Only contacts with a group or social referent are reported here.)

India – Have you ever personally contacted some member of the Panchayat/municipality or some other person of influence in the village/town about some need or problem? (Only contacts with a group or social referent are reported here.)

Japan – Number of local elites the respondent has ever contacted. (Only contacts with a group or social referent are reported here.)

Netherlands – Here is a list of persons who are for some reason important in this municipality. Did you ever contact any of them about a problem? For whom did you raise this matter? (Only contacts with a social referent are reported here.)

Nigeria – Have you ever personally contacted – that is, gone to see or spoken to – some member of the divisional government unit or some other person of influence in the community about some need or problem? (Only contacts with a social referent are reported here.)

United States – We were talking earlier about problems that you and the people of this community have – have you ever personally contacted some member of the local community about some need or problem? (Only contacts with a social referent are reported here.)

III.H *Contacted extralocal official with social referent*

Austria – (Same as III.E) (Only contacts with social referent are reported here.)

India – Have you ever contacted some representative or government official at the block/district/state level? What were the most important problems discussed? (Only contacts with a social referent are reported here.)

Japan – Number of extralocal elites the respondent has ever contacted. Problems discussed: (Only contacts with a social referent are reported here.)

Table B–1 *(cont.)*

III.H *(cont.)*

Netherlands – Here is a list of persons who have for some reason national importance [respondent is shown a list of names]. Can you tell me for each of those whether you have ever been in contact with him/her to talk about a certain problem? (Only contacts with a social referent are reported here.)

Nigeria and United States – What about some representative or government official outside of the local community? Have you ever contacted or perhaps written to any of them on some need or problem? (Only contacts with a social referent are reported here.)

IV   **PARTICULARIZED CONTACTS**

IV.A *Contacted local official with particular referent*

Austria – (Same as III.D) (Only contacts with a particular referent are reported here.)

India – (Same as III.G) (Only contacts with a particular referent are reported here.)

Japan – (Same as III.G) (Only contacts with a particular referent are reported here.)

Netherlands – (Same as III.G) (Only contacts with a particular referent are reported here.)

Nigeria – (Same as III.G) (Only contacts with a particular referent are reported here.)

United States – (Same as III.G) (Only contacts with a particular referent are reported here.)

IV.B *Contact extralocal official with particular referent*

Austria – (Same as III.E) (Only contacts with a particular referent are reported here.)

India – (Same as III.H) (Only contacts with a particular referent are reported here.)

Japan – (Same as III.H) (Only contacts with a particular referent are reported here.)

Netherlands – (Same as III.H) (Only contacts with a particular referent are reported here.)

Nigeria and United States – (Same as III.H) (Only contacts with a particular referent are reported here.)

where Z_1 stands for the standardized variable of *I.A.*, Z_2 for *I.C.*, and Z_3 for *I.D.* of Table B–1.

The overall participation scale was constructed in a similar way by combining the component scales. In order to salvage as much data as possible in constructing scales, we have estimated some of the missing information in individual items. The principle followed in estimating missing information was to replace the missing information with the least squares predictor from other

Table B-2. *Weighting factors used in constructing composite indices of various participation measures*

	Austria	India	Japan	Netherlands	Nigeria	United States	Yugoslavia[a]
I. Voting							
A. Vote in national election (1)	.34575	.7071	1.0	—[d]	.7071	.38631[b]	[d]
B. Vote in national election (2)	—	—	—	.7071	—	.39291[c]	
C. Vote in provincial elections	.35177	—	—	.7071	—	—	
D. Vote in local elections	.34924	.7071	—	.7071	.7071	.37085	
II. Take part in campaign activities							
A. Persuade others for a candidate	.42679	—	—	.30057	—	.26383	
B. Ever worked for a party	.43737	.49380	.51312	—	—	.31354	
C. Attended political meetings or rallies	.43640	.51082	.49067	.38033	—	.28424	
D. Given money in a campaign	—	.37287	—	.35865	—	.26369	
E. Member of a political club or organization	—	—	.37047	.35757	—	.28536	
F. Display or distribute campaign posters or leaflets	—	—	—	—	—	—	
III. Cooperative activities							
A. Active member of organization engaged in solving community problems	.29717	—	—	—	—	—	
B. Worked through group on a community problem	—	.36450	.37934	.38059	.35654	.41081	
C. Helped form local group to deal with a community problem	—	.37942	.33865	—	.35314	.38649	
D. Contacted local official with others	—	—	—	—	—	—	
E. Contacted extralocal official with others	—	—	—	.36169	—	—	
F. Worked through a group on an extralocal problem	.34334	—	—	—	—	—	
G. Contacted local official with social referent	.36995	.37542	.40609	.34578	.27759	.36591	
H. Contacted extralocal official with social referent	.35360	.36564	.34921	.42054	.30223	.31931	
I. SOCREFEL	—	—	—	—	.32014	—	
IV. Particularized contacts							
A. Local official on personal matter	.7071	.7071	.7071	.7071	.7071	.7071	
B. Extralocal official on personal matter	.7071	.7071	.7071	.7071	.7071	.7071	

Table B-2 (*cont.*)

	Overall participation variable						United	
	Austria	India	Japan	Netherlands	Nigeria	States	Yugoslavia[a]
Voting	.31740	.19918	.30977	.35823	.59625	.37354	.36270
Campaign	.49788	.46781	.49838	.53804	—	.46998	.46216
Communal	.46801	.43327	.45275	.50287	.57975	.44253	.53666
Part. contact	.32678	.36278	.26245	.18170	.32742	.13391	.19985

[a] See Table 8–3 for data on Yugoslavia.   [b] Presidential vote in 1964.   [c] Presidential vote in 1960.   [d] No entry indicates a case in which a particular item was not asked.

Table B–3. *Political participation: Yugoslavia*

I.	*Voting*	
A.	Votes regularly	1.0
II.	*Communal*	
A.	Member of an electoral nominating committee	.25371
B.	Contacted an official about community problem	.21691
C.	Member of local community council	.23475
D.	Member of municipal self-government councils	.23540
E.	Attended voters' meetings	.29896
III.	*Self-management*	
A.	Member of an apartment or a house council	.7071
B.	Member of workers' council	.7071
IV.	*Particularized contact*	1.0

available variables plus a random component whose expected variance is equal to the error of estimate.

More specifically, the inserted value is:

regression estimate + random component
$$= \text{predicted value} + \text{error term}$$

In order to simulate the degree of uncertainties inherent in the data, the error term is created by a (pseudo) random number with the mean $= 0$, and variance = the error of estimate in multiple regression. (See Kim and Curry, 1977.)

Index of socioeconomic resource level

This index was created by adding two items, level of formal education and family income. The resulting index was made to have a mean $= 0$, and variance $= 100$. When the information was available in a grouped data form, as was the case in several countries, we have converted these categories into estimated mean values for the category. Then each item was standardized before being added together. In short, the index reflects equally both the respondent's educational and economic resources.

Index of psychological involvement in politics

The index of psychological involvement is created by combining the following variables: (1) index of political interest, (2) the degree to which the respondent engages in political discussions, (3) the index of political knowledge and information, and (4) the degree to which the respondent can articulate community and national problems. The weights for combining these variables

Table B–4. *Weights for creating psychological involvement index*

	Austria	India	Japan	Netherlands	Nigeria	United States	Yugoslavia
Political interest	.490	.259	.415	.648	.648	.320	.576
Political information	.085	.336	.159	.174	.174	.259	.419
Political discussion	.309	259	.205	.203	.203	.297	—
Awareness of national needs	.249	.214	.257	—	—	.187	—
Awareness of community needs	.136	.147	.172	.059	.097	.172	.100

into a simple index were based on the loadings on the first principal component, and the index was adjusted to have a mean = 0, and a variance = 100.

The four items that constitute the overall index are themselves in turn created by combining various indicators. The index of political interest was created by combining items such as "degree of interest in local or national politics," "following the political news," and so forth. The index of information and knowledge was created by adding several items such as being able to name elected officials and being able to identify legal requirements for voting, and so on. The last subindex was created by counting the number of national and community needs the respondent can identify as a response to open-ended questions.

A summary of items used in the construction of the psychological involvement index and their relative weights are given in Table B-4.

APPENDIX C

Sampling design, sample weights, and data base of basic tables

The Cross-National Participation Project is a complex and multifaceted re-search program. As such, there were many different objectives that influenced the overall design. In each nation we generated a national representative sample of a cross section of the citizenry, a set of mini-community samples for 60–100 communities, a sample of elites for each of these communities, and finally numerous types of information on the demography and structure of each of the communities. A detailed description of each facet of the design would take many pages. Because, however, this book almost exclusively con-centrates on the national cross-section samples, we shall limit our description here to these cross-section samples and the factors that influenced the way we drew them.

In Austria, Japan, the Netherlands, and the United States the cross-section samples are representative of the entire nation. In the other three nations the samples pertain to specified subnational regions. Due to the enormity of the cultural diversity and sheer physical size, only four states were sampled in India: Andhra Pradesh, Kujarat, Uttar Pradesh, and West Bengal. The cross section is, however, representative of the citizenry of those four states. For similar reasons the study was conducted in only four of six republics of the Yugoslavian Federated Nation, in Croatia, Macedonia, Serbia, and Slovenia. The situation with regard to Nigeria is even more complicated. Although we had originally planned a study of the entire nation, severe political tensions began to escalate rapidly as we entered the period of our actual field work. The situation degenerated, particularly in the North, where violence broke out while we were still in the field. This added to our already difficult task of obtaining interviews with women in the Muslim North, lowering the response rate to a point at which we felt it was unwise to employ the data from northern Nigeria in our analysis. All data from Nigeria reported in this work, therefore, exclude that region of the country.

In all of the countries except the United States the cross-section samples are multistaged area probability samples to the level of the individual. Due to cost considerations and because of our long experience in doing surveys in this country, the U.S. sample is a multistaged area probability sample to the block level, with block quota techniques employed for the final selection of respond-ents.

349

The sample design began by stratifying according to region, culture, language, degree of urbanization and development, as well as other relevant characteristics as required in each nation to obtain a sample containing the full national or subnational variation. Within each strata the Primary Sampling Units (PSUs) were selected with probability proportional to size. In those countries where PSUs represent relatively large areas, a second-stage selection of second sampling units was drawn, once again with probability proportional to size.

There was in our design a continuing tension between two objectives of the study: to produce a highly reliable national cross-section sample that would enable us to describe and compare participatory systems of each of the nations, while at the same time to maintain the ability to focus on local communities as the most relevant and immediate context for understanding political activity.

The first objective calls for a maximum number of sampling points with a minimum amount of clustering, whereas the second necessitates a more limited number of sampling points, that is, local communities with a relatively large number of respondents from each community. We resolved the tension between these two objectives by increasing the number of interviews in each country beyond that which would normally be collected for a cross-section national sample. However, we clustered these additional interviews in that subset of our PSUs targeted as our sample of small communities. Thus we enlarged or augmented the number of respondents interviewed in communities under 50,000 population. Although the sampling details vary from country to country, this general procedure has the following main consequences:

1 The additional interviews, although adding somewhat to the quality and precision of the samples, do not have as much positive impact as they would have had had they been spread out over all or most of the PSUs.

2 The additional interviews in the small communities require weighting interviews in the large urban centers. However, in order not to misrepresent the power and efficiency of our samples, we have divided all weights by a constant so that the number of weighted respondents reported in our analyses is equal almost exactly to the number of respondents actually interviewed.

In addition, there were the following deviations from pure probability sampling. In India, in the sample for the state of Kujarat, the selection probabilities were increased by 50 percent in order to obtain an adequate sample of this small yet politically important urban state. Similar increases in the selection probabilities were also carried out for the Republics of Slovenia and Macedonia within the Yugoslavian sample. These two republics are very small, particularly when compared with Croatia and Serbia, and increases of 100 percent in the selection rates were necessary in order to take account of reasonable internal variation. Finally, in both Nigeria and India rural residents and women were undersampled relative to urban residents and males. Consequently, rural women were undersampled by substantial proportions.

The experience of both national teams suggested three main reasons for undersampling rural residents in general, all women, and particularly rural women. First, responses of the rural population and of women each tend to be highly homogeneous in content. In the rural sectors of these nations it is extremely difficult to gain access to women to conduct interviews in the first place. Low literacy rates in rural areas and the absence of any form of "outside the home" social activity for women, tend to create large numbers of "don't know" and "inapplicable" responses for these segments of the population.

As in the case of prior deviation from probabilistic selection weights, these deviations are adjusted in a similar way by sample weights during the analysis phase. Detailed information on each national sample design follows.

Austria

The cross section consisting of 1,769 interviews was collected by the Institute für Empirische Sozialforschung (IFES), Vienna. The universe sampled represents the noninstitutionalized Austrian population consisting of citizens over eighteen and under seventy-one years of age. Interviews were clustered in fifty-seven communities, which were selected from three different strata: (1) communities under 50,000 in population that contain 66 percent of the target population; (2) communities with a population between 50,000 and 1 million that contain 11 percent of the population; (3) Vienna, a city with over 1 million population consisting of 22.6 percent of target population. (The Voralberg Province, with 3 percent of the Austrian population, was excluded from the target.) The number of communities, target samples, and completed interviews for each stratum are presented in Table C–1.

The selection of communities from the first stratum was done with further classification of communities according to the population size. The respondents were randomly selected from voting lists in these fifty seven communities. In Austria, all eligible citizens are automatically registered to vote; therefore, these lists included all adult citizens. In a few communities, the lists have not been

Table C–1. *Number of communities, target sample, completed interviews, and response rate by type of strata: Austria*

Type of strata	Sample communities	Target sample	Completed interviews	Response rate (%)
Communities, with population less than 50,000	40	1,650	1,260	76
Communities with population between 50,000 and 1 million	6	244	196	80
Vienna	1	377	313	83
Total	57	2,271	1,769	78

updated since the 1966 national elections; in most communities, provincial elections were held in 1968 or 1969. There is, then, some variability, believed to be very minor, in the representativeness of the voting lists.

In this selection, citizens in Vienna (the largest stratum) were undersampled by one-third and citizens from the second stratum were undersampled by one-tenth.

India

Selection of a representative sample for the entire nation of India posed administrative problems beyond our resources, particularly because of the multiplicity of languages, the difficulty of getting adequate personnel for conducting the interviews, and a government ban on citizen interviews in some states such as Kashmir and Assam. Our aim was to obtain an Indian sample that would be representative enough for cross-national comparisons. As an initial step, one state from each of the four main geographic regions was chosen. These were Andhra Pradesh, Gujarat, West Bengal, and Uttar Pradesh. An attempt was made to introduce as much variance as possible into the sample of states, in terms of cultural, geographical, and socioeconomic aspects. It is hoped that some amount of national representativeness can be presumed to exist. Each state was then divided into rural and urban areas; actual sampling of communities and individuals was done by treating these two types of areas as separate universes.

From the outset it was decided to undersample females relative to males and to oversample urban residents relative to rural residents. The guidelines used were to select 2 per 100,000 for rural males; 5 per 100,000 for urban males; 1 per 200,000 for rural females; and 2 per 100,000 for urban females. The reasons for undersampling female respondents were twofold: the difficulty of obtaining interviews, and the assumed homogeneity (general low level of political involvement) of the female population. Urban residents were oversampled in order to secure a sufficient number of interviews from urban areas, which constitute only about one-fourth of the whole country.

Urban sample

Urban areas are classified into three groups: (1) state capitals, (2) towns with populations of 50,000 and over, and (3) towns with populations under 50,000. In each case the state capital was selected automatically. Within each district (see the description on rural sampling for the selection of districts), two towns of type (2) were randomly selected, the probability of selection being proportional to the population size of the type (2) towns. Also within each district two towns were selected from type (3) – one from the larger towns and another from the smaller towns – after type (3) towns were stratified into two groups, using the median split. Interviews were clustered by wards in the state capitals, and by towns with populations over 50,000. More specifically, 10 percent of the wards were selected if the town contained more than 30 wards, 25 percent if the total number of wards was 20–29, and 50 percent if the total wards were fewer than 20. The selection of wards was made proportionate to the population size of the wards, and the allotment of interviews was also made proportionate to their relative size. In the towns with populations under 50,-000, the entire town was treated as a single unit or ward. All in all, the urban sample contains four state capitals, eight towns with populations over 50,000, and eight towns with populations under 50,000. The total number of urban interviews in each state was distributed among the three types of towns proportionate to the state population staying in all towns of that type in each state. After having allocated the number of interviews in this way, however, we distributed the number of interviews for a particular town according to the relative size of the two towns selected in each type.

The total urban sample selected was 1,293, out of which 974 were male and 319 were female. For the female sample, it was decided to interview only in three cities in each state, the capital, and one out of the two selected towns in each of the other two categories. The selection was made randomly.

Rural sample

Rural sampling was done in four stages: districts, blocks, villages, and individuals in each village. First, the districts in each state were stratified according to the level of socioeconomic development, using an index developed by M. N. Pal and C. Subramaniam for the Indian Statistical Institute in New Delhi. Using these data, we arranged the districts in each state from low to high in levels of social development and then applied a median split to obtain two categories before randomly selecting the districts from each category. The total number of districts selected for our sample was twenty-five, and the number of districts selected from each state was roughly proportionate to their respective population base. In consequence, there were five districts from Andhra Pradesh, four from Gujarat, four from West Bengal, and twelve from Uttar Pradesh. (In the case of Andhra Pradesh, one district was selected randomly out of the total list.) Furthermore, the probability of selection of districts from each category of the developmental level was made proportionate to their population size.

Within the selected districts, community development blocks were stratified on the basis of their distance from the district headquarters. The list of blocks and the data on distance were obtained from the district government. One block from each stratum was randomly chosen. Selection probability was again made proportionate to the size of the block. Within each block the villages were ranked in terms of their size, and once again, by splitting at the median, villages were stratified into large and small villages. One village was then randomly selected from each stratum.

Finally, individuals were randomly selected from each village from the list of eligible voters. The number of interviews to be obtained was determined by

Table C–2. *Number of interviews by various strata: India*

	Rural		Urban	
	Male	Female	Male	Female
Andhra Pradesh	2@4	68	136	50
Uttar Pradesh	646	147	217	69
West Bengal	249	52	157	50
Gujarat	246	56	163	47
Total	1,425	323	673	216 = 2,637

the size of the state, district, and block to which the village belongs. That is, the state sample quota is proportional to the relative state population (an exception being the smallest state – Gujarat – which was given fifty more than its share based on the population size). The state sample quota was distributed proportionately into block quotas. Likewise, a block quota was distributed proportionately into village quotas. The final result is that the size of the sample in a village is not strictly proportionate to the size of the selected villages, but rather to the underlying characteristics employed for stratification.

Female sample. Because of the smaller intended sample size of females in rural areas, we have interviewed them only in about one-fourth of the villages selected. In selecting the villages from which female respondents were to be interviewed, each combination of district and block types is represented. But in some cases, only a large village or a small village was selected from each combination, although an equal number of small and large villages was included in the state sample.

The distribution of samples by state, urban and rural areas, and sex are as shown in Table C–2.

Japan

The whole country was first stratified into metropolitan, urban, and rural areas. The metropolitan areas were then stratified by their administrative units, such as Tokyo, Kyoto, Yokohama, and so on; the urban areas were first grouped into two regions (West vs. East), each region then being categorized into small or large cities, depending upon whether their predominant industry was primary, secondary, or tertiary; the rural areas were first stratified by the prefecture, and second by population size.

After the entire country had been stratified with accompanying cumulative population size, it was then divided into 200 sample strata, each stratum being similar in population size. (When the natural unit – such as the metropolis –

Table C–3. *Number of completed interviews for various strata: Japan*

Primary strata	Completed interviews
Metropolitan	508
Urban	1,351
Rural	810
Total	1,669

is larger than the average sample stratum, it was included in the stratum and the size was doubled.)

From each of the 200 survey strata, one sample unit was randomly selected. (When the sample stratum was doubled, two units were selected.) The sampling units were wards in metropolitan areas, cities in urban areas, and towns or villages in rural areas. When the voting district was smaller than these units, one voting district was selected from each unit, except in urban areas, where two were selected – one representing the old section of the city, the other the new section.

Each sampling unit was assigned an average of about fifteen interviews. These fifteen interviewees were selected systematically with a random start from the voter registration list. To adjust for the anticipated lower rate of successful interviews in urban and metropolitan areas, two additional interviews were assigned from the beginning. Table C–3 presents the primary strata and the number of successful interviews.

The Netherlands

The cross-section sample consists of the second-wave interviews of a four-wave panel, three of which were conducted by the Catholic University at Tilburg (in collaboration with the University of Michigan). A total of 1,746 interviews were obtained from 79 municipalities during the months of February and March of 1971. Of the total second-wave sample, 944 had been previously interviewed in the first wave, and 842 were new. The first wave was administered subsequent to the elections for the provincial legislatures in 1970. The sample for all waves was drawn prior to these elections and was intended to represent the Dutch population over twenty-one years of age as of January 1, 1970.

Sampling was done in two stages in order to obtain samples of both municipalities and individual voters. In order to ensure representation of a variety of municipalities, all of them were stratified (1) by twelve primary urbanization strata as defined by the Central Bureau of Statistics, (2) within each stratum by eleven provinces, (3) (for the six least urbanized categories) by the percentage of the population living within the largest built-up area, and (4) by the percentage of votes cast in 1967 for the three main religious parties. After having stratified the municipalities according to these four characteristics, we chose target municipalities and individuals in these municipalities as follows.

In order to limit transportation costs, it was determined (by the designers of the four-wave panel mentioned previously) that a minimum cluster of 15 would be selected from each municipality in the sample. As the desired target sample size was 2,500, this value divided by 15 yielded about 167 clusters. Then the total number of eligible voters was divided into 167 strata, each containing approximately 44,700 voters. Within each stratum a random number was chosen, representing a hypothetical voter, and the municipality in which this hypothetical voter lived was chosen as one of the target municipalities. Such a process yielded about 100 municipalities, since some contained more than one stratum. According to the initial sample design, the number of target interviews would be determined by 15 times the number of strata falling into the municipality.

This basic design was modified slightly to fit the needs of the participation study. It was determined that, for our purposes, it is desirable to have at least 25 interviews from each municipality. Because it would have been too costly to have increased the target sample size for each stratum to 25, we randomly dropped one-third of the strata and increased the target sample size to 25 for every target municipality containing only one stratum. Consequently, the larger municipalities containing more than two strata are underweighted by the ratio of 15 to 25.

Within each municipality selected, a systematic sample of individuals was obtained from the population registration list. From a random start, every nth person was selected provided that the nth person was an eligible voter. Since almost half of the population is not eligible to vote, an interval was designated that would yield a sufficient number of eligible voters.

The number of completed interviews, the target population size, and the selection probabilities by the categories of municipalities are given in Table C-4.

Table C-4. *Sampling information: Netherlands*

Type of municipality	Number of municipalities in the sample	Completed interviews	Approximate probability of section
Large	16	510	1/8,333
Small	63	1,236	1/5,000
Total	79	1,746	

Nigeria

The sampling plans for Nigeria utilized the sample spots of two surveys carried out by the government with the assistance of United Nations advisers. One survey covers urban, the other, rural areas.

The proportion of urban dwellers in Nigeria ranges from 5 percent in the North to 40 percent in the West; the overall proportion is about 12 percent. Therefore, to obtain an adequate sample for urban dwellers, it was decided to oversample them, making the target sample size 1,000 for urban and 1,500 for rural residents.

Urban sample

We used the sample of urban communities drawn by the Demographic Survey of the Federal Office of Statistics in Lagos, which is a survey ancillary to the 1962 Federal Population Census. Forty-six towns were selected, with a total of 54 clusters and 270 enumeration areas. The towns were selected with probability proportional to the number of enumeration areas that are about equal in size.

Because of a lack of resources, some urban communities had to be eliminated on linguistic grounds. The remaining urban areas were stratified according to their age and economic characteristics. Every other urban area was picked from the stratified list, giving about 22 urban areas. In the second stage, enumeration areas were selected within each of the 22 urban areas, the number so chosen being proportional to the number of enumeration areas per urban area. Respondents from each enumeration area were in the ratio of three adult males to every adult female. The number of interviews set as a target depended upon the size of the place; in 45 percent of them, at least 45 interviews were obtained; in 68 percent of them, at least 36 interviews were obtained, and in 86 percent of the urban places, 26 interviews were obtained. The average number of interviews per urban place was 47.

Rural sample

The Federal Rural Economic Survey Sample of 204 villages constitutes our sampling base. The sample was drawn from a list of villages in the federation, stratified by region and type of economy. Fifty-four villages were eliminated from our target, either because of less widely known languages or geographic isolation. The remaining 150 villages were stratified into three groups according to voter turnout for the 1959 federal elections. About one-third of the villages were chosen, giving all together 40 villages or sampling points. All 40 villages were weighted in proportion to their population, and the number of respondents was apportioned according to their population weight. An average of 22 interviews was obtained from each village; in 80 percent of the communities, either 21 or 22 interviews were obtained. The

Table C–5. *Final sample points selected (villages and towns): Nigeria*

Region	Town	Village	Total
East	6	11	17
Midwest	3	7	10
West	6	9	15
Lagos	1	9	1
Total	15	28	43

Table C–6. *Completed interviews and completion rate: Nigeria*

Completed samples	Urban		Rural		
	Male	Female	Male	Female	Total
East	247	140	110	109	606
Midwest	103	86	75	68	332
West	234	154	105	73	566
Lagos	101	54	—	—	155
Total	685	434	290	150	1,659

final choice of respondents was obtained as follows. Using a random table, the number of households was picked from the list of households prepared for the selected villages. In every third household so selected, a female was interviewed instead of a male, yielding the ratio of 2 to 1 male over female.

In the middle of our interviewing, which was conducted in the summer of 1966, disturbances broke out in the northern cities and the interviewing in the North was interrupted before the sample was completed. Therefore, we decided to delete the data from the North from our analysis. (The data for Nigeria are presented in Tables C–5 and C–6.)

United States

The cross-section data consisting of 2,549 interviews were collected by the National Opinion Research Center (NORC) in some 200 separate locales in March 1967. The universe sampled was the total, noninstitutionalized population of the United States, twenty-one years of age or older. The sample was a standard, multistaged, area probability sample to the block or segment level. At the block level, however, quota sampling was utilized (to reduce costs to a tolerable level) based on sex, age, race, and employment status statistics of the census tract or division within which the block fell. The primary sampling units consist of a Standard Metropolitan Statistical Area (SMSA) or a county if the county lies outside the SMSA. Out of these primary sampling units, about 200 are selected, using the probabilities proportionate to their population size. (For more detailed information about the NORC master sample and population adjustment, see Verba and Nie, 1972, Appendix A.)

Within each selected PSU, localities were ordered according to: (1) cities with block statistics, (2) other urban places, (3) urbanized Minor Civil Divisions (MCDs), and (4) nonurbanized MCDs, with the places ordered by the 1960 population for each of these categories. Localities were selected from this list, using a random start and applying a designated skip interval to the cumulative 1960 population. This provided stratification according to the size and urban type of locality and at the same time selection with probability proportionate to population size.

Where available, 1960 block statistics were used. Blocks were selected with probability proportionate to the population. In places without block statistics, census enumeration districts were selected with probabilities proportionate to the number of households. The selected districts were then divided into segments, and estimates of the number of households within each segment were obtained by field count. The election of respondents was then made with probability proportionate to the number of households. The sample of 1,500 was then divided into about 200 localities, the exact size of the sample being proportionate to the population size of the last block or segment. This means that the average sample size per block determined in this way was about 7.5.

Out of the communities and localities included in this sample, 67 localities with populations of less than 50,000 were randomly selected. An additional 1,100 respondents were then sampled out of these 67 localities. This is partly to enlarge the overall sample size, but mostly to ensure having the proper number of cross-section interviews for the target communities. This modification was necessary because the overall design of the larger study requires community-specific analysis as well as the comparison between the cross-section interviews and elite interviews within each community. In these target communities the average sample is about 27.

Once the number of respondents to be selected from each block or segment is determined, the interviewer fills a quota by beginning his interview at a random dwelling unit that has been previously designated in the block, and proceeding in a specified direction until his quotas have been filled. In the South, segments were selected by the race of respondents. This was done because the accuracy of responses increases when blacks are interviewed by black interviewers in the South. Elsewhere the interviewer is given no race quotas.

The quotas call for approximately equal numbers of men and women, with the exact proportion of each location to be determined by the 1960 census. For women the additional requirement is imposed that there be the proper proportion of employed and unemployed women in the location. For men the additional requirement is that there be the proper proportion of men over and under thirty in the location. These particular quotas have been established because past experience has shown that employed women and younger men under thirty are the most difficult to find at home for interviewing. This seems to provide a suitable balance of precision and economy. Although sampling errors cannot be computed directly, past experience suggests that for most purposes a sample of 1,500 could be considered as having about the same efficiency as a simple random sample of 1,000.

Yugoslavia

Since Yugoslavia is a country of different nations and of nationalities with different cultural-historical backgrounds, it was difficult to secure sample respondents that would be representative of the entire country. Therefore, the target population was initially limited to four republics – Croatia, Macedonia, Slovenia, and Serbia – which contitute a fairly diverse set of republics. Within each republic selected, the final sampling was done in three stages: selection of communes, selection of local communities within each commune, and individual voters from each local community. Because of the importance of communes in Yugoslavian politics, it was decided to select as many communes as possible. The number actually selected was about one-third (125 communes) of the 374 communes existing in the four republics. In each commune, three local communities were selected, and in each local community, eight voters were chosen randomly.

The selection of communes was done after stratifying entire communes in each republic by the proportion of the agricultural population. Then a systematic sample of 125 was made, giving the probability of selection of each commune proportional to its relative population size. Because of the difference in the population size of these republics, it was decided to select about proportionately twice as many communes in Macedonia and Slovenia as in Croatia and Serbia to ensure an adequate number of communes for the smaller republics in our sample.

The cross-section data were collected in the months of March and April 1971, and the total number of communes, local communities, and respondents by each republic are shown in Table C–7.

Table C–7. *Number of communes, communities, and interviewers: Yugoslavia*

	Croatia	Macedonia	Slovenia	Serbia	Total
Number of communes	29	18	24	54	125
Number of local communities	87	54	72	102	375
Respondents	696	432	576	1,291	2,995

Weighting cases

Since the probability of being included in a sample was not uniform for each group in all countries except Japan, therefore the sample cases were weighted. The sample weights were assigned in such a way that the sample reproduces the population distribution (on characteristics employed as sampling criteria) and the actual size of the sample obtained.

When the selection probabilities are based on a single criterion *and* the

Table C–8. *Sample weights*

Austria
1. Communities with populations of less than 50,000   .9084
2. Communities with a population between 50,000 and 1 million   1.0094
3. Vienna   1.3627
Actual and Weighted Sample Size = 1,769

Japan
No weighting. Actual Sample Size = 2,657

Netherlands
1. Large urban areas   1.395
2. Other   .8369
Actual and Weighted Sample Size = 1,746

United States
1. Communities with populations of less than 50,000   .8236
2. Others   1.6472
Actual and Weighted Sample Size = 2,549

Yugoslavia
1. Macedonia and Slovenia   1.2023
2. Croatia and Serbia   .612
Actual and Weighted Sample Size = 2,995

	Rural		Urban	
	Male	Female	Male	Female
India				
Andhra Pradesh	.8476	3.4957	.3795	.9861
Uttar Pradesh	.8171	3.2963	.3878	.9889
West Bengal	.8781	3.9666	.5152	1.1329
Gujarat	.5124	2.1523	.2770	.8615
Actual and Weighted Sample Size = 2,637				
Nigeria				
Western	2.0406	2.8461	.5370	.6981
Midwestern	.8055	.9666	.1074	.1074
East	2.4702	1.7924	.2148	.2363
Lagos	—	—	.2578	.3007
Actual and Weighted Sample Size = 1,659				

completion rates do not fluctuate widely from group to group, the weights are made inversely proportional to the initial selection probabilities. Such a weighting was applied to the United States, the Netherlands, Austria, and Yugoslavia. Likewise, when the selection probabilities are uniform and there is no wide variation in completion rates, no weights are applied, as was the case with Japan. However, when varying selection probabilities are combined with somewhat fluctuating completion rates, we applied the weights in such a way that both the selection rates *and* the completion rates are adjusted, as with India and Nigeria. The weights are reproduced in Table C–8.

The completion rate of interviews varied from country to country. For instance, in Yugoslavia, the completion rate was almost perfect, whereas in the United States, owing to the quota-sampling, the completion rate was not particularly meaningful. For other countries the following completion rates were obtained: Austria – 78 percent; India – 95 percent; Japan – 82 percent; Netherlands – 76 percent; and Nigeria – 77 percent.

Marginal frequencies for basic tables

In Tables C–9 through C–21 we present marginal frequencies for the basic tables used in the text, first, for the actual samples obtained, and, second, for the weighted samples. These tables may be used in evaluation of the data bases of various tables used in the text. Actual frequencies for the tables in the main text may vary slightly from the frequencies shown in these tables, mainly because of missing values in some other variables involved. Unless it is specifically noted in the main text, the reader may assume that the frequencies shown in these basic tables can be used safely as appropriate data bases for the corresponding analysis tables.

Table C-9. *Data base for Austria: unweighted*

	Sex			Institutional affiliation				
	Male	Female	Total	1	2	3	4	Total
SERL								
(1) Low	205	384	589	97	164	175	153	589
(2) Medium	306	289	595	74	113	160	248	595
(3) High	324	260	584	110	94	174	206	584
Total	835	933	1,768	302	371	541	554	1,768
Inst. affil.								
(1)	119	184	303					
(2)	105	266	371					
(3)	249	292	541					
(4)	362	192	554					
Total	835	934	1,769					

	Sector										
	1	2	3	4	5	6	7	8	9	10	Total
Sex											
Male	95	62	274	35	108	64	187				825
Female	116	121	235	44	90	80	177				863
Total	211	183	509	79	198	144	364				1,688
Inst. affil.											
(1)	22	32	79	9	38	20	85				285
(2)	54	45	110	14	25	32	71				351
(3)	57	72	159	23	58	47	100				516
(4)	78	34	161	33	77	45	108				538
Total	211	183	509	79	198	144	364				1,688
SERL											
(1) Low	148	91	188	16	38	21	31				533
(2) Medium	46	74	210	24	72	46	114				586
(3) High	17	18	111	38	88	77	219				568
Total	211	183	509	78	198	144	364				1,687

Table C–10. *Data base for India: unweighted*

	Sex			Institutional affiliation				
	Male	Female	Total	1	2	3	4	Total
SERL								
(1) Low	487	174	661	307	60	243	33	643
(2) Medium	670	180	850	302	77	341	114	834
(3) High	943	181	1,124	255	107	402	336	1,100
Total	2,100	535	2,635	864	244	986	483	2,577
Inst. affil.								
(1)	543	323	866					
(2)	186	58	244					
(3)	860	126	986					
(4)	478	5	483					
Total	2,067	512	2,579					

	Sector										
	1	2	3	4	5	6	7	8	9	10	Total
Sex											
Male	174	113	176	223	145	79	473	330	160	167	2,040
Female	31	33	19	67	36	29	77	125	20	73	510
Total	205	146	195	290	181	108	550	455	180	240	2,550
Inst. affil.											
(1)	73	52	71	94	66	35	174	122	58	85	830
(2)	17	15	24	37	15	17	32	53	9	21	240
(3)	93	48	64	93	65	38	211	171	80	103	966
(4)	21	26	33	57	35	16	125	99	31	26	469
Total	204	141	192	281	181	106	542	445	178	235	2,505
SERL											
(1) Low	113	62	79	62	44	18	102	22	63	54	619
(2) Medium	68	48	74	93	69	23	217	78	68	90	828
(3) High	24	36	42	135	67	66	231	355	49	96	1,101
Total	205	146	195	290	180	107	550	455	180	240	2,548

Table C-11. *Data base for Japan: unweighted*

	Sex			Institutional affiliation				
	Male	Female	Total	1	2	3	4	Total
SERL								
(1) Low	422	539	961	306	130	328	182	946
(2) Medium	393	413	806	205	119	270	200	794
(3) High	485	403	888	174	126	372	203	875
Total	1,300	1,355	2,655	685	375	970	585	2,615
Inst. affil.								
(1)	235	452	687					
(2)	181	194	375					
(3)	519	451	970					
(4)	343	242	585					
Total	1,278	1,339	2,617					

	Sector										
	1	2	3	4	5	6	7	8	9	10	Total
Sex											
Male	231	297	332	179	137	42					1,218
Female	294	95	359	97	85	66					996
Total	525	392	691	276	222	108					2,214
Inst. affil.											
(1)	159	53	166	76	64	10					528
(2)	70	0	100	64	63	4					301
(3)	180	186	285	91	69	22					833
(4)	114	148	127	37	24	72					522
Total	523	387	678	268	220	108					2,184
SERL											
(1) Low	278	83	195	124	30	52					762
(2) Medium	100	129	174	103	64	90					672
(3) High	81	180	322	49	128	20					780
Total	525	392	691	276	222	108					2,214

Table C-12. *Data base for the Netherlands: unweighted*

	Sex			Institutional affiliation				
	Male	Female	Total	1	2	3	4	Total
SERL								
(1) Low	184	159	343	77	57	104	105	343
(2) Medium	380	288	668	139	134	190	205	668
(3) High	338	303	641	150	138	182	171	641
Total	902	750	1,652	366	329	476	481	1,652
Inst. affil.								
(1)	156	231	387					
(2)	160	185	345					
(3)	303	204	507					
(4)	330	177	507					
Total	949	797	1,746					

	Sector										
	1	2	3	4	5	6	7	8	9	10	Total
Sex											
Male	110	165	103	119	99	215	137				948
Female	102	170	107	105	76	174	63				797
Total	212	335	210	224	175	389	200				1,745
Inst. affil.											
(1)	77	73	37	38	13	124	24				386
(2)	40	62	45	40	21	86	51				345
(3)	52	108	61	61	53	108	64				507
(4)	43	92	67	85	88	71	61				507
Total	212	335	210	224	175	389	200				1,745
SERL											
(1) Low	33	64	40	53	30	81	42				343
(2) Medium	89	137	70	79	73	145	75				668
(3) High	77	115	83	81	66	142	76				640
Total	199	316	193	213	169	368	193				1,651

Table C–13. *Data base for Nigeria (excluding North): unweighted*

	Sex			Institutional affiliation				
	Male	Female	Total	1	2	3	4	Total
SERL								
(1) Low	77	247	324	126	125	73		324
(2) Medium	225	225	450	141	185	124		450
(3) High	669	255	924	209	333	382		924
Total	971	727	1,698	476	643	579		1,698
Inst. affil.								
(1)	227	255	482					
(2)	362	283	645					
(3)	386	193	579					
Total	975	731	1,706					

	Sector										
	1	2	3	4	5	6	7	8	9	10	Total
Sex											
Male	129	226	1	5	76	132	28	48			645
Female	74	171	6	22	57	95	21	31			477
Total	203	397	7	27	133	227	49	79			1,122
Inst. affil.											
(1)	42	128	6	16	25	48	12	20			297
(2)	68	124	0	5	63	114	19	35			428
(3)	93	145	1	6	45	65	18	24			397
(4)											
Total	203	397	7	27	133	227	49	79			1,122
SERL											
(1) Low	51	84	5	19	42	10	4	8			223
(2) Medium	71	90	1	2	60	41	24	15			304
(3) High	80	223	1	6	31	175	21	56			593
Total	202	397	7	27	133	226	49	79			1,120

Table C–14. *Data base of the United States: unweighted*

	Sex			Institutional affiliation				
	Male	Female	Total	1	2	3	4	Total
SERL								
(1) Low	422	427	849	119	226	286	213	844
(2) Medium	373	434	807	135	145	261	261	802
(3) High	436	456	892	113	76	304	385	878
Total	1,231	1,317	2,548	367	447	851	859	2,524
Inst. affil.								
(1)	179	188	367					
(2)	185	262	447					
(3)	416	435	851					
(4)	439	421	860					
Total	1,219	1,306	2,525					

	Sector										
	1	2	3	4	5	6	7	8	9	10	Total
Sex											
Male	267	270	89	97	102	260	19	117			1,221
Female	274	224	90	111	93	289	22	144			1,247
Total	541	494	179	208	195	549	41	261			2,468
Inst. affil.											
(1)	69	89	13	26	34	84	7	28			350
(2)	64	87	54	39	48	71	5	53			421
(3)	173	143	68	72	65	197	13	95			826
(4)	223	172	44	71	47	192	15	84			848
Total	529	491	179	208	194	544	40	260			2,445
SERL											
(1) Low	91	186	85	57	77	158	2	149			805
(2) Medium	135	171	53	73	78	181	12	77			780
(3) High	315	137	41	77	40	210	27	35			882
Total	541	494	179	207	195	549	41	261			2,467

Table C–15. *Data base for Yugoslavia: unweighted*

	Sex			Institutional affiliation				
	Male	Female	Total	1	2	3	4	Total
SERL								
(1) Low	390	480	870	579	260	31		870
(2) Medium	538	492	1,030	464	454	112		1,030
(3) High	561	399	960	241	431	288		960
Total	1,489	1,371	2,860	1,284	1,145	431		2,860
Inst. affil.								
(1)	559	808	1,367					
(2)	665	529	1,194					
(3)	340	94	434					
(4)								
Total	1,564	1,431	2,995					

	Sector										
	1	2	3	4	5	6	7	8	9	10	Total
Sex											
Male	517	312	452	46							1,327
Female	325	312	570	23							1,230
Total	842	624	1,022	69							2,557
Inst. affil.											
(1)	326	132	667	28							1,153
(2)	398	269	326	38							1,031
(3)	118	223	29	3							373
(4)											
Total	842	624	1,022	69							2,557
SERL											
(1) Low	125	10	661	2							798
(2) Medium	455	90	307	22							874
(3) High	234	519	30	16							799
Total	814	619	998	40							2,471

Table C-16. *Data base for Austria: weighted*

	Sex			Institutional affiliation				
	Male	Female	Total	1	2	3	4	Total
SERL								
(1) Low	190	368	578	92	154	168	144	558
(2) Medium	301	291	591	95	111	195	190	591
(3) High	340	279	619	121	98	186	214	619
Total	830	938	1,768	308	363	549	547	1,768
Inst. affil.								
(1)	122	187	309					
(2)	106	257	363					
(3)	248	301	549					
(4)	354	193	547					
Total	830	939	1,769					

	Sector										
	1	2	3	4	5	6	7	8	9	10	Total
Sex											
Male	86	59	272	34	112	61	196				821
Female	105	114	244	43	94	78	191				869
Total	192	173	516	77	206	140	387				1,690
Instit. affil.											
(1)	20	30	81	9	41	20	91				292
(2)	49	43	111	13	24	30	74				344
(3)	52	69	164	23	62	46	109				523
(4)	71	31	160	33	79	44	113				530
Total	192	173	516	77	206	140	387				1,690
SERL											
(1)	134	84	184	15	37	20	31				504
(2)	42	71	212	23	73	44	118				583
(3)	15	18	120	38	96	76	238				602
Total	192	173	516	76	206	140	387				1,689

Table C–17. *Data base for India: weighted*

	Sex			Institutional affiliation				
	Male	Female	Total	1	2	3	4	Total
SERL								
(1) Low	362	506	868	500	73	242	23	839
(2) Medium	466	428	894	398	104	295	80	876
(3) High	548	323	871	270	83	304	195	851
Total	1.375	1,257	2,633	1,168	260	842	297	2,566
Inst. affil.								
(1)	381	791	1,172					
(2)	116	144	260					
(3)	568	274	841					
(4)	290	7	297					
Total	1,355	1,216	2,571					

	Sector										
	1	2	3	4	5	6	7	8	9	10	Total
Sex											
Male	135	69	132	130	116	45	342	156	124	82	1,331
Female	96	88	61	128	126	71	223	195	61	153	1,201
Total	230	156	193	258	242	116	565	351	185	235	2,532
Inst. affil.											
(1)	102	87	88	115	105	39	249	139	80	119	1,122
(2)	27	9	25	36	23	29	35	41	8	24	256
(3)	86	41	54	67	86	35	182	119	75	75	820
(4)	15	15	24	30	28	8	89	44	22	13	290
Total	230	152	191	249	242	112	555	344	184	231	2,488
SERL											
(1) Low	139	97	83	82	61	27	110	32	78	90	799
(2) Medium	71	42	72	92	102	31	236	76	61	89	872
(3) High	20	17	38	81	76	57	219	242	16	56	856
Total	230	156	193	258	239	115	565	351	185	235	2,528

Table C–18. *Data base for the Netherlands: weighted*

	Sex			Institutional affiliation				
	Male	Female	Total	1	2	3	4	Total
SERL								
(1) Low	185	157	342	81	57	105	100	342
(2) Medium	379	288	667	136	140	190	202	667
(3) High	342	299	641	155	138	180	168	641
Total	907	744	1,650	372	335	475	469	1,650
Inst. affil.								
(1)	154	239	393					
(2)	168	185	353					
(3)	305	200	506					
(4)	325	169	494					
Total	952	794	1,746					

	Sector										
	1	2	3	4	5	6	7	8	9	10	Total
Male	108	153	98	116	93	231	153				951
Female	100	161	105	98	72	186	72				794
Total	209	313	204	214	165	417	224				1,745
Inst. affil.											
(1)	73	69	37	38	14	134	28				392
(2)	44	57	44	38	20	94	56				353
(3)	52	103	59	57	49	115	72				506
(4)	40	84	64	81	83	73	69				494
Total	209	313	204	214	165	417	224				1,745
SERL											
(1) Low	34	61	36	52	27	85	47				342
(2) Medium	87	126	70	76	70	156	83				667
(3) High	75	109	80	76	62	153	85				640
Total	196	296	186	203	160	394	215				1,650

Table C–19. *Data base for Nigeria (excluding North): weighted*

	Sex			Institutional affiliation				
	Male	Female	Total	1	2	3	4	Total
SERL								
(1) Low	112	458	571	208	236	127		571
(2) Medium	254	286	541	119	257	165		541
(3) High	392	194	586	107	225	254		586
Total	759	939	1,698	434	718	546		1,698
Inst. affil.								
(1)	143	298	441					
(2)	280	439	719					
(3)	339	207	546					
Total	762	944	1,706					

	Sector										
	1	2	3	4	5	6	7	8	9	10	Total
Sex											
Male	178	136	0	3	161	55	14	20			567
Female	135	149	20	32	149	71	13	8			578
Total	313	285	20	36	310	126	27	28			1,145
Inst. affil.											
(1)	69	82	20	20	49	21	8	8			277
(2)	107	103	0	11	156	82	8	11			478
(3)	138	99	0	5	105	24	10	9			390
Total	313	285	20	36	310	126	27	28			1,145
SERL											
(1) Low	98	82	19	30	107	22	3	4			365
(2) Medium	113	75	1	2	135	29	12	0			373
(3) High	100	127	0	4	68	75	12	18			404
Total	310	285	20	36	310	126	27	28			1,142

Table C-20. *Data base for the United States: weighted*

	Sex			Institutional affiliation				
	Male	Female	Total	1	2	3	4	Total
SERL								
(1) Low	423	419	842	117	214	292	214	838
(2) Medium	371	439	810	135	150	264	257	806
(3) High	436	459	894	120	75	306	376	878
Total	1,230	1,317	2,547	372	439	863	847	2,522
Inst. affil.								
(1)	182	190	372					
(2)	178	261	439					
(3)	421	442	863					
(4)	436	413	849					
Total	1,217	1,306	2,523					

	Sector										
	1	2	3	4	5	6	7	8	9	10	Total
Sex											
Male	255	250	78	93	98	269	27	150			1,221
Female	268	208	78	106	84	290	32	184			1,251
Total	523	458	156	199	182	559	59	334			2,472
Inst. affil.											
(1)	71	85	12	26	31	85	10	37			356
(2)	62	78	46	35	44	77	7	63			414
(3)	168	136	60	70	61	198	21	124			839
(4)	209	156	39	68	44	193	20	109			838
Total	510	455	156	199	181	553	58	334			2,448
SERL											
(1) Low	82	175	72	53	68	163	2	184			801
(2) Medium	128	156	47	72	77	182	20	103			785
(3) High	313	128	37	72	36	214	37	47			885
Total	523	458	156	198	182	559	59	334			2,470

Table C-21. *Data base for Yugoslavia: weighted*

	Sex			Institutional affiliation				
	Male	Female	Total	1	2	3	4	Total
SERL								
(1) Low	418	526	944	629	283	32		944
(2) Medium	532	470	1,002	443	450	450		1,002
(3) High	537	382	919	227	405	288		919
Total	1,487	1,378	2,865	1,298	1,137	429		2,865
Inst. affil.								
(1)	557	819	1,377					
(2)	665	522	1,187					
(3)	337	94	431					
(4)								
Total	1,559	1,436	2,995					

	Sector										
	1	2	3	4	5	6	7	8	9	10	Total
Sex											
Male	504	308	471	44							1,327
Female	316	304	598	23							1,242
Total	820	612	1,069	68							2,569
Inst. affil.											
(1)	312	126	702	27							1,167
(2)	391	262	338	38							1,029
(3)	117	224	29	3							373
(4)											
Total	820	612	1,069	68							2,569
SERL											
(1) Low	132	11	723	1							867
(2) Medium	450	88	294	23							855
(3) High	213	507	29	13							763
Total	794	607	1,046	37							2,484

Bibliography

Aaron, Henry. 1967. "Social Security: International Comparisons." Pp. 13–48 in Otto Eckstein, ed., *Studies in the Economics of Income Maintenance*. Washington, D.C.: Brookings Institution.

Aberbach, Joel D., and Jack L. Walker. 1973. *Race in the City*. Boston: Little, Brown.

Adamany, David W., and George E. Agree. 1975. *Political Money: A Strategy for Campaign Financing in America*. Baltimore: Johns Hopkins University Press.

Adelman, Irma, and Cynthia Taft Morris. 1973. *Economic Growth and Social Equity in Developing Countries*. Stanford, Calif.: Stanford University Press.

Alford, Robert A., and Harry M. Scoble. 1968. "Community Leadership, Social Status and Political Behavior." *American Sociological Review* 32: 259–72.

Alker, Hayward R., Jr. 1969. "A Typology of Ecological Fallacies." In Mattai Dogan and Stein Rokkan, eds., *Quantitative Ecological Analysis in the Social Sciences*, pp. 69–86. Cambridge, Mass.: M.I.T. Press.

Almond, Gabriel A., and Sidney Verba. 1963. *The Civic Culture*. Princeton, N.J. Princeton University Press.

Althauser, Robert P., and Michael Wigler. 1972. "Standardization and Component Analysis." *Sociological Methods and Research* 1 (August):97–135.

Andersen, Kristi. 1975. "Working Women and Political Participation, 1952–1972." *American Journal of Political Science* 19 (August):439–53.

Apter, David Ernest. 1971. *Choice and the Politics of Allocation: A Developmental Theory*. New Haven, Conn.: Yale University Press.

Barbic, Ana. 1975. *Predsedniki Krajevnih Skupnosti–Njihova Politicna Naravnanost in Aktivnost* [Political Activity of Local Community Leaders]. Ljubljana: Institut Za Sociologijo in Filozofijo Pri Univerzi v Ljubljani.

Barbic, Ana, et al. 1973. *Druzbenopolitica Aktivnost Obcanov v Krajevni Skupnosti* [Sociopolitical Participation in Local Communities Yugoslav Report]. Ljubljana: Institut Za Sociologijo in Filozofijo Pri Univerzi v Ljubljani.

Bendix, Reinhard. 1964. *Nation-Building and Citizenship: Studies of Our Changing Social Order*. New York: Wiley.

Berelson, Bernard, Paul F. Lazarsfeld, and William N. McPhee. 1954. *Voting*. Chicago: University of Chicago Press.

Berger, Joseph, Morris Zelditch, Jr., and B. Anderson. 1966. *Sociological Theories in Progress*. Vol. 1. Boston: Houghton Mifflin.

Bhatt, Anil. 1975. *Caste, Class and Politics*. Delhi: Manohar Book Service.

Blalock, Hubert M., Jr. 1964. *Causal Inferences in Nonexperimental Research*. Chapel Hill: University of North Carolina Press.

376

Bluhm, William T. 1973. *Building an Austrian Nation: The Political Rights of a Western State.* New Haven, Conn.: Yale University Press.

Blumberg, Paul. 1968. *Industrial Democracy: The Sociology of Participation.* New York: Schocken Books.

Booth, John A. 1976. "A Replication: Modes of Political Participation in Costa Rica." *Western Political Quarterly* (December): 627–33

Budge, Ian, Ivor Crewe, and Dennis Farlie, eds. 1976. *Party Identification and Beyond: Representations of Voting and Party Competition.* New York: Wiley.

Burnham, Walter Dean. 1965. "The Changing Shape of the American Political Universe." *American Political Science Review* 61: 7–28.

– 1974. "Theory and Voting Research." *American Political Science Review* 68 (September).

Butler, David Edgeworth, and Donald Stokes. 1969. *Political Change in Britain: Forces Shaping Electoral Choice.* New York: St. Martin's.

Campbell, Donald T. 1969. "Perspective: Artifact and Control." In *Artifact in Behavioral Research,* edited by Robert Rosenthal and Ralph L. Rosnow. New York: Academic Press.

Campbell, Donald T., and Julian C. Stanley, 1963. *Experimental and Quasi-Experimental Designs for Research.* Chicago: Rand McNally.

Charlot, Jean, and Monica Charlot. 1961. "Politisation et Depolitisation en Grande Bretagne." *Revue Francaise de Science Politique* 11 (September): 609–41.

Cobb, Roger W., and Charles E. Elder. 1972. *Participation in American Politics: The Dynamics of Agenda Building.* Boston: Allyn and Bacon.

Cole, G. D. H. 1920. *Guild Socialism Restated.* London: L. Parsons.

– 1921. *The Future of Local Government.* London: Cassell.

Coleman, James S. 1971. "Political Money." *American Political Science Review* 65: 1074–87.

Converse, Philip E., P. E. Clausen, and W. E. Miller. 1965. "Electoral Myth and Reality: The 1964 Election." *American Political Science Review* 59: 321–36.

Curtis, Gerald. 1971. *Election Campaigning Japanese Style.* New York: Columbia University Press.

Cutright, Phillips. 1965. "Political Structure, Economic Development, and National Social Security Programs." *American Journal of Sociology* 70 (March): 537–50.

Daalder, Hans, and Jerrold Rusk. 1972. "Perception of Party in the Netherlands." In *Comparative Legislative Behavior,* edited by John Wahlke and Samuel C. Patterson. New York: Wiley.

Dahl, Robert A. 1967. "The City in the Future of Democracy." *American Political Science Review* 61 (December): 958–70.

– 1970. *After the Revolution?* New Haven, Conn.: Yale University Press.

– 1971. *Polyarchy: Participation and Opposition.* New Haven, Conn.: Yale University Press.

Dahl, Robert A., and Edward R. Tufte. 1973. *Size and Democracy.* Stanford, Calif.: Stanford University Press.

Denitch, Bogdan. 1973a. "Notes on the Relevance of Yugoslav Self-Management." *Politics and Society* 3 (Summer): 473–91.

– 1973b. "Mobility and Recruitment of Yugoslav Leadership: The Role of the League of Communists." Chapter 4 in *Opinion-Making Elites in Yugoslavia,* edited by Allen H. Barton, Bogdan Denitch and Charles Kadushin. New York: Praeger.

Deutsch, Karl. 1961. "Social Mobilization and Political Development." *American Political Science Review* 55 (September): 493–514.

Dietz, Henry A. 1975. "Some Modes of Participation in an Authoritarian Regime." Paper prepared for delivery at the annual meeting of the American Political Science Association, San Francisco.

Duverger, Maurice. 1955. *The Political Role of Women.* Paris: UNESCO Report.

Eckstein, Harry. 1961. *A Theory of Stable Democracy.* Princeton, N. J.: Princeton University, Center of International Studies.

Engelmann, Frederick C. 1966. "Austria: The Pooling of Opposition." In *Political Oppositions in Western Democracies,* Robert A. Dahl, ed. New Haven, Conn.: Yale University Press.

Faul, Erwin, ed. 1960. *Wahlen und Wähler in Westdeutschland* [Elections and Voters in West Germany]. Villingen: Ring-Verlag.

Field, John O. 1972. *Partisanship in India: A Survey Analysis.* Unpublished Ph.D dissertation, Stanford University.

– Forthcoming. *Consolidating Democracy: Politicization and Partisanship in India.* New Dehli: Manohar Book Service.

Fieldder, Maureen. 1975. "The Participation of Women in American Politics." Paper prepared for delivery at the annual meeting of the American Political Science Association, San Francisco.

Flanagan, Scott. 1977. "The Genesis of Variant Political Cultures: Contemporary Citizen Orientation in Japan, America, Britain and Italy." In *The Citizen and Politics,* edited by Sidney Verba and Lucian Pye. Stamford, Conn.: Greylock.

Flanagan, Scott C., and Bradley M. Richardson. 1977. *Japanese Electoral Behavior: Social Cleavages, Social Networks and Partisanship.* Beverly Hills, Calif.: Sage Professional Papers in Contemporary Political Sociology.

Goel, M. Lal. 1975. *Political Participation in a Developing Nation – India.* New York: Asia Publishing House.

Greenstein, Fred. 1965. *Children and Politics.* New Haven, Conn.: Yale University Press.

Gruberg, Martin. 1968. *Women in American Politics.* Oshkosh, Wisc.: Academia Press.

Haavio-Mannila, Elina. 1970. "Sex Roles in Politics." *Scandinavian Political Studies* 5.

Hart, David K. 1972. "Theories of Government Related to Decentralization and Citizen Participation." *Public Administration Review* 32 (October): 603–21.

Hess, Robert, and Judith Torney. 1967. *The Development of Political Attitudes in Children.* Chicago: Aldine.

Hibbs, Douglas A., Jr. 1975. *Economic Interest and the Politics of Macroeconomic Policy.* Cambridge: Massachusetts Institute of Technology, Center for International Studies.

– 1976. *Long-Run Trends in Strike Activity in Comparative Perspective.* Cambridge: Massachusetts Institute of Technology, Center for International Studies.

Himmelstrand, Ulf, Albert Imohiosen, and Martin Igbozurike. Forthcoming. *Options and Constraints of Development: The Case of Nigeria.*

Holter, Harriet. 1970. *Sex Roles and Social Structure.* Oslo: Universitets-forlaget.

Hunnius, Gerry. 1973. "Workers' Self-Management in Yugoslavia." In

Workers' Control, edited by Gerry Hunnius, G. David Garson, and John Case. New York: Vintage.

Huntington, Samuel P., and Joan M. Nelson. 1976. *No Easy Choice: Political Participation in Developing Countries.* Cambridge, Mass.: Harvard University Press.

Igbozurike, Martin. 1976. *Problem-Generating Structures in Nigeria's Rural Development.* Uppsala: The Scandinavian Institute of African Studies.

Inkeles, Alex. 1969. "Participant Citizenship in Six Developing Nations." *American Political Science Review* 63: 1120-41.

Inkeles, Alex, and David H. Smith. 1974. *Becoming Modern: Individual Change in Six Developing Countries.* Cambridge, Mass.: Harvard University Press.

Irwin, Galen. 1974. "Compulsory Voting Legislation: Impact on Voter Turnout in the Netherlands." *Comparative Political Studies* 7 (October): 292-315.

Jackman, Robert W. 1975. *Politics and Social Equality: A Comparative Analysis.* New York: Wiley.

Jensen, Richard J. 1971. *The Winning of the Midwest: Social and Political Conflict, 1888-1896.* Chicago: University of Chicago Press.

Kaase, Max. 1976. "Party Identification and Voting Behavior in the West German Election of 1969." Chapter 5 in *Party Identification and Beyond: Representations of Voting and Party Competition,* edited by Ian Budge, Ivor Crewe, and Dennis Farlie. New York: Wiley.

Kelley, Stanley, Jr., Richard E. Ayres, and William G. Bowen. 1967. "Registration and Voting: Putting First Things First." *American Political Science Review* 61: 359-77.

Kesselman, Mark. 1966. "French Local Politics: A Statistical Examination of Grass-Roots Consensus." *American Political Science Review* 60 (December): 963-73.

Kim, Jae-On, Norman Nie, and Sidney Verba. 1974. "The Amount and Concentration of Political Activity." *Political Methodology* 1 (Spring): 105-32.

Kim, Jae-On, John R. Petrocik, and Stephen Enockson. 1975. "Voter Turnout Among the American States: Systemic and Individual Components." *American Political Science Review* 69 (March): 107-31.

Kim, Jae-On, and Charles W. Mueller. 1976. "Standardized and Unstandardized Coefficients in Causal Analysis: An Expository Note." *Sociological Methods and Research* 4 (March): 428-38.

Kim, Jae-On, Norman Nie, and Sidney Verba. 1977. "A Note on Factor Analyzing Dichotomous Variables: The Case of Political Participation." *Political Methodology* 4 (Spring): 39-62.

Kim, Jae-On, and James Curry. 1977. "The Treatment of Missing Data in Multivariate Analysis." *Sociological Methods and Research* 6 (November): 215-40.

Kirkpatrick, Jeanne. 1974 *Political Women.* New York: Basic Books.

Kleppner, Paul J. 1970. *The Cross of Culture: A Social Analysis of Midwestern Politics, 1850-1900.* New York: Free Press.

Kolaja, Jiri Thomas. 1965. *Workers' Councils: The Yugoslav Experience.* London: Tavistock.

Kothari, Rajni. 1970 *Politics in India.* Boston: Little, Brown.

Lancelot, Alain. 1968. *L'Absentionnisme Electorale en France.* Paris: Armond Colin.

Lane, Robert A. 1959. *Political Life: Why People Get Involved in Politics.* New York: Free Press.

Lerner, Daniel. 1958. *The Passing of Traditional Society.* New York: Free Press.

Liepelt, Klaus. 1971. "The Infra-structure of Party Support in Germany and Austria." In *European Politics,* edited by Mattei Dogan and Richard Rose. Boston: Little, Brown.

Lijphart, Arendt. 1975. *The Politics of Accommodation: Pluralism and Democracy in the Netherlands.* 2d ed. rev. Berkeley and Los Angeles: University of California Press.

Lipset, Seymour Martin, and Stein Rokkan. 1967a. "Cleavage Structures, Party Systems and Voter Alignment." In *Party System and Voter Alignment,* edited by S. M. Lipset and Stein Rokkan. New York: Free Press.

Lipset, Seymour M., and Stein Rokkan, eds. 1967b. *Party Systems and Voter Alignment.* New York: Free Press.

Little, Kenneth. 1965. *West African Urbanization: A Study of Voluntary Associations in Social Change.* Cambridge: University of Cambridge Press.

Lorwin, Val. "Segmented Pluralism." 1967. Mimeographed. Stanford, Calif.: Center for Advanced Study in Behavioral Sciences.

McCrone, Donald J., and Charles F. Cnudde. 1967. "Toward a Communications Theory of Democratic Political Development: A Causal Model." *American Political Science Review* 61 (March): 72–79.

McRae, Kenneth, ed. 1974. *Consociational Democracy: Political Accommodation in Segmented Societies.* Toronto: McClelland and Stewart.

Marrow, A. J., D. G. Barrows, and S. E. Seashore. 1968. *Management by Participation.* New York: Harper & Row.

Matthews, Donald R., and James W. Prothro. 1962. *Negroes and the New Southern Politics.* New York: Harcourt, Brace and World.

Michels, Robert. 1968. *Political parties: A Sociological Study of the Oligarchical Tendencies of Democracy.* Translated by Eden and Cedar Paul. New York: Free Press.

Milbrath, Lester W. 1965. *Political Participation.* Chicago: Rand McNally.

Milbrath, Lester W., and M. L. Goel. 1977. *Political Participation.* 2d ed. Chicago: Rand McNally.

Miller, Philip. 1975. *An Analysis of the Impact of Organizational Activity on Black Political Participation and on the Level of Black Political Influence.* Unpublished M.A. thesis, The University of Chicago.

Molleman, Henk. Forthcoming. *Action Groups in Dutch Politics.*

Mulder, Mauk. 1971. "Power Equalization Through Participation?" *Administrative Science Quarterly* 16 (March): 31–38.

Needler, Martin C. 1968. "Political Development and Socioeconomic Development: The Case of Latin America." *American Political Science Review* 62:889–97.

Nettle, John Peter. 1967. *Political Mobilization: A Sociological Analysis of Methods and Concepts.* London: Faber.

Neubauer, Deane. 1967. "Some Conditions of Democracy." *American Political Science Review* 61 (December): 1002–9.

Nie, Norman H., Bingham G. Powell, and Kenneth Prewitt. 1969. "Social Structure and Political Participation: Developmental Relationships. Parts 1 and 2." *American Political Science Review* 63:361–78, 808–32.

Nie, Norman, Sidney Verba, and Jae-On Kim. 1974. "Participation and the Life-Cycle." *Comparative Politics* 6 (April): 319–40.

Nie, Norman H., Sidney Verba, and John R. Petrocik. 1976. *The Changing American Voter.* Cambridge, Mass.: Harvard University Press.

Olson, Mancur. 1965. *The Logic of Collective Action.* Cambridge, Mass.: Harvard University Press.

Parry, Gerain, ed. 1972. *Participation in Politics.* Manchester: Manchester University Press.

Pateman, Carole. 1970. *Participation and Democratic Theory.* Cambridge: Cambridge University Press.

Peil, Margaret. 1976. *Nigerian Government: The People's View.* London: Cassell.

Petrocik, John. 1976. *Changing Party Coalitions and the Attitudinal Basis of Alignment.* Unpublished Ph.D. dissertation, The University of Chicago.

Pickles, Dorothy. 1953. "The Political Role of Women." *International Social Science Bulletin* 5: 75–104.

Powell, G. Bingham, Jr. 1970a. *Social Fragmentation and Political Hostility: An Austrian Case Study.* Stanford, Calif.: Stanford University Press.

– 1970b. *Social Fragmentation and Political History.* Stanford, Calif.: Stanford University Press.

– 1976. "Political Cleavage Structure, Cross-Pressure Processes, and Partisanship." *American Journal of Political Science* 20 (February): 1–24.

Pryor, Frederick L. 1968. *Public Expenditures in Communist and Capitalist Nations.* Homewood, Ill.: Richard D. Irwin.

Przeworski, Adam, and Henry Teune. 1966. "Establishing Equivalence in Cross-National Research." *Public Opinion Quarterly* 30.

– 1970. *The Logic of Comparative Social Inquiry.* New York: Wiley.

Ranney, Austin. 1972. "Turnout and Representation in Presidential Primary Elections." *American Political Science Review* 66: 21–37.

Richardson, Bradley M. 1973. "Urbanization and Political Participation: The Case of Japan." *American Political Science Review* 67 (June): 433–52.

– 1976. *The Political Culture of Japan.* Berkeley and Los Angeles: University of California Press.

Robinson, W. S. 1950. "Ecological Correlations and the Behavior of Individuals." *American Sociological Review* 15 (June): 351–57.

Rokkan, Stein. 1962. "The Comparative Study of Political Participation: Notes Towards a Perspective on Current Research." In *Essays in the Behavioral Study of Politics,* edited by Austin Ranney. Urbana, Ill.: University of Illinois Press.

– 1970. *Citizens, Elections, Parties.* Oslo: Universitets-forlaget.

Rose, Richard. 1974a. *Electoral Behavior: A Comparative Handbook.* New York: Free Press.

– 1974b. "Comparability in Electoral Studies." In *Electoral Behavior,* edited by Richard Rose. New York: Free Press.

Rose, Lawrence. 1976. *Patterns of Political Perceptions and Behavior in Two Norwegian Communities.* Unpublished Ph.D. dissertation, Stanford University.

Rose, Richard, and Derek, Urwin. 1969. "Social Cohesion, Political Parties and Strains in Regimes." *Comparative Political Studies* 2:1.

Rosenthal, Robert, and Ralph L. Rosnow. 1969. *Artifact in Behavioral Research.* New York: Academic Press.

Scheuch, E. K. 1968. "The Cross-Cultural Use of Sample Surveys: Problems of Comparability." Pp. 176–209 in *Comparative Research Across Cultures and Nations,* edited by Stein Rokkan. Paris: Mouton.

Schoenberg, Richard. 1972. "Strategies for Meaningful Comparison." In
 Herbert L. Costner, ed., *Sociological Methodology,* pp. 1–35. San
 Francisco: Jossey-Bass.

Shabad, Goldie. 1976. *Participatory Democracy: The Case of Yugoslavia.*
 Unpublished Ph.D. dissertation, The University of Chicago.

Sharkansky, Ira, and Richard Hofferbert. 1969. "Dimensions of State
 Politics: Economics and Public Policy." *American Political Science Review*
 63: 867–79.

Sklar, Richard L. 1963. *Nigerian Political Parties: Power in an Emergent
 African Nation.* Princeton, N.J.: Princeton University Press.

Steiner, Kurt. 1972. *Politics in Austria.* Boston: Little, Brown.

Stiefbold, Rodney P. 1972. "Segmented Pluralism and Consociational
 Democracy in Austria: Problems of Political Stability and Change." In
 Martin O. Heisler, ed. *Politics in Europe: Structures and Processes in Some
 Industrial Societies.* Boston: David McKay.

Sullerot, Evelyne. 1971. *Women, Society and Change.* New York: McGraw-
 Hill.

Supek, Rudi. 1973. "The Statist and Self-Managing Models of Socialism."
 Chapter 11 in Opinion-Making Elites in Yugoslavia, edited by Allen H.
 Barton, Bogdan Denitch, and Charles Kadushin. New York: Praeger.

Tarrow, Sydney. 1971. "The Urban-Rural Cleavage in Involvement: The
 Case of France." *American Political Science Review* 65 (June): 341–57.

Teune, Henry. 1968. "Measurement in Comparative Research."
 Comparative Political Studies 1.

Thomassen, Jacques. 1976. "Party Identification as a Cross-National
 Concept: Its Meaning in the Netherlands." Chapter 4 in *Party
 Identification and Beyond: Representations of Voting and Party Competition,*
 edited by Ian Budge, Ivor Crewe, and Dennis Farlie. New York: Wiley.

Townsend, James Roger. 1967. *Political Participation in Communist China.*
 Berkeley: University of California Press.

Verba, Sidney. 1969. "The Uses of Survey Research in the Study of
 Comparative Politics: Issues and Strategies." Chapter 2 in *Comparative
 Survey Analysis,* by Stein Rokkan, Sidney Verba, Jean Viet, and Elina
 Almasy. Paris: Mouton.

– 1971. "Cross-National Survey Research: The Problem of Credibility." In
 Comparative Methods in Sociology: Essays in Trends and Applications, edited
 by Ivan Vallier. Berkeley: University of California Press.

– 1978. "The Parochial and the Polity." In *The Citizen and Politics: A
 Comparative Perspective,* edited by Sidney Verba and Lucian Pye.
 Stamford, Conn.: Greylock.

Verba, Sidney, Richard Brody. 1970. "Participation, Preferences and the
 War in Vietnam." *Public Opinion Quarterly* 34: 325–32.

Verba, Sidney, Norman H. Nie, and Jae-On Kim. 1971. *The Modes of
 Democratic Participation: A Cross-National Analysis.* Beverly Hills, Calif.:
 Sage Professional Papers in Comparative Politics 2, no. 01–013.

Verba, Sidney, Bashiruddin Ahmed, and Anil Bhatt. 1971. *Caste, Race and
 Politics: A Comparison of India and the United States.* Beverly Hills, Calif.:
 Sage.

Verba, Sidney, and Norman H. Nie. 1972. *Participation in America: Social
 Equality and Political Democracy.* New York: Harper & Row.

Verba, Sidney, Norman H. Nie, Ana Barbic, Galen Irwin, Henk
 Molleman, and Goldie Shabad. 1973. "The Modes of Participation:
 Continuities in Research." *Comparative Political Studies* 6: 235–50.

Verba, Sidney, and Goldie Shabad. 1975. "Workers' Councils and Political Stratification: The Yugoslav Experience." Paper presented at the annual meeting of the American Political Science Association, San Francisco, September.

Verba, Sidney, and Lucian Pye, eds. 1978. *The Citizen and Politics: A Comparative Perspective*. Stamford, Conn.: Greylock.

Vogel, Ezra Feivel. 1963. *Japan's New Middle Class: The Salary Man and His Family in a Tokyo Suburb*. Berkeley: University of California Press.

Wandruszka, Adam. 1954. "Oesterrichs Politiche Struktur." In Heinrich Benedikt, ed., *Geschichte der Republik Osterreich*. Verlag für Geschichte und Politik, 289–485.

Watanuki, Joji. 1967. "Patterns of Politics in Present Day Japan." In *Party Systems and Voter Alignment*, edited by S. M. Lipset and Stein Rokkan. New York: Free Press.

Weiner, Myron. 1971. "Political Participation: Crisis of the Political Process." In *Crises and Sequences in Political Development*, edited by Leonard Binder, James S. Coleman, Joseph LaPalombara, Lucian Pye, Sidney Verba, and Myron Weiner. Princeton: Princeton University Press.

Welch, Susan. 1975. "Dimensions of Political Participation in a Canadian Sample." *Canadian Journal of Political Science* 8 (4): 553–59.

White, James W. 1975. "Status Differences in Political Participation in Tokyo." Paper prepared for delivery at the annual meeting of the American Political Science Association, San Francisco.

Wilensky, Harold L. 1975. *The Welfare State and Equality: Structural and Ideological Roots of Public Expenditures*. Berkeley: University of California Press.

Wilson, James Q. 1975. *Political Organization*. New York: Basic Books.

Zelditch, Morris, Jr. 1971. "Intelligible Comparisons." In *Comparative Methods in Sociology: Essays in Trends and Applications*, edited by Ivan Vallier. Berkeley: University of California Press.

Zukin, Sharon. 1975. *Beyond Marx and Tito: Theory and Practice in Yugoslav Socialism*. London and New York: Cambridge University Press.

Cross-National Program in Participation

The analyses reported in this volume deal with one central aspect of the data collected in our cross-national studies of participation. Other publications have dealt with other issues cross-nationally as well as with issues and problems within individual nations. The following is a list of these works.

Comparative works

Verba, Sidney, Norman Nie, and Jae-On Kim. 1971. *The Modes of Democratic Participation: A Cross-National Comparison.* Beverly Hills, Calif.: Sage Publications.

Verba, Sidney, Bashiruddin Ahmed, and Anil Bhatt. 1971. *Caste, Race and Politics: A Comparison of India and the United States.* Beverly Hills, Calif.: Sage Publications.

Kim, Jae-On, Norman Nie, and Sidney Verba. 1974. "The Amount and Concentration of Participation." *Political Methodology* (Spring).

Nie, Norman, Sidney Verba, and Jae-On Kim. 1974. "Participation and the Life-Cycle." *Comparative Politics* 1 (April): 319–40.

Nie, Norman, and Sidney Verba. 1975. "Political Participation." In *Handbook of Political Science,* edited by Fred Greenstein and Nelson Polsby. New York: Addison-Wesley.

Verba, Sidney. 1971. "Comparative Survey Research: The Problem of Credibility." In *Comparative Methods in Sociological Research,* edited by Ivan Vallier. Berkeley: University of California Press.

– 1976. "Organizational and Methodological Issues in the Cross-National Study of Participation." In *Cross-National Comparative Survey Research,* edited by A. Szalai and R. Petrella. Oxford: Pergamon Press.

– 1978. "The Parochial and the Polity: Political Demands by Apolitical People." In *The Citizen and Politics,* edited by Sidney Verba and Lucian Pye. Stamford, Conn.: Greylock Publishers.

Verba, Sidney, Norman Nie, Ana Barbic, Galen Irwin, Henk Molleman, and Goldie Shabad. 1973. "The Modes of Participation: Continuities in Research," *Comparative Political Studies* (July).

Kim, Jae-On, Norman Nie, and Sidney Verba, 1977. "A Note on Factor Analyzing Dichotomous Variables: The Case of Political Participation." *Political Methodology* 4 (Spring): 39–62.

Austria

Powell, G. Bingham. 1972. "Incentive Structures and Campaign Participation: Citizenship, Partisanship, Policy and Patronage in Austria." Paper prepared for a conference on political participation, University of Leiden, March.

- 1976. "Political Cleavage Structure, Cross-Pressures, Processes and Partisanship: An Empirical Test of a Theory." *American Journal of Political Science* (February): 1–24.
Powell, G. Bingham, and Linda W. Powell. Forthcoming. "Citizen-Elite Linkages in Austrian Communities." In *The Citizen and Politics: A Comparative Perspective,* edited by Sidney Verba and Lucian Pye. Stamford, Conn.: Greylock.
Powell, G. Bingham, Jr., with Rodney P. Stiefbold. 1977. "Anger, Bargaining, and Mobilization as Middle-Range Theories of Elite Conflict Behavior," *Comparative Politics* 9 (July): 379–98.

India
Bhatt, Anil. 1975. *Caste, Class and Politics: An Empirical Profile of Social Stratification in Modern India.* Delhi: Manohar Publishers.
- 1972. *Caste and Politics in India.* Unpublished Ph.D. dissertation, The University of Chicago.
Field, John O. Forthcoming. *Consolidating Democracy: Politicization and Partisanship in India.* New Dehli: Manohar Book Service, 1978.
- 1976. "Politicization and System Support in India: The Role of Partisanship." Monograph C/74-12. Center for International Studies, M.I.T.

Japan
Ikeuchi, Hajime, Ichiro Miyake, Joji Watanuki, and Jun-ichi Kyogoku. 1974. *Politicization in Japan* [in Japanese]. Tokyo: University of Tokyo Press.
Hirose, Hirotade. 1974. *The Structure of Political Cuture in Japan.* Ph.D. dissertation, The University of Tokyo.
Miyake, Ichiro. 1972. "Political Economy of Urban Problems – Japan and the U.S." Special issue of *Toyo-Keizai-Jiho* [in Japanese] (March).
Watanuki, Joji. 1972. "Social Structure and Political Participation in Japan." Research Paper, Institute of International Relations, Sophia University, Tokyo [in English].

Netherlands
Irwin, Galen. 1974. "Waarheen, Waarvoor, Voor Wie: Contacten van de burger met de lokale overheid." *Bestuurswetenschappen,* 28e jaargang, nr. 1 (January) (met R. B. Andeweg en W. Braak).
- 1975. "Political Efficacy, Satisfaction, and Participation." Mens en Maatschappij, 50e jaargang, nr. 1.
Irwin, Galen, and Henk Mollemann. 1972. "Political Participation in the Netherlands: A Preliminary Report." Paper presented to the meeting of the Dutch Political Science Association, Amsterdam (November).

Nigeria
Himmelstrand, Ulf, Albert Imohiosen, and Martin Igbozurike. Forthcoming. *Options and Constraints of Development: The Case of Nigeria.*
Igbozurike, Martin. 1976. *Problem-Generating Structures in Nigeria's Rural Development.* Uppsala: The Scandinavian Institute of African Studies.
Himmelstrand, Ulf. 1970. "Ethnicity, Political Power, and Mobilization: The Case of Nigeria." Paper presented at the Seventh World Congress of Sociology, Varna, Bulgaria (September).

- 1971. "Tribalism, Regionalism, Nationalism and Secession: Options of Political Development in Nigeria, 1960–67." The University of Uppsala.

United States
Verba, Sidney, and Norman Nie. 1972. *Participation in America: Political Democracy and Social Equality.* New York: Harper & Row.
Hansen, Susan B.. 1972. *Citizens and Leaders: A Study of Community Responsiveness.* Unpublished Ph.D. dissertation, Stanford University.
- 1975. "Participation, Political Structure and Concurrence." *American Political Science Review* (December): 1181–99.
Nie, Norman. 1971. *Citizen Participators: A Study of the Dimensions of Popular Participation in American Society.* Unpublished Ph.D. dissertation, Stanford University.
Verba, Sidney, and Richard Brody. 1970. "Policy Preferences, Participation and the War in Vietnam. " *Public Opinion Quarterly* (Fall).

Yugoslavia
Barbic, Ana, et al. 1973. *Druzbenopoliticna Aktivnost Obcanov v Krajevni Skupnosti* [Sociopolitical Participation in Local Communities]. Ljubljana: University of Ljubljana.
Barbic, Ana. 1972. "Druzbenopoliticna Aktivnost Zensk v sr Sloveniji" [Political Activity of Women in Slovenia]. Ljubljana: University of Ljubljana.
- 1975. "Political Participation of Citizens in Four Yugoslav Republics, Unity v. Diversity." Paper presented at annual meeting of the American Political Science Association, San Francisco (September).
- 1975. *Predsedniki Krajevnih Skupnosti–Njihova Politicna Naravnanost in Aktivnost* [Political Activity of Local Community Leaders]. Ljubljana: Institut za Sociologijo in Filozofijo pri Univerzi v Ljubljani (December).
- 1976. "Political Activity and Political Attitudes of Local Leaders Related to Structural and Developmental Characteristics of their Local Communities." Paper prepared for delivery at SOECO (International Sociological Association), research committee on social ecology. Ljubljana (August 1–12).
Shabad, Goldie. 1976. *Participatory Democracy: The Case of Yugoslavia.* Unpublished Ph.D. dissertation, University of Chicago.
- 1977. "Participation as Education: Learning Democratic Norms in Yugoslavia." Paper presented at the Conference on Southeastern Europe, Ohio State University (April 7–9).
Verba, Sidney, and Goldie Shabad. 1975. "Workers' Councils and Political Stratification: The Yugoslav Experience." Paper presented at the annual meeting of the American Political Science Association, San Francisco (September).
- Forthcoming. "Workers' Councils and Political Stratification: The Yugoslav Experience." *American Political Science Review.*

Index

Aaron, Henry, 3
Aberbach, Joel D., 13
action groups (Netherlands), 129
Adamany, David W., 9
Adelman, Irma, 3, 4
age distribution: education 69n4; sex differences, 265–6; welfare spending, 4
aggregate data, 28, 30, 32
Agree, George E., 9
Ahmed, Bashiruddin, 42n4, 60, 73n8, 213
Alford, Robert A., 47
Alker, Hayward R., Jr., 29n1
Almond, Gabriel A., 34, 47, 48, 330
Anderson, B., 12
Anti-Revolutionary Party (ARP, Netherlands), 185, 186, 187
Apter, David Ernest, 21n6
ARP, see Anti-Revolutionary Party
association(s) (voluntary): national variation, 79; participation rates, 81; voting, 74; see also organization(s) (private)
Austria: activity modes, 75; campaign activity, 79, 115, 116, 117, 118, 119, 120, 132, 150, 155, 156, 207, 287; communal activity, 61, 125, 126, 128, 129, 287; discussion, 104, 111, 138; education, 67, 68, 238; factor analysis, 322; institutions, 108, 109, 110, 111, 135, 208, 247; interviews, 351; involvement (psychological), 140, 177–82, 256; leadership, 297, 298; organizational membership, 101, 102, 103, 105, 106; participation, 58–9; party, 60, 95, 96, 97, 98, 104, 105, 146, 147, 148, 150, 151, 154–5, 172, 175–6; political rights, 20, 48; rural/urban, 272, 273, 279, 351–2; segmentation (cleavage), 164, 165–6, 167, 172–7; sex differences, 235, 238, 247, 256; status/participation correlation, 18, 65, 66, 77, 79, 152; voting, 60, 61, 76, 79, 122, 151, 235, 287
Austrian Freedom Party (FPÖ), 175, 181n8
Ayres, Richard E., 60

Barbic, Ana, 217n1, 269n1
Barrows, D. G., 9n2
Barton, Allen H., 219

Bendix, Reinhard, 5
Berelson, Bernard, 47
Berger, Joseph, 12
Beyond Marx and Tito: Theory and Practice in Yugoslav Socialism (Zukin), 30
Bhatt, Anil, 42n4, 60, 73n8, 210n15, 213, 269n1
blacks, *see* race
Blalock, Hubert M., Jr., 66n2, 261n6
Bluhm, William T., 111
Blumberg, Paul, 219
Booth, John A., 335, 336
Bowen, William G., 60
Brody, Richard, 301
Budge, Ivan, 154
Burnham, Walter Dean, 271, 308–9
Butler, David Edgeworth, 107

campaign activity: community size, 274, 280, 281, 282–3; cross-national, 57, 60–1, 76, 77, 78–9, 114–19, 132–3, 288; institutions, 74, 75, 77, 81, 83, 92, 119, 124, 130, 294; leadership recruitment, 298; "locking out," 115, 117, 118; party system, 114, 119, 150, 152, 156; questionnaire, 341; research strategy, 53, 56, 73, 313; segmentation, 179, 180, 181, 190, 191, 197, 199, 204, 205, 212, 287; SERL scale, 43, 114–19, 134, 206–7, 288, 294; sex differences, 287; Yugoslavia, 54, 61, 217, 223
campaign contributions, 9–10
campaign laws, 48
Campbell, Donald T., 33, 79n11
caste, 73n8, 210
Catholic Party (KVP, Netherlands), 97; organizations, 105, 106; segmentation, 185, 186, 187
Catholic People's Party (ÖVP, Austria), 145; membership, 146, 148, 165; organizational ties, 104, 105; policy, 167; segmentation, 174, 175, 176, 177. 181
Center for Political Studies (University of Michigan), 96n2
Charlot, Jean, 271
Charlot, Monica, 271
Christian Historical Party (Netherlands), 185, 186, 187
Civic Culture study, 18, 63
class: communal activity, 129; institutions, 83–4, 88–91, 134, 208;

387

class: *(cont.)*
  party system, 144–5; political activity,
    41, 113; segmentation, 174, 194; *see
    also* stratification (socioeconomic)
Clausen, P. E., 301
cleavage (social): groups, 163, 165;
    inequality, 169–70; institutions, 169,
    208; party, 161, 163–8; *see also*
    segmentation
Cnudde, Charles F., 47, 271
Cole, G. D. H., 271n3
communal activity: community size,
    275–7; cross-national analysis, 58–9,
    61, 76–7, 287, 294; institutions, 74,
    75, 124–9, 130; "locking out," 128,
    129; party system, 129, 156n1;
    research strategy, 54, 56, 73; SERL
    scale, 124–9, 288, 294; survey(s),
    342–4; Yugoslavia, 62, 217, 223, 287
Coleman, James S., 311
Communist Party (Austria), 146
Communist Party (Japan), 146;
    membership, 97
Communist Party (Yugoslavia), *see*
    League of Communists
community organizations, 100; Japan,
    102, 104, 111
community size: campaign activity, 274,
    280, 281, 282–3; political activity,
    272–3, 275–7, 279; voting, 271, 274,
    281–3, 284
conflict: equality, 157–8, 198, 308;
    political participation, 53, 56, 311–12
Congress Party (India), 39, 100, 146;
    base, 168; membership, 147;
    segmentation, 209; SERL/voting, 153
Conservative Party (U.K.), 4
Converse, Philip E., 301
cooperative activity, 312, 314–15
Costa Rica, 335–6
Crewe, Ivor, 154
cross-national (cultural) analysis
    (variation): activity/involvement
    dichotomy, 76–7, 137; activity/status
    correlation, 63; campaign activity, 57,
    60–1, 76, 77, 78–9, 114–19, 132–3,
    288; communal activity, 58–9, 61, 76–
    7, 287, 294; education, 68;
    institutions, 94; organizational
    membership, 100–1; political rights,
    48; problems of, 32–3, 57; SERL/
    participation relationship, 80–1, 136;
    subsistence needs, 303; techniques of,
    27–8, 39; voting, 120–4
Curtis, Gerald, 9, 48, 60, 167, 199n12
Cutright, Phillips, 3

Daalder, Hans, 111, 146, 183
Dahl, Robert, 3–4, 219, 271
decline-of-community model, 269, 270–
    5; political activity, 275, 283–4

democracy: equality, 28, 29, 308;
    evolution of, 5; measures of, 29;
    participation and, 47, 301;
    redistribution, 3
Democratic Party (U.S.), 145;
    macroeconomic policy, 4;
    membership, 97, 147, 148, 154; race,
    166; segmentation and, 202, 203;
    SERL/voting, 152
Democratic Socialist Party (Japan), 97
Denitch, Bogdan, 218, 219, 221
Deutsch, Karl, 270n2
development (economic): organizational
    membership, 101; participation, 61;
    political mobilization, 21–2, 47;
    welfare expenditures, 3
Dietz, Henry, 336
discussion (political): cross-national
    differences, 76, 78, 104, 111, 138–9;
    institutions, 75, 80, 81, 113, 136–7;
    involvement measure, 73; SERL scale,
    135, 142
Duverger, Maurice, 234, 236

Eckstein, Harry, 30, 48
ecological fallacy, 28n1
economic development, *see* development
    (economic)
education: age distribution, 69n4;
    economic development, 21; leader
    recruitment, 69–70, 299, 300;
    motivation, 11, 12, 75; participation,
    64, 66–9, 86, 91, 158, 206; party
    system, 149; sex differences, 237, 238,
    239, 257–9; survey, 97n3; variable,
    63; voter turnout, 7–8; Yugoslavia,
    216
elections: control by, 47; Nigeria, 49
Engelmann, Frederick, 165, 166, 179n6
Enockson, Stephen, 28n1
equalitarianism: democratic systems, 1;
    stratification hierarchies, 3
equality: cleavage, 169–70, 198; conflict,
    157–8, 198, 308; democracy, 29, 308;
    institutions, 130–3, 157, 206, 208,
    290; participation, 30, 90, 119, 161;
    sources of, 28, 50
ethnicity: affiliation by, in Nigeria, 111;
    political participation, 157

factor analysis, 40; of acts, 317–27;
    political participation, 52, 54, 63n1;
    relations among factors in, 328–31
Farlie, Dennis, 154
Faul, Erwin, 271
Field, John O., 39, 111
Fielder, Maureen, 337, 338, 339
Flanagan, Scott C., 111, 167, 193n10,
    194n11
FPÖ, *see* Austrian Freedom Party (FPÖ)
free-enterprise ideology, 17

388

390

voting: *(cont.)*
  sex differences, 235, 244–5, 250–1, 256; turnout, 6–9, 46–7, 48–9; Yugoslavia, 49, 218–19, 222, 224
VVD, *see* Liberal Party (Netherlands)

Walker, Jack L., 13
Wandruszka, Adam, 165
Watanuki, Joji, 193
Weber, Max, 2
Weiner, Myron, 47
Welch, Susan, 332, 333
welfare expenditures, 3–4
White, James W., 336, 337
whites, *see* race
Wilensky, Harold L., 3, 4
Wilson, James Q., 170n3
women, *see* sex differences
workers' councils, 9n2, 49, 60, 62, 217; participation, 219, 227–32
World Data Analysis Program (Yale University), 28
World War I, Austria, 165
World War II: Austria, 165; Yugoslavia, 221

Yale University, 28
Yugoslavia: activity modes, 75; campaign activity, 54, 61, 217, 223; communal activity, 62, 217, 223, 287; education, 67, 68, 238, 239; factor analysis, 323–7; institutions, 217–18, 222, 226, 229, 232, 247; interest, 76; involvement (psychological), 72, 256; leadership, 297, 298; participation, 58–9, 216–17; party system, 95, 108n9, 168n2, 215, 220–1; political rights, 20, 49; rural/urban, 272, 273, 279, 281; sample selection, 360; self-management activities, 57, 60, 62; SERL scale, 216; sex differences, 238, 239, 247, 256; status/participation correlation, 18, 30–1, 63–4, 65, 66, 77, 79; survey, 218–19; voting, 226, 287; workers' councils, 9n2, 49, 60, 62, 217, 219, 227–32

Zelditch, Morris, Jr., 12, 25, 36, 78
Zuilen (pillars), 166, 182
Zukin, Sharon, 30, 31–2